£14.40 TW/2

SOCIAL CHANGE AND POLITICS IN TURKEY

A STRUCTURAL-HISTORICAL ANALYSIS

SOCIAL, ECONOMIC AND POLITICAL STUDIES OF THE MIDDLE EAST
ÉTUDES SOCIALES, ÉCONOMIQUES ET POLITIQUES DU MOYEN ORIENT

VOLUME VII

SOCIAL CHANGE AND POLITICS IN TURKEY

A STRUCTURAL-HISTORICAL ANALYSIS

BY KEMAL H. KARPAT
AND CONTRIBUTORS

LEIDEN
E. J. BRILL
1973

SOCIAL CHANGE AND POLITICS IN TURKEY

A STRUCTURAL-HISTORICAL ANALYSIS

BY

KEMAL H. KARPAT
AND CONTRIBUTORS

With 52 Tables

LEIDEN
E. J. BRILL
1973

Comité de rédaction—Editorial committee

F. BARTH (University of Bergen), E. GELLNER (London School of Economics), C. ISSAWI (Columbia University), S. KHALAF (American University of Beirut), M. F. AL-KHATIB (Cairo University), P. MARTHELOT (Ecole Pratique des Hautes Etudes, Paris), S. H. NASR (Arya-Mehr University of Technology, Tehran), M. SOYSAL (Ankara University), M. ZGHAL (Université de Tunis).

Rédacteur—Editor

C. A. O. VAN NIEUWENHUIJZE

Le but de la collection est de faciliter la communication entre le grand public international et les spécialistes des sciences sociales étudiant le Moyen-Orient, et notamment ceux qui y résident. Les ouvrages sélectionnés porteront sur les phénomènes et problèmes contemporains : sociaux, culturels, économiques et administratifs. Leurs principales orientations relèveront de la théorie générale, de problématiques plus précises, et de la politologie : aménagement des institutions et administration des affaires publiques.

The series is designed to serve as a link between the international reading public and social scientists studying the contemporary Middle East, notably those living in the area. Works to be included will be characterized by their relevance to actual phenomena and problems : whether social, cultural, economic, political or administrative. They will be theory-oriented, problem-oriented or policy-oriented.

ISBN 90 04 03817 5

Copyright 1973 by E. J. Brill, Leiden, Netherlands

All rights reserved. No part of this book may be reproduced or translated in any form, by print, photoprint, microfilm, microfiche or any other means without written permission from the publisher

PRINTED IN BELGIUM

*In honor of the fiftieth year of the
Turkish Republic
1923-1973*

TABLE OF CONTENTS

Tables VIII
List of Contributors XI

Introduction — KEMAL H. KARPAT 1

PART I
THE STRUCTURAL AND HISTORICAL FOUNDATIONS OF CONTEMPORARY TURKISH POLITICS

I. Structural Change, Historical Stages of Modernization, and the Role of Social Groups in Turkish Politics — KEMAL H. KARPAT 11
II. The Modernization of Turkey in Historical and Comparative Perspective — DANKWART A. RUSTOW 93

PART II
THE SOCIAL GROUPS AND CHANGE IN ROLES

III. The Middle Classes in Turkey — NEZİH NEYZİ 123
IV. Labor in Turkey as a New Social and Political Force — BÜLENT ECEVIT 151
V. The Integration of the Villager into the National Life of Turkey — JOHN KOLARS 182
VI. The Free Boarding (Leyli Meccani) Schools — ILHAN BAŞGÖZ 203

PART III
THE POLITICS AND IDEOLOGY OF SOCIAL GROUPS

VII. Social Groups and the Political System after 1960 — KEMAL H. KARPAT 227
VIII. Turkish Provincial Party Politics — FRANK TACHAU . . 282
IX. Ideology in Turkey after the Revolution of 1960 — KEMAL H. KARPAT 317

Index of Names 367
Index of Subjects 371

TABLES

Table 1.1.	Number of troops and military expenditure, 1528-1670	35
Table 1.2.	Trade of Marseille	39
Table 1.3.	Occupation of Turkish males, fifteen years and over	63
Table 1.4.	Economically active population, fifteen years and over, 1927-1965	64
Table 1.5.	Percentage change in occupation over base period 1927	66
Table 1.6.	Economically active population by occupation	66
Table 1.7.	Agricultural machinery, equipment, and land in use in Turkey	68
Table 1.8.	Gross national product and per capita G.N.P.	70
Table 1.9.	Net national product and its origin	70
Table 1.10.	Sector origin of national income	71
Table 1.11.	Net national income, population, and per capita income	71
Table 1.12.	Government revenues and expenditures	73
Table 1.13.	Urban population	73
Table 1.14.	Urban administrative centers of provinces and districts	75
Table 1.15.	Transportation and communication in Turkey	76
Table 1.16.	School attendance by levels and type of education	78
Table 1.17.	Ages of Justice Party and Republican People's Party Deputies	81
Table 1.18.	General occupations of Justice Party and Republican People's Party Deputies	81
Table 1.19.	Specific occupations of Justice Party and Republican People's Party Deputies	82
Table 1.20.	Chain index numbers of major indicators of development	84
Table 1.21.	Index numbers of major indicators of development	85
Table 1.22.	Political indicators : participation and freedom	86
Table 1.23.	Political participation : political parties and elections	87
Table 3.1.	Estimated number of the middle class in Turkey based on earnings	128
Table 3.2.	Income brackets in Ereğli	129
Table 3.3.	Selected household items at Ereğli	129
Table 3.4.	Increase in the Civil Service	132
Table 3.5.	Pay scale of Civil Servants, 1968	134

Table 3.6.	Percentage of Civil Servants receiving no supplementary compensation	134
Table 3.7.	Salaried and nonsalaried middle income group	135
Table 3.8.	Income tax declarations	136
Table 3.9.	Registrants to the Chamber of Commerce of Istanbul	139
Table 3.10.	Savings pattern of Turkish laborers in Germany	142
Table 3.11.	Credits granted by Central Bank to institutions	145
Table 3.12.	Special funds created by the Ministry of Finance	145
Table 3.13.	Private enterprise credits	146
Table 3.14.	Credits according to sectors	146
Table 4.1.	Number of workers affiliated with the Confederation of Trade Unions of Turkey (Türk-İş), 1960-68	177
Table 4.2.	Employers' unions, workers' trade unions, and collective bargaining contracts enacted	178
Table 4.3.	Labor strikes 1963-67.	179
Table 4.4.	Average wages for workers covered by Social Security	180
Table 4.5.	Social Security and minimum wage	181
Table 6.1.	Students attending free boarding elementary schools, 1924-39	212
Table 6.2.	Free boarding students in Lises	214
Table 6.3.	Free boarding students in trade schools	215
Table 6.4.	Boarding students in teacher training schools	215
Table 6.5.	Students in the Village Institutes	216
Table 6.6.	Boarding students in other vocational secondary schools, 1946-47	216
Table 6.7.	Boarding students at universities in 1939-40 and 1943-44	218
Table 8.1.	Members of provincial executive committees	285
Table 8.2.	Members of provincial executive committee from twelve selected provinces, February to August, 1964	288
Table 8.3.	Members of provincial executive committees, by party, from twelve selected provinces	291

LIST OF CONTRIBUTORS

ILHAN BAŞÖZ, Associate Professor, Department of Uralic and Altaic, Indiana University, Bloomington, Indiana.

BÜLENT ECEVIT, Former Minister of Labor and Chairman General of People's Republican Party, Ankara.

KEMAL H. KARPAT, Professor of History, University of Wisconsin, Madison, Wisconsin.

JOHN KOLARS, Professor of Human Geography, Department of Geography, University of Michigan, Ann Arbor, Michigan.

NEZIH NEYZI, Director of PEVA-Market Research Organization, Istanbul.

DANKWART A. RUSTOW, Distinguished Professor of Political Science, City University of New York, New York, N.Y.

FRANK TACHAU, Professor of Political Science, Illinois State University, Chicago.

INTRODUCTION

This book deals with one basic issue : the correlation between economic and social development and politics, and the role of social groups in this process which we define as modernization. We have studied this problem collectively relative to one specific country, namely Turkey. Although we focus mainly on developments after the revolution of 1960, nevertheless we deal also, rather extensively, with broader historical and conceptual problems, as well as with relevant political developments occurring at earlier stages. The basic idea advanced is that structural differentiation is the dynamic of change which under certain conditions becomes modernization, that this modernization occurs in successive stages of development which are qualitatively and quantitatively different from each other, and that each stage is marked by the leadership of a specific social group. This situation was illustrated in Turkey after 1945 by the gradual loss of power by the intellectual bureaucratic elites and the economic and political ascendancy of the economic entrepreneurial groups. Thus, the conflict between the bureaucratic and economic elites is central to the study of politics in Turkey.

The establishment of modern states and the creation of new political identities and loyalties, that is, the process of nation formation, corresponds more or less to a precise stage of historical and structural development in the third world. This process was and still is carried out in large measure under the leadership of some new social cadres, such as the intelligentsia and the bureaucracy. These groups, which may be called "statist," "administrative," or "directing," have emerged as the by-product of various economic, social, and political stimuli preceding the formation of independent national states. In their own turn these groups have created new political institutions, and established new patterns of decision making and national goals. Also they have created a national framework of economics and accelerated the structural change which has affected, finally, both the country's social composition and political culture, and the very political and social position and roles of the elites. These "modernist" elites—intelligentsia bureaucracy—have become, in fact, a new type of upper class by monopolizing governmental power. Consequently, it is fallacious to refer to these groups as "the middle classes." Unlike true middle-class groups, such as those which emerged in Europe and engaged in the politics of compromise with the lower and upper groups, the intelligentsia and bureaucratic elites in the third world, including Turkey, are generally authoritarian and ideologically oriented, although their ideology, aiming at economic development, is more pragmatic than doctrinaire. They tend to assume control of the economic resources based on government power and the defense of increased welfare for the masses rather than on property rights as was the case with the traditional middle classes.

The processes of nation formation and economic and social development initiated by the statist elites produce eventually new occupational groups whose political outlook and economic philosophy may conflict with those of the ruling elites. We refer to these new groups in this study as economic and entrepreneurial—including the professionals—and regard them as the natural consequence of economic growth and social change as well as the representatives of a set of special political values. These new groups may not achieve political power overnight. The ideology of the ruling groups, personalities, and international circumstances may hasten or delay the outcome of the political struggle between the statist elites and the economic and entrepreneurial groups. The demands for recognition and power by these groups will manifest themselves openly in a democratic regime whereas in a totalitarian regime they may appear in a variety of guises. Yet, the indirect impact of the economic groups on the social strata, and the tensions and pressures generated by their activities, sooner or later affect the ruling elites and compel them to make a series of political compromises and adjustments. These views, it must be stated, derive not only from observations in Turkey but also from a close survey of structural changes and the action of social groups elsewhere in the Middle East and in Latin America.

This book contains repeated references to the political struggle in Turkey between the statist elites and the economic entrepreneurial groups, as well as to the term "middle classes." We have used the term "middle classes" sparingly throughout this study, to describe a series of occupations, attitudes, and interests rather than a rigid hierarchy of groups. The pattern of social stratification, the nature of economic development, the political ideology, and the sociocultural bases of the system in Turkey, as in many developing nations, are such as to preclude yet the formation of the rigidly separated and antagonistic social classes seen in Western Europe. Although we refer repeatedly to the political conflicts between the bureaucratic elites and the economic groups we do not regard these conflicts as being a classic class struggle stemming chiefly from the clash of economic interests. The economic entrepreneurial groups, which included a substantial number of professionals, struggled for a degree of social and political recognition and for inclusion into the ranks of the ruling elite. In a way this was a new development since historically Turkey had a variety of communal and religious elites but these did not share government power. The new economic groups were supported by the lower strata and eventually succeeded in drastically changing the very meaning of elitism. The new economic groups in Turkey reflected to some extent the impact of the forces which created them.

The process of structural change or modernization in the third world today is relying more and more on economic development based on the adoption of technology and industrialization, the use of state power for the mobilization of national resources, and the qualitative improvement of manpower through education. Accelerated social mobility, increased participation, political mobilization, the establishment of social and cultural goals and of expanded national welfare programs make this modernization not only broader in scope but also, theoretically at least, more egalitarian and democratic. One may assume, therefore, that these tendencies are reflected in one way or another in the political attitudes of all social groups as seen in the rise of the economic entrepreneurial groups in Turkey and especially in their demand for participation in decision making at the government level. And in fact the economic entrepreneurial-professional groups, or the new middle class, played a major role in redirecting Turkish politics toward a more participatory and democratic pattern, even if only to consolidate their own position.

The term "economic entrepreneurial groups" covers the actual entrepreneurs, businessmen, upper income farmers, and a variety of other groups that use their capital, training, and skills, coupled with personal initiative, as the bases for participation in economic life. We included such divergent groups in one broad category because we used as classification criteria the position and functions of these groups in the economic process, and their political attitudes and social status as related to their occupation. Having risen against the statist elites, the leadership of the economic entrepreneurial groups mobilized the lower social strata through promises of freedom from pressure and abundant economic opportunities. However, in the actual struggle for recognition and power, the economic entrepreneurial groups became imbued with, and were often compelled to adopt, many of the new social and political ideas disseminated by the statist elites. Indeed, mainly after 1960, many of the statist elites, put on the defensive, turned to the left and adopted a series of egalitarian, social, and political ideas broader in scope than those of the new entrepreneurial groups, ideas that they had, incidentally, ignored during their own political supremacy between 1920 and 1945. Despite mutual accusations and bitter attacks, in practice the economic entrepreneurial groups played a major role in generating pressure and eventually in assuming political leadership from 1945-1960, and again after the military take-over in 1961. A similar pattern developed after the military forced the Justice Party government to resign in March 1971. Hence in Turkey's present stage of development and modernization the economic entrepreneurial groups appear to have acquired leading economic and political positions. These groups seem to realize that in order to maintain their own positions they have to rely on mass support and on a well-sustained effort to recruit and induct new and increasingly numerous elements into a pattern of economic and political life germane to their own interests and cultural orientation. Consequently, they are involved in a search for economic, technical, and managerial means to serve their own purposes, and incidentally, further reshape the social structure and change the attitudes of the intelligentsia according to their own image of society. The resulting changes, which may appear at first sight as a consequence of planned social engineering, are actually the accidental by-products of economic activity, since so far the entrepreneurial groups lack the intellectual capacity and the organizational sophistication necessary for a fundamental reshaping of the social structure. Nevertheless, sustaining Joseph Schumpeter's observations on social classes, one may say that the new middle-class groups in Turkey are presently striving to the best of their ability to create by participation and consensus a material complement to their social position, whereas in the past practically all elites in Turkey acquired *by force* that material complement which had been created by other groups. The composition and size of the entrepreneurial groups change continuously. Hence, a general study of the "middle classes," besides filling a sorely felt theoretical gap, could clarify the special nature of social stratification and of politics in the new nations.

The concepts and methodology used in this book stem in large measure from the nature of the subject and the desire to place it in broad perspective. Consequently, we have relied heavily on a historical and structural approach and used quantitative data extensively in order to illustrate clearly the idea of stages and the dominant role played by a specific social group at each stage. We have stressed the fact that development occurred in stages, that each stage was marked by the reorganization of economic-technological forces, and that all this culminated in the rise of new social groups and their assumption of political roles. The concept of historical stages of development seems to be of vital analytical importance in understanding the qualitative changes and the factors responsible for them in the modernization process. In order to illustrate this point we have outlined social changes in the Ottoman state and Turkey, not only to show the existence of some continuity in the form of social situations inherited from previous groups, but also to indicate, according to our own concepts and approach, the differences between various stages of modernization and the groups responsible for those differences.

We have made in this work a rather consistent effort to relate political development to certain tangible economic and social factors as manifest in the action of various groups. However, in so doing we have not started from any *a priori* judgment but tried to visualize the correlation statistically between economic and social factors, and politics in the light of conditions specific to the place and time. Yet, we must state from the very beginning that we have not found everywhere a direct and mechanical correlation between statistically measurable growth and political phenomena. The correlation between economic and social growth and politics appears to be a cumulative process, which manifests itself after varying periods of time. The cultural factors seem to play an essential role in conditioning the form and intensity of this manifestation. Thus, we do not ignore the impact of cultural forces on politics but see them in large measure as subordinate to the socioeconomic factors. As explained further, the correlation between socioeconomic factors and politics is often manifest in the types of social groups which emerged as a consequence of the socioeconomic change and in their political attitudes and philosophies. In other words, the social groups embody on one hand the very forces which created them while on the other they interpret those forces in the light of their own social, political, historical, and cultural background. But this background culture, while outwardly preserving its original features, undergoes constant change too.

One may rightly ask the reason for not emphasizing the cultural forces underlying Turkey's politics. We have partly compensated for this shortcoming by adding a chapter on ideological changes. However, the main reason for not considering the cultural factors in depth *at this time* is the fact that most of the studies on Turkey have relied heavily on cultural factors in explaining the changes in the country. Turkey's history of transformation for the past one hundred and fifty years has been, for most scholars, an effort to adopt Western institutions. The Turks' performance was measured often according to their willingness to give up their own traditions and adopt European habits, dress, manners, and culture. The need for a new approach to the history of change in Turkey, as elsewhere, was obvious. Hence, the effort to view the contemporary politics of Turkey in the light of concrete social, economic, and historical forces so that a proper balance may be restored between cultural and economic determinism.

This book is in good measure the product of cooperation between several scholars in the United States and Turkey, and individuals engaged either in policy making or in the analysis of various aspects of Turkish society. Books such as this consisting of several studies undertaken by different people have been criticized in the past as being disjointed, and as reflecting divergent approaches, styles, and analytical methods. There is truth in such views. Yet, although we feel that if the contributions were to revolve around a central theme or analyze the various facets of the same problem under the conceptual guidance of one man a certain thematic unity could be achieved, we also believe that views expressed by different people on the same subject, in this case on the structural differentiation and emergence of new social groups in Turkey, may give the major theme a multidimensional perspective which a single person might be less able to achieve. This I believe has been accomplished to a large extent in this work.

Since the original introduction was written and the manuscript updated in 1969, Turkey has undergone some important changes. Economic development has been maintained at a steady growth rate of 6 to 7 percent, thus enabling the smaller Anatolian towns and cities to integrate themselves more fully into the market economy. A new segment of the entrepreneurial class coming from these towns and cities has joined forces with those in the larger cities and, politically speaking, it has assumed leadership positions. The victory of the Justice Party in the elections of 1969, due to these groups, has been countered by growing resistance and opposition by the intelligentsia and civil and military bureaucracies. The intelligentsia in the university establishment has moved from theory to violent action, under the slogans of antiimperialism and anticapitalism, that is, opposition to the alignment with the West and to the entrepreneurial-capitalist system of economy. They have drawn much of their ideological nourishment from Marxism, Maoism and Turkish nationalism, however paradoxical that may sound. The bureaucracy on the other hand has used the legal system, notably the constitutional court and the administrative court *Danıştay*, to invalidate not only laws deemed to be "unconstitutional" but also various acts of government which it considered likely to strengthen the private sector of the economy or to enhance the cultural and political power of the entrepreneurial groups. There cannot be a better example than the Turkish case in which a democratic system of controls has been so effectively used by a handful of judges and government officials to debilitate and eventually render powerless a popularly elected assembly. The military intervention and the resignation of the Demirel government on March 12, 1971, was a consequence of these background developments. The government formed subsequently by Nihat Erim aimed in theory at enhancing the power of the Executive and at achieving social reform and accelerating economic development at the same time. The Erim government was the synthesis of the struggle between the statist and economic elites, which will continue under the new government though in a different form. This government represents, in fact, the beginning of a new phase in Turkish political life, one of systematization, and rationalization of the economic life still within a middle class philosophy despite symptoms indicating the existence of new currents of thought. Even if the Erim government is changed the general direction of development may not alter significantly its course.

The book consists of nine studies, most of which are based on original research, field investigation, and surveys. Six studies are by the contributing Turkish and American scholars, researchers, and politicians and the remaining three by the editor. These studies have been organized in three sections: the historical and structural background; the major social groups; and finally, the ideology and political action of these groups since the Revolution of 1960.

The original studies were presented and discussed in a conference sponsored by the Social Science Research Council and the Department of Politics of New York University, and held at NYU in May 1965. Some of the original papers have been drastically revised, brought up to date, and rewritten in the light of the conference discussions and more recent research. The two studies on theoretical problems and ideology were added later, while two other papers presented to the conference were not included. We wish to thank the Committee on the Middle East of the Social Science Research Council which financed the conference and the Department of Politics at New York University which cosponsored it, as well as the discussants and participants at the conference. Thanks go also to Professor Howard A. Reed for his suggestions and criticism, as well as to Mr. Engin Akarli who labored patiently in gathering, organizing, and checking the statistical data.

Madison, April 16, 1969.   KEMAL H. KARPAT

PART I

THE STRUCTURAL AND
HISTORICAL FOUNDATIONS OF
CONTEMPORARY TURKISH POLITICS

CHAPTER ONE

STRUCTURAL CHANGE, HISTORICAL STAGES OF MODERNIZATION, AND THE ROLE OF SOCIAL GROUPS IN TURKISH POLITICS

Kemal H. Karpat

Political development in Turkey since the revolution of 1960 represents a new phase in the country's social and political development in particular and modernization in general. We shall view these developments as part of a broad process of structural change occurring in various historical stages, each one differentiated from the previous one by the action of a particular social group.

This is, thus, in essence a historical-structural study of political development centered on a specific society : Ottoman-Turkish. We have adopted a historical view of political development not in order to prove or disprove the existence of an evolutionary law or of a unilinear sequence of generic periods of development but rather to theorize about the forces causing the political growth and decay of a particular society. Consequently, we have regarded the stages of development in the history of the Ottoman-Turkish society not as a straight path leading to "progress" or "modernity" but rather as a dialectical process subject to a variety of internal and international forces. The study does not have any pretensions. It is an effort to evaluate the historical forces conditioning the current political performance of a national state—Turkey.

It is obvious that the rate of economic and political development in any society is subject not only to the policies of the government but also to its historical preparedness. We feel that the failure of most students of development to devise a proper approach to the use of "history" is one of the causes accounting for the lack of a basic theory of development. Some of the existing theories appear rather useless when applied to societies other than those studied by the respective authors, or when historically tested. Certainly the role of theory consists not only in the systematization of information, or in the arrangement of facts in a logical order for the scholar's benefit, but also in providing meaningful explanations and a sense of direction for events occurring now or in the past.

A proper use of history may help solve some of the key theoretical problems of development and modernization. The changing capacity of a given developmental factor grows or diminishes in time. The independent variables become dependent. The policies which produce growth in some societies may cause decay in others, thus indicating that these latter societies are in different stages of development, or that their structures are not mutually responsive to the stimulus, or that they are not favored equally by international factors. All these plead in favor of a historical view of development based on quantitative data, new concepts rather than new chronology.[1] The comparison of Japan with the Ottoman Empire is a good example. The so-called "modernization" in the Ottoman Empire began at least one century earlier than in Japan, but the latter quickly surpassed Turkey. Finally, the proper use of history—the remarriage of history and political science—may lead to the development of basic concepts of development applicable to all societies and all periods.

The study of Ottoman society as a model for historical development is warranted not only by the fact that it would place contemporary Turkish political development in proper historical perspective, but also because it would help to explain the patterns of change and development in most of the states in the Balkans, the Middle East, and even North Africa. It is a well-known fact that the peoples of at least twenty of the contemporary national states in the area, including those of Turkey, were subject to the *direct* rule of Ottoman bureaucracy for several centuries. Their social structure, and especially their patterns of development, despite variations and local differences, appear strikingly similar when viewed in longer time perspectives.

The study of Ottoman-Turkish development in this work is based on four hypotheses which draw heavily on the theories and ideas developed previously by economists, sociologists, and political scientists. We shall attempt to use these theories, as well as various empirical studies, within an integrated historical model framed according to the Ottoman-Turkish experiment in development and modernization. (Modernization is here considered a stage of development.)

The basic hypotheses underlying this study are the following : 1) development, political or otherwise, should rest first upon a basic cause-

---

[1] The research projects on the use of quantitative data for historical studies are listed in the *Historical Methods Newsletter*: *Quantitative Analysis of Social, Economic and Political Development*, published by the Department of History, University of Pittsburgh. The functionalist analysis of history is in S. N. Eisenstadt, *Political Systems of Empires* (Glencoe: Ill., 1963). See also Guenther Lewy, "Historical Data in Comparative Political Analysis," *Comparative Politics*, October 1968, pp. 103-10.

factor applicable to all societies; 2) this factor should be historically present in various degrees in all the phases of change; 3) the various forces contributing to change, as well as the change itself, should be quantitatively measurable; and, 4) political developments and changes in the structure should correlate and be quantitatively measurable. (This does not prejudice the political system's ability to become the independent, causative variable.)

In the light of these ideas we have studied the processes of development in the Ottoman Empire and Turkey in general as being caused first by structural change or differentiation, manifest in the form of shifts in occupations, power, roles, and status among various social groups. Second, we have regarded the structural change as having followed a historical sequence which could be divided into several major stages; every stage in turn may be further subdivided into substages. We have defined a stage of development as being "major" if a new factor were added to the process of change. We regarded the substages, though often more intensive and widespread in appearance than the stage itself, as having resulted from the interaction of existing factors rather than the introduction of an original developmental factor. Third, we considered the changes in the social structure, hence the historical sequences of development in the Ottoman Empire and Turkey, to have been caused by concrete factors, manifest in a series of real situations. Consequently, we expected these structural changes to be quantitatively measurable at all times, provided the data were available. Finally, we have viewed political activity in each stage of development as being the consequence of the activities of specific social groups. We have regarded the contemporary political development of Turkey as corresponding to a specific historical stage of development, that is, to the stage in which the political system begins to act as an independent (causal) variable and conditions the rate of structural differentiation. Briefly, the process can be placed in this causal paradigm: technological-economic stimuli; structural differentiation (occupational diversification and emergence of new groups); a new stage of development quantitatively more complex than the previous one; political development. We shall attempt to analyze each of the four phases and the factors conditioning them along with the hypotheses mentioned above and apply these to the history of Ottoman-Turkish development.[1]

---

[1] For a comparative historical study of modernization see Robert E. Ward and Dankwart A. Rustow, eds., *Political Modernization in Japan and Turkey* (Princeton, 1964).

1. Structural Change as the Dynamics of Development

Development in Turkey as elsewhere consists of a process of structural change, a corresponding differentiation of functions and reassignment of statuses, roles, and responsibilities among individuals and social groups. Structural change is caused by technological or economic factors, as well as by the response of social, political, and cultural systems to the political challenge rooted in these factors. Structural change is taken to mean changes in occupations, in production methods, in the patterns of stratification, and a corresponding justification of authority and group solidarity. The main consequences of these changes appear in the form of new social groups, in the establishment of new power relationships, and in the re-evaluation of sociopolitical roles and statuses often in competition with older social groups. The ancient groups, if viewed in the light of Ottoman-Turkish developmental history, tend to adapt to new conditions through a series of functional adjustments. In fact, these are often the human bases from which the new groups emerge.

Technological innovation is taken to mean the introduction of a new technical material element in the major field of activity. Historically speaking, such innovations seem to have been stimulated by the need to increase the government's military potential or were the consequences of internal structural pressures. A technologically superior society seldom attributes its superiority to factual causes, but rather to the uniqueness of its social and cultural system. Thus, the Ottoman Empire achieved superiority over the Byzantines in the fifteenth century and later over Persians and Mamluks by using gunpowder and artillery in a manner and volume unknown to its enemies. But it attributed its victory to the superiority of its own society and culture, supposedly resulting from compliance with divine commandments. In the eighteenth and nineteenth centuries, Europe claimed that its superiority over the Ottomans resulted from the high virtue of its culture and not technology, armament, or economic power. The latter were considered to be the consequences of culture.

We regard structural transformation as the fundamental cause of political development. This derives in part from our own ecological view of development, and in part from the need to find a constant variable against which other variables can be measured and the changes in the quality of political development linked more precisely to given factors. The cultural determinists were probably right as far as their methodology was concerned because they tried to explain all change by relying on one basic factor.[1] We adopted the same approach by substituting structure for culture and regarding the latter as being subject to the former. Obviously both "culture" and "structure" are composed of many parts which can be analyzed separately, but this leads one to the dilemma of the "tree" and the "forest" or the egg and the chicken. Moreover, the role of personality and leadership in the political process cannot be ignored. But the question of the individual's adjustment to altered circumstances (all of which form the basis of the behavioristic theory of cultural continuity and diffusion, and clarify specific problems and conflicts caused by growth), and his leadership performance is superseded by, and in fact subject to, structural change.

The idea of structural change as the prime cause of social and political transformation seems to be present in one way or another in the reasoning of most historians and social scientists who adopt a quantitative view of development. It is the fundamental idea in Barrington Moore's work, *Social Origins of Democracy and Dictatorship*. One may certainly disagree with Moore's overemphasis on peasants and landlords as the key factors in the transformation of certain agrarian societies, but not with his basic concept that structure is the fountainhead of all social and political development. His idea that the key feature of both the American and French revolutions was the "development of a group in society with an independent economic base" is essential, despite his bias in favor of an ultimate democratic order which was to emerge from this development.[2]

The idea of structural change as the key factor in development is accepted in a variety of forms by other social scientists. Karl Deutsch stated that social mobilization "accompanies the growth of markets, industries, and towns, and eventually of literacy and mass communication." [3] Elsewhere he referred to social mobilization as being the "process

---

[1] See William F. Ogburn, *Social Change* (New York, 1950), and Otis Dudley Duncan and Leo F. Schnore, "Cultural Behavior and Ecological Perspectives in the Study of Social Organization," *The American Journal of Sociology* LXV (September 1959), pp. 132-46.

[2] See Barrington Moore, Jr., *Social Origins of Dictatorship and Democracy* (Boston, 1966), and on change from estates to classes see Eugene and Pauline Anderson, *Political Institutions and Social Change in Continental Europe in the Nineteenth Century* (Berkeley, 1967), pp. 3-25.

[3] Karl W. Deutsch, *Nationalism and Social Communication* (Cambridge, Mass., 1966), p. 188. See also Chapter 6.

in which major clusters of old social, economic and psychological commitments are eroded or broken and people become available for new patterns of socialization and behavior." [1] Deutsch's indicator of social mobilization, namely the shift from agricultural to industrial occupations, is a typical case of structural change, and consequently part of the restructuring process of a society, and eventually of its value system. But this shift from agriculture to industry, to be dealt with later, is a key indicator of development only in modern or contemporary societies. It cannot explain the changes in history. Consequently, one must adopt a broader view of structural change which can be applied to development throughout history.

Seymour M. Lipset saw social stratification and the assumption of political roles by the middle classes in Latin America—manifest in a change in the social structure from an elongated pyramid into a diamond shaped one—as the effect of industrialization.[2] This, in fact, was another way of viewing structural transformation as a cause-effect relationship and of regarding it as the prime cause of political development. Thus, Lipset's well-known indices separating a democratic society from a nondemocratic one, such as the rate of industrialization, wealth, education, and urbanization do not fall in the same category. The first indicator is, in fact, the cause and the following three are the effects of structural transformation.

Phillip Cutright, though critical of Lipset's simple indices, developed his own indicators of political development still rooted in structural change.[3] Cutright's basic premise was that a politically developed nation had more complex and specialized institutions, and that a proper index of political development should correlate with the variables of other social institutions. The national indices used by Cutright, such as developoment of education, urbanization, communication, economic growth, and labor force characteristics, do not follow a logical sequence. Like Lipset, he confuses the basic cause of structural change with its effects. Thus, economic growth and change in labor force characteristics are

---

[1] Karl W. Deutsch, "Social Mobilization and Political Development", *American Political Science Review* LV (September 1961), pp. 493-514.

[2] Seymour M. Lipset, "Some Social Requisites of Democracy: Economic Development and Political Legitimacy," *American Political Science Review* LIII (March, 1959), pp. 76, 83.

[3] Phillip Cutright, "National Political Development: Measurement and Analysis," *American Sociological Review* 28 (April, 1963), pp. 253-64. See also: Leo F. Schnore, "The Statistical Measurement of Urbanization and Economic Development," *Land Economics* XXXVII (August 1961), pp. 229-45.

inseparably the original causes of structural change, while education, urbanization, and communication depend on and become, in fact, qualitative expressions of economic growth and changes in the labor force. After a certain degree of development, education may provide powerful stimuli for additional change. Nevertheless, Cutright's view that political development is measurable and that each nation can be visualized within a process of a continuum of development is an implicit recognition of the historical dimension of development.

It was Bert F. Hoselitz who, building on J. Schumpeter's theory of social groups, referred specifically to the basic relationship which exists between the complexity of productive activities and the alterations in other fields of social organization and structure, above all in social stratification. This last is determined by occupational roles or membership in a specialized collectivity.[1] The most characteristic aspect of a pre-industrial stratification system, according to Hoselitz, was evident in the sharp polarity of the social strata, resulting in an extreme gap between mass and elite, and in the disregard for economic performance as an important status-conferring variable. Incidentally, both these social characteristics apply to the Ottoman Empire.

Thus, if one accepts structural transformation as the central factor present at all stages of development in all societies at all times, a certain conceptual unity in time and space may be established.

It is necessary to interject into the discussion at this point the special role performed by the political system in accelerating structural transformation through massive introduction of technology into society. One of the chief characteristics of the modern political system is the role it assumes in deliberately initiating structural change as a means for establishing a new social order, and for assigning roles and responsibilities according to the new exigencies of production, solidarity, action control, value preservation, and transmission. But viewed historically, the very modern state appears as the by-product of a long process of structural transformation and functional differentiation.

Most of the current work on the new nations deals either with the immediate political processes which preceded the establishment of modern statehood or with the postindependence problems of national integration and consolidation, political identity, and loyalty. These studies ignore, for the most part, the structural changes which culmi-

---

[1] Bert F. Hoselitz, "Social Stratification and Economic Development," *International Social Science Journal* XVI (2) (1964), pp. 237-51. See also, William Kornhauser, *The Politics of Mass Socicty* (Glencoe, 1959).

minated in the establishment of a modern state as a form of political response to prior structural differentiation. The reshaping of ethnic, religious, or tribal loyalties and identities into national-political ones, and the idea of territorial statehood occurring in a variety of ways were preceded by basic changes in the structure of the native society.

Yet modern statehood is a definite watershed in the modernization process. It marks the end of a series of previous stages of structural change and the beginning of new ones by maximizing the interdependence between social, economic, and political structures and the deliberate use of power for societal goals. Modern statehood stands between the various preparatory stages of "modernity" and "modernity" itself. A modern political system has indeed the potential to adopt technology in all its aspects, and thus to speed up structural differentiation on behalf of new national goals. It is the stage, as Deutsch described it, when administratively skilled talent and available economic resources begin to rise above popularly expressed demands. It is also the stage in which man's view of himself and the universe is desacralized to the extent of recognizing the human being as having an unlimited capacity to transform nature, society, and himself.

Many of the differences separating the developed West from the third world are bound to disappear when the latter reaches full modern statehood, and achieves an optimum rate of economic development through the adoption of technology and industrialization. We believe that the basic difference between the developed countries and the third world stemmed from the early organization of the West in a system of modern statehood and its subsequent adoption of technology and of industrialization, the latter being the economic consequence of technology. In fact, much of the economic, cultural, and social superiority of the West may be related to its technology and political system geared to fulfill also the needs of the first rather than exclusively to the inherent superiority of its cultural values. It is difficult to explain the cultural and political differences between France and England when compared to one another, and the similarities in their "way of life" when compared to that of an underdeveloped country in Asia or Africa. On the other hand, it is difficult to understand why Asiatic Japan is far more developed than, say Lebanon, despite the pervasive Western influences of Catholicism and French culture in the latter. Lebanon is in good measure Europeanized and Westernized, but only partly developed, while Japan is not "Westernized" but quite developed. Japan's initial advantages over other countries, including the Ottoman Empire, lay in the presence of structural conditions (facilitated in turn by special geographic and demographic circumstances) conducive to full modern nationhood and subsequent technological advance.[1]

The modern state is the framework in which the political system can maximize its ability to achieve structural change through the rational integration of social groups into the system, the assignment of roles and statuses, and the definition and legitimization of authority according to the functional needs and goals of these groups. In fact, today, the degree of "modernity" is commensurate with the ability of a society to achieve modern nationhood and economic development, and meet welfare goals. The idea of Gabriel Almond that the difference between "developed" and "underdeveloped" political systems results from the degree of the complexity of differentiation and functions, is too simple as well as historically incorrect. The ancient systems of Asia, including the Ottoman state, were extremely complex structures, performing a variety of representative and symbolic functions not encountered in the modern systems. One may, however, point to the fact, noted also by Almond and Coleman, that the input of the old political systems was much greater than the output, while in the modern systems the opposite is true. In summary, we view the formation of modern statehood both as the result of prior structural change and as a new major stimulus to intensified social differentiation and development in general.

The idea that structural differentiation is the basic cause of political development needs further elaboration. We regard the structural change as being manifest, among other things, in the form of social groups. Political action is the action of social groups. It is the social group which develops as the consequence of social restructuring and becomes eventually the incubator from which individual leadership emerges. Leadership has been omnipresent in all stages of history. Yet, a leader cannot be conceived without relating him to a specific social group. There is a continuous generic relationship between technology and economics and the resulting structural differentiation of which social groups and their leaders are a natural consequence.

The emphasis placed on social groups in this study as the embryos of social and political development in the Ottoman Empire and Turkey stems not only from theoretical considerations but also from an actual division of society into social estates. For centuries, Middle Eastern society was divided into four major estates, which were assigned specific

---

[1] Ward and Rustow, *Political Modernization*, pp. 259-60.

roles, statuses, and functions. Thus the men of the pen, including the doctors of religion, writers, and accountants, and the men of the sword, that is the military, were charged with the maintenance and transmission of culture, religion, and tradition, and the defense of territory. The merchants and artisans had the duty of manufacturing and exchanging goods, whereas the fourth estate, comprising the peasants and the husbandmen, were considered food producers. The basic responsibility of the political system—composed primarily of the first two groups—was to see to it that each individual maintained his place in the respective group, that he performed his group functions, and that social mobility was kept at a minimum. If social mobility occurred because of personnel needs in the ruling estates and occupational change, it had to follow a precise, rigid procedure. The sociopolitical system also accepted the interdependence of social groups. In the ultimate analysis the chief function of the political system was to preserve the status quo through a rigid, prescriptive control of social mobility and stratification. This was relatively easy as long as the forces of change were constant and the process of transformation followed a known cycle. The challenge to the system began to arise about the sixteenth century when new forces such as the technology coming from the West and changes in routes of trade and inflow of gold and silver changed the traditional economic structure and brought about new patterns of social stratification. This was, in fact, the beginning of a gradual transition of the traditional society from social estates to a class organization. It proved to be a fundamental social and political movement toward modernity. (European society's ancient division into various estates such as noble, clerical, burgher, or peasant, was not very different in substance from that of society in the Middle East.)

2. Historical Evolution or Stages of Development

In the preceding discussion we have tried to bring into focus two major aspects of politics. First, structural differentiation appears as a basic cause of social and political development. Second, this structural differentiation is occurring in a historical continuum which can be divided into several stages. Each new stage is characterized by the addition of a new element in the process of development, thus rendering it more complex and differentiated. It is important to note from the very start that the idea of stages of development enjoys great popularity among economists and some social scientists. Thus, Walt W. Rostow's idea of five stages of socioeconomic growth—traditional society, preconditions to takeoff, takeoff, the drive towards maturity, and mass consumption—is in essence a historical concept of staged development.[1] Simon S. Kuznets, though critical of Rostow's views, developed his own theory of stages by placing special emphasis on the impact of the historical heritage, especially in his concept of *economic epoch* and the epochal innovation, the first consisting of the interaction between technological, institutional, and social change. Another view of stages of development in which education was given a special role was advanced by John K. Galbraith.[2]

Political scientists and sociologists have dealt with the idea of historical stages of development. A. F. K. Organski believed that modern nations have undergone four distinctive stages of political development since the sixteenth century: the politics of primitive unification, the politics of industrialization, the politics of national welfare, and the politics of abundance.[3] All countries had to go through these stages of development and must be in one of the stages. Organski's views largely followed Rostow's stage theory of economic development and tended to overemphasize the government's economic role, while disregarding the rise and impact of social groups in history.

Dankwart A. Rustow found it necessary to deal also with the "problem of sequel" within the context of the formation of modern nation states. According to Rustow, the most critical set of alternatives confronting modernizing societies are the timing for authority, for identity, and for participation and equality. He believes that these three political ingredients of the modern nation state are more effectively assembled one by one, that is to say, in stages, rather than all at once, and that political participation and equality should be the last crowning achievement in the total process.[4] Rustow, however, qualifies his view of stages by indicating that the sequence of authority, identity, and equality should not be regarded as stages in time and quantity but as qualitative expressions. In other words, Rustow limits his remarks to noting certain sequences

---

[1] Walt W. Rostow, *The Stages of Economic Growth: A Non-Communist Manifesto* (Cambridge, Mass., 1960). *Politics and the Stages of Growth* (Cambridge, 1971) appeared after the manuscript went to the publisher and was not used.

[2] Simon S. Kuznets, *Modern Economic Growth: Rate Structure, Spread* (New Haven, 1966). See also J. K. Galbraith, *Economic Development in Perspective* (Cambridge, Mass., 1962).

[3] A. F. K. Organski, *The Stages of Political Development* (New York, 1965).

[4] Dankwart A. Rustow, *A World of Nations, Problems of Political Modernization* (Washington, D.C., 1967), pp. 120-32.

of political development without dealing with the historical socioeconomic causes of that development. Elsewhere, however, while dealing in a more concrete fashion with political events in the Ottoman Empire and Turkey, he refers to five "periods" of development.[1] Frederick W. Frey, in a study of Turkish elites, openly alludes to stages of political development as being somehow necessary since in the development process countries travel the same road, some a little behind, others ahead, and suggests that "there seem to be regularities in the sequence of political changes actually observed in many of the new nations over the world".[2] C. E. Black, one of the few to deal with development in historical perspective, saw seven patterns of modernization with four successive phases in each one; challenge of modernity, consolidation of modernizing leadership, economic and social transformation, and social integration.[3]

Finally, one must mention Daniel Lerner's theory of modernization, not only because he gave a new twist to the concept of stages but also because he dealt specifically with Turkey and the Middle East. Lerner began with the *a priori* idea that Middle Eastern "traditional" society, whatever that may be, was passing away by adopting new modes of communicating ideas and attitudes through the mass use of tabloids, radio, and movies. Consequently, he generalized by stating that the less developed societies would achieve Westernization by passing in a unilinear process through four stages of development. The first stage was urbanization, which tended to increase literacy; rising literacy tended to increase media exposure; and media exposure went with wider economic and political participation. This modernization, according to Lerner, was stimulated by the West and followed the Western model of an efficient society.[4] Lerner's major hypothesis was that high emphatic capacity was the predominant personal style of the individual only in a modern society which was distincly industrial, urban, literate, and participant.[5]

Daniel Lerner's theory suffers from serious drawbacks. He sees modernity and traditionalism as two exclusive modes of life in which the latter is doomed to perish. It is ethnocentric, for it accepts Western development

---

[1] Dankwart A. Rustow, "Political Parties and Ruling Elites in Turkey," in J. La Palombara and M. Weiner, eds., *Political Parties and Political Development* (Princeton, 1966), pp. 112-13.

[2] Frederick W. Frey, *The Turkish Political Elites* (Cambridge, Mass., 1965), pp. 407 ff.

[3] Cyril E. Black, *The Dynamics of Modernization: A Study in Comparative History* (New-York, 1966).

[4] Daniel Lerner, *The Passing of Traditional Society* (Glencoe, Ill., 1964) pp. 45 ff.

[5] *Ibid.*, pp. 46, 50.

as a unique model of modernization and it combines data acquired through sampling with a variety of available statistical information merely to prove a point. Finally, the nebulous concept of empathy ignores totally the fact that Middle Eastern society had its own version of the same. From the viewpoint of this study, Lerner's major shortcoming lies in the fact that his theory of stages of modernization based on the correlation between industrialization, urbanization, literacy, and mass exposure is not historically correct. First, the Middle East had a rather high level of urbanization in the fifteenth to seventeenth centuries without having much industry or widespread literacy. Urbanization declined in the late eighteenth and early nineteenth centuries due to the disintegration of the crafts industries and changes in trade patterns. Then it began to rise in the late nineteenth century due to trade with the West, and in the twentieth century because of industrialization and increased administrative and commercial activities.[1] Urbanization in the past did not seem to have much of an impact on literacy, which remained at less than 20 percent until 1920. In the recent period, from 1950 onward, the rate of urbanization in Turkey, for instance, rose from roughly 18 percent to about 35 percent by 1968, while the rate of literacy remained constant at about 40 percent between 1950 and 1960, and then went up to 48 percent, due largely to political pressures. On the other hand, total newspaper circulation remained constant at less than half a million in the period 1927 to 1945, despite an increase of literacy from 10 to 29 percent in the same period. Yet, after the establishment of opposition parties in 1945-46, newspaper circulation in Turkey rose to about 1.5 million by 1960, while the literacy rate went up to barely 39.5 percent. The number of radio sets, which stood at about 176,000 in 1945, rose to over 1.3 million in 1960 and went up to over 2.4 million in 1965, simply because of the introduction of inexpensive transistor sets and de facto abolition of a radio tax. On the other hand, political participation (voting) remained constantly very high, in fact reaching the highest point in 1950 and 1954, when the radio and the newspaper barely touched the villagers and literacy was low. Similar discrepancies in Lerner's "modernization" and "stage" indicators may be found in analyzing relevant data in other Middle Eastern countries.

The correlation between urbanization, literacy, media communication, and participation as seen by Lerner may, in fact, depend on some

---

[1] For historical background see William R. Polk and Richard L. Chambers, eds., *Beginnings of Modernization in the Middle East: the Nineteeenth Century* (Chicago, 1968).

prerequisites, such as technological change and the rise of new social groups. Indeed, the four indicators actually describe special functions occurring as a result of the prior rise of groups. The communication process itself seems not to be basic but derivative in origin, seldom gaining the status of an independent variable as seen by Lerner. One may draw rather different conclusions from the available studies of communications in Turkey.[1]

But we are not concerned here as much with how a particular scholar defines the stages of development as with the reasons which induce a man to think in terms of stages of development. Indeed, the recurrent theme of stages of social, economic, or political development among scholars dealing with modernization is of capital importance and deserves close scrutiny.

The theory of stages carries with it the implicit idea that the development process does not follow a uniform trend but is broken into several periods which are qualitatively and quantitatively different from each other. Economists Rostow and Kuznets, whatever their approach, seem to agree that the differences in stages of development result from growth and that growth is caused by the addition of new tangible social (new groups), and economic (capital, labor, planning) factors into the development process, and that each addition creates a different stage of change. However, the economists fail to point out how this economic growth transforms itself into social and political stituations through the interaction of social groups. In other words, an integral theory of development should indicate how the new groups rise and how their leadership, their economic and social functions alternate in each stage. E. E. Hagen tried to focus on the group characteristics of development in his theory of social change, advocating the "withdrawal of status" as a condition for economic development. He is, in fact, pleading for the creation of a modern entrepreneurial class which would stimulate the development process through the massive and rational use of economic resources. It seems that E. E. Hagen, and also David McClelland, who stressed the roles of entrepreneurs, are concerned only with the present stage of economic development. Following Schumpeter's ideas, they idealize the entrepreneur's developmental role but fail to analyze the conditions which facilitated the rise but also conditioned the political competence of the entrepreneur in time and space.[2]

---

[1] Frederick W. Frey, *The Mass Media and Rural Development in Turkey*, Report Number 3 (Cambridge, Mass., 1966), pp. 32 ff.

[2] E. E. Hagen, *On the Theory of Social Change: How Economic Growth Begins*

It seems to us that the rise of the modern entrepreneur is due not only to psychological cultural factors, but also to concrete economic forces, and the social structuring occurring in history. In developing nations the self-reliant, innovating type of ideal entrepreneur may not come into being, at least not in accordance with the Western model. Though we stress the role of entrepreneurs in the current stage of political development in Turkey, we regard them as rising not only through personal effort but especially because of specific government policies and carrying the peculiarities of the sociohistorical process.

We can summarize our view by saying that development takes place in stages. A new stage begins through the addition of a new element into the development process. This may be a technological or economic factor which, while increasing the complexity of the social structure, does not always lead to growth, that is to say to rise in economic activity or production, though its effects are felt in all layers of society through the action of some social groups. Thus, the economic or material factor is always present in a process of change and is reflected in a variety of social and political manifestations.[1] Each developmental stage coincides with the rise of a new social group and with its involvement in social, economic, and political activity. (In the premodern Middle Eastern society, involvement in political activity was reserved to a small elite and it occurred under prescribed rigid regulations. The beginnings of modern politics may be found in the political claims of new social groups created by new types of economic forces. This is discussed in Chap VII).

The group's manner and the timing of its involvement in politics through claims for positions and status, the development of group consciousness of solidarity and a rational view of economic interest are conditioned in good part by the rate of exposure to the stimuli, and by ideological preparedness. Thus, new technological and/or economic factors and the subsequent rise of a new social group are the distinguishing features of each new stage of development.

(Homewood, Ill., 1962), and David C. MacClelland, *The Achieving Society* (New York, 1961).

[1] In a recent study of political development, the author who disagrees with Lipset's correlation between wealth and democracy finds that constitutionalism and popular participation in politics parallel gradually the level of economic development. Martin C. Needler, "Political Development and Socio-Economic Development: the Case of Latin America," *American Political Science Review*, September, 1968, pp. 895, 897.

3. The Quantitative Measure of Stages and of Development

Technological innovation, economics, and social groups are intimately interrelated key factors of political development. They appear in the form of concrete, tangible situations and consequently their presence and activity should be factually determined, and quantitatively measured. The differences between the stages of development, and in fact the entire stage theory, become tenable only if the quantitative differential is factually determined, and statistically measured. It is interesting to note that the theory of stages of development is supported by some available quantitative studies. For instance, the authors of *World Handbook of Political and Social Indicators*, though without adopting any particular scheme of stage theory, have arrived at the same by using current development statistics with regard to 114 countries. The data accumulated led the authors to distinguish five stages of economic and political development: "traditional primitive" societies, "traditional civilizations", "transitional societies", "industrial revolution" societies, and "high-mass consumption" societies. The authors agree that "a more direct and dependable method for examining stages would be to look at developmental data for many countries over long periods of time, to substitute longitudinal for cross-sectional data".[1] Indeed, the five types of societies or stages of development, defined by the authors of the *World Handbook* strictly on the basis of quantitative statistics, correspond roughly to the stages of development in the Ottoman Empire. The authors did not intend to produce a theory of stages but an aggregate of economic, political, and social data for use in studies of development. But in the end they did provide enough statistical data to show that there was an intimate relationship between quantitative growth and stages of development, and that the process can be historically studied.

There are, in addition to the *World Handbook*, a series of other studies dealing with the measurement of social and political development. Most of these, however, tend to regard the current stage of development as absolute, if not final, and are often inadequate for use in historical analyses of development and do not apply to many contemporary societies of the third world.[2] Obviously, measurement indices developed

---

[1] Bruce M. Russett, H. R. Alker, Jr., K. W. Deutsch, and H. D. Lasswell, *World Handbook of Political and Social Indicators* (New Haven, 1966), pp. 294-303.

[2] S. M. Lipset, "Research Problems in the Comparative Analysis of Mobility and Development," *International Social Science Journal* XVI, no. 1 (1964), pp. 35-48.

in accordance with the complex structure of contemporary society, and often *ex post facto*, are oriented toward the measurement of performance in the nation state and cannot be applied to a situation arising several centuries ago. Most of these indicators, particularly the political ones, are overly elaborate and hardly useful in historical studies of development. Some of the currently used indicators, such as per capita income established in the framework of market economy, or the size of urban centers, or of unemployment, already varying in effect from country to country, would have a great margin of error if used for historical studies of development.[1] Moreover, these indicators often fail to take into account the differences of development which exist among various regions of the same political unit.[2] Finally, some broad theories of development, formulated on the basis of observation in a single Asian or African country, become rather useless when applied to a different region or to comprehensive historical situations.[3] There is not yet a concept or generally accepted set of indicators to be used in a study of historical stages of development, though the use of quantitative methods in historical

---

See also Philip E. Converse, "New Dimensions of Meaning for Cross-National Sample Surveys in Politics," *International Social Science Journal* XVI (1964), pp. 19-34. See also Paul F. Lazarsfeld and Morris Rosenberg, eds., *The Language of Social Research* (Glencoe, 1955).

[1] Donald V. McGranahan, "Comparative Social Research in the United Nations," in *Comparing Nations: The Use of Quantitative Data in Cross-National Research*, Richard L. Merritt and Stein Rokkan, eds. (New Haven, 1966), pp. 529-30.

[2] This idea may be confirmed by a study concerning Spain. The authors found seven types of regions in Spain: bourgeois, proletarian in transition, classes medias in transition, classes medias, gentry in transition, gentry and proletarian. Madrid was a special eighth area. See Juan J. Linz and Amado de Miquel, "Within-Nation Differences and Comparisons: The Eight Spains," in Merritt and Rokkan, *Comparing Nations*, pp. 267-319.

[3] One must confess in full candor that theories of modernization based on the analysis of contemporary development in one or two countries of Africa, for instance, have limited relevance to Latin America or Asia, unless one stresses the fact that the theory was based on the qualitative analysis of a specific stage of development, or of a particular society and not of the modernization of a continent as a whole. On the other hand, certain aspects of social and political development in the Middle East, Latin America, and Asia show striking similarities, suggesting that their stages of development coincide. Furthermore, the level of development in one country varies from one region to another. One may assume that these differences are compatible with the structural changes which correspond historically to a more or less precise stage of differentiation. Thus, the quantitative and qualitative data used to measure development or to devise a theory of modernization, if not properly defined according to the specific stage of development it purports to analyze, could lead to erroneous conclusions.

research as mentioned before is gradually spreading.[1] The studies on the Ottoman Empire are even less conceptually and quantitatively oriented. But the lack of truly operational concepts and of complete statistical data on the Ottoman Empire is partly compensated for by the existence of empirical studies and a few statistics which are sufficient to formulate general hypotheses.[2] The following brief survey of the stages of development in the Ottoman Empire, therefore, is based mostly on such special studies and some statistics, while the section on modern Turkey makes wider use of economic and social indicators, as used in current quantitative research.

4. THE STAGES OF DEVELOPMENT IN THE OTTOMAN STATE

A) *The Frontier Marches* : *Uç beyler* ("*frontier lords*")

The history of the Ottoman state if viewed from the standpoint of structural differentiation, and the action of social groups which determined the specific features of each stage, may appear radically different from most of the opinions hitherto held.[3] The spectacular rise of the

---

[1] Sten Sparre Nilson, "Measurement and Models in the Study of Stability," *World Politics* (October 1967), was able to study the political role played by some 180,000 freeholders in the eighteenth century in England. He used statistics which show their shift between Whigs and Tories. He associates these shifts with the changes in the interest position of the freeholders. (See also page 11, n. 1)

[2] We acknowledge our indebtedness to the works of Professors Omer L. Barkan of Istanbul University, Halil Inalcik of Ankara University, Bernard Lewis of the University of London, and many others from various institutions in Europe and the United States. Detailed bibliographical references to these and other studies on Ottoman history may be found in some of my own following articles and papers : Kemal H. Karpat, "The Ottoman Parliament of 1877 and its Social Significance", in the *Actes du premier congres international des études Balkaniques*, IV (Sofia, 1969), pp. 247-257; "The Land Regime, Social Structure, and Modernization in the Ottoman Empire," in Polk and Chambers, *Beginnings of Modernization*, pp. 69-90; and the introduction in Kemal H. Karpat, *Political and Social Thought in the Contemporary Middle East* (New York, 1968). Mention should be made also of quantitative research presently being carried out by Mr. Bruce McGowan concerning taxation in the 16th century Ottoman Empire. Finally, I must mention my own unpublished research on the social history of Gaziantep (Ayntab) Province in Turkey, based on a variety of sources including the civil court registers which has enabled me to fathom better the historical dimensions of development.

[3] Practically all students of the Ottoman Empire divide its history into several periods based largely on the sequence of political events. For instance, the noted Turkish historian Halil Inalcik, in an unpublished study entitled "The Periods of Ottoman History," distinguishes six periods : formative 1300-1402, consolidation and

Empire in the late thirteenth and early fourteenth centuries resulted from the evolution of petty lords, local and nomadic chieftains, family heads and their followers into a ruling group of military lords. East of the Ottoman territory there were several small, but well developed, feudal Turkish states which had been subject to the Seljuk, and then to the Mongolian-Turkic rulers located farther East in Anatolia and Central Asia. In the West there was the feeble and rapidly decaying Byzantium, whose feudal system, based on rigid control of the land and the population, had degenerated into an oppressive rule. Consequently, the newly established principality in 1299 under the leadership of the house of Osman relied heavily on the above groups. Their leaders came to be known eventually as the *uç beyleri* (literally the "lords of the points" frontiers) who were instrumental in conquering and ruling the territories in the West. The early Ottoman state, in fact, was just a frontier principality like many other Turkish states existing at that time. The *ahis*, the virtuous organizations of the craftsmen and artisans, which spread throughout Anatolian towns, seemed to have played a major role in the establishment of the early Ottoman state. The basic role of the central authority embodied in the ruling dynasty of Osman was to achieve military cooperation, to assign responsibilities, and to act as the supreme arbiter among the frontier beys. We lack precise information about the early beys of the thirteenth century. But in the following century we encounter a series of families such as the Evresnoğulları (the extensive area around the Vardar River in the Balkans was called "Evrenos territory" as late as the eighteenth century), Djandarlı, Turakhanoğulları, Malkoçoğulları, and Mihaloğulları, which constituted the backbone of the early Ottoman socio-political system. These formed a special type of "nobility" in control of vast territories in the Balkan penisula where the Empire's main territory lay after 1357, and in Anatolia.

The peasant, working on the conquered lands, usually owned by the state but controlled by the bey, found himself in a position of relative freedom. He was no longer a vassal as in the early Byzantine feudal system, but a kind of tenant as far as the usage of the land was concerned.

---

reorganization 1402-81, attempt at a world-wide empire 1481-1671, crisis and development struggle 1581-1699, defeat and acceptance of European superiority 1699-1826, abolition of Janissaries to Abdulhamid's overthrow 1826-1909. Halil Inalcik, "Osmanli Tarihinin Devirleri" ("The Periods of Ottoman History"), mimeographed paper, 1957.

The bey raised an army, usually from his territory, and commanded it in the field in case of war under the orders of the central authority, the throne. The latter depended on the bey's cooperation for carrying out its military and administrative functions, though theoretically the sultan, as the highest ranking bey, retained ultimate decision-making power. Thus, the early Ottoman state was based on the cooperation of all beys. This cooperation assured to the bey security for his land holdings and political power for the throne.

The beys appeared as the basic group in this stage. One must mention the fact that in the fourteenth century the central Ottoman government had neither a large standing army nor a large bureaucratic organization, but relied heavily on the cooperation of the beys. It is true that the embryos of the future vast centralized bureaucracy appeared rather early. The special recruitment system, *devşirme*, paved the way for the high government officials, usually converted to Islam, and personally attached to the Sultan (the *kul* or servant) to replace the Turkish elements in the bureaucracy; the *timar* holdings (land owned by the state and administered through appointed officials) became a quasi feudal economic-social system in its own right, while the judiciary strove to apply a set of general but flexible rules derived from Islamic law and local custom applicable to the heterogeneous society. Agricultural land was the economic basis of society and the foundation of the beys' power.

Thus, on one hand, there was the central authority bent on increasing its own authority, and on the other, the frontier lords eager to preserve their autonomy. This situation was the source of continuous tension, but it contained also the dynamics of development for the latter-day Ottoman state.

The Ottoman Empire, according to a new theory, developed out of economic tensions.[1] The coastal towns around the Sea of Marmara and the immediate inland areas, according to this theory, formed a new economic unit combining sea trade with agriculture. This developed a special dynamic life of its own which left out the main Anatolian inland. Consequently, various groups engaged in economic occupations were affected negatively by this change and eventually migrated to join the new economic unit under the Ottomans in the West. These groups gave the Ottoman sultanate its unusual economic strength which made

---

[1] Mustafa Akdağ, "Osmanlı imparatorluğunun kuruluş ve inkişafı devrinde Türkiye'nin iktisadi vaziyeti" *Belleten* 51 (1949), pp. 497-571; 55 (1950), pp. 319-418. See also the criticism by Halil Inalcık in *Belleten* 15 (1951), pp. 629-90. See also Bernard Lewis, *The Emergence of Modern Turkey* (London, 1968).

possible rapid military expansion. The nomads were settled in the conquered areas and acquired new economic habits. The author of the theory thought that the Seljuk Turks, the predecessors of the Ottomans, were a socioeconomic cadre, whereas the Ottomans themselves were a politico-economic cadre. He thus implied, rightly, that there were some qualitative differences between the Ottoman and Seljuk social structures. He tried to point this out by stressing the political aspect of the Ottoman state.[1]

The central authority could not depend permanently on the cooperation of the frontier beys, who were ready to engage in new wars in order to expand their power, as well as their land holdings. The beys, on the other hand, were fearful of a powerful centralized authority which would deprive them of power. The growing tension and suspicion between the central authority and the beys were contained partly by fear of crusades from the West. This fear was relieved after a major crusade was decisively defeated at Nicopolis in 1396. The victorious Sultan Beyazid I (1389-1402), encouraged by his prestige, decided to curtail the power of frontier beys by expanding the size of the imperial army and by increasing the authority of the central institutions. But in the crucial battle of Ankara in 1402, the frontier beys and their armies lent little support to Beyazid, who was defeated, taken prisoner by Timur (Tamerlane) and died in capitivy.

The Ottoman Empire subsequently went through a period of disintegration caused by the struggle for power among Beyazid's sons and various categories of beys. Indeed, behind each of the sultan's four sons (another one appeared later) stood several groups of beys. The Anatolian beys under Mehmet, who relied on the central authority and on the support of inland towns, eventually defeated the Balkan beys who had backed Suleyman. Finally, Mehmet I (1413-21), after defeating with some difficulty the last brother, Musa, became Sultan and brought the fighting to an end. It is important to note that the beys under Suleyman represented the latinized lords of the Balkans who had instituted a feudal regime of their own. Musa had behind him the combined Muslim-Christian lower classes of the Balkans and inflicted several defeats on his adversaries. He lost in the end because some of the beys who sided with him changed sides and supported Mehmet.[2]

---

[1] For a different viewpoint see Paul Wittek, *The Rise of the Ottoman Empire* (London, 1938).

[2] See Paul Wittek, "De la defaite d'Ankara à la conquête d'Istanbul", *Revue des*

The development of the Ottoman system under Murat II (1421-51) and especially Mehmet II (1451-81) was conditioned largely by the situation described above. Mehmet II enacted a series of basic laws ("*Kanunname*") to give the Ottoman Empire its basic administrative structure, which survived until the nineteenth century. This basic legislation (in theory supplementing but at times altering the Islamic Shar'iah), which had developed in large part as a response to the relationship between the beys and central authority and the land system, set the stage for future structural changes.

Basically, this legislation can be defined as the instrument through which the beys were bureaucratized and the land subjected to strict regulation. The quasi-autonomous frontier beys were replaced by a much larger group of officials who formed the backbone of the provincial bureaucratic structure. The major body of the bureaucracy was recruited through the *devşirme* system and enjoyed much higher prestige than the frontier beys. The early Ottoman nobility, composed mostly of the beys, was drawn mostly from Turkish-Muslim stock. They lost political power in the fifteenth century but preserved their land as well as social position in the countryside. The large bureaucratic order loyal to the throne isolated them from direct participation in decision making.

The basis of this sociopolitical system was the land. Indeed, Mehmet's legislation had turned the land into the economic foundation which generated social and political developments. The relationship between economics, social structure, and politics may be summarized as follows :

The central authority established its supremacy through the expansion of the imperial army. Sultan Mehmet II backed by his bureaucracy expanded the Janissary corps, increasing their pay but also their training and discipline. He installed in each provincial center Janissary units to back the representatives of the central governement. The Sultan established a hierarchical and impersonal type of bureaucracy which functioned through a system of councils.

The title to the land was defined precisely and registered in perpetuity in the state's name in registers whose quality attests to the high level of bureaucratic efficiency.

The administrator of the state land, or *timar*, was the *sipahi*, usually a cavalryman who had shown valor on the battlefield. The *sipahi* could be removed at any time since his administrative position was not hereditary, but subject to the government's decision. The *sipahi's* duty

---

études islamiques, 1 (1938). For earlier periods see Claude Cahen, *Pre-Ottoman Turkey* (London, 1968).

was to preserve the state land title, rent the land to farmers, collect taxes, and see that the land was continuously cultivated. In case of war, the *sipahi* had to produce a given number of soldiers and supplies according to the *timar's* revenue.

Thus in one and a half centuries the Ottoman state acquired its basic structure. A military-bureaucratic group headed by the Sultan held the power. The villager, who had been the vassal of the former Byzantine or Balkan feudal lords, first became a kind of semi-tenant to the bey and then a full tenant to the state. His status deteriorated later. The peasantry or *raya* was assigned the status of a social group in accordance with the traditional theory of estates and was thus integrated into the system. The position of the military bureaucracy was also precisely defined except for the fact that its members were given some supervisory economic functions which in some ways violated the stringent rule that the social estates should not have overlapping functions. The place and functions of scholars and merchants were also clearly defined according to the ancient organization of the social estates as mentioned earlier. Mehmet II established also the *millet* system whereby each major religious group—Orthodox, Armenian, and later Jewish—chose its religious leaders and regulated autonomously its own cultural and religious affairs.

B. *The Centralized Quasi-Feudal Stage*

The frontier beys who had constituted the key social group for more than a century were superseded by a large centralized bureaucracy in the second half of the fifteenth century. The *sipahis* appeared now as the most strategically situated group. Though the *sipahi*'s authority ranked well below that of most of the officials in the capital and provincial administrators, his economic and social functions—that is, his role in agricultural production and leadership in the rural areas—gave him an unusually influential position. Consequently, any change in the *sipahi*-land-peasant relationship would have had drastic repercussions upon the existing sociopolitical system. Indeed, the adoption of guns and artillery caused basic changes in the relationship.

The introduction of small firearms into the Ottoman army in the late fifteenth and sixteenth centuries was a technological event of far-reaching consequences. The rifle made the foot soldier the backbone of the military organization. The old land organization which provided the economic support for the cavalry ("*sipahi*") and the provincial army became politically disfunctional, while its economic importance grew as a source of revenue for the imperial, central army based on gun-carrying infantry.

The major problem now was to utilize the land in such a fashion as to supply enough revenue for the government to buy the modern firearms and support the ever increasing number of foot soldiers, or the *kuls*, servants of the Sultan. (The translation of *Kul* as "slave" is wrong since this relationship between the *kul* and the Sultan was not one of ownership but service.) The legal title of the state to the *timar* lands and the social status of the peasantry were formally maintained, though the old functional relationship between the socioeconomic structure and the politicomilitary system ceased to exist. Social disintegration followed in a few years at the end of the sixteenth century as all of Anatolia entered a period of social turmoil from which it never quite recuperated. The Ottoman historian Naima attributes the rebellions to the fact that many *sipahis* not joining or deserting the campaign against Austria were deprived of their land holdings and tried to regain them by enlisting in their service the bands of deserters and auxiliary troops (*sekbans*, *levends*) roaming through Anatolia. These rebellions, known as *Jelali*, were actually peasant uprisings led in some cases by disgruntled *sipahis*, scions of feudal families and governors, but also by commoners. They were, in fact, the natural outcome of the breakdown of the ancient estate system and the beginning of a long evolution leading to new social reorganization based on class characteristics.

The reliance of the state for defense on foot soldiers armed with firearms had several other major effects. It led to increases in the size of the central imperial army or the *kapıkulus*. It necessitated new expenditures for armament and maintenance, and eventually led to a thorough reorganization of the government apparatus. Table 1.1. illustrates best the increases in the number of imperial troops and of military expenditure.[1]

---

[1] O. L. Barkan, "Les particularités du système financier ottoman et son évolution du XVe au XVIIe siècle," *L'impôt dans le cadre de la ville et l'état* (*Collection Histoire— Historische Uitgaven*), no. 13, (1966), p. 272. For the sources of these statistics see "H. 933-934 Tarihli Bütçe Cetveli ve Ekleri," *Iktisat Fakültesi Mecmuası*, Vol. 15, 1-4 (n.d.) pp. 1-51; "1079-1080 (1669-1670) Mali Yılına Ait Bir Osmanlı Bütçesi ve Ek'leri," *Ibid.*, Vol. 17, 1-4, (1961), pp. 1-79. For the uses of artillery see Carlo M. Cipolla, *Guns and Sails in the Early Phase of European Expansion* (London, 1965), and D. Ayalon, *Gunpowder and Firearms in the Mamluk Kingdom* (London, 1956). For revolts see M. Akdağ, *Celali Isyanları 1550-1603* (Ankara, 1963); also B. Lewis, "Ottoman Observers of Ottoman Decline," *Islamic Studies* (Karachi, 1962), pp. 71-87.

Table 1.1
Change in Number of Troops and Military Expenditure
1528-1670

	1528	1563	1582	1670
Number of imperial troops	21,519	38,599	44,468	88,382
Expenditure for troops in aspers	57,707,666	117,917,392	115,039,203	236,605,688

One asper is equivalent to two dollars.
The revenue in 1527 was about 538 million aspers while in 1653 it was still 537 million. Actually, due to inflation the buying power was five-eighths to two-thirds less.

The imperial army developed to the detriment of the *sipahi* by usurping in the countryside the former *timar* lands. The state used its legal title to exploit the land and the peasant in order to secure the highest revenue from agriculture. It was interested primarily in cash revenue and not in the direct exploitation and administration of the land, as it had been during the heyday of the *timar* system when the politicomilitary organization and the social and economic systems were so harmoniously interwoven.

A new social order was to rise from this situation, despite the fact that the *timars* survived formally until 1831. The number of *timars* was drastically reduced and many of the lands were given as reward or in lieu of salary to government dignitaries and the Sultan's favorites. For instance, the *vilayet* of Erzurum, which had 5,618 *timars* in 1653, lost two-fifths, or a total of 2119 *timars* at once in 1715. By 1804 the total number of surviving *timars* was barely 3,575 and these were used often by the Sultan to reward the commanders of the army of the New Order or *Nizam-ı Cedit*. According to Professor Halil Inalcik, the total number of *sipahis*, that is, holders of *timars*, in 1475 was 63,000; it decreased to 45,000 in 1610 and by 1630 it was only between 7,000 and 8,000. Meanwhile, the number of *kapıkulu* imperial bodyguards, some of whom held land, went up from 12,800 in 1475 to 92,206 in 1630. The old structure on which the Ottoman state was based had all but disappeared.[1]

---

[1] For the total number of *timars*, based on the official *yoklama* ("census"), in 1605-6 and 1607-8, and in 1804 and 1805, along with a statistical analysis, see V. P. Mutafcieva and Strazimir Dimitrov, *Sur l'état du système des timars des XVII*e*-XVIII*e*ss.* (Sofia, 1968). Also, Halil Inalcik, "The Breakdown of the Ottoman Economic and Social Structure" (Unpublished paper, 1967).

The birth of the next social group, which spawned a new stage of development, may be found in this situation brought about by economic and technological forces. Before dealing with this next group it may be important to point out a few characteristics of the stage under study.

The fifteenth and sixteenth centuries saw the rise of an Ottoman civilization evident in the rapid development of cities and cultural establishments, a medical school with its surgery room and a hospital were established in Edirne by Beyazid II (1481-1512); trade and industry flourished, while the Empire's political power extended to Europe, Western Asia, the Indian Ocean, Sumatra, North Africa, and even Mombasa. Such development may be defined as growth. But more important was the underlying structural development, namely the differentiation and tensions which rose within the bureaucracy and the society at large. The provincial administrative apparatus began to be identified with the economic and social problems in the countryside and gradually fell under the influence of new social groups, the *ayans*, which acquired de facto control of the land.

The gradual fall of the *timars* and the rise of the *ayans* occurred more or less simultaneously, providing thus a typical case of what Samuel Huntington would call simultaneous political development and political decay.[1] The process intensified in the following centuries.

C) *Provincial Autonomy and the Ayans*

The situation described above provided the basis for restructuring and reorienting the economic-functional relationships of a group long in existence. Indeed, beginning toward the end of the seventeenth century, the social and political effect of the economic factor in the differentiation process became increasingly evident in the person of the *ayan*.[2] It must be stressed that this qualitative transformation, that is, the transformation of the economic factor from a semidependent variable to an independent one, occurred to the detriment of the personality factor.

---

[1] Samuel P. Huntington, "Political Development and Political Decay," *World Politics*, XVII, no. 3 (April 1965), pp. 386-430.

[2] *Encyclopedia of Islam*, new edition, s.v. "Ayan" and bibliography. Çagatay Uluçay, *Saruhan'da Eşkiyalık ve Halk Hareketleri* (Istanbul, 1944). For the old *ayan*, see also L. Fekete, "XVI Yüzyılda Taşralı Bir Türk Efendisinin Evi," *Belleten* 29, 116 (1965), pp. 615-38. For the new "economic"-minded *ayans* of the 18th and 19th centuries and their social origin, see Cemal Gökçe, "Edirne Ayanı Dağdevirenoğlu Mehmed Ağa," *Istanbul Universitesi Edebiyat Fakültesi Tarih Dergisi* XVII, no. 22 (March 1967), pp. 97-110 and Avdo Suceska, *Ajnai* (Sarajevo, 1965).

In other words, leadership came to be identified more with a group rather than with a person. Indeed, all classical histories of the Ottoman Empire agree that the era of "good" sultans ended and the reign of "weak" or "bad" sultans began in the second half of the sixteenth century. The change corresponded to the complexity of structural differentiation. This, indeed, was the period in which various elements of the bureaucracy became the chief policy-making bodies of the center, whereas in the countryside a new social group acquired economic power, chiefly because of its control of land.

The notables in the countryside and towns had been known for long in the Middle East as *ayans* or *ashraf*. These were communal leaders, often organized in a local administrative board, whom the central government frequently used as intermediaries in its dealings with the villagers and town dwellers. The eclipse of the *sipahi* as land administrator, and the change of the land from being the direct source of men and supplies into a source of cash in the form of taxes, gave the *ayan* a new role. He became eventually the tax collector, usually farming out part of the tax and then supervising the rental of state lands to peasants while maintaining his position as intermediary between the peasants and the bureaucracy. The title of *ayan* was awarded through a special charter by the government. Thus, the *ayans* developed not as a totally independent group but through the action of the government. The *ayans* early in the seventeenth century belonged to the old ruling families, some of which had been heads of the feudal Turkish states of Anatolia prior to their inclusion in the Ottoman Empire. These consolidated their power to the detriment of the central authority for a while, but in the eighteenth century they were overwhelmed by lesser *ayans*.[1] The latter were often former soldiers of the imperial army stationed in the provinces, or officers of the same units who became local notables, or town dwellers and even upper class peasants. They could invest their money in auctioning tax farming rights over a region, and thus were able to consolidate further their economic position.

The *ayans*' power rested in their economic control of rural resources, as well as in their influence among the town people and the peasantry, but especially in their usefulness to the government. While not yet a true social class, the *ayans* became rich enough by the end of the 18th century to be able to lend money to the government, as in the war with Russia in 1768. Some were exerting de facto control over their

---

[1] See Karpat, "Land Regime".

areas. It is wrong to look upon the *ayan* as a feudal lord. He was part of the rising social strata, rooted not only in agricultural occupations but also in the trade and manufacturing which accompanied the diversification of professions and rise of small towns in the eighteenth century.[1] The proof that the *ayan* was the outgrowth of structural differentiation can be found in the fact that this institution was generalized both among Muslims and Christians. Thus, in the Balkans, particularly in Bulgaria, the *djorbaji* or *çorbacı* often played identical roles to the *ayans* in Muslim areas, as intermediaries between the government and the local community. The *djorbajis* were landowners, often had small shops, and were engaged in local trade. These *djorbajis* eventually became important elements in Christian nationalist movements for independence in the Balkans during the nineteenth century. Other groups, such as the *Celep* (known as Jelepi in the Balkans), charged by the government with raising and collecting cattle and supplying the army and town with meat, were exempted from this duty at the end of the eighteenth century as a result of the emergence of a market economy. Nevertheless, they continued to raise the cattle on their own and eventually became businessmen, trading often in foreign markets.[2]

The *ayans* became the key element which supported the revolts staged by provincial administrators against the central government in the eighteenth and nineteenth centuries. Eventually the *ayans*, backed by their own private armies stationed outside Istanbul, were able to secure from the government in 1808 a special charter, *Sened-i Ittifak* or Pact of Alliance, recognizing as hereditary their rights over the land and forbidding government officials from interfering in their affairs.

Parallel to the rise of the latter-day *ayans* there occurred two other crucial developments. The technological and economic superiority of

---

[1] See the following on this subject: Christo Gandev, "L'apparition des rapports capitalistes dans l'économie rurale de la Bulgarie du nord-ouest au cours du XVIIIe S.," *Études Historiques* (Sofia, 1960), pp. 208 ff; and Traian Stoianovich, "The Conquering Balkan Orthodox Merchant," *The Journal of Economic History* XX (June, 1960), pp. 234-313. See also for Syria: Herbert L. Bodman, Jr., *Political Factions in Aleppo, 1760-1826* (Chapel Hill, N.C., 1963); M. D'Ohsson, *Tableau Général de l'Empire Ottoman*, 7 vols. (Paris, 1788-1824); and Bernard Lewis, "Some Reflections on the Decline of the Ottoman Empire," *Studia Islamica* (1958) pp. 111-27.

[2] The complex process of economic and social development in the Balkans is well illustrated in a series of excellent translations from original sources by Doreen Warriner, ed., *Contrasts in Emerging Societies* (London, 1965). For the emergence of the national states see Dimitrije Djordjevic, *Révolutions nationales des peuples Balkaniques 1804-1914* (Belgrade, 1965).

the West brought about a series of Ottoman defeats and led to the establishment of new military units and the adoption of new weapons in the eighteenth century. All this increased further the need for additional revenues, which were derived as usual from the exploitation of land resources.

The growth of trade with Europe was the most powerful economic stimulus which shaped the Empire's social structure and politics. Concomitant with the rise of the *ayans* and the *djorbajis* and all other similar groups in the countryside, there developed a merchant group, first in the Balkans and then in the coastal cities. Trade eventually affected the economic functions of the upper agrarian groups by transforming them into producers for the market economy or into small manufacturers. The *ayans* and *djorbajis* controlling the production sector of the economy had an interest in the expansion of trade and appeared as an ally of the merchant against the central authority and its taxes. Liberalism was the merchants' political philosophy.

Behind the emerging market economy there was, as mentioned before, the ever increasing stimulus, trade with the West. It was this trade, based on special extraterritorial rights granted to Western powers (including the trade arrangement with England in 1838) and on a merchant-manufacturing class composed of Christian town dwellers, which decided the destiny of the Ottoman social structure and the state itself in the eighteenth and nineteenth centuries.

The increase in trade and the change in the import-export patterns between Izmir (Smyrna) and Marseille illustrates the point (Table 1.2).[1]

Table 1.2

Trade of Marseille

	Imports to Marseille in francs	Exports from Marseille in francs	
1700	2,087,304		—
1750	5,629,076	(1749)	4,222,984
1766	10,611,300	(1765)	5,695,921
1789	12,805,603		9,545,793
1839	17,029,000		35,856,000
1850	31,031,000		36,227,000
1860	59,663,000		46,159,000
1872	86,846,000		121,671,000
1874	112,263,000		98,489,000
1877	77,060,000		117,051,000
1881	116,403,000		104,600,000

[1] Demetrius Georgiades, *La Turquie actuelle* (Paris, 1892), pp. 218, 224-5. See

The trade of Salonica, which was about 600,000 piastres in the period of 1700-1718, went up to 2 million between 1750 and 1770 and from 1786 to 1800 reached 8 million. The Greeks became the leading trade group in the area and replaced the Jews and Armenians who had been the chief merchants in the past.[1] In a study of trade in Salonica in the eighteenth century and of the socioethnic groups active in the economic life of the area, Nicolas Svoronos supports fully the view that trade with the West stimulated the growth of urban population, that a new powerful merchant class rose there and that these groups professed freedom of trade and gained political consciousness along ethnic lines.

The total trade of the Ottoman Empire with Europe in 1783 was £ 4.4. million. By 1845 it had reached £ 12.2 million, and £ 54 million in 1876, and £. 63.5 million in 1911, despite considerable loss of territory by the Empire.[2] The population growth of coastal cities accompanied the rise in trade volume. For instance, the population of Izmir, which was barely 30,000 in 1800, went up to over 200,000 in 1892. Beirut's population of 6,000 in 1782 went up to about 12,000 in 1846 and to 100,000 in 1885.[3]

The socioeconomic development of the Ottoman Empire in the eighteenth century, stimulated by trade, affected first the Balkans, then the coastal areas along the Mediterranean, and finally the inland towns. The Christian population—Greeks, Armenians, Copts, Maronites, and to a lesser extent Jews—inhabiting these regions received favorable treatment from the British and the French trading interests. Many came to represent or work for the Western commercial interests and opened their own offices in the Mediterranean and the Black Sea ports as well as in cities in the interior of Europe, such as Vienna. In the Balkans the Christian small merchants, manufacturers, and landlords inhabiting the towns formed a new relatively wealthy structure out of which grew an intellectual-military group. These had little in common with the medieval estates and could hardly expect to remain under Ottoman rule. The ruling political order, on the other hand, not reformed from within, and bent on maintaining the ancient organization of social

---

also A. Ubicini, *Letters on Turkey* (London, 1856), and A. Velay, *Essai sur l'histoire financière de la Turquie* (Paris, 1903).

[1] Nicolas G. Svoronos, *Le commerce de Salonique au XVIIIe siècle* (Paris, 1956), p. 323. P. Masson, *Histoire du commerce français dans le Levant* (Paris, 1911).

[2] Charles Issawi, *The Economic History of the Middle East, 1800-1914* (Chicago, 1966), p. 30.

[3] Georgiades, *La Turquie.*, p. 223; Issawi, *Economic History.*, p. 232.

estates as well as its cultural religious outlook, could not think of true reform but only of change to restore the status quo, as clearly revealed in Selim III's (1789-1807) imperial directives.

The political consequences of the above situation were as expected. First, in Serbia Kara George in 1804 and then Miloş Obrenovich in 1815, both engaged in livestock trade with Austria, headed the Serbian revolution movement. The Greek revolt of 1821, which began in Russia, was helped greatly by the rich Greek merchant colony of Odessa. The Balkan national states were on the rise. Yet, the same social structure which enabled them to reach independence and nationhood prevented their advancement. The basis of the new states was an agricultural, peasant society dominated by the town—in which the educated together with the landed groups monopolized political power. The society did not generate technological drive or industrialization, but was content to maintain a patriarchal-romantic view of the world and of itself. The politics of the area emerged eventually as a struggle for the emancipation of the peasant who in turn, once free, was happy to work his land and perpetuate the village traditions. A cursory look at the Balkan literature suffices to show that the intellectual taste had not gone beyond the tales of *haiduks* ("Robin Hoods"), the saga of liberation in which anti-Turkish sentiment played a great role. They saw the Ottoman Empire in their own national image though Turks had not yet acquired national consciousness. The Balkans could not break away from this peasant rural mould until recently.

The remaining sections of the Ottoman Empire failed to produce a well-established merchant or intellectual class, or even develop economically until late in the nineteenth century. This, in fact, proved to be a blessing in the long run. The lack of class differences and the parochial attachment to land and village facilitated rapid social mobility and restructuring according to the needs of modern industry and mass society.

Thus, in the stage of development under consideration, trade was the major economic stimulus while the land and the groups controlling it such as the *ayans* and their subgroups played a major role in structural change and political development.

D) *National Statehood : Modern Bureaucracy and the Intelligentsia*

Practically all scholars who studied the political development in the Ottoman state in the nineteenth century referred invariably to this stage as the beginning of modernization. In other words, they accepted implicitly the view that political development moved to a more complex stage of differentiation and acquired new qualities which gave it "modernistic" features. The idea that this was the beginning of all "modernization" cannot be accepted at face value, since the very stage of "modernization" was the consequence of previous structural changes. The distinguishing characteristics of this phase of development, called "modernization," lay in the emergence of a centralized, multifunctional government and a series of social groups created as its consequence. This is, incidentally, the stage in which the political system becomes increasingly the most effective factor of change, or the independent variable. It is also the beginning of the transition to modern statehood and nationhood.

In a different work we have studied the political transformation of the Ottoman state late in the eighteenth and throughout the nineteenth centuries in the light of structural change and functional adjustment.[1] We have pointed out in that work that Sultan Selim III (1789-1807) attempted to meet the challenge posed by the *ayans* in the interior (and Russia and Austria abroad) through a drive toward centralization based first on the establishment of a modern army. This attempt failed, but Selim's nephew and successor, Mustafa IV (1807-08) intervened, Mahmut II (1808-39) was able to establish a modern army, and he then proceeded to subdue the *ayans* mercilessly and confiscate their property. But he left intact the process which produced the *ayans*. In fact, his suppression of the Janissaries in 1826, of the *timars* in 1831, and his bringing the *vakfs*, the old Islamic social service institutions, under government control, facilitated the rise of a broadly based middle class. The functions assumed by the government in the field of education, agriculture, social services, etc., which had been discharged in a variety of ways and in varying degrees by voluntary organizations, or had not existed at all, opened new employment outlets for specially trained personnel. These attempts have been praised in various studies as the "modernization" measures undertaken by an enlightened Sultan who finally realized that he had to borrow ideas and institutions from the most advanced civilization of his time, that is, the West, if the country wanted to survive at all. Actually, if studied with reference to the particular functions embodied in these reforms, one would realize that these measures answered in good part both the Sultan's need for effective central authority and the demands of the rising commercial and agrarian groups for a new

---

[1] Kemal H. Karpat, "The Transformation of the Ottoman State", *International Journal of Middle East Studies*, 3 (July 1972) pp. 243-81.

regulatory system, rather than being the blind imitation of an advanced civilization. The Tanzimat edict of 1839, long hailed as the turning point in the Empire's modernization, was in reality a promise to respect life as well as property rights, that is to say, to assure the most powerful economic groups, as well as peasants in the Balkans, that their economic and personal security would not be impaired. Outwardly, the edict appeared as a declaration by the new Sultan, Abdulmecid (1839-1861), to institute a regime of law. In fact, this was the institutionalization of various structural developments which had taken place in the past century.

The structural development meanwhile continued its own course. The rapid penetration of the Anatolian markets by Western goods, the increased influence of foreign banks, and the further expansion of trade with the West stimulated economic activity. The rate of urbanization in the Anatolian towns accelerated. The flourishing coastal cities acquired distinctive Western features, becoming centers of export and import, while the towns in the interior remained largely agricultural, and, while preserving the traditional outlook stagnated.

The basic agricultural resource, the land, was still owned by the state. Left outside the normal commercial transactions it was unable to respond properly to the stimulus of the liberal economy, as repeatedly stressed by Western advisors and local merchants. The idea of increasing the circulation of state lands and improving their cultivation, and thus enhancing their monetary value, prompted the government to enact an agrarian law in 1858. This law, considered a turning point in the Empire's life, preserved in principle the state title to lands considered *miri* (mostly former *timar* and *vakf* estates), but liberalized greatly the tenants' rights. Eventually, the law was amended so as to make the tenants' rights subject almost to the same rules as those governing the sale and transfer of private land property.[1] This was, in fact, a fundamental transition from state ownership toward private economy.

Far-reaching consequences resulted from these changes. In Iraq and other areas which used the land in common according to tribal customs, the sheik or the tribal chief registered the land in his own name and became a landowner. Elsewhere the land was mortgaged, sold, or bought according to the cultivators' needs and the supply and demand law of a market economy. Rural capital in the form of land was thus accumulated largely in the hands of the Muslim-Turkish agrarian

---

[1] Karpat, "Land regime".

town elites, while in the coastal cities of Anatolia and the Eastern Mediterranean, trade, especially the import-export business, remained largely, but not exclusively, in the hands of the non-Muslims.

The political roles and ideology of the intelligentsia and the bureaucracy, composed mostly of Muslims and Turks, can be properly understood only in the light of the above social and economic background. This group came into being largely in response to the government's need for technically trained personnel. It became eventually the elite which engineered the political transformation. While it is true that the upper bureaucracy consisted mostly of the descendants of the old imperial bureaucratic families, the lower ranks, and especially the new services, were filled by the sons of the agrarian town elites and lower urban groups. This new bureaucracy, most of which was Muslim and Turkish, was expected to fulfill regulatory services according to the needs of an expanding market economy of which the Christian commercial groups formed the upper crust, while the Muslims formed the lower—and in most cases the agricultural—estate. Understandably enough, when Westerners described the Muslim-Turkish element, they saw it either in the role of a political magnate or of a humble peasant. The structural transformation in Anatolia and the Middle East, in the second half of the nineteenth century, notably after the Paris Treaty of 1856, shows striking similarities to the social changes which occurred one century earlier in the Balkans, but not to the political ones. The Balkan states created their own political system in the form of national states. In the remaining areas under Ottoman rule the government structure and the social strata, still under monarchic rule, became ideologically and culturally separated from each other.

The so-called "modern" educational system appeared at this period as the chief means of recruitment into the bureaucracy.[1] Established after 1839, and greatly expanded after 1869, the educational system appeared more as an avenue for gaining social position and status than a means for acquiring the skills necessary to perform practical tasks. The attitudes

---

[1] These schools adopted a view of the world and of their own society that reflected the condescending intellectual outlook of other societies of the West. If one regards the Western education system as being partly the expression of a highly diversified social and technological order and industrialized economy, it is obvious that its ideas could not be properly assimilated and interpreted by the native intelligentsia nor transmitted to the masses. Deprived of the technological, economic, and social bases on which Western education stood, the intelligentsia often interpreted the West in a superficial and fragmentary fashion as an ideal rather than a normal way of life.

and the philosophical outlook of the new intelligentsia, when rated as "modern" or "Western" by outside observers, were not based on a realistic appraisal of their professional quality but on the degree of alienation from their native culture, and adoption of Western ways, including dress. Modern education caused alienation and was thus resented both by conservatives and nationalists, though their reasons were different. The position of the bureaucratic intelligentsia as an "elite" was a completely new situation both with respect to the traditional Ottoman Empire and Europe. Indeed, the social and economic environment in which they had to operate, as well as their philosophic outlook stemming from these conditions, was different from their own traditional past as well as from the European social and cultural milieu. This group was, in fact, the forerunner of the elites in the third world of our time but without their advantages as far as experience was concerned.

The isolation of the intelligentsia from the masses was further intensified because the relationship between the government institutions, the philosophy of the elites, and the needs and aspirations of the social strata were not functionally harmonized. Indeed, attempts at industrialization and the modernization of agriculture, which could have created some basic structural change, failed. This failure may be attributed in part to subtle European interference, and in part to the inability of the bureaucracy to relate the problems arising from expanded trade, urbanization, or land ownership, to the idea of functional government. All this produced economic and military weakness which was rendered worse by inability to provide a new integrative principle, a rallying idea.

The Ottoman Empire was not a national state. It was a multinational state based on the co-existence and the mutual balance among various ethnic and religious and social groups. Consequently, it could not adopt without danger of self-dismemberment the ideas of nationalism and liberalism based on ethnicity, class differentiation and economic motivation as developed by the French Revolution and the Russians' sense of nationality based on religion successfully borrowed by the Christian intelligentsia. It is true that the Young Ottomans (1865-1876), who represented a segment of the liberal-minded bureaucracy-intelligentsia, advocated political and cultural integration through representative institutions, and through the adoption of a Muslim-Ottoman nationalism that would embody the society's cultural and social characteristics. They also used the newspaper, and the modern literature developed after

1860, to disseminate their opinions and enlist popular support.[1] But these feeble attempts at political socialization could not bridge the ever-widening gap between the bureaucracy-intelligentsia and the agrarian commercial groups, which was rendered worse by the deepening chasm between Muslims and Christians. The debates in the parliament established between 1876 and 1878 as the consequence of a short-lived experiment in constitutionalism, indicate the differences between the bureaucracy and the countryside notables, and the representatives of occupational groups in towns. Though without organized mass support and without a program of political action, the latter insisted on establishing legislative control over the Executive. This parliament was prorogued in 1878.

The structural change, meanwhile, accelerated and eventually affected the intelligentsia itself. The agrarian and commercial groups expanded rapidly in size as did the intelligentsia. The general education decree issued in 1869, by Sultan Abdulaziz (1861-1876) not only swelled the ranks of the educated but also brought a slight differentiation between the bureaucracy and the intelligentsia proper, through emphasis on professionalization. By about 1885, sections of the intelligentsia began to voice some of the cultural and political opinions of the countryside as well as the aspirations of some urban groups. This was, in fact, the beginning of Turkish nationalism, which began formally, like most other similar ideologies, as a linguistic-literary movement. This nationalism had anti-Western and anti-Christian as well as liberal features. The interference of Western powers in the Empire's affairs, the special privileges accorded to Christian commercial groups as a result of Western pressure, and their superior economic status, as well as the claims for independence of the Christian ethnic groups still under Ottoman rule, accounted for the negative aspects of Turkish nationalism. That nationalism's liberal features stemmed from the intelligentsia's claim to reinstate the Parliament and the Constitution of 1876 and to establish a regime of freedom. The Young Turks' revolt of 1908, staged by army officers and countryside notables in the Salonica and Monastir areas against the

---

[1] Real newspapers appeared in 1843 (*Ceride-i Havadis*) and especially in 1860 (*Tercuman-i Ahval*) and 1862 (*Tasviri Efkar*). *Tasvir* had a circulation of 24,000 copies. By 1870 the Empire had a score of newspapers and periodicals, though no major increase in literacy occurred despite demand for education among the intelligentsia. It is significant that the demand for professional education was voiced chiefly by the representatives of the rising middle classes such as the journalist Mithat Efendi. See Kemal H. Karpat, "The Mass Media," *Political Modernization*, pp. 255-282.

Sultan, was the consequence of these structural-ideological developments. It was the first modern-type revolution in the Empire. The Young Turks' secret organization, the Union and Progress Committee, acquired de facto control over the government and one year after the revolution it was able to replace Sultan Abdulhamit II (1876-1909) with a more congenial ruler. The Union and Progress Committee officially became a political party in 1913, and although faced with a score of opposition parties it remained the chief representative of the modernist, nationalist intelligentsia, and also of the rural groups which had established and dominated the local party branches in the agrarian towns throughout the Empire. The dissolution of this party in 1918, after the Empire's defeat by the Allies in World War I was followed by the establishment of *Mudafaa-i Hukuk Cemiyetleri* ("Associations for Defense of Rights"). These organizations, headed first by rural notables and later, after the partial demobilization of the reserve officers in 1918-1919, by teachers and other local intellectuals, proved the major media for mobilizing popular support for the successful movement of national liberation headed by Mustafa Kemal (Atatürk). [1] The War of Liberation (1919-22), waged against Greece, France, and England, brought together the notables, the intelligentsia, and lower sections of bureaucracy and the military, as well as the population, for the first time since the early days of the Ottoman Empire. It was the first egalitarian, participatory, political movement, and from it Republican Turkey was born. This was the traumatic phase of transformation from which the basic characteristics of Turkish modern national statehood emerged. Eventually, in 1922-1923, the Associations were transformed into a political party, the People's Republican Party, which became the ruling body of Turkey in the period 1923-45, based still on the coalition of town notables and urban bureaucracy-intelligentsia. This was in fact a Turkish national middle class, which divided into several groups in the next decades.

The Republican regime established in 1923 replaced the centuries-old monarchy, and it was followed by a series of cultural reforms which appeared designed to consolidate the newly established Turkish national state. Geographic regions were integrated under a centralized national Turkish government, and emphasis was placed on a secular, national sense of political identity and loyalty above all other forms of allegiance.

---

[1] This is a topic of fundamental importance. A study of the Gaziantep branch of the Union and Progress Committee undertaken by this writer shows how tightly politics and economics were interwoven in the countryside. For background information see also Marc J. Swarz, *Local -Level Politics* (Chicago, 1968).

Domestic and international goals were defined according to the new needs. From 1923 to 1945 the bureaucracy and the intelligentsia, using the Republican Party as their organizational basis, inducted segments of the urban and some rural groups into the political culture of modern national statehood through an intensive campaign of political socialization.[1] The political system consequently reached an advanced degree of institutionalization by becoming resistant to stress and by developing a professional bureaucracy, which theoretically at least remained above group conflict.[2]

The political developments in Turkey in the decade 1920-1930 appear as monumental developments to an impressionistic observer. They are monumental indeed if the rate of development is measured according to the changes in the political institutions. But if viewed from the standpoint of structural differentiation and the action of social groups, the second half of the nineteenth century, as well as the period 1908 to 1930, do not appear to show a new stage of development, but the culmination of a developmental stage which began with Sultans Selim III and Mahmud II. The entire period from 1800 to 1945 was marked by the slow emergence of a "modern" bureaucracy, then of an intelligentsia, and the subsequent transformation of both through the broadening of the bases of recruitment, education, and politization. Sons of the urban groups, rural notables, and upper class peasants, as mentioned, joined the elite order chiefly through education. The upward mobility intensified but did not change the relationship of the rising elite to the masses. In fact, as mentioned before, the differences between the two sharpened and the sense of alienation increased since the intelligentsia's values were determined not by the social group from which it was born but by the ruling one it had joined.

The situation could be illustrated much better if one analyzed the position of the intelligentsia from the viewpoint of group ideology. Indeed, from the second half of the nineteenth century until well into

---

[1] The political socialization followed a pattern similar to that described by Herbert H. Hyman, *Political Socialization* (Glencoe, Ill., 1959). See also Gerald J. Bender, "Political Socialization and Political Change," *Western Political Quarterly*, June 1967, pp. 390-407.

[2] For this we have used mainly William Flanigan and Edwin Fogelman, "Patterns of Political Development and Democratization: A Quantitative Analysis", and Michael C. Hudson, "Some Quantitative Indicators for Explaining and Evaluating National Political Performance" (papers read at the American Political Science Meeting, Chicago, 1967). The authors' kindness in making these papers available is gratefully acknowledged.

the 1940s the intelligentsia's elitist philosophy competed with the pragmatic, utilitarian, semiliberal ideology of the economic strata of the middle classes, first the Christians, and then mainly after 1923 the Turkish-Muslim groups. The intellectuals, having monopolized power, position, and the mass media, disseminated their own viewpoint. Their often-used idea of populism, "*halkçılık*", despite its democratic connotation, did not then go beyond being an ideology of mobilization against the outside enemy and eventually against the imperial bureaucracy, but not against the economic elites.[1] Later it was used as an integrative device to achieve mass following and national cohesion. The ideas of participation and social equality were not part of populism, despite a few instances where attempts were made to achieve it.

All these developments do not undermine our main argument that this massive political change in Turkey does not represent a truly new phase of development. Indeed, many of the reforms carried out in the Republic were proposed as early as the end of the nineteenth century and then elaborated upon from 1908 to 1918, and partly implemented. Some of the legal reforms carried out in the Republic fulfilled regulatory demands voiced by the economic groups in the 1840s.[2] The sections on property and inheritance of the Swiss Code Civil, and especially the Code of Obligations adopted in 1926, following on the footsteps of previous commercial codes, provided for precise procedures in business transactions, and established uniform, predictable rules for the acquisition, protection, and transfer of private property. Incidentally, this Code made a special point of indicating that the Land Code of 1858 was abolished.

The establishment of a European system of private property and the regulation of business activities geared to the principle of free enterprise consolidated and sanctioned legally the pattern of social stratification based on economic power which had been in the making for more than a century. Eventually, in the Republic, this system of private property conditioned the rise of new economic activity, group interest and consciousness, and political action. But the elite legitimized its power and

---

[1] There is a new school of thought in Turkey which regards the struggle for national liberation of 1920-22 as an anti-imperialist social uprising of the Anatolian masses under the leadership of a military-intellectual group. Sabahaddin Selek, *Anadolu Ihtilali*, 2 vols. (Istanbul, 1964).

[2] There is abundant literature on this period. For bibliographical information see Bernard Lewis, *The Emergence*, and Kemal H. Karpat, *Turkey's Politics* (Princeton, 1959).

reforms, based not on a social and economic doctrine but on the model of a contemporary civilization, namely the West, although few knew what the West really meant. There is a subtle difference between Ataturk's reference to the West as a model and that of his followers. He spoke of the need to rise to the level of *contemporary civilization* and pointed to the West as being situated at its most advanced end. After his death the West was taken as a model to be imitated without qualification.

Thus, the legal system appeared as a normative regulatory apparatus adopted to the social diversification and stratification which had begun one and a half centuries earlier. It became also one of the factors stimulating future differentiation in fostering the growth of new groups with their distinct mentality. The school of law in Istanbul was expanded and a new one established in Ankara in order to train lawyers, judges, and civil servants. Trade, land survey, and a number of other professional schools expanded rapidly after 1930 as the demand for trained personnel rapidly exhausted the available skilled manpower. Yet these developments, though impressive when compared with earlier ones, ended in a relative impasse.[1]

By 1930, the dynamism and creativity evident during the previous decade was replaced by the rulers' complacency and self-satisfaction, and their dedication to the consolidation and preservation of the new social system. The cycle of development had reached its zenith. One could not expect another advance without the introduction of a significant new structural stimulus which could thrust society into another stage of transformation.

However, before we deal with this structural stimulus it is necessary to point out that developments between 1908 and 1930, and their underlying secularist philosophy played a major role in conditioning the nature of demands and preparing for the transition to a new stage of development. These demands appeared in the form of requests for increased material welfare and higher professional performance. It seemed as though the ancient mystical predisposition to seek reward in the next world was replaced by a sudden awareness that material satisfaction in this world was preferable and possible. The concentration of power in the hands of the government, coupled with its secularist-positivist

---

[1] Frederick Frey distinguishes six phases of political development in Republican Turkey: formation of national identity, struggle for national independence, post-independence realignment, tutelary regimes, initial democracy, and consolidation of democracy. *Turkish Political Elites*, p. 408. These are, in our view, the formative and consolidation phases of modern statehood.

philosophy, and the empirical and secular outlook in education seem to have maximized the belief in the system's ability to provide material satisfaction for all demands. Several latent elements in the native culture which could produce a new "protestant ethic" in business seemed also to have moved to the surface due largely to the "desacralizing" impact of secularism, achievement orientation, and interest in material welfare.[1] Somehow in the air there was the expectation that one stage of development was about to end and another to begin.

E) *The Making of a New Stage: Industrialization, Entrepreneurial Groups, and Political Development*

Industrialization, which started in 1931, was the dominant technological economic force which gradually reshaped the social structure and gave Turkey's development a new quantitative and qualitative outlook. There are distinctive differences in Turkish political development before and after industrialization. The process of nation formation under the leadership of a bureaucratic political elite sustained by agrarian town notables was the dominant feature of the period before 1931. In the second period, beginning roughly in 1931 and gradually accelerating from 1949 to 1958 and from 1962 to 1970, there was a higher level of economic growth and ideological ferment, all reflected in intensified political activity.

The same kind of difference in the quality of political development can be seen in other developing countries as reflected in the literature on the subject. Thus, the writings dealing with countries in the early stage of political development stress the problems of nation formation, integration and identity, and loyalty to the new government over all other forms of tribal ethnic and religious allegiances. The intelligentsia and the military are regarded in this phase as the chief social groups performing key political roles. On the other hand, the studies of countries in Latin America, Asia, and the Middle East, which underwent the initial phase of political development and industrialization, tend to stress participation and equality as the dominant features of politics.

The brief historical analysis of Ottoman and Turkish political development indicated that the process of modern nationhood which began

---

[1] Robert Bellah, *Tokugawa Religion: The Values of Pre-Industrial Japan* (Glencoe, Ill., 1957), speaks about the religious factors which prepared Japan for the industrial revolution. There is no parallel development in Turkey between 1930 and 1950. Perhaps in the future one may see also in Turkey the search for new religious values in order to develop a kind of middle-class ethic.

in the nineteenth century as a transition "from empire to nation," to use Rupert Emerson's expression, conferred upon the intelligentsia and the military bureaucracy special political functions which in turn determined their status and power. We will first sketch some of the main points in this process, then discuss them in more detail.

The propertied groups in earlier periods, though providing economic support for the system and benefiting economically from their association with the bureaucratic-intellectual order remained in the background as far as political power was concerned.[1] But the economic performance of this group from 1908 to 1918, and from 1923 to 1930, measured in the light of demand and expectation, was unsatisfactory since it lacked the dynamic, innovational characteristics of modern entrepreneurs. The explanation for the economic passivity of the members of the group, despite their wealth, may be found, among other things, in their reliance upon land ownership as the primary source of economic power, and limited access to technology.

The industrialization process which began after 1931 acted as a new technological-economic element of change and increased production while altering drastically the patterns of social mobility and stratification. It also moved Turkey's political development to another stage and level. The economic factor eventually became the most influential variable in determining the course of political development. The effect of industrialization was seen in the birth of a labor class (to be studied separately in chapter IV) and the rapid growth of a modern entrepreneurial group, as well as in the changes occurring in the structure, functions, and ideology of the intelligentsia. The rate of professional and technical specialization among the intelligentsia increased together with a definite economic reorientation of their philosophy.

The entrepreneurial sectors of the middle class groups engaged in manufacturing and trade and some of the agrarian sections grew rapidly in size. The inital industrialization which began under a rigid, costly, and restrictive type of state capitalism controlled by an economic

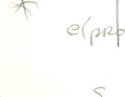

---

[1] We believe that E. E. Hagen's view that the "withdrawal of status respect" as a condition for the rise of the entrepreneurial class is not proven by the Turkish case since the entrepreneurs rose from the lower urban strata and from the towns in direct competition with the old bureaucratic elites and the propertied groups without the military losing their prestige until about 1953. An entrepreneur is in our view a "person holding a managerial position in a firm giving him ultimate decision-making power by virtue of his share of ownership in the enterprise." Alec P. Alexander, *Greek Industrialists: An Economic and Social Analysis* (Athens, 1964), p. 19.

bureaucracy was attuned after 1947, in part through the subtle pressure of the United States, to the needs and laws of a free market economy. Gradually the entrepreneurial groups were recognized as participants and beneficiaries of the developing economic and political system. By 1947 Turkey had fully abandoned the tutelary one-party system and embraced a rather liberal multiparty life in which the economic groups acquired important political roles. The general political effects of this transformation were evident in the emphasis placed on participation, equality, and freedom. Participation meant not voting rituals, as in the era of tutelary politics, but an actual involvement in politics as individuals, groups, and organizations formed on the basis of interest and solidarity. Equality was regarded not as consisting merely of formal rights and free access to courts, but of the actual availability of economic and social opportunities, of the abolition of the invisible but everpresent cultural and educational barriers perpetuating the rule of the bureaucratic elites, and of the acceptance of achievement, including the economic one, as a criterion for status and position. Freedom covered not only the right to voice discontent and criticize authority, but also the liberty to inquire into the bases and legitimization of power, and to organize and defend one's interests and views through political action. The institutionalization of participation, equality, and freedom, with due respect to the social and economic conditions which engendered them, was a crucial political development which emerged after the revolution of 1960. It is necessary now to expand upon the above points.

The industrial basis of the Republic was minimal.[1] The census of 1913 and 1915 of some cities (Istanbul, Bursa, Izmir, Uşak, Manisa, Bandırma) showed the existence of only 264 (1915) industrial establishments. More than half of these or 55.4 percent processed food and textiles. On the other hand 214 of these industrial establishments belonged to private individuals, 28 to corporations, and only 22 to the government, indicating thus the dominant position of the private entrepreneurs. Some 93.9 percent of these enterprises utilized some sort of mechanical energy. The total number of workers employed was 16,309 in 1913, and only 13,485 in 1915, due to the war conscription. The total value of industrial production of 229 and 175 establishments in 1913 and 1915 was 67,081 and 75.704 million liras respectively.[2]

---

[1] The only study on industry in the early period, that is Tanzimat, is by Omer Celal Sarç, "Tanzimat ve Sanayimiz," *Tanzimat* (Istanbul, 1931), pp. 1123-40. It appears in translation in Issawi, *Economic History*, pp. 48-59.

[2] The figures are taken from one of the lesser-known but essential studies on the

A national census of industry taken in 1921 indicated the existence of 33,058 establishments employing 76,216 people. The important industrial centers—Istanbul, Izmir, Adana, and Bursa—under foreign occupation, were excluded from the census. But another census taken in 1927, after the national boundaries were established, counted a total of 65,245 manufacturing and business sites employing a total of 256,855 people or roughly 2 percent of the population. But only 2,060 or slightly over 3 percent of these establishments employed 11 or more people. Of the remaining, 78 percent employed 1 to 3 people, indicating that they were small shops which could not be called industrial. This is also shown by the fact that only 2,822 establishments used any kind of machine.

In 1927, a total of 13,683 institutions employing four or more workers belonged to 10,941 individuals or entrepreneurs, of whom 10,259 were Turks and 642 foreigners.[1] We know that some capital had been accumulating in the country, partly because important sums of money were brought in by Turks migrating from the Balkans, who managed to sell their land. K. J. Jiricek, the outstanding authority on Bulgaria, reports that in 1879-1883 sales of land in Eastern Rumelia, which was soon incorporated into Bulgaria, amounted to 108 million krus. Of this amount 72 million krus represented sale by the Muslims (Turks) to Christians (Bulgarians). In the district of Stara Zagora alone the total value of land sale between 1877 and 1885 amounted to 50.5 million krus, of which 40 million represented land sales by Turks to Bulgarians. Indeed, a substantial number of Turkish entrepreneurs, bankers at the turn of the century, originated in the Balkans.[2]

The above figures indicate that the industrial foundations of Turkey from 1923 to 1927 were hardly suitable for a structural revolution. Agriculture was overwhelmingly dominant. But this industry, aside from a few state owned establishments, was in the hands of private individuals. This small private sector seems to have been extremely active as indicated by the number of banks in operation.[3] It gained some additional momen-

---

economy of Turkey by the noted economist and social scientist Ismail Hüsrev Tokin, *Rakamlarla Türkiye* (Ankara, 1949), pp. 20-38. A recent excellent publication is Vedat Eldem, *Osmanlı İmparatorluğunun İktisadi Şartları Hakkında Bir Tetkik*, (Ankara, 1970).

[1] *Ibid*. p. 54.

[2] K. J. Jirecek, *Cesty po Bulharsku* ("*Travels in Bulgaria*") (Prague, 1888). Sections translated in Warriner, *Contrasts in Emerging Societies*, pp. 244-45.

[3] The commercial secretary of the British High Commission reported that "in spite of the serious political and economic stituation which has existed in Turkey during the year, new branches of four banks have been established, and, in addition, arrange-

tum from the abolition of the capitulations through the Lausanne Treaty in 1923. It benefited also from the freedom to set up tariffs which became enforceable in 1929.

The political elites responsible for creating the political conditions for economic development pinned their hopes on the private sector's self-generated capabilities as indicated by Ataturk in his address to the economic convention of Izmir in 1923.

Economic independence appeared as a corollary to political independence, but the world economic crisis of 1929, which brought loss of faith in private enterprise, and the great popular support received by Fethi Okyar's Free Party changed the political elite's views on freedom and on economic development. Established through Ataturk's own initiative in order to open a safety valve for internal pressure, Okyar's party acquired enough strength in four months to seriously challenge the ruling order. The party was disbanded in the same year. Concerned with this unexpected opposition, Ataturk took a three-month trip throughout Anatolia to discover the causes of this popular discontent. Fortunately, we have a general record of Ataturk's talks with the people and group leaders.[1] Limited economic opportunities, unemployment, taxes, bureaucratic pressure, restrictive state monopolies, and domination by various groups seemed to have been the main causes of complaints of the small-town leaders heading the opposition.

These developments culminated in a convention of the Republican Party in 1931 which aimed at defining economic policy and at providing an ideology to support it as well as the regime as a whole. Subsequently, republicanism, nationalism, populism, secularism, statism, and reformism were defined as the principles embodying the regime's ideology. Actually statism was the major outcome of the convention. It envisaged the assumption of extensive authority by the government in the economic field through a program of industrialization. The decision was followed by the gradual rise to power within the Republican Party of a group headed by Celal Bayar, one of the founders of the Democratic Party in 1946, who had advocated a program of economic action through the cooperation of the government and private enterprise as early as 1924.

Economic development through statism, though slow and very costly

---

ments have been made for the establishment of two early in 1921." There were 22 large banks and eight individually owned at the time. C. H. Courthope-Munroe, *General Report on the Trade Economic Conditions in Turkey*, (London, 1921), p. 12.

[1] Ahmet Hamdi Başar, *Atatürk'le Üç Ay ve 1930 dan Sonra Türkiye* (Istanbul, 1945). Also Karpat, *Turkey's Politics*, pp. 64 ff.

at the beginning, was the major factor in enlarging the scope and quality of structural change.[1] The census of 1932-1939 shows that privately owned industrial establishments declined from 1,473 to 1,144. A new criterion was used to describe "industrial establishments," such as the use of mechanical energy and the number of workers eligible to benefit from the industrial law. This census did not consider the small family type of enterprise, but concentrated on larger industrial outfits. By 1941 the number of privately owned industries had further declined to 1,052. But the value of production in these enterprises as well as the total number of workers and employees had tripled, showing thus that these establishments were rationalized and were expanding toward becoming fully industrial.

The state enterprises established according to the five-year development plan of 1934, covered mostly consumer industries. This policy aimed at self-sufficiency stimulated first the rapid growth of the entrepreneurial class among upper class farmers. The continuing high demand for raw materials and high profits yielded by cash crops induced them to specialize in these fields by expanding the cropped area and adopting machinery. For instance, the land for sugar beet cultivation increased from 22,667 ha. in 1935, to 44,213 ha. in 1941. The state goods, distributed through privately owned enterprises, further augmented the size of the entrepreneurial groups. The structure of the economic sectors of the middle class, represented originally by agrarian groups and crafts, diversified through the growth of manufacturers, suppliers of industrial crops, and banking enterprises.

The economic middle class groups, which consisted originally of small merchants, guild members of the Ottoman period, came to be increasingly dominated by manufacturers, merchants, and entrepreneurs of the Republican vintage whose economic activity was related in one way or another to industry. Richard D. Robinson, in an interesting study of manpower in Turkey, strongly influenced by Hagen's theory of withdrawal of respect, lumps together all middle class groups without considering the sequence and the special characteristics of each new group appearing between 1930 and 1960.[2] Obviously, their political activities were to

---

[1] See Z. Y. Hershlag, *Turkey: An Economy in Transition* (The Hague, 1963), and the revised edition of the same publication, *Turkey, the Challenge of Growth* (Leiden, 1968), which unfortunately does not correlate economics, social strata, and politics.

[2] Richard D. Robinson, *High Level Manpower in Economic Development: The Turkish Case* (Cambridge, Mass., 1967).

reflect a new mentality and a new view of the world, at least of their own business world as it related to the rest of society.

Meanwhile, the increase in the number of industrial workers, chiefly because of the industrialization undertaken by the government through state owned and operated enterprises, gradually pushed up the rate of urbanization. A new lower urban strata, consisting mainly of newcomers from the villages, was developing in the cities. Technical innovation, enterprise, and bold planning undertaken for the purpose of gaining economic security were the only means which most of these people had to break away from poverty, rise up the social ladder, and provide their children with a better future. The *gecekondu* or the squatter settlements of rural migrants represent the best example of this form of mobility.[1]

Furthermore, the management of the state enterprises necessitated the creation of a new bureaucracy as well as a new intelligentsia versed in national planning and possessing high technical skills. Consequently, the technical professions such as engineering and architecture began to provide high income and acquired superior social prestige.

The first political manifestation of these structural changes, as mentioned before, was evident in the adoption of a multiparty system between 1945 and 1960. We have repeatedly attributed the decision of Ismet Inönü, then President, to permit the establishment of opposition parties to the need to ease the social unrest among all groups, but especially the entrepreneurs, peasants, and industrial workers. Inönü's own account of the multiparty system clearly supports our contention.[2]

The intensive political activity in Turkey and the high percentage of political participation (voting was 89-92 percent from 1950 to 1957) cannot be explained satisfactorily merely because of the rise in urbanization or literacy, since these only began to correlate after 1960. We have already pointed to Lerner's incorrect reasoning on these points. The rise of new leadership cadres in the middle classes, which had a widespread following in the peasantry and lower urban groups, as well as the belief in the efficacy of political action, account for this high level of political participation. Indeed, a new type of leadership, with an achievement orientation, had already developed in towns and lower urban groups.[3]

---

[1] A comprehensive study of the Turkish squatter town has been prepared for publication by the writer. See also C. W. M. Hart, "Peasants Come to Town," *Social Aspects of Economic Development* (Istanbul, 1964), pp. 58-71.

[2] See the text of Inönü's speech translated in Kemal H. Karpat, *Political and Social Thought*, pp. 315-17.

[3] In the list of achievement-orientation of developing countries, Turkey has an

National leaders of the major political parties established before or after 1946, such as the Republican, Democratic, and Nation parties, were initially intellectuals, former bureaucrats, professionals, or members of agrarian groups. Eventually, with the electoral victory of the Democratic Party in 1950, the landlords and the professionals acquired government power and replaced the bureaucratic intelligentsia. The new political mandarins relied initially on small landowners, merchants, and craftsmen, and families with an established social status in the local community. But the influence of what may be called "traditional" leaders in this group gradually vanished as rapid economic and social growth during the Democrats' rule, from 1950 to 1960, brought to the fore new leaders whose claims to status were based on wealth and who gained political power by effective work in local party branches.

The Democratic Party rule was indeed a period of quantitative growth in every field. The workers reached the proportions of a true social class and differentiated into various categories and skill ranges while urbanization and exposure to mass media increased. One social mobility index which stood at 173 in 1938, and went up barely to 208 in 1948, soared to 521 in 1955.[1]

The most important structural development in the period 1950 to 1960, indicating the change in modes of production and income distribution and considered to be the key to economic development,[2] was the relative decline of agricultural labor, and the growth of the labor force in industry and services. The income from agriculture, industry, and services, which was 4.5, 1.4, and 3.6 billion liras in 1950, rose to 7.3, 2.8, and 6.6 billion liras respectively in 1960. The mechanization of agriculture, after an upsetting start in 1952, entered a slow but steady course as indicated by the respective statistics. The introduction of technology in agriculture changed and intensified social differentiation and stratification at the rural level. It accelerated rural migration into towns, while creating an unprecedented demand for technical skills at the grass-root level. While the state industries and various government services, such as the road building program, needed high level technicians, the

---

index of 2.16, and occupies the first place, whereas most other indicators place her usually in the lower half. Russett, *Handbook*, p. 194.

[1] Robinson, *High-Level Manpower*, p. 5.

[2] Simon S. Kuznets, "Industrial Distribution of National Product and Labor Force," *Economic Development and Cultural Change* V (July, 1957), pp. 10 ff. See also Kuznets, *Modern Economic Growth: Rate, Structure and Spread* (New Haven, 1966).

mechanized sectors of agriculture and the small manufacturing enterprises, operated mostly by private entrepreneurs, demanded mid-level technicians to process a variety of goods and handle machinery. As a consequence of all this, mid-level technicians, self-trained mechanics, small-machine operators, and personnel in a variety of services coming from the lower social strata developed rapidly to form a new social group. Their need for capital and more advanced management further spurred the development of entrepreneurial and banking groups and placed an even higher premium on technical knowhow. The entrepreneurs, managers, small manufacturers, and new businessmen as a group were markedly different from the landlords, professionals. bureaucrats, and intellectuals who had formed the backbone of the Turkish political elites and decided the destiny of Turkey until the mid-fifties. This development was somewhat similar to the rise of the "middle sectors" in Latin America. J. J. Johnson has pointed out that lawyers, doctors, writers, publishers, and the like dominated Latin American politics in the period of transition from neo-feudal agriculture to semindustrial capitalism. The situation in Latin America changed drastically when the need for different skills permitted the representatives of commerce and industry to enlarge their groups through the recruitment of members from marginal groups.[1] The emergence of the new-type technically oriented middle classes in Latin America and Turkey may resemble a similar occurrence in England about a century and a half earlier,[2] suggesting once more the existence of some parallelism or even a certain regularity in structural changes and thus supporting the theory of historical stages of development.

The demands for social justice, rapid economic development, industrialization, and scientific and national reorientation of political life, all expressed during the Turkish election campaign of 1957, indicated clearly that the economic and social bases of Turkish politics had undergone profound changes and that a qualitative readjustment was in the making. A new middle class, whose rational modes of thought and political philosophy resembled its counterpart elsewhere in the world, was making its bid for power. The near defeat of the Democratic Party in the election of 1957 was caused by the shift of these entrepreneurial groups in the countryside—which had limited political loyalty—to the opposition

---

[1] John J. Johnson, *Political Change in Latin America, the Emergence of the Middle Sectors* (Stanford, 1958). Also Jacques Lambert, *Amerique latine structures sociales et institutions politiques* (Paris, 1968).

[2] See W. J. Reader, *Professional Men: The Rise of the Professional Classes in Nineteenth Century England*, (New York, 1966).

parties. The same groups tried to acquire power in the party convention of 1955 but failed, since at this time the agrarian sections of the Democratic party still had the upper hand.[1]

The Revolution of 1960, therefore, appears to be a natural corollary to the above developments. Though it was not engineered by the new middle-class groups, it ended by institutionalizing practically all the political and social demands voiced by them. Thus, the revolution marked the full ascendance to power of the technically oriented, entrepreneurial groups engaged in the production process, as well as the acceptance of science and technology as major forces of material progress. These may be considered the main determining social forces in the fifth stage of development in Turkey.

The Revolution of 1960, as far as its immediate causes are concerned, stemmed chiefly from the system's limited capacity for conflict resolution. It can be viewed from three different viewpoints: first, as an intervention by the military to end party strife and restore democracy, as the junta proclaimed idealistically after the take over; second, as the reaction of the urban, secular groups of intellectuals and bureaucrats, that is the old elites, to the political and economic rise of the new middle-class groups and their cultural conservatism; and third, as a violent political, social, and cultural-ideological readjustment and group realignment caused by structural change. This readjustment took the form of a new constitution and institutional innovation followed by cultural and ideological reorientation.[2] All these tended to integrate the new groups into the political system and allowed them to share power under constitutional guarantees. Both political and social equality and participation were the guiding principles of the system emerging after 1960.

In our view the Revolution of 1960 does not represent a new stage of development, although it brought about a wider political participation and use of technology and generalized the faith in science. To be con-

---

[1] See Kemal H. Karpat, "The Turkish Elections of 1957," *Western Political Quarterly* 14 (June 1961), pp. 436-459.

[2] For the relationship between structural change and ideology see chap. 9. George K. Park and Lee Solton, "Politics and Social Structure in a Norwegian Village," *The American Journal of Sociology* 67 (September, 1961), pp. 152-54, have studied the relationship between structure, ideology, and values in a socialist regime. They discovered that the regime's ideology removed income and wealth as bases of stratification and instead compelled a new social ranking based on occupational differences. In Turkey the opposite happened. For a study of the revolution of 1960 see K. H. Karpat, "The Military and Politics in Turkey, 1960-64: the Socio-Cultural Analysis of a Revolution," *American Historical Review*, October 1970, pp. 1654-83.

sidered a new stage of development according to our criteria, the revolution should have introduced a new technological element and established the bases for the creation of a truly new social group which could play a major political role. But the revolution definitely did help remove from power the old agrarian and bureaucratic-professional groups, thus perhaps unwittingly enabling the entrepreneurial groups of the middle classes to acquire political supremacy. This is clearly demonstrated by the case of the Justice Party, which began as a direct successor of the Democratic Party's rural organizations in 1961, and reflected the agrarian political outlook of its predecessor.[1] But in the convention of 1964 the technocrats and the professionals won control by giving the chairmanship of the party to a man who symbolized the changes in the party and the country. Süleyman Demirel, born in a village—his parents are still there—was an engineer who had shown remarkable administrative skill while directing the state water works.

The revolution also established the economic institutions whereby demands for economic development, social justice, literacy, and technology could be more satisfactorily met. The State Planning Organization was established in 1960—it has grown to mammoth proportions since—with the purpose of providing solutions to all these problems through a rational and planned use of economic and human resources. Finally, the revolution paved the way for a new constitutional framework which incorporated the workers and peasants into the political system and established new institutions for conflict resolution.

All these political changes, important as they are in themselves, occurred in a rather advanced level of the fifth stage of development. Indeed, all the political changes in the earlier periods, regardless of whether they were peaceful or violent (such as the Tanzimat of 1839, the Parliament of 1876, or the Young Turk Revolution of 1908) occurred not at the beginning but at an advanced stage of development. Usually a new stage begins to emerge imperceptibly on the foundations established in a previous stage. The length of stages varies considerably, but in the Ottoman-Turkish case the mean length appears to have been about one

---

[1] See W. B. Sherwood, "The Rise of the Justice Party in Turkey," *World Politics* 20 (October 1967), pp. 54-65. In the general convention held in December 1968, the right wing in the party representing the conservative town groups was decisively defeated in its efforts for a comeback. Eventually it was expelled from the JP and formed its own Demokratik Party in an effort to capitalize on the loyalty felt to Menderes's Democratic Party.

and one-half centuries. The trend suggests that major changes seem likely to occur at shorter intervals henceforth.

One can say that the present stage of political development in Turkey has not reached its peak and that it will continue to develop further as the new middle-class groups create their own intellectual order, including a new type of professionally minded and technically skilled intelligentsia. In fact, this is now occurring. Both the intelligentsia and the middle classes seem to agree on the rapid conversion of the agricultural society into a technically oriented mass society. But while a part of the intelligentsia looks upon the mass society in the light of its own leftist ideology, the entrepreneurial class regards it as a source for additional power and profit. The political conflict between the two is raging furiously as clearly indicated by ideological debates in chapter IX.

F) *Quantitative Indicators of Structural Change in Turkey*

Occupational differentiation in our view is the most important determinant and indicator of social and political development. Occurring in the past and in our time—under the impact of technological and/or economic stimuli—it manifested itself in the form of new social groups corresponding functionally to the nature of the stimuli.

The gross national product (GNP) and per capita income, though vital indicators of economic growth and eventually of social differentiation, do not alone produce the qualitative transformation associated with political development. The rapid growth of the GNP in Kuwait and Saudi Arabia have produced no political development worthy of mention, yet. Such developments can occur only if occupational change reaches an advanced level of quantitative and qualitative differentiation. GNP, urbanization, communication, and literacy become politically effective only if they are manifest in a wide range of technical and professional occupations. The idea that the measure of political development would consist merely of the levels of "capabilities, conversion functions, and system maintenance and adaptation functions, and the interrelation among these three kinds, or levels, of functions," as claimed by Gabriel Almond, becomes meaningful only if there are occupations and social groups to which these functions are relevant,[1] as discussed later in this chapter.

---

[1] Gabriel Almond and G. Bingham Powel, *Comparative Politics* (Boston, 1966), p. 30.

The statistical data on Turkey supports these contentions. Indeed, the data available after 1927, the year in which the government began to issue regular statistics, covers occupations in the crucial period of transition from the stage of nation formation, in which the bureaucratic intellectual elite was dominant, to the politics of participation, equality and freedom, in which the entrepreneurial middle-class groups became dominant. Tables 1.3, 1.4, 1.5, and 1.6, compiled from various sources, indicate that the percentage of government and administrative personnel was quite high until 1945, that is during the period of one-party rule and state capitalism. But after 1945 the percentages as well as the gross number of professionals, technicians, and personnel employed in trade, industry, and services increased rapidly. Indeed, Table 1.4 indicates that categories A (professionals and technicians), G (manufacturers, craftsmen, and maintenance men), and I (services) went up several hundred percent. The total percentage of agricultural employment (Table 1.6) went up about 58 percent between 1945 and 1965, but most of the increase actually occurred from 1945 to 1950, whereas afterwards the rise in agricultural employment remained even or declined slightly, despite the sharp rise of population.[1]

Table 1.3

Occupation of Turkish Males, Fifteen Years and Over
(in percentages)

Years	Professional and technical	Government and administrative	Agriculture	Service	Trade industry, and commerce	Unknown
1927	1.3	1.6	64.2	2.5	12.7	17.7
1935	1.1	7.0	64.0	0.8	18.5	8.6
1940	1.6	10.1	68.4	0.9	14.3	4.7
1945	1.5	10.1	59.8	0.6	17.4	10.7
1950	1.5	5.8	69.3	2.3	15.2	6.0
1955	1.9	2.8	65.0	3.2	19.8	7.2
1960	2.2	3.8	60.6	4.1	21.2	8.1
1965	2.7	3.9	57.8	4.8	24.2	6.5

Sources : 1927-55 : İstatistik Yıllığı 1959. Publication No. 380 of the State Institute of Statistics, (Ankara, 1959), p. 87, table 37.
1960 : İstatistik Yıllığı 1963. Pub. No. 490, p. 67, table 53.
1965 : 24 Ekim 1965 Genel Nüfus Sayımı 0/01 Örnekleme Sonuçları (1% Sampling Results of General Population Census, Oct. 24, 1965). Publication No. 508 of the State Institute of Statistics (Ankara, 1963)., pp. 16-7, table 14.

---

[1] See also Robinson, *High-Level Manpower*, table 23, p. 51, for figures for 1955-62.

Table 1.4

Economically Active Population Fifteen Years and Over 1927-65
(in thousands)

M : Male; F : Female; T : Total.   2.5 % sapmling.

a : Only self-employed persons and judges. b : Excludes entrepreneurs and nonofficials. c : Includes entrepreneurs and executives. d : Only communications personnel. e : Includes members of the armed forces and protective services. f : Includes the operators of hotels, coffeehouses, and similar places. g : Self-employed and working alone. h : Excludes self-employed and working alone. i : Excludes agricultural labor, port employees, and sanitary engineers. j : This figure appears in the source as only 551,000 which is a typographical error. The figure is corrected.

Occupations		1927	1935	1940*	1945	1950	1955	1960	1965
A. Technical, Professional, and related	M	53	51	77	81	92	138	179	229
	F	7	11	11	16	21	29	39	60
	T	60 a	62	89	97	114	167	218	289
B. Managerial, administrative, and clerical	M	63	309	494	556	200	367	309	326
	F	1	6	8	12	26	25	33	44
	T	64 b	315 b,e	502 b,e	569 b,e	392	226	342	370
C. Salesman and related	M	237	204	189	264	83 g	270	322	379
	F	9	11	13	11	4	6	4 a	5
	T	246 c	215 c	203 c	274 c	87	277 h	326	384
D. Farmers, fishermen, lumbermen, hunters and related	M	2,551	2,844	3,356	3,302	4,390	4,738	4,983	4,858
	F	1,638	2,734	3,049	4,058	4,581	5,062	4,942	4,885
	T	4,190	5,578	6,405	7,360	8,971	9,800	9,925	9,743
E. Workers in transportation and communication	M	15	117	80	134	106	184	247	273
	F	—	3	3	3	1	2	3	3
	T	15 d	120 c	83 c	138 c	107	186	250	276
F. Miners, quarrymen, and related	M	33	33	33	49	29	46	52	65
	F	1	1	1	1	—	1	1	0
	T	34 c	34	34	50	29	29	53	65

Table 1.4 (continued)

Occupations		1927	1935	1940*	1945	1950	1955	1960	1965
G. Craftsmen, production process workers or repairmen	M	254	399	361	489	560	685	864	1,021
	F	31	97	85	68	92	114	135	148
	T	286 c	496 c	446 c	557	651	799	999	1,169
H. Manual workers elsewhere classified	M		71	39	24	185	260	261	298
	F		23	6	6	27	17	16	7
	T		94	53	30	212	277	277	305
I. Service workers	M	100	36 f	44 f	34	144	237	340	405
	F	16	23	15	14	16	25	30	33
	T	117	59 f	59 f	48	160	262	370	438
J. Workers in occupation unidentifiable or not reported	M	703	382	321	592	377	525	666	550
	F	3,150	2,141	2,212	1,653	1,829	2,024	2,901	1
	T	3,853 e	2,523	2,443	2,246 e	2,205	2,549 e	3.567 j	3,551
TOTAL	M	3,976	4,445	4,906	5,526	6,333	7,283	8,224	8,405
	F	4,854	5,050	5,412	5,842	6,595	7,306	8,104	5,181
	T	8,830	9,495	10,318	11,369	12,929	14,589	16,328	16,592

Sources: 1927-55 : *İstatistik Yıllığı* 1959. Publication No. 380 of the State Institute of Statistics, p. 87, table 37.

1960 : *İstatistik Yıllığı* 1963, no. 490, p. 67, table 53.

1965 : *24 Ekim 1965 Genel Nüfus Sayımı % 1 Örnekleme Sonuçları* (1 % Sampling Results of General Population Census, Oct. 24, 1965), no. 508, pp. 16-17, table 14.

There are differences between various censuses in defining and classifying the data. In order to make the results comparable some changes have been undertaken. The information about these changes is given in *Bulletin No. 33*, and in the *10 % Sampling Results of General Population Census of 1955*.

Table 1.5

Percentage Change in Occupation over Base Period 1927
(1927 = 100)

Occupation*	1927	1933	1940	1945	1950	1955	1960	1965
A	100.0	103.3	148.3	161.6	190.0	260.9	846.6	481.6
B	100.0	492.2	784.3	889.0	612.5	353.1	543.3	578.1
C	100.0	86.9	82.0	111.3	32.9	112.6	132.5	156.0
D	100.0	133.1	152.8	175.6	214.0	233.8	236.8	232.5
E	100.0	800.0	553.3	920.0	713.5	1240.0	1666.6	1840.0
F	—	100.0	100.0	141.1	85.2	138.1	155.8	191.0
G	100.0	173.4	155.9	159.0	227.5	279.3	349.3	409.9
H	—	100.0	56.3	31.9	225.5	294.6	294.6	324.4
I	100.0	50.4	50.4	41.1	136.7	224.0	316.2	374.3
J	100.0	65.4	63.4	58.3	57.2	66.1	92.4	92.0
Total op 1.4	100.0	107.5	110.6	129.0	146.4	176.5	184.9	187.9

* For explanation of categories see Table 1.4.

Table 1.6

Economically Active Population by Occupation
(As percentages of total)

Occupation*	1927	1935	1940	1945	1950	1955	1960	1965
A	0.68	0.65	0.86	0.86	0.88	1.15	1.34	1.74
B	0.72	3.31	4.87	5.00	3.03	1.55	2.10	2.23
C	2.78	2.26	1.97	2.41	0.67	1.90	2.00	2.31
D	47.47	58.74	62.07	64.74	69.16	67.17	60.79	58.73
E	0.17	1.26	0.83	1.22	0.83	1.27	1.53	1.67
F	—	0.37	0.34	0.45	0.23	0.32	0.32	0.39
G	3.23	5.22	4.32	4.90	5.03	5.47	6.12	7.04
H	—	0.99	0.51	0.23	1.44	1.90	1.70	1.84
I	1.32	0.62	0.56	0.43	1.34	1.80	2.26	2.64
J	43.63	26.58	23.67	19.76	17.39	17.47	21.84	21.41
Total	100.00	100.00	100.00	100.00	100.00	100.00	100.00	100.00

* For explanation of categories see Table 1.4.

The bases for the compilation of these statistics changed from year to year, as several occupational groups were shifted from one category to another. For instance, the armed forces were included in 1927, 1950 and 1955 in category J or the "unidentifiable," whereas in the period 1935-40 they were put in category B together with the managerial and clerical groups. Category B showed an increase of 481.6 percent in the period 1926-65. The entrepreneurs were excluded from category B and included in other categories, not on the basis of entrepreneurship but occupation. Nevertheless, despite these inconsistencies in classification, the statistics do indicate in general that the percentage of technicians, professionals, and service personnel increased much more rapidly than other occupational categories.

There was a qualitative improvement of manpower which manifested itself in sharper political consciousness, in broader political participation, and grass-roots leadership. Initially, from 1923 to 1945, the developments associated with modernization centered in a few cities, while the villages and the small towns lent economic support to the process without participating in decision-making. After 1945 even the small agrarian towns and villages aspired toward fuller participation in politics and economics and were subject to their effects.

We do not have reliable statistics to indicate the structural change and the occupational diversification of the manpower employed in agriculture. But we do possess a series of figures on agricultural machinery which gives a fair idea of the penetration of technology in rural areas. Table 1.7 shows a rather dramatic rise from 1944 to 1965 in the number of tractors, cultivators, and combined thresher-harvesters, as well as of the land cultivated by tractors. (The primitive wooden ploughs registered as "in existence" by the census takers, are less and less in use.) One can presume that the number of mechanics, technicians, repair and maintenance men, and of businessmen selling machine parts, fuel, etc., has also increased in accordance with the rate of mechanization. The machinery is used mostly in the west, in some sections of the south and central Anatolia, and much less in the southeast and east.)

In summary, the figures on occupational change correlate with political development among the economic entrepreneurial groups, as illustrated best by the introduction of a multiparty system in 1945-46, and the politics of participation, equality, and freedom after 1960. This politics coincides with the rise of a wide-range middle-class group in economic, technical occupations and with differentiation within the intelligentsia, that is, the growth of the professional and technical group at the top, and the increasing mobility and technical specialization oı the labor force at the mid- and even grass-roots levels. This transformation was reflected also in the thought process, as the symbolic, mythical, and historically oriented type of nationalist ideology, encountered in the initial process of nationhood, diversified and polarized in the form of liberalism and free enterprise on one hand and socialism on the other.

Table 1.7

Agricultural Machinery, Equipment, and Land in Use in Turkey

Years	Agricultural machinery and equipment						Land in use	
	Ploughs (wooden)	Ploughs (steel)	Tractors	Cultivators	Primitive threshing machines	Combined Thresher Harvester	Land-Sown (Fallows excluded) (1000 hectars)	Land cultivated with tractors (1000 hectars)
1933		266,314			2,947			
1936		410,365	961		2,078		7,941	72
1940		432,071	1,066	2,744	7,240		9,610	80
1944		419,445	956	3,367	5,155		8,170	72
1948		537,493	1,756	6,171	11,220	1,291	9,477	132
1955	2,123,750	1,026,388	40,282	16,622	24,742	8,607	14,205	3,021
1960	1,991,259	1,159,232	42,136	38,268	28,498	11,127	15,305	3,160
1965	2,031,400	1,379,600	65,103 (1966)	47,880	54,900	15,340	15,294	4,100

Sources : *Tarım İstatistikleri Özeti, 1966 (The Summary of Agricultural Statistics)*, Publication No. 526 of the State Institute of Statistics (Ankara, 1967).

İstatistik Yıllığı (Statistical Yearbook), Publication of State Institute of Statistics.
  Publication No. 332 (Ankara, 1951), p. 233.
  Publication No. 460 (Ankara, 1960-62), p;. 233.
  Publication No. 490 (Ankara, 1963), pp. 197, 229.

Production Yearbook, Publication of the United Nations Food and Agriculture Organization 1966.

The bureaucratic intelligentsia, that is the salaried groups in government service such as officials and teachers, shifted to the left and adopted socialism in the form of welfare statism as their group ideology. The professionals and technicians, many of whom became entrepreneurs, as well as the manufacturers and commercial groups, defended free enterprise and a special kind of economic liberalism which still depended on the government for tariff protection, credits, and foreign exchange. (The ideological position of the industrial workers, of the bureaucratic intelligentsia and the entrepreneurial groups is discussed in detail in chapter IX.)

The second indicator of quantitative growth is GNP and per capita income, and distribution. Table 1.8 shows that the growth in the period between 1929 and 1938 appears to have been rather slow. But the increase of GNP in the next three decades, even if one discounts the inflation factor, is very high. Table 1.9, showing the net national product compiled at factor cost indicates that this growth was due chiefly to the increase of industrial production and services. Table 1.10 indicating the sectoral origin of national income supports this view. Interesting to note is the fact that after 1950 there was also a steady growth in agricultural income. This occurred in large measure—leaving aside the fluctuations due to seasonal factors—because of the steady mechanization of agriculture and specialization, which resulted in increased agricultural production.

Heavy capital investment not supported by a diversified and specialized occupational network will produce neither real growth nor political development. Trained and specialized manpower, on the other hand, can effectively increase the GNP and create conditions for a more democratic form of political development. Turkey stands probably as a good case for the Middle East. Not endowed with any major source of foreign exchange, such as oil (she buys most of her oil from abroad) and beset perennially by various economic problems, Turkey's per capita income, nevertheless, is higher than that of most of the Middle Eastern countries. Her political development has also been well sustained, by most standards. This is due in part to the fact that after 1960 the major aim of the development plan was to improve the quality of trained manpower.

Table 1.11, however, indicates that per capita income barely doubled between 1927 and 1965. This table in our estimation should be revised upward. Nevertheless, it still indicates that the average individual's real income did not increase as much as one would expect. This very fact

Table 1.8

Gross National Product and per Capita G.N.P.
(At market prices)

Years	Population (1,000)	G.N.P. (1,000,000 TL)	Per Capita G.N.P. (TL)
1929	14,200	1,800	127
1935	16,158	1,300	80
1938	17,016	1,953	115
1944	18,790	7,586	403
1948	20,049	10,067	502
1950	20,947	10,384	496
1955	24,065	21,059	875
1960	27,755	50,970	1,836
1965	31,391	79,779	2,541
1967	33,044	103,780	3,141

Sources: *Türkiye Milli Geliri* ("*The National Income of Turkey*") *1938, 1948-67*, Publication No. 536 of the State Institute of Statistics (Ankara, 1968), p. 12. Zvi Yehuda Herschlag, Turkey: *An Economy in Transition* (The Hague, 1963), Table xxiv, p. 163. *İstatistik Yıllığı* (*Statistical Yearbook*) *1963*, Publication No. 490 of the State Institute of Statistics (Ankara, 1967).

Table 1.9

Net National Product and its Origin
(At factor cost of 1948, per million Turkish liras)

Years	Agriculture	Industry and construction	Services	Net National Product *
1927	2,561.5	248.1	1,639.0	4,448.6
1935	3,523.2	611.7	1,976.0	6,110.9
1940	4,428.7	923.0	2,336.6	7,690.3
1945	3,551.2	1,026.2	1,730.0	5,941.7
1950	4,551.2	1,468.8	3,098.9	9,098.3
1955	5,607.5	2,116.3	4,638.1	12,333.9
1960	7,403.5	2,776.7	6,534.9	16,677.3
1965	11,137.4	2,864.5	6,971.7	20,926.1

* The differences among the totals of agricultural, industrial, and services product and net national product derive from expenditures and earnings abroad, tourism, savings of workers, and capital transfers.

Sources: 1950-1965: *Türkiye Milli Geliri, Toplam Harcamaları ve Yatırımları, 1938, 1948-1967* ("National Income, Total Expenditure and Investment of Turkey"), Publication No. 536 of the State Institute of Statistics (Ankara, 1968).

1927-1955: Aysel Yenal, *Türkiye'nin İktisadi Gelişmesi, 1927-60* (Economic Development of Turkey), (Professorial diss., The University of Istanbul, 1963), p. 25.

Table 1.10

Sector Origin of National Income
(*At factor costs of 1948*)

Years	Agriculture	Industry	Construction	Commerce	Communication and transportation	Free professions and services	Real estate taxes	Public services
1927								
1935								
1938	3,680	890		1,980				
1948	4,360	1,040		2,470				
1950	4,660	1,100		2,530				
1955	5,607.5	1,428.3	688.0	1,205.5	923.6	626.4	357.1	1,224.3
1960	7,403.5	1,795.2	981.5	1,678.1	1,253.5	791.4	735.4	1,633.9
1965 [a]	25,434	11,743	4,250	5,671	5,139	3,676	3,325	6,869
1966 [a]	29,305	13,574	4,909	6,544	5,674	4,182	3,691	7,464

All figures for 1965 and 1966 are at current prices.

Sources: *İstatistik Yıllığı* ("Statistical Yearbook"), Publication of the State Institute of Statistics Publication No.332 (Ankara, 1951), p. 337. Publication No. 460 (Ankara, 1960-62), p. 431.

Economic Indicators of Turkey, 1962-66, Published by Iş Bankası (Ankara, 1967), pp. 1, 7, 8.

Table 1.11

Net National Income, Population, and per Capita Income
(*At factor cost of 1948*)

Years	Net national income (TL)	Population	Per capita income (TL)
1927	4,448.6	13,648,270	325.95
1935	6,110.9	16,158,018	378.20
1940	7,690.3	17,820,950	431.53
1945	5,941.7	18,790,174	316.22
1950	9,098.3	20,947,188	434.35
1955	12,333.9	24,064,763	512.52
1960	16,677.3	27,754,820	600.88
1965	20,926.1	31,391,207	666.62

Sources: 1927-1960: *İstatistik Yıllığı, 1963* (Statistical Yearbook) Publication No. 490 of the State Institute of Statistics (Ankara, 1963), p. 42.

1965: *24 Ekim 1965 Genel Nüfus Sayımı % 1 Örnekleme Sonuçları* (1 % Sampling Results of Oct. 24, 1965, General Census), Publication No. 508 of the State Institute of Statistics (Ankara, 1965), p. 3. See also Table 1.9.

is clearly reflected in the quality of political development. Indeed, the rise of leftist groups, and of socialism in general after 1960, was stimulated not only by the slow rise of actual personal income but also by its unbalanced distribution, though this is now somewhat corrected (see the rise of wages in Chapter IV). The share of agriculture in the GNP also increased, thus depriving the urban areas of some of their unearned income.[1]

The rise of GNP was reflected also in the increase of government revenue and expenditure. Table 1.12 shows that the state budget increased close to ten billion liras between 1945 and 1965. Actually most of the increase occurred between 1960 and 1965, making government expenditure a chief stimulus of economic activity. Thus, with relatively great economic resources at its disposal, the government can now set the course of structural change and of political development in the desired direction. Consequently, the mastery of political power is not any longer a question of authority, of law and order, as from 1923 to 1950, but a condition for controlling patronage, the distribution of contracts, the maintenance of a high level of economic activity and of establishing the political conditions necessary for the survival and proliferation of the new economic groups. In fact, most of the new groups are an inherent part of this economic-political process and regard its maintenance as the major condition for their own prosperity and survival.

The third indicator of growth, urbanization, follows on the steps of occupational change and the increase in GNP and income. Table 1.13 shows that the rate of urbanization between 1927 and 1950 went up very slowly. In 1960 the rate was 31 percent, about 35 percent in 1965 and higher in 1970. The rapid population growth distorts the true significance of these percentages. Actually, the total number of city-dwellers increased more than three times (Table 1.13, Column 4) from 1927 to 1960. This column shows that the real growth occurred in cities with a population over 10,000, that is, in the potential centers of industry and trade and politics, which came to harbor over two-thirds of the urban

---

[1] Abraham Hirsh and Eva Hirsh, "Changes in Terms of Trade of Farmers and Their Effect on Real Farm Income Per Capita of Rural Population in Turkey, 1927-60," *Economic Development and Cultural Change*, pp. 440-57. These authors may wish to revise their views regarding farm income, though in some sections of Turkey, notably in the east and southeast the increase is negligible. See also "Changes in Agricultural Output Per Capita of Rural Population in Turkey, 1927-60," *Ibid.* XI, no. 4 (July 1963), pp. 372-394. See also Frederic C. Shorter, ed., *Four Studies on the Economic Development of Turkey* (London, 1967).

CHANGE AND MODERNIZATION OF SOCIAL GROUPS 73

Table 1.12

Government Revenues and Expenditures

Years	State Budget in TL	
	Revenue (Actual Collection)	Expenditures (Actual Payments)
1927	202,239,236	198,951,159
1935	231,391,323	259,589,193
1940	550,209,438	535,863,786
1945	658,759,214	600,676,044
1950	1,419,449,408	1,467,382,531
1955	3,148,365,193	3,308,864,355
1960	6,933,254,375	7,320,286,000
1965	13,833,000,000	14,692,000,000
1966	16,401,000,000	16,548,000,000

Sources: *İstatistik Yıllığı* (Statistical Yearbook), Publication of the State Institute of Statistics.
Publication No. 332 (Ankara, 1951), p. 337.
Publication No. 460 (Ankara, 1960-62), p. 431.
Economic Indicators of Turkey: 1962-66, Published by İş Bankası (Ankara, 1967), pp. 1, 7, 8.

Table 1.13

Urban Population

Years	(1)	%*	(2)	%*	(3)	%*	(4)	%*
1927	3,305,046	24.2	3,189,339	23.4	2,782,291	20.4	2,236,085	16.4
1935	3,802,642	23.5	3,676,148	22.8	3,241,842	20.1	2,684,197	16.6
1940	4,346,249	24.4	4,201,451	23.6	3,737,305	21.0	3,202,987	18.0
1945	4,687,102	24.9	4,533,182	24.1	4,006,050	21.3	3,441,895	18.3
1950	5,244,337	25.0	5,090,666	24.3	4,538,000	21.7	3,871,834	18.5
1955	6,927,343	28.8	6,777,922	28.2	6,158,607	25.6	5,324,397	20.9
1960	8,859,731	31.9	8,714,323	31.4	7,993,011	28.8	6,999,026	25.2

* Percent of total population.
(1) Urban administrative centers of provinces and districts.
(2) Urban administrative centers of provinces and districts with population over 2,000.
(3) Urban administrative centers of provinces and districts with population over 5,000.
(4) Urban administrative centers of provinces and districts with population over 10,000.

Sources: 1927-35: *İstatistik Yıllığı* (Statistical Yearbook) 1952. Publication of the State Institute of Statistics (Ankara, 1952), p. 79.
1940-60: *23 Ekim 1960 Genel Nüfus Sayımı Kati Sonuçları*, ("Final Results of the General Population Census of Oct. 23, 1960"), Publication of the State Institute of Statistics (Ankara, 1964), p. xxxv.

population. This figure can be elaborated upon. Table 1.14 shows that in 1940 Turkey had only three cities with a population over 100,000 —Istanbul, Ankara, and Izmir—six towns with a population between 50,000 and 100,000, and 21 towns with a population between 25,000 and 50,000. In 1955 the number of cities with a population over 100,000 went up to six, those with 50,000 to 100,000 to eleven, and those with 25,000 to 50,000 to twenty-six. In 1960, the number of the large cities increased rather dramatically to nine, eighteen, and thirty respectively. Thus, the main increase occurred in the relatively large cities with population between 50,000 and 100,000. In 1940 only 392,532 people lived in these cities, while in 1960 the total number had risen to 1,222,719. This development has its political significance. The small rural town, which was the dominant type of urban settlement until the mid-fifties and the center of political activity in the countryside, was replaced by the industrial and trading city as the center of economic life and politics. We have repeatedly stressed the fact that after 1960 politics in Turkey broadened its scope and quality and that this was the result of qualitative change in the population. Indeed, the rise of relatively large cities, and the fact that many of the new groups of entrepreneurs, businessmen, technicians are active in them account for the change in the quality of Turkish politics. This trend has accelerated since 1960. The preliminary results of the census of 1970, indicating that the population of Turkey went up to 36.2 million, tends to support fully the above views.

The fourth indicator of growth is transportation and communication (Table 1.15). Indeed, physical communication, that is to say the highway system, the bus and truck, stand as the most powerful agents of economic, social, and cultural change in Turkey. One has to see the small modern settlements with electricity, running water, repair shops, and even motels and restaurants clustered around the gas stations throughout Anatolia to realize the revolution caused by transportation. The increase in road mileage is not very impressive at first sight. Actually, the main achievement in the road program was to transform country roads into all-weather paved highways. The railroad did not match the highway development since economic reasons and terrain conditions favored highway construction. Transportation was one of the first factors causing occupational change, since much of the maintenance and repair work, and a variety of technical jobs developed first around the transportation services. The number of trucks and buses increased rather insignificantly until 1945. But in the following two decades it went up 30 to 50 times. One should stress that real increase occurred after 1960. According

Table 1.14

Urban administrative centers of provinces and districts
and their inhabitants by population groups

Population Groups	1940 Number of cities	1940 Population	1945 Number of cities	1945 Population	1950 Number of cities	1950 Population	1955 Number of cities	1955 Population	1960 Number of cities	1960 Population
10,001- 15,000	42	515,247	41	504,133	42	509,917	35	422,538	47	555,666
15,001- 20,000	14	238,590	17	292,983	19	325,956	32	550,123	22	385,185
20,001- 25,000	10	229,430	11	240,165	10	224,090	11	252,216	22	475,539
25,001- 50,000	21	692,244	19	622,150	20	693,987	26	902,216	30	997,442
50,001-100,000	6	392,523	6	396,018	16	397,275	11	763,138	18	1,222,719
100,001- +	3	1,134,953	4	1,386,446	5	1,729,609	6	2,434,166	9	3,362,475

Source: 23 Ekim 1960 Genel Nüfus Sayımı Kati Sonuçları ("Final Results of the General Population Census of Oct. 23, 1960"), Publication of the State Institute of Statistics (Ankara, 1964), p. xxxv.

See also Malcom D. Rivkin, *Area Development for National Growth* (New York, 1965), who uses urbanization as a major indicator of growth.

On population see also Orhan Türkay, *Türkiye Nüfusu* (Ankara, 1960), and Ruşen Keleş, *Türkiye'de Şehirleşme Hareketleri, 1927-1960* (Ankara, 1961).

Table 1.15

Transportation and Communication in Turkey

Years	Roads (km) (highways)	Passenger km	Railroads (km)	Passenger km (millions)	Trucks	Cars	Buses	Telephone Subscriptions	Radios	Newspapers and magazines (circ. in 1000 nds)
1927	22,053		4,637	224 (1925)				12,265		
1935	39,583		6,639	630				18,622	29,000	149
1940	41,582		7,381	2,113	3,882 (1938)	4,573 (1938)	1,044 (1938)	22,964	78,237	338
1945	43,511		7,515	1,545	4,479	3,406	988	28,875	176,262	336
1950	47,080		7,671	2,516	13,201	10,071	3,185	58,189	320,853	647
1955	55,008	12,911	7,802 (1956)	3,917	24,429	29,990	6,848	116,455	998,662	—
1960	61,542	10,880	7,895	4,396	57,460	45,767	10,981	180,030	1,341,272	1,658
1965	48,638 (1963)	25,650	9,301	4,075	79,121	87,584	54,668	241,848	2,442,919	1,722 (1963)

Sources: *Statistical Yearbook of UN*, Publication of the UN Statistical Office (New York, 1967), p. 755. *Economic Indicators of Turkey, 1962-1966*, Türkiye İş Bakası (Ankara), p. 9. *Statistical Yearbook of Turkey*, Publication of the State Institute of Statistics.
  Publication No. 490 (Ankara, 1964), pp. 474, 515, 526, 527.
  Publication No. 460 (Ankara, 1963), pp. 419, 427, 507, 519.
  Publication No. 380 (Ankara, 1959), pp. 453, 482, 525.
  Publication No. 342 (Ankara, 1952), pp. 479, 519.
  Publication No. 332 (Ankara, 1951), p. 468.
  Publication No. 255 (Istanbul, 1942-45), pp. 449, 526, 535.
  Publication No. 88 (Istanbul, 1935-36), p. 466.
  Publication No. 77 (Istanbul, 1934-35), p. 613.
Encyclopedia Britannica, Chicago 1947, p. 375, 11th ed., s.v. "*İsmet İnönü, Turkey, 1937-1946 : Ten Eventful Years.*"
The International Yearbook and Statesmen's Who is Who, 1967 (London, 1967), p. 492.
Kemal H. Karpat, "The Mass Media," *Political Modernization in Japan and Turkey* (Princeton, 1964).

to informal information, about 3 million people know how to operate tractors, cars, and buses. (Fiat and Renault are building cars in Turkey, while an older manufacturer, the maker of Anadol, the Koç enterprise, has shifted to truck making.) This number, which comprises roughly eight percent of the population, acquires its true significance only if viewed in the light of Turkey's agricultural background. But in ideal terms all this growth is hardly satisfactory as most Turks are ready to acknowledge.

The increase in the number of radios and newspaper circulation was relatively low during the most extensive period of cultural reforms, 1923 to 1935. Moreover, the radio was an expensive item. Under official control, it broadcast music and educational programs geared to the tastes of the urban elite. Then, in the span of fifteen years, 1950 to 1965, the number of radios went up drastically, though the rate of urbanization and literacy did not match it. The interest in radios and newspapers increased after the introduction of a multi-party system in 1945-46. Today the possession of a radio or transistor is a common occurrence.

The fifth indicator of development is literacy, and especially the type of education provided in schools (Table 1.16). We feel that literacy plays a truly transforming role only if the rate of literacy is accompanied by a similar increase in professional and technical education. Literacy in Turkey, after a rapid increase from 1927 to 1950, from 10 percent to about 33 percent, went up to a mere 48 percent in 1965, despite the growth of GNP, communication, and urbanization. So, literacy does not necessarily correlate with these indicators. But there is a definite correlation between professional education, occupational diversification, and technical specialization and politics. Statistics support this assertion. The total enrollment in the university, which is considered the highest level of specialization at the academic level, went up four times between 1950 and 1965 and redoubled from 1965 to 1970. During the same period the number of university students enrolled in technical branches went up also about four and one-half times. A somewhat similar situation prevailed in higher secondary education. The *lise* or the high school enrollment, on the other hand, increased about five times from 1950 to 1965.

The *lise* is a theoretical elitist-minded school which was the key educational institution for recruitment into the ruling urban bureaucratic elite between 1923 and 1950. In fact, the causes for the relative apathy toward general education after 1950 on the part of the Democratic Party government may be found in the fear that the expansion of literacy

Table 1.16

School Attendance by Levels and Type of Education

Years	Literacy	Primary Schools (İlk) Urban	Primary Schools (İlk) Rural	Junior High (Orta) Theoretical training	Junior High (Orta) Technical and vocational Number	Junior High (Orta) Technical and vocational % of total	High Schools (Lise) (Preparatory for universities or equivalent)	Universities Total (including technical and professional)	Universities Technical Number	Universities Technical % of total	Others who do not attend regular school (Public technical education)
1927	10.7										597,010
1935	19.6	318,777	369,325	19,858	7,718	28.0	3,819	3,918	2,281	74.2	51,106
				52,386	9,229	14.9	13,622	7,277	4,461	61.3	(1928)
1940	22.4	377,553	578,404	95,332	20,264	17.5	24,862	12,844	7,781	60.5	56,922
1945	29.2	437,999	919,741	65,608	54,248	45.2	25,515	19,273	11,266	58.4	90,531
1950	33.5	467,925	1,148,701	68,187	53,289	43.6	22,169	24,815	13,989	56.3	60,677
1955	40.6	686,919	1,296,749	133,217	72,675	35.3	33,412	36,998	19,534	52.8	80,446
1960	43.7	1,050,061	1,816,440	291,266	108,221	27.0	75,632	65,297	37,793	57.8	170,683
1965	48.0	1,406,818	2,517,508	433,210	182,476	29.6	114,641	97,308	59,611	61.2	39,342 *

* Incomplete

Sources: *Milli Eğitim Hareketleri, 1927-1956* ("Changes in National Education"), Publication No. 517 of the State Institute of Statistics (Ankara, 1967).

See also: *Turkey: Country Projects, Mediterranean Regional Project, Organization for Economic Cooperation and Development* (Paris, 1965), p. 160; Andreas N. Kazamias, *Education and the Quest for Modernity in Turkey* (London, 1966), p. 271; *İstatistik Yıllığı* ("Statistical Yearbook 1951"), Publication No. 332 of the State Institute of Statistics (Ankara, 1952), p. 185.

under the existing educational system might strengthen the old elites. (See Chapter VI on the social roles of education.) There was, however, after the mid-1950's a growing interest in technical and professional education as clearly indicated by the proliferation of public and private engineering and a variety of other professional schools. The pressure for building the *lises* came from towns, where relatively prosperous new groups clamored for the education of their offspring. Because of long-entrenched habits, they still considered education the best avenue for upward mobility. After the revolution of 1960 the idea of fighting illiteracy at grass-roots levels, and of adopting a more democratic educational philosophy prevailed. The educational program was to be supplemented by specialized, technical, and professional education. The educational statistics indicate that this program has begun to be implemented although as a whole the educational system of Turkey is far behind the country's practical and technological needs. It remains one of the most obsolete, uncreative, and unproductive institutions of Turkey.

G. *Political Development and its significance*

It is necessary at this point to place the correlations between political development and economic and social growth in proper perspective. The idea of regarding voting as the major form of political participation and of associating it with various indicators of growth has not been sustained by this study. We have pointed out repeatedly that in the case of Turkey there was not any *direct* correlation between GNP, literacy, and communication on one hand and political participation on the other. The rise in political participation was caused by considerations which were more or less independent of the growth in other sectors. The voting percentage, for instance, was 89.3 percent in 1950 and decreased to 81.4 percent in 1961 and 71.3 percent in 1965. During the same periods, notably from 1961 to 1965, GNP, urbanization, and communication accelerated and in some cases doubled or tripled. Thus, the idea of automatic correlation between various indicators of growth and political participation (voting) is not supported by our findings. The high level of voting percentage can be easily explained in terms of accumulated resentment against the bureaucratic elite order and the ability of the leadership of the economic-entrepreneurial groups to mobilize the masses against it. There is, nevertheless, an indirect, cumulative relationship between economic growth and political activity and the spread of a modern political culture. This relationship, in our estimation, can be established only through a survey of the changes in the quality of political leadership, which occurs within a period of time among a chosen social group. In this case the immediate effects of occupational diversification, growth in GNP, communication, etc., become politically meaningful and ascertainable as such, if analyzed within the framework of the political activity of the middle class groups. In other words, most of the growth and the structural transformation dealt with here acquires political relevance mainly in connection with political leadership. This political leadership, as repeatedly stressed throughout this work, was the bone of contention between the statist-intellectual elites and the newly rising economic entrepreneurial groups. It is interesting to note that the structural and political changes in Turkey received due attention much more in the Soviet Union than in the West, and served considerably in shaping the Soviet foreign policy toward Turkey.[1]

It is only too obvious that a variety of other social groups outside the old or new elites felt the consequences of social and economic change and showed political reactions of various kinds and intensity. But these reactions were not articulated and expressed by their own group leaders. The views and aspirations of the lower strata were expressed chiefly by the leaders of the middle class groups in the Justice Party and the Republican Party which together control almost 90 percent of the electorate. Historical and structural conditions created a special, and possibly transitional situation in which large segments of the lower urban groups, peasants, and the bulk of the industrial workers supported and are still supporting the economic entrepreneurial groups. This support may diminish or shift when the historical causes which prompted the informal political coalition lose their immediacy. For the time being, however, large segments of the population and the new leadership groups are part of one political front directed against the bureaucratic elites.

It is evident from the foregoing that the effects of occupational diversification, growth of GNP, communication, and urbanization, although affecting the population as a whole, correlate chiefly with the changes in and the quality of political leadership of the economic-entrepreneurial groups. Throughout this study we have tried to point

---

[1] D. I. Vdovichenko, *Natsionalnaya Burzhuaziya Turtsii* ("*Turkish National Bourgeoisie*") (Moscow, 1962). N. Rozaliyev, *Klassy i Klassovaya Bor'ba Turtsii*, ("*Classes and Class Struggle in Turkey*") (Moscow, 1966). Y. Rustamov, *Sovremennaya Turetskaya Burzhuaznaya Sotsiologiya* ("*Modern Turkish Bourgeois Society*") (Baku, 1967). D. I. Vdovichenko, *Bor'ba Politicheskikh Partiy v Turtsii* ("*The Struggle of the Political Parties in Turkey*") (Moscow, 1967).

out first, how landed interests and ancient families of notables acquired the leadership of most political parties and, then, how this leadership passed to professionals, technicians, and similar groups. These were of younger age and represented a great diversity of occupations and a relatively more advanced degree of specialization and also a more rational and politically conscious outlook on life. The changes in the

Table 1.17

Ages of Justice Party and Republican Peoples Party Deputies in Percentages

Ages	JP 1961	JP 1965	PRP 1961	PRP 1965
31 - 35	18.1	7.1	7.1	3.7
36 - 40	35.6	22.6	28.2	13.5
41 - 45	15.5	33.0	23.5	33.6
46 - 50	14.1	17.2	15.9	14.9
51 - 55	8.7	10.9	10.6	17.9
56 - 60	5.4	4.6	5.9	6.7
61 - 65	1.3	3.4	6.5	3.7
66 +	1.3	1.2	2.3	6.0
Total	100.0	100.0	100.0	100.0
Mean	43	41	46	48
Mode	40	44	43	45
Median	39	44	39	41

Table 1.18

General Occupations of Justice Party and Republican Peoples Party Deputies in Percentages

Occupation	JP 1961	JP 1965	PRP 1961	PRP 1965
Government [a]	18.5	24.7	15.0	30.1
Professions	48.4	48.5	54.4	53.4
Agriculture	6.6	5.0	12.6	6.8
Industry, commerce [b]	24.5	19.3	16.8	9.0
Other	2.0	2.5	1.2	0.7
Total	100.0	100.0	100.0	100.0

[a] Physicians, engineers excluded; agricultural engineers included.
[b] Engineers included.
Source: T[ürkiye] B[üyük] M[illet] M[eclisi] Albümü, 2 vols. (Ankara, 1962, 1965).

profession and age of members of parliament may be taken as an indication of the effects of economic and social growth upon political leadership. Table 1.17 indicates that the Justice Party deputies were originally of younger age but then became "established" and grew in age, and that industry and trade acquired a larger percentage of representation. It is

Table 1.19

Specific Occupations of Justice Party and Republican Peoples Party Deputies in Percentages

Occupations	JP 1961	JP 1965	PRP 1961	PRP 1965
Teachers [a]	3.3	6.3	3.6	5.3
Military [a]	6.0	3.8	4.8	12.0
Public administrators [a]	9.3	14.3	6.6	12.8
Lawyers, judges [b]	35.8	34.7	32.9	36.8
Physicians, dentists [b], druggists	7.9	6.7	16.1	10.5
Publishers, journalists [b]	4.6	7.1	5.4	6.0
Farmers [c]	6.6	5.0	12.6	6.7
Engineers, architects [d] (1)	2.0	2.5	1.2	1.5
Contractors [d]	6.0	2.9	1.2	1.5
Industrialists [d]	4.6	2.9	2.4	0.8
Tradesmen [d]	11.9	10.9	12.0	5.3
Other (labor leaders)	2.0(0.7)	2.9(1.7)	1.2	0.8
Total	100.0	100.0	100.0	100.0

(1) Contractors excluded.
[a] Classified in Table 1.4 as "Government."
[b] Classified in Table 1.4 as "Professions."
[c] Classified in Table 1.4 as "Agriculture."
[d] Classified in Table 1.4 as "Industry and Commerce."

Source: T[ürkiye] B[üyük] M[illet] M[eclisi] Albümü, 2 Vols. (Ankara, 1962, 1965). See chapter VII, pp. 246-48.

also quite clear that the elections of 1965 brought about a new realignment in the leadership of the two major political parties. The Republican Party, the traditional citadel of the bureaucratic elites, attracted a higher percentage of the military, former judges, and also farmers, and the usual landowners, but fewer businessmen. This change was caused by the shift of the party to a policy of "left of center" ("*ortanın solu*") after 1965, intended to attract the left-oriented younger intelligentsia and the lower classes. The attempt was unsuccessful as far as voting was concerned but it did realign the party with its traditional bureaucratic supporters. On the other hand, the age of deputies in both parties showed some increase in 1965, indicating thus that the old leaders perpetuated themselves in power. However, it would be rather misleading to take the professions and the ages of deputies as the only major indicators of changes occurring in the leadership of the economic entrepreneurial groups. The true political leaders, the real "kingmakers," are not nowadays very interested in becoming deputies. After a period of prestige and popularity a deputy seat has lost its appeal, somewhat, as deputies are being regarded and used as spokesmen and defenders of the views and interests of their constituents. Many deputies nowadays complain that the pursuit of the electors' business in various government offices takes much of their time and that considerable amounts of their salaries (about $ 390 a month before taxes in 1970) are spent on entertaining in the opulent Turkish fashion—visiting constituents, including delegations from villages.

The true change in the quality of political leadership occurred in the party organizations at the provincial and especially at the district level. It is here that a new group of leaders, reflecting the occupational diversification in society and sharpening of group consciousness and interest orientation have acquired the upper hand. If the scanty data in hand (see Chapter VIII) were to be supplemented with additional extensive surveys of party leaders at the local level, this point would most probably be fully supported.

Furthermore, occupational diversification and economic and social growth have affected the political process by greatly increasing the number and the kind of issues which are expected to be decided upon politically. Tables 1.20, 1.21 and 1.22 represent in general terms the economic and table 1.23 the political developments in Turkey from 1927 to 1969. These are given here not as proof of the correlation among various indicators but rather as a broad panorama of the political process in which the economic entrepreneurial groups rose to power. Thus, table 1.22 indicates that, with the exception of sporadic freedom from 1923 to 1925 and in 1930, the one-party regime had all the characteristics of a quasi dictatorship. Freedom was limited, opposition parties did not exist, leftist parties were suppressed, while rightist (nationalist) ones flourished. The voting percentage, because of the indirect system, was insignificant. The unicameral legislature was dominated by officials. Then in the period 1945 to 1950 the picture changed abruptly. The voting system became direct, political freedom was liberalized, opposition parties mushroomed, elections were relatively free, the number of leftist, rightist and religious publications increased while the voting percentage soared. Thus, Turkey which in 1944 met none of the qualifications for democracy used by one study, such as electoral or parliamentary succession of the chief executive, competition between political parties, universal suffrage and political suppression, had turned around and met all of them by 1946.[1] Obviously, this unique and spectacular adoption of democracy cannot be explained without recourse to historical background and changes in leadership.

The major force behind this relatively successful adoption of democracy, as already explained, was the gradual structural transformation which created the social groups —the new entrepreneurial middle-class groups—which could demand freedom and provide the leadership necessary to achieve it. A series of other secondary causes, such as the political education provided by the one-party regime, the dissatisfaction caused by political restrictions, and the victory of democracies in World War II, also prepared the ground for democracy. However, the main concrete pressure came from the upper agrarian, business, entrepreneurial, and some intellectual groups which mobilized the masses to struggle for a regime of freedom. The result of all this was the liberalization of 1946-47, and then the Democratic Party's electoral victory in 1950. But this democratic appearance was deceptive. The system gave to the Executive extensive powers and did not allow for the political representation of groups and ideologies which differed from those in power. The unicameral Assembly, based on the constitution of 1924, theoretically concentrated all the power in its own hands, but in reality it was dominated by the Executive through the party in power. Checks and balances did not exist. Consequently the Democratic Party government of Adnan Menderes was able to curtail many freedoms from 1957 to 1960, and despite criticism and opposition it maintained itself in power.

Significantly enough, the first opposition to Menderes, as mentioned before, came from his own party in 1955 and almost made him lose the election of 1957. This writer investigated throughout Anatolia the social groups within the Democratic Party which rose against Menderes in 1957. Small entrepreneurs, merchants, artisans, mechanics, technicians, and professionals, usually between twenty-five and forty years of age, formed the bulk of this opposition. Consequently, after the Revolution of 1960 these men, who had been in the lower echelons of the Democratic Party, which was banned, established the Justice Party overnight and vied successfully for power. Hence the young age of deputies elected

---

[1] William Flanigan and Edwin Fogelman, "Patterns of Democratic Development: An Historical Comparative Analysis" (Paper presented to the Annual Meeting of the American Political Science Association, Washington, D.C., September, 1968).

CHANGE AND MODERNIZATION OF SOCIAL GROUPS 85

Table 1.20

Chain Index Numbers of Major Indicators of Development *

Years	Net National income [1]	Urbanization [2]	Communication and Mass media — Radios	Communication and Mass media — Newspapers and magazines	Transportation — Highways	Transportation — Railroads	Occupational Diversification [3] — Professional and technical	Occupational Diversification [3] — Service workers	Occupational Diversification [3] — Trade, industry and commerce	Occupational Diversification [3] — Government and administrative	Occupational Diversification [3] — Agriculture	Literacy [4]
1927	100.0	100.0	—	—	100.0	100.0	100.0	100.0	100.0	100.0	100.0	100.0
1935	137.4	120.0	100.0	100.0	179.5	143.2	84.6	32.0	145.7	437.5	99.7	183.2
1940	125.8	119.3	269.8	226.8	105.0	111.2	145.5	112.5	82.2	147.3	106.9	114.3
1945	77.3	107.5	225.3	99.4	104.9	101.8	93.8	66.7	126.8	100.0	87.4	130.4
1950	153.3	112.5	186.2	195.2	108.2	102.1	100.0	383.3	87.4	57.4	115.9	114.7
1955	135.6	137.5	311.2		116.8	101.7	126.7	139.1	130.3	48.3	93.8	121.2
1960	135.2	131.5	134.3	256.3	111.9	101.2	115.8	128.1	107.1	135.6	93.2	107.6
1965	128.5		182.1	103.9 (1963)		117.8	122.7	117.1	114.2	102.6	95.4	109.8

* Chain index numbers show percentage increases from period to period, compiled on the basis of preceding tables.
[1] Per capita income chain index numbers are as follows : (100.0), (116.0), (114.1), (73.3), (137.4), (120.3), (117.2), and (110.9).
[2] Numbers in this column indicate the changes in numbers of people living in provinces and districts with population over 10,000. Chain index numbers of the percent of total population living in provinces and districts with population over 10,000 are as follows : (100.0), (101.2), (108.4), (101.7), (101.1), (113.0), (120.6).
[3] Numbers indicate changes in percentages of total working population.
[4] Numbers in this column indicate the changes in literacy as percent of total population. Chain index numbers of the literate population are as follows : (100.0), (216.7), (126.0), (137.4), (109.7), (162.4), (124.1), (124.2).
Chain index numbers for percent of political participation are as follows : insignificant up to 1946; 1946 = 100; 1950 = 119.1; 1954 = 99.2; 1957 = 86.7; 1960 = 105.7; 1961 = 100.5; 1965 = 87.6.

Table 1.21

Index Numbers of Major Indicators of Development

* Provinces and districts with population over 10,000.
** Percentages of eligible votes. Election years are 1946, 1950, 1954, 1957, 1960, 1961, 1965 respectively.

Years	Net national income	Per capita income	Urbanization: Population living in urban centers *	Urbanization: % of total population living in urban centers	Transportation: Highways	Transportation: Railroads	Communication and Mass media: Radios	Communication and Mass media: Newspapers × magazines	Occupational Diversification: Professional × technical	Occupational Diversification: Service workers	Occupational Diversification: Trade, industry and commerce	Occupational Diversification: Government × administrative	Occupational Diversification: Agriculture	Literacy: Literate population	Literacy: Percent of total population	Political participation **
1927	100.0	100.0	100.0	100.0	100.0	100.0	Insignificant	—	100.0	100.0	100.0	100.0	100.0	100.0	100.0	Insignificant
1935	137.4	116.0	120.0	101.2	179.5	143.2	100.0	100.0	84.6	32.0	145.7	437.5	99.7	183.2	216.7	
1940	172.9	132.4	143.2	109.7	188.6	159.2	269.8	226.8	123.1	36.0	112.6	631.2	106.5	209.3	273.4	
1945	135.6	97.0	153.9	111.6	197.3	162.1	607.8	225.5	115.4	24.0	137.8	631.2	93.1	272.9	375.0	100.0
1950	204.5	133.3	173.2	112.8	213.5	165.4	1,106.4	434.2	115.4	92.0	119.7	362.5	107.9	313.6	412.0	119.1
1955	275.0	156.6	238.1	127.4	249.9	168.3	3,443.7	—	146.2	128.0	155.9	175.0	101.2	379.4	669.0	118.1
																102.1
1960	374.9	184.3	313.0	153.7	279.1	170.3	4,625.1	1,112.8	169.2	164.0	119.8	237.5	94.4	408.4	829.8	108.0
																108.5
1965	470.4	204.5				200.6	8,423.9	1,155.7 (1963)	207.7	192.0	190.6	243.8	90.0	448.6	1,031.8	95.1

CHANGE AND MODERNIZATION OF SOCIAL GROUPS   87

Table 1.22. *Political Indicators: Participation and Freedom*

+ = Full freedom	D = Direct election	O = Restricted
— = No freedom	I = Indirect election	O+ = Freedom recognized but somewhat restricted in practice
A = One Chamber assembly	M = Line indicating the end of one party system under People's Republican Party	R = Religious
AS = Assembly and Senate	N = Nationalist	S = Sporadic
C = Continuous at least two years		

Periods	Election years	Election system	Freedom of press, political activity, and association	Number of opposition parties (brackets = months of activities)[1]	Number of free elections and degree of freedom	Major ideological parties on left with program and following	Major ideological parties on right with program and following[2]	Number of major leftist reviews and dailies	Number of major rightist and/or religious reviews and dailies	Voting percentage	Types of legislature
1923-1930		I	O	2 (6)		2		6 S	2 N	Insignificant	A
1930-1935		I	O					2 C	6 N	»	A
1935-1940		I	O						8 N	»	A
1940-1945		I	O							»	A
1945-1950	1946 1950	D	O+	3	2+	2	1	8 S	4 N 3 R	80.0 89.3	A
1950-1955	1954	D	+	3	1+				4 N 5 R	88.6	A
1955-1960	1957	D	O+	4	1 O+				3 N 5 R	76.6	A
1960-1965	1961 1965	D	+	5	2+	1	1	5	2 N 2 R	81.0[3] 81.4[4] 71.3	AS

[1] The independents usually representing minority views or interests but seldom going beyond 3 percent of the total vote are not included.
[2] There are more than a dozen small parties on the right with limited following, which may fall in this category. Religious parties are not included here. *World Handbook* gives the religious vote for 1957 and 1961 as 10.6 percent, but this percentage is debatable.
[3] This refers to the Constitutional Referendum.
[4] This drop of percentage is due to an extremely cumbersome voting procedure especially designated to cut down the peasant vote and weaken the Justice Party. This artificial reduction can be seen from comparing this percentage with the referendum and election of 1961.

Table 1.23

Political Participation: Political Parties and Elections

[1] This refers to the Constitutional Referendum.
[2] Numbers in parentheses are percentages of total valid votes.
[3] Tentative results. (Actual numbers of votes received by each party do not include votes from Hakkari province. All other figures are nation-wide).

Election Years	1950	1954	1957	1960 [1]	1961	1965	1969 [3]
Eligible votes	8,905,743	10,262,063	12,078,623	12,747,901	12,925,395	13,679,753	14,692,581
No. of votes cast	7,953,085	9,095,617	9,250,949	10,321,111	10,522,716	9,748,678	9,454,676
% of participation	89.3	88.6	76.6	81.0	81.4	71.3	64.4
Democratic Party	4,241,393 (53.3) [2]	5,151,550 (56.6)	4,372,621 (47.3)				
Justice Party					3,527,435 (34.8)	4,921,235 (52.9)	4,184,814 (46.5)
People's Republican Party	3,176,561 (39.9)	3,161,696 (34.8)	3,753,136 (40.6)		3,724,752 (36.7)	2,675,785 (28.7)	2,465,554 (27.4)
Nation Party	250,414 (3.1)						
Peasant's Party		57,011 (0.6)	350,597 (3.8)				
Republican Nation Party		434,085 (4.8)	652,064 (7.0)			582,704 (6.3)	294,655 (3.2)
Freedom Party			346,881 (4.0)				

Post Revolution = (New Constitution, Broader Representation, Ideological Phase)

CHANGE AND MODERNIZATION OF SOCIAL GROUPS 89

Table 1.23 (Continued)

Election Years	1950	1954	1957	1960[1]	1961	1965	1969[3]
New Turkey Party					1,391,934 (13.7)	346,514 (3.7)	202,042 (2.2)
Republican Peasant's Nation Party					1,415,390 (14.0)	208,696 (2.2)	
Turkish Labor Party						276,101 (3.0)	238,741 (2.7)
Reliance Party							577,026 (6.6)
National Action Party							278,220 (3.0)
Union Party							228,586 (2.8)
Independents	383,282 (4.8)	137,318 (1.5)	4,994 (0.1)		81,732 (0.8)	296,528 (3.2)	508,733 (5.6)

Post Revolution = (New Constitution, Broader Representation, Ideological Phase)

Sources: 1950-65: *1950-65 Milletvekili ve 1961, 1964 Cumhuriyet Senatosu Üye Seçimleri Sonuçlari* ("The Results of 1950-1965[1] Deputy Elections and the Senate Elections 1961, 1964"), Publication No. 513 of the State Institute of Statistics (Ankara, 1966), p. vii.

1969: *Cumhuriyet*, October 15, 1969. Walter F. Weiker, "Turkey's Elections, May Bode Ills," *Mid East*, December, 1969, pp. 10-13, 32-34.

Also see: Kemal H. Karpat, "The Turkish Elections of 1957," *The Western Quarterly*, 14 (June 1961), p. 459; Michael Steed and Nermin Abadan, "Four Elections of 1965," *Government and Opposition*, May 1966, p. 343; Walter F. Weiker, *The Turkish Revolution, 1960-61: Aspects of Military Politics* (Washington, D.C., 1963), p. 166.

on the JP slate in 1961. The political rise of the entrepreneurial middle class groups occurred through, and despite, the military revolution of 1960, and despite the insistence of some of the intelligentsia on retaining the military regime under the justification of radical social reforms. The system which emerged after the new constitution was accepted in 1961 enlarged the sphere of participation and brought equality by allowing for the free expression of different opinions, and for the parliamentary representation of various social groups. Eventually, a leftist party (Labor Party) entered Parliament while publications of all tendencies were freely issued. A bicameral Parliament (Assembly and Senate) was formed and a series of checks and balances thus established (see Chapter VIII). So the Revolution of 1960, engineered by the military, and the Constitution of 1961 framed under their quasi tutelage, ended by establishing and consolidating a political regime which theoretically corresponded to the social, economic, and cultural aspirations and world view of the economic-entrepreneurial groups. But this was not really the victory of one class over another as in the classical class struggle but the emergence of a new social stratum which fought for and eventually achieved recognition. It marked, in fact, the emergence of a new type of society without rigidly formed classes, and without an aristocracy, a kind of modern mass democratic society which may well be the prototype of society emerging in the third world.

The relations between the economic entrepreneurial groups and the statist ones as well as with other groups have been analyzed here within the context of Western concepts of politics and society. But there are rules, conventions, attitudes, and unwritten laws deriving from the society's own "traditional" political culture and history which were and are equally instrumental in governing relations among social groups. These could be subject to lengthy analyses. But there is one feature, a pattern of struggle inherited from the so-called "traditional" society which was evident throughout the process analyzed in this study. The history of the Turks, from the early days in Central Asia to the Republic, has been marked by the role of statist elites. The rank and file, the masses, obeyed the rulers and acquiesced in their power. At times (and history being written from the viewpoint of the ruling elites seldom mentions it or if it does is pejorative) leaders and social movements sprang up from the masses only to be crushed by or absorbed into the ranks of the rulers. The ruling establishment had developed incredibly refined methods for attracting and assimilating popular leaders, and if these leaders proved recalcitrant, for annihilating them at the opportune moment.

In our day a new social stratum has appeared and with popular support it has acquired the power which it still retains. Its power roots are in the masses but its political philosophy is hazy at best. It is ideologically almost powerless under the assault of the statist elites. The political future of Turkey will be decided by the ultimate power struggle between the statist elites and the newly rising groups. Will the economic entrepreneurial groups preserve their informal coalition with the masses and develop a new type of society or will they bow to the statist elites and accept their political supremacy as in the past? The pull of tradition, the lure of security, and the desire to enjoy their riches may be too strong to resist. Already events in 1971 indicate that all these forces are headed toward a synthesis as demonstrated by the resignation of the Demirel government under military pressure and its own failure at providing leadership (see Preface). If so, the Turkish masses' millenary struggle for the recognition of man's dignity and freedom as man, for spiritual liberty, will resume but with greater vehemence. The intricate psychological and political undertones of this conflict among the masses and elites in Turkey are fully and bluntly spelled out in the following lengthy excerpt from an article by Feyzi L. Karaosmanoğlu, a scion of an ex-feudal family, a liberal politician, an ex-Minister in the Democratic Party and a rebel against the Menderes group in 1955. In Turkey, says Karaosmanoğlu :

"There are not yet [social] classes born from the social and economic causes that we know. Even if [such classes] exist, thank God, we do not see their struggle. But beyond these, and quite distinct from them, there are in our country two classes whose smouldering struggle sometimes openly, sometimes secretly, even if not acute, continues. One of these classes is the ruling group and the other is the ruled. The ruled group comprises the entire population engaged in their own [routine] occupations, regardless of whether or not they are educated. The struggle...does not appear in the form of resistance to the ruling group. On the contrary it is in the form of an offensive, oppression and pressure on the part of [the ruling group] who act as though they have been charged by divine order to rule the [other] people. The ruling ones may come from villages, may rise from cities but whatever their place [of origin] and manner of [political] ascendancy, and whatever their upbringing, they have the same attitudes, the same mentality and habits. These, once they are entangled in the wheels of the organization called State, adopt, from the youngest to the oldest, an unsmiling face, a grumbling voice and attempt to direct and to rule the big masses as they please regardless of their position and origin. They do not care whether the masses are hurt and suffer... Actually the [rulers] come from among the people and boast of it [their social origin] all their life. They claim to have studied and been brought up in order to rule. These are either politicians who have come to power through...elections or are officials who started low and rose by promotion... [but] once they [thus] separate themselves from the ruled groups...the commanding attitude and manner betakes them. Instead of marching with the masses which they are supposed to guide, they pass opposite them...as reformists, educators, and like a man holding the reins [of a horse] they start to crack the whip and pull the reins. From there on God forbid... This is a disease. It is the disease of the so-called intelligentsia [elites] who think from the youngest to the oldest, that they have been created to rule the nation.[1]

The political future of Turkey may in fact be determined on one hand by this permanent philosophy of society and government and the new social groups created and motivated by the modern economic forces on the other, as well as by their concepts of nationhood, equality, freedom, and modernity.

---

[1] Fevzi L. Karaosmanoğlu, "İdare Edenler ve Edilenler" *Dünya* (March 31, 1962).

CHAPTER TWO

THE MODERNIZATION OF TURKEY IN HISTORICAL AND COMPARATIVE PERSPECTIVE

Dankwart A. Rustow

I

Modernization is a term that has gained currency among social scientists to designate a cluster of historic changes, including industrialization, rationalization, secularization, bureaucratization, and many others. It is a convenient term because, unlike the other polysyllables that pick single strands from the tangled web of human affairs, modernization draws attention to change throughout the tapestry. And it is preferable to a term such as "development," which can either designate generally any sort of change (the barbarian invasions of Rome, the alienation of contemporary urban life, and the erosion of topsoils in Anatolia each "developed" over a number of centuries), or specifically change in a direction held to be desirable (for example, toward affluence or democracy); for modernization is far less than change as such, and it may be considered morally ambiguous. Modernization may be defined as the transformation of three of man's basic relationships—to time, to his physical environment, and to his fellow man. Modern man looks on time not as repetitive or cyclical, but as a process: a pattern at once of continuity and change. He looks on his physical environment as amenable to man's progressive understanding and control. And he looks on his fellow man as a potential partner in a division of labor—a division of labor aimed at the control of nature within a purposeful pattern of temporal change. As modern man interacts more intensely with his fellows, he may interact with them for greater material comfort, for wider spiritual exchange, and for more savage physical destruction. Society as a whole cannot engage in modernization without accepting its ingredients as beneficial or its totality as inevitable. The student of modernization, however, need not concur in these judgments; his study is amply justified if modernization, for good or for ill, is acknowledged as the most potent force of his age.[1]

---

[1] I have elaborated this view of modernization in several other writings: Robert E. Ward and Dankwart A. Rustow, eds., *Political Modernization in Japan and Turkey*,

To the student of modernization and of the policy choices that it poses, Turkey offers one of the most fruitful locales, for in few other countries has modernization been so comprehensive and deliberate. This is not to say that the Turks have been the world's most successful modernizers; that distinction, surely, is shared by Westerners and Japanese. But even the mistakes the Turks have made and the obstacles they have encountered suggest important lessons.

Modernization began in Europe in the ages of the Renaissance and the Reformation, of absolutism and the early industrial revolution. As pioneers in a world-wide transformation, the Europeans experienced modernization as a process of discovery and invention rather than of response and adaptation. Others were to resort to modernization from a sense of weakness; to the Europeans it gave a heady sense of superiority. In a world of warring societies, Europe derived an inestimable competitive advantage from its tighter social organization and its more effective technology. Modernization, therefore, spread to other continents in the wake of European expansion, as a result of colonial rule and overseas settlement. Turkey, however, was one of the few countries able to resist European conquest—at the price of deliberately espousing important elements of Western culture.

The first historical comparison that suggests itself, therefore, is one between Turkey and other settings of "defensive modernization," such as Russia, Japan, China, Iran, Afghanistan, and Thailand. Of these, Russia shared much of Europe's medieval heritage and, as one of the borderlands of Christendom, participated in the imperialist explosion of the sixteenth to nineteenth centuries. To Turkey and to China indeed, the European imperial threat was mainly a Russian threat, and victory over Russia in 1904-05 was a major landmark in Japan's self-assertion against Europe. Nevertheless, the Russian reforms of Peter I (reigned 1689-1725) and his successors remain the classic instance of defensive modernization, with its induced and often frantic changes from the top of the social structure downward and from the surface of culture inward, with its initial preoccupation with military and administrative reforms, with its ambivalent attitude of admiration and hate toward an intrusive alien civilization. Turkey like Russia bordered on Europe, and, by virtue of its Muslim religion and its succession to Byzantium, shared

---

(Princeton, 1964), pp. 3-13; *A World of Nations: The Dynamics of Modern Politics* (Washington, 1967); and "The Political Impact of the West," *Cambridge History of Islam*, Peter M. Holt, Anne K. S. Lambton, and Bernard Lewis, eds. (Cambridge, 1970), part IX, chap. II.

much of the Hellenistic and Judaeo-Christian heritage. Unlike Japan or the Americas, it did not have to be "discovered" or "opened up" by the arrival of Western ships at distant shores. There had been recurrent warfare and intermittent cultural interchange with Europe since early Muslim and Ottoman times. The beginnings of a one-sided Western impact on Turkey, nonetheless, can be quite precisely dated—not from the first establishment of contact but from a shift in the balance of power within the traditional pattern of contact. The turning point was loss of Hungary to the Habsburgs in 1783-99 and of the Ukraine and the Crimea to the Romanovs in 1768-83—defeats which, for the Ottomans, involved something far more precious than territory or strategic position. They posed a fundamental problem in statecraft and even in theodicy; they threatened the very basis of self-confidence. For the first time, Ottomans had occasion to question the rationale of a state founded on Muslim conquest of Christians and of a religious revelation that promised its believers prosperity and power on earth as well as salvation in the hereafter. In matters of warfare at least, it now was painfully clear that Ottoman Muslims must learn from the despised infidel.

Military reform—the most urgent item on the agenda of defensive modernization—was as sweeping in Turkey as it was in Russia and in Japan, but because of Turkey's focal location its results were far more tenuous than in those peripheral areas. While the Ottomans were exerting themselves to ward off the might of Habsburg emperors and Romanov tsars, France under Napoleon, Britain under Canning, Palmerston, and Disraeli, and Germany under Bismarck and William II appeared on the scene. Foreign pressure and domestic reform, moreover, conspired to spread the ideal of the nation-state first among Balkan Christians, then among Armenians, Albanians, and Arabs, and at last among the Turkish-speaking Ottomans themselves; and nationalism was bound to be a destructive force in an empire that for centuries had united the most diverse nationalities and denominations under a single cosmopolitan ruling class. The Ottoman sultans of the nineteenth century thus were quite unable to match the record of the tsars with their continental policy of conquest and russification, or of the Meiji emperor (reigned 1867-1912), secure in his insular location and supported by a population whose cultural and linguistic unity antedated written history. Rather, the "Sick Man on the Bosphorus" resembled the emperors of China, the kings of Thailand, the shahs of Iran, or even his own nominal vassals, the khedives of Egypt. Like those other hapless rulers, he was the recipient now of condescending advice and now of blunt threats from Western ambassadors, a victim of capitulations and unequal treaties, the prey of unscrupulous concession hunters and usurious bankers, a ward at length of international committees of creditors, ruler in his realms by virtue not of his own strength but of the rivalries among his foes, free agent no longer on the diplomatic stage but a mere supernumerary in the sombre denouement of the "Eastern Question."

Clearly, the short-run effects of the early reforms were far from encouraging. The juxtaposition of European-inspired with traditional Ottoman institutions produced much conflict and disarray. Selim III (reigned 1789-1807), first of the modernizing sultans, lost his throne and his life in the fight against traditional forces of resistance. The new army of Mahmud II (reigned 1808-1839) lost more decisive battles than had the rebellious and rapacious Janissaries. The European-trained diplomats of the nineteenth century were forced into piecemeal surrender of the empire's territory and sovereignty. Solemn promises of civic equality and legal reform failed to deflect the subject nationalities from their course of rebellion and secession. And the newly trained administrators and tax collectors did not stave off imperial bankruptcy. It is a tribute to the Ottoman's resolute spirit of pragmatism that these setbacks did not turn them against reform but only spurred them to greater effort.

Only by the 1920's and 30's did modernization at long last confer upon Turkey a degree of domestic strength and foreign prestige not attained at the time by Egypt, Iran, Thailand, or even China. This vindication of the modernization program came as result of the transition from multinational empire to nationalist republic—a strategic retrenchment that converted defeat in World War I into victory in the War of Independence and that allowed reform to proceed more intensively on a more manageable geographic scale. With the establishment of the Republic in 1923, modernization reached a climax—and, in a sense, came full circle. The heirs of the new army that Selim III had founded in 1793 deposed his cousin's grandson and pronounced the Ottoman Empire defunct. Reform, which had started out as a selective expedient for the defense of tradition against the Western onslaught, had become an instrument for the destruction and the wholesale transformation of tradition itself.

II

Turkish modernization began as a deliberate policy to wipe out the defeats inflicted by Prince Eugene of Savoy and the generals of Catherine

II, a concerted effort to redress the humiliations imposed by the treaties of Carlowitz in 1699 and of Küçük Kaynarca in 1774. But by slow and logical stages, military reform expanded into cultural transformation, the policies initiated by sultans engulfed society as a whole, defensive modernization turned into integral modernization. The Ottomans found, as Arnold Toynbee was to put it with charming simplicity, that "in the game of cultural intercourse... one thing lead[s] to another." [1]

The forces that propelled the movement of change far beyond its original intent were both external and internal. In Ottoman Turkey, as later in Japan, the rising might of Europe provided the stimulus for reform. But Japan witnessed the West's military and commercial pressure on China at some distance and later suffered a single, galvanizing intrusion by Commodore Perry's squadron, whereas Turkey was a victim not a witness, and the pressure on her was both massive and direct. The defeats of 1683-99 and 1711-18, it is true, were followed by a half-century interval of peace unique in Ottoman history and interrupted only by a brief and victorious campaign in 1735-39. But after 1768, military defeat piled upon military defeat and territorial loss upon territorial loss for a century and a half right down to the final collapse of 1918. There were wars with Russia (1768-74, 1787-92, and 1806-12); the French expedition in Egypt (1798-1801); uprisings in Serbia (1804-07), Arabia (1811) and Greece (1821-29); attacks by Egypt (1831-33 and 1839-41); the Crimean War (1853-56); a general rising in the Balkans (1775-1878); the occupation of Tunis by the French (1881) and Egypt by the British (1882); a war with Greece (1896-97); repeated uprisings toward the turn of the century by Macedonians, Armenians, Yemenis, and Albanians; the Italian occupation of Libya (1911-12); the two Balkans Wars (1912-13); and, after only a year's respite, the Ottoman Empire's fatal involvement in World War I (1914-18). The outcome of these campaigns was rarely in Ottoman hands, and even on the few occasions when the Empire was on the winning side (as in 1801, 1856, and 1897), further territorial losses resulted. Napoleon's expedition in Egypt was thwarted more by British naval than Ottoman military action, and in its wake an Ottoman-Albanian soldier, Muhammad Ali, established himself as Egypt's virtually independent ruler. Muhammad Ali helped defeat the Wahhabis in 1811 and the Greeks in the 1820's, but British and Russian intervention secured Greek independence in 1829-30. Pressure from Britain and France checked Muhammad Ali's advance in 1840-41, but the Russian

---

[1] Arnold J. Toynbee, *The World and the West* (New York, 1953), p. 75.

invasion of 1876-78 converted initial Ottoman victory into defeat. Step by step the Ottoman Empire was forced to surrender its wealthiest provinces in Europe and in Africa. By 1913, the Empire in Europe was limited to Istanbul and its hinterland in Thrace. World War I entailed the loss of the Arab provinces, and, except for Turkish victory in the subsequent War of Independence (1919-22), might have brought an end to Turkish sovereignty. Even that signal success was due in large part to the war-weariness, over-extension, and discord among the victors of World War I.

For two centuries, therefore, the Empire's efforts to match the military power of its European enemies resembled the pursuit of a rapidly receding target. In the eighteenth century, the Ottomans would have done well to resist the Habsburgs and the Romanovs. By the early twentieth century that goal still eluded them, but meanwhile Austria and Russia themselves had slipped to the second rank of military power behind Germany, France, and Britain. Nonetheless, the Ottoman military reform effort was steadily expanded and increased. At first European experts, such as the Comte de Bonneval in the 1730's and the Baron de Tott in the 1770's, were invited to improve the performance of the artillery. In 1793 Selim III established a body of new troops, entirely trained in the European style. Later, Mahmud II revived the experiment and used the new troops to destroy the anti-reformist Janissaries (much as Peter of Russia had destroyed the Streltsi and Mehmet Ali of Egypt the Mamluks). From the 1830's a network of military schools was instituted to train a professional officer corps, and from the 1840's conscription was applied to the Muslim population. Individual foreign instructors such as Hellmuth von Moltke, the later Field Marshall, had taught at the military college from the start. In 1884 another Prussian officer, Colmar von der Goltz-Pasha, was made inspector of the military schools, and by 1909 Germans outnumbered Turks on the staff of the military college. After the Balkan War defeat, General Otto Viktor Karl Liman von Sanders was called in for a further reorganization of the Ottoman forces; and in World War I, German officers served as commanders or chiefs of staff of most Ottoman military units from army group down to regiment and batallion.

While the military reform program proceeded in this fashion, three distinct sets of internal pressures pushed modernization far beyond the military sphere. The first of these was the pressure of traditional resistance to change, the second the pressures of technical requirements, and the third the pressure of new social groups called into life by the reforms themselves.

Selim III's reforms foundered against the resistance of Janissaries and *ulema*, and this traditional resistance was closely related to the disintegration of central authority throughout the empire. Toward the end of the eighteenth century, independent foci of power had emerged in all the provinces—the Mamluk oligarchies in Egypt and Iraq; governors such as the Azm family (1724-1783) and Jezzar Pasha (1790-1804) in Syria and Ali Pasha of Tepedelen (d. 1822) in Epirus; leading Kurdish clans such as the Babanzades at Suleymaniye and the Bedirhan family at Bitlis and Cizre; the corsairs of Tripoli and Algiers; Janissary garrisons in Belgrade, Aleppo, and other cities; nomadic tribes on the Arabian peninsula; and numerous landowners, taxfarmers, and other notables throughout Anatolia. The sultan's authority at times extended little beyond the capital city, and in the double revolution of 1807-08 a coalition of provincial notables came close to taking control of Istanbul as well. But in two decades of tenacious struggle, Mahmud II subdued all the provinces except Egypt, Greece, and Serbia. And the power thus wrested from obstreperous vassals and headstrong feudatories was reposited in the hands of a new bureaucracy, trained at first in the embassies at Paris, London, and Vienna and the translation chamber at the Sublime Porte, and later in higher schools in Istanbul and other cities of the Empire.

Meanwhile, "by a compelling logic the program [of autocratic reform] slowly spread. The army could not be reformed in isolation from the rest of the body politic. The new soldiery needed officers schooled in mathematics, French, and geography, and army surgeons with *alla franca* medical training. Military conscription required a tightening of administration in the provinces... The costs of the new army and administration had to be borne by systematic taxation. An entire new school system was instituted to prepare the future officers, administrators, and tax collectors for their tasks. The schools required more money—and yet more schools for the training of teachers".[1] These new systems of administration and education were instituted during the Tanzimat period (1839-1876) and elaborated during the reign of Abdulhamid (1876-1909) who strengthened them further through introduction of telegraphs and railways—the rudiments, that is, of a modern system of communication. Henceforth young men of talent from all parts of the country were trained in Istanbul as military officers, administrators, tax collectors, or school teachers to be transferred from province to

---

[1] Ward and Rustow, *Political Modernization*, p. 353.

province at regular intervals of two to three years. It was this new military and civilian bureaucracy with tentacles throughout the Empire that consolidated Mahmud's work of political centralization.

The European-style educational system of Tanzimat did far more, however, than facilitate the staffing of the centralized public service. It also created a new social class that adopted European tastes in dress and in social intercourse, in literature and in thought. This new ruling class differed significantly from its predecessors. The Ottoman ruling class of the classical period had been trained in the palace schools in the exclusive service of the sultan; the Janissaries and provincial officials of the period of Ottoman decadence had been eager to establish their independent and hereditary power in the provinces. The new elite of the nineteenth century was firmly centered upon Istanbul—reassignment to the capital remained the dream of every official forced to win his spurs in the provinces—but it acquired a consciousness of group identity quite apart from its official function in the imperial service. Its members became the bearers of public opinion on important matters of state, and they soon proceeded to form political associations to give expression to such opinions.

No career illustrates better these side-effects of the Tanzimat reforms than that of İbrahim Şinasi (1824-1871). As a young man, Şinasi had been a clerk in the imperial artillery school and had learned French from one of the foreign military instructors. Sent to Paris to study public finance, he became an enthusiastic admirer of the romantic poetry and the liberal politics of men like Alphonse de Lamartine and Victor Hugo. Back in Istanbul, he served intermittently in various government posts but spent most of his energy on his literary and political pursuits; in 1860 he became the first Turkish editor of a private daily newspaper. Trained initially within the new military establishment, Sinasi became the father of the movement known as the New Literature (*edebiyat-ı cedide*), the Ottoman originator of European-style drama, poetry, journalism, and political polemics.

Şinasi's example was followed by a group of political malcontents —an Egyptian prince and several younger bureaucrats and *ulema*—who founded the New Ottoman Society in 1865. After some years in exile, members of this movement seized power in two military coups d'état in 1876, which gave the Ottoman Empire the first written representative constitution to be adopted in any non-Western country. Following the suppression of that constitution by Abdülhamid in 1878, the movement was resumed by the secret Society of Union and Progress (1889), by a growing group of political exiles known to Europeans as the Young

Turks, and by a renewed military-civilian conspiracy in Macedonia (1906) which restored the constitution in 1908. It was significant that the Society of Union and Progress was founded at the military medical college, the most technical branch of the new army; that the leading Young Turk exile, Ahmed Riza, had been a provincial director of education; and that the prominent revolutionaries of 1906-08 included men like Talat, a telegraphy clerk, Cemal, a military inspector of railways, and Cavid, a teacher and journalist. The reformed army, education, and communications remained the seedbeds of modernizing innovation and of political organization. In short, "by the end of nineteenth century [the] higher schools had produced a new elite of officers and officials to whom Europeanizing reform was no longer an occasional expedient for preserving tradition but an instrument for transforming tradition itself. Modernization, starting out as the command of an autocrat, had become the project of ministers and at last the fervent mission of a new social class. In laying the foundation for military reform, the sultans, like the sorcerer's apprentice, had released a process which became increasingly autonomous and which they eventually became unable to control".[1] The external stimulus to modernization had been fully internalized and thus produced a self-propelling momentum.

III

How can this state be saved? *bu devlet nasıl kurtarılabilir*? This was the fateful, nagging question that preoccupied the late Ottomans for a century and a half. The immediate threat was military, and so were the initial countermeasures. But for military measures to attain their end, they must be undertaken by a restored central authority, buttressed by reforms in administration and education, and actively supported by new social groups outside the narrow confines of palace and ministry. The sequence of reform from Mahmud II to the Tanzimat, the Young Turks, and the Kemalists thus followed a clear logic—but it followed a teleological logic, not a deterministic one. It was not the only logic possible; rather it was a logic forged in a series of purposeful human choices. And these choices gave rise to recurrent conflict.

Radically opposite conclusions could be drawn at any given moment from the overwhelming fact of foreign pressure and domestic weakness. The first conflict was one between reformers and champions of tradition.

---

[1] *Ibid.*, p. 359.

To the *ulema* and Janissaries of the turn of the eighteenth century, Selim's New Order signified betrayal rather than salvation, a surrender to the execrable ways of the Frankish enemy. The provincial potentates and notables, moreover, saw in Mahmud's program of centralization an intolerable encroachment upon their vested rights. After the destruction of the Janissaries and the provincial notables, the conflict of reform vs. tradition gave way to conflicts among divergent courses of reform, among competing blends of tradition and modernity, among alternative sequences of modernization. The Tanzimat ministers championed the sultan's absolute power as the most effective force for enlightened reform. The New Ottomans believed, on the contrary, that absolutism opened the doors wide to corruption and the squandering of public funds, to subservience to foreigners, and to imperial bankruptcy. They found in constitutions and parliaments, in a free press and public criticism the true secrets of European strength, and they were determined to make these the basis of sound reform in the Ottoman state.

The clash between enlightened despotism and upper class constitutionalism intensified as the pressure from foreign powers and from secessionist nationalities mounted during the next generation. The Russian attack of 1877-78 provided Abdülhamid II with a ready rationale for suspending the constitution and dismissing a parliament that introduced dangerous dissension at a moment of supreme danger to the Empire. While forcefully promoting administrative and material aspects of modernization—military training, higher education, telegraphs, and railways—he suppressed elections, criticism in the press, and political organization. To the Young Turks, on the contrary, the Anglo-Russian rapproachement of 1907 and the danger of renewed risings on the Balkans provided an added incentive for reimposing parliamentary restraints upon a ruler whose policies of favoritism and domestic espionage were sapping the morale of the army and setting the subject nationalities against one another. Midhat Pasha, the chief author of the basic law of 1876, had conceived of a constitutional empire based on a common set of Ottoman loyalties embracing Turks, Albanians, and Arabs, Muslims, Balkan Christians, and Armenians. His program was taken up by liberal constitutionalists such as "Prince" Sabahaddin (1877-1948) and the Freedom and Accord Party (Entente Libérale) of 1911, who were convinced that the dangerous times called for an administrative decentralization such as would bring about a reconciliation of the nationalities, a true "union of the elements" (*ittihad-ı anasır*). In the eyes of their radical antagonists, the treachery of Christians, of Albanians, and later of Arabs confirmed that union and progress could result only from a tightening of administration and from a strict reliance on the Turkish national element.

The desperate situation after the defeat of 1918 produced an even sharper political divergence. Sultan Mehmed VI Vahideddin (1918-22) and his ministers hoped to secure lenient peace terms by conceding any and all demands of the victorious Allies. The younger military leaders, such as Mustafa Kemal, and the patriotic societies in the provinces were convinced that the Allies, bent on occupation and partition, would respect only armed resistance rooted in popular organization. The two groups, moreover, diverged in their aims as well as their methods : the Istanbul politicians were concerned to save faith and dynasty (*din ve devlet*), the leaders who rallied in Anatolia were concerned to save fatherland and nation (*vatan ve millet*). The decisive showdown came in the Anatolian civil war of the summer of 1920—the bloodiest of all internal conflicts in Turkish history.

Disagreement did not cease with the establishment of the Republic in 1923. The leaders of the Progressive Party of 1924-25 believed, in the words of Ali Fuat Cebesoy, that "the Gazi would have administered the revolutionary program better by remaining an impartial head of state." [1] But Kemal himself, except for a brief departure in 1930, remained convinced that only a unified party organization could impose his program of radical Westernizing reforms, that any organized opposition would lead at length to demands for the restoration of the caliphate and of religious tradition. Within Kemal's Republican People's Party itself, some interpreted revolutionary populism as an approximation of communism or of fascism; others saw in it a necessary preparation for parliamentary democracy. In the 1930's and 40's some believed that the needs of economic development required strong state initiative within a mixed (or etatist) economy; others argued the virtues of liberalism and private enterprise. In the 1950's and 60's the makers of economic policy have had to choose between giving priority to agriculture or to industry, to current consumption or to investment, to increased production or to equalized distribution, and to civilian or to military needs.

Some of the bitterest recent conflicts have been fought over basic constitutional questions. The concepts of democracy held by Adnan Menderes (1899-1961, prime minister 1950-60) amounted at first to an extreme majoritarianism: agricultural development and retrenchment

---

[1] A. F. Cebesoy'un, *Siyasi Hatıraları*, (Istanbul, 1957), I, p. 2316.

of secularism to satisfy the demands of the rural voters regardless of liberal safeguards concerning the independence of judges, the freedom of the press, or the tenure of professors. In Menderes' later years there was a headlong rush toward personal autocracy with religious overtones—a system under which any public criticism or organized opposition came to be treasonable or even blasphemous. Whereas to Menderes and his followers any policies endorsed by the majority of rural voters were, *ex hypothesi*, democratic, his critics saw in the religious conservatism of the rural voter clear evidence that Turkey was not yet ready for democracy. And in 1960-61 the predominant military and civilian groups deduced from the miscarriage of the first democratic experiment the need to reestablish democracy more securely on a system of checks and balances including guarantees of civil rights, bicameralism, proportional representation, and judicial review. Others concluded that there was a clear need for a renewed imposition of authoritarian methods.

Many Turkish observers have interpreted these recurrent conflicts over policies of modernization as a single protracted contest between two perpetual and distinct forces: Progress vs. Reaction, or Enlightenment vs. Obscurantism. There is, of course, an undeniable continuity among those whom this view identifies as progressive—Mahmud II, the Tanzimat ministers, the Young Turks, and Kemal Atatürk. As successive rulers of the country, each of these necessarily had to build on the accomplishments of his predecessors. But Abdülhamid II—whom this conventional view of history castigates as a reactionary—also belongs in that line of continuity. (Once when asked how he had won the war of independence, Mustafa Kemal replied, only half jokingly, "with the telegraphy wires";[1] those wires had been strung at the orders of Abdülhamid to provide tighter control over his governors in the provinces.) Nor did successive opponents of the prevailing political trend have very much in common with one another—except for their greater attachment to religious tradition. Typically, indeed, the opponents of one period were dissidents from within the group that had just previously come to power. The leaders of the opposition of 1909-1918 (e.g. Colonel Sadık, Prince Sabahaddin, and Ahmed Riza) had opposed Abdülhamid as vigorously as had the members of the Union and Progress Party, or had taken leading roles in the 1908 revolution. The Progressives who opposed Mustafa Kemal in 1924-25 included his closest associates of

---

[1] Quoted by Enver Behnan Şapolyo, *Kemal Atatürk ve Milli Mücadele Tarihi*, 3d ed. (Istanbul, 1958), p. 349; cf. Lord Kinross, *Atatürk: The Rebirth of a Nation* (London, 1964), p. 165.

1919-20. And Bayar, Menderes, and other leading Democrats of the 1950's had been members in good standing of the Republican Peoples' Party of the 1930's.

The conventional view errs, above all, in likening the course of modernization to the labors of Sisyphus, in disregarding the many issues that in fact have been settled. This settling of old issues has come about in a number of different ways.

First, some policies were clearly proven right and others just as clearly proven wrong by the course of subsequent events. The best example is provided by the aftermath of the defeat of 1918. The assumption behind Vahideddin's policy of cooperation with the Allies was strikingly disproven by the punitive terms of the Treaty of Sèvres which his government was forced to sign in August 1920. Conversely, the diplomatic recognition or support which the nationalists received in 1920 and 1921 from the French, Italians, Russians, and even British was the clearest vindication of Kemal's course of nationalist resistance.

Second, some policies may or may not have been right when first formulated, yet once adopted, they served, to some extent, as self-fulfilling prophesies. The facile way in which the Union and Progress movement after 1908 equated Ottomanism with Turkish nationalism served to antagonize further all the non-Turkish groups; and the heavy-handed repression of Albanians, Armenians, and Arabs confirmed each of these groups in their course of rebellion and secession. By 1918 it was obvious, as it was not in 1908, that only Turks could be relied upon to remain loyal to the state.

Third, some contestants and their policies clearly won and others clearly lost in direct, forcible confrontations. The provincial notables and the Janissaries were destroyed by Mahmud II; hence any future opposition (such as the New Ottomans) could form only within, not against, the modernized bureaucracy. Similarly, Vahideddin's miscalculations and Mustafa Kemal's cautious but resolute policies in 1919-22 destroyed the political base of the sultanate. It is remarkable that, after a half century during which fundamental opposition and exile had become a perennial feature of Turkish politics, no loyalist opposition formed at home or abroad for the restoration of the sultanate.

Fourth, conservatism being a relative position, the values defended by Turkish conservatives have changed from generation to generation. The conservatives of 1808 extracted from Mahmud II a solemn undertaking to share his power with the provincial notables; those of 1908 were defending the centralized monarchy of Mahmud and Abdülhamid against demands that the sultan share power with parliamentary representatives from the provinces. The fez, which Mahmud had forced on his bureaucrats as a newfangeld Western form of headdress in place of the turban, a century later was abolished as the most visible symbol of traditionalism.

Finally, a number of political ideals and symbols have been accepted by nearly all political protagonists whatever their position within the current spectrum. Turkish nationalism was an extremist fringe position in 1897 when Mehmed Emin [Yurdakul] (1864-1944), in a bellicose poem, proclaimed, "I am a Turk, my faith, my race are sublime." As late as 1920 Mustafa Kemal himself felt compelled to reprimand one of his ministers for implying that the current war was a national struggle of the Turks and to close the ensuing parliamentary incident in the Ankara Assembly by disavowing Turkish nationalism in favor of a multiethnic Islamic nationalism.[1] In the 1930's nationalism still was freely invoked as justification for various cultural, economic, or foreign policies. Today, nationalism is so widely accepted that the term rarely is used in political discourse. Secularism remained controversial into the 1930's and beyond; yet by the 1950's even religious conservatives were arguing their case from secularist premises (e.g. that true secularism implies freedom of religious organization). Needless to say, Atatürk has become a universal patriotic symbol claimed alike by authoritarians and democrats, by secularists and even religious conservatives.[2] In the last two decades democracy, too, has become widely accepted—a symbol claimed by Menderes and by the military junta that overthrew him and by each of the major parties today. There are indications that "social justice," the ideal proclaimed in the preamble of the constitution of the Second Republic,

---

[1] His words bear quoting: "Gentlemen, with the request that this question should not arise again I should like to make clear two things. What is intended here...is not only Turks, not only Circassians, not only Kurds, not only Lazes, but the Islamic ethnic elements comprising all of these, a sincere community...The nation the preservation and defense of which we have undertaken is not only composed of one ethnic element. It is composed of the various Islamic elements" (*Atatürk'ün Söylev ve Demeçleri* Ankara, 1945-54), I, 70 ff. For a similar statement by Kemal see *inbid.*: I, 28; for the full text of the parliamentary debates see the reprint of the proceedings of the National Assembly (*T.B.M.M. Zabıt Ceridesi, Devre I, İçtima senesi 1*, 3d printing (Ankara, 1959), I, pp. 165 ff. (Note that the "T" for "Türkiye," in the title is an anachronism). The statements were made on May 1 and April 24, 1920, respectively.

[2] For recent examples of religious conservatives invoking secularism and Atatürk see Dankwart A. Rustow, "Politics and Islam in Turkey," in *Islam and the West*, ed. Richard N. Frye (The Hague; 1957), pp. 65n, 103, 106.

will be enjoying similarly unrestricted currency in the foreseeable future. Many political protagonists, of course, will tax their opponents with paying mere lip service to Atatürk's memory, to democracy, to secularism, or to social justice. But the words that come frequently over a man's lips have a subtle and steady way of influencing the thoughts in his mind.

It is important in this connection to place in proper perspective the upsurge of Islamic sentiment that manifested itself in the period of multiparty competition between 1945 and 1960 and that often is cited as a major reversal of Turkish modernization. It is doubtful, first of all, that Islamic sentiment in fact increased; rather, with the relaxation of official restraints, such sentiment as had survived two decades of enforced secularism became more vocal. Secondly, the policies adopted by the Republican People's Party (RPP) government in 1947-50 and under Menderes in the 1950's were in the nature not of a revival but a very limited restoration. And thirdly, to the peasant majority new water wells, new feeder roads, new village mosques, and a high support price for wheat were all so many facets of the general movement of rural self-assertion after millenia of urban dominance. As wells and roads enable the peasants to produce for a national market and, in growing numbers, to migrate to the towns, the peasants too are becoming engulfed in the overall sweep of modernization and secularization.

The ideological inventory just attempted reveals an important difference between the Turks and most other defensive modernizers. The nineteenth-century Japanese tried to adopt Western technology while preserving or even reinforcing traditional elements of social and spiritual culture. The twentieth-century Russians and Chinese have embraced a radically dissident Western ideology which could be used in the political struggle against the West. The Turks, by contrast, have drawn no such distinction and made no such heretical substitution. Their ambition, for the better part of a century, has been to become accepted as Europeans, and Marxism has only very recently found a responsive echo among their intellectuals. The assumption that has prevailed among most Ottoman and Turkish modernizers was well stated by Abdullah Cevdet (1869-1932), cofounder of the Society of Union and Progress, and most farsighted of the Young Turk political writers: "There is no second civilization: civilization means European civilization, and it must be imported with both its roses and its thorns." [1] It is for this reason that

---

[1] Cited by Bernard Lewis, *The Emergence of Modern Turkey* (London, 1961), p. 231, from *İçtihad*, 89 (Istanbul, 1329 = 1913).

at the outset of this essay I called the Turkish program of modernization one of the most deliberate and comprehensive of its kind.

IV

Fuad Pasha (1815-1868), the great *vezir* of the Tanzimat period, once boasted to a European statesman : "Our state is the strongest state. For you are trying to cause its collapse from without, and we from within, but still it does not collapse." [1] His bitter jest expressed a profound truth. For centuries, the Ottoman Empire had been the foremost power at the juncture of Europe, Asia, and Africa—the largest, best administered, and most durable realm west of China since the fall of Rome. The chief asset that the Ottomans brought to the task of modernization was this legacy of political rule, of governmental responsibility. This tradition also furnished the main argument with which Mustafa Kemal in 1919 and 1920 spurred the population of the Anatolian rump of the defeated empire to a new effort at state building. A people that has ruled for over six hundred years—so he proclaimed in his travels throughout Anatolia—will not willingly submit to becoming a colony.[2]

The specific content of the Ottoman political tradition—the secret of early Ottoman success—had been a comprehensive military organization and a vast educational program for the training of public servants in army and administration. Following an interval of stagnation in the sixteenth to eighteenth centuries, these same devices were harnessed to the task of modernization. And military organization and education became again the chief vehicles of the transition from empire to republic. After the avalanche of defeats from 1683 to 1913, it was no mean accomplishment for the Ottoman armies to delay the empire's final collapse so as to coincide with that of its Romanov and Habsburg rivals. And at the end of a decade of almost continuous fighting (in Libya 1911-12, in the Balkans 1912-13, and in World War I), the victory over French, Armenian, and Greek forces in the War of Independence was an even more impressive achievement. Meanwhile, of all the nineteenth century innovations, the new educational system most consistently proved its worth in the long run. For amidst defeat, rebellion, and bankruptcy, it was the products of the schools founded during the Tanzimat period—the officers trained at the Harbiye and the civil servants graduated from the

---

[1] Cited by Roderic H. Davison in Ward and Rustow, *Political Modernization*, p. 103 from Abdurrahman Şeref, *Tarih Musahabeleri* (Istanbul, 1339 = 1923), p. 104.

[2] *Atatürk'ün Söylev*, I, 4; II, 3, 8.

Mülkiye—who provided the leadership in the Kemalist regeneration. Nor was this crucial role of education an incidental by-product; rather it was the result of a deliberate strategy of modernization. Although he could not have foreseen what form the eventual regeneration would take, the role of education in that process was clearly seen by Küçük Said Pasha (1838-1914), perennial grand *vezir* during the Hamidian period. In a memorandum of 1880, Said Pasha analyzed the imperatives of reform as follows : "As long as public education is not disseminated, there will be no leaders capable of directing the internal and external affairs of the Empire soundly, no judges who can administer the public laws justly, no commanders who can run the Army efficiently, and no finance officers who can show how to manage and increase the sources of revenue in accordance with economic principles, and none of the institutions and operations that serve public prosperity and wellbeing can be brought into existence as long as education is not disseminated." [1]

The greater strength and political stability of the First Turkish Republic compared with other Ottoman successor states, both in the Balkans and in the Middle East, was due more than anything else to the Ottoman political and educational legacy. Of the trained public servants of the late empire, 85 percent of the administrators and 93 percent of the staff officers continued service in the Turkish Republic, most of the remainder in Syria and Iraq, and hardly any in the Balkan countries.[2] In 1919 and 1920 the Turkish nationalist movement was led by Ottoman generals and colonels, the Arab nationalist movement around Sharif Faysal by Ottoman captains and lieutenants. The Anatolian resistance movement was a civilian organization (composed chiefly of the local remnants of the disbanded Union and Progress party) with a military apex. "Victory on the battlefield over European foes, moreover, provided self-assurance that facilitated the wholesale acceptance of European ways"[3] —whereas the Arabs' frustration in their national aims engendered smoldering anti-Western resentment. Once the Turkish War of Independence was won and the republic founded, Mustafa Kemal concentrated on an educational effort to give the new Turkey a thoroughly Westernized, modern image.

Mustafa Kemal's stature as Turkey's most resolute and most successful modernizer remains beyond dispute; yet his methods were entirely

---

[1] Quoted by Lewis, *Modern Turkey*, p. 175 ff., from *Said Paşanın Hatıratı* (Istanbul, 1328 = 1912), I, 423.

[2] Ward and Rustow, *Political Modernization*, p. 388.

[3] *Ibid.*, p. 383.

within the classic Ottoman tradition. Like the early sultans he combined the three roles of victorious battlefield commander, state founder, and chief sponsor of a large-scale educational establishment. Two symbolic acts of the Ankara government made manifest (unwittingly, no doubt) this organic link between Kemalism and the earliest Ottoman tradition. After the decisive victory over the Greeks on the Sakarya in 1921, the National Assembly conferred upon Kemal the title of *Gazi* ("Victor")—the very appellation that the Turkish-Muslim frontier warriors who founded the Ottoman state in the thirteenth century had earned in their encounter with Greco-Christian enemies on the same Bithynian battlefields. And just as Sultan Mehmed II (reigned 1451-1481) after the conquest of Istanbul proceeded to establish his famous palace school, so the Ankara government in November 1928 adopted a decree concerning the "Organization of a National School." Article 3 of that remarkable and concise document provided that "Every Turkish citizen, man and woman, is a member of this organization"; article 4 appointed that "The headmaster of the National School is the President of the Republic, His Excellency Gazi Mustafa Kemal." [1] (It was the time of the enforced transition from Arabic to Latin letters, and soon the Gazi could be seen, chalk on the blackboard, teaching the new alphabet to his citizen pupils.)

Ottoman political maturity as applied to the task of modernization bore fruit in a responsible foreign policy, in effective political organization, and in careful selection of the sequence of issues taken up by the modernizers. Whereas many postcolonial states have resorted to a boisterous and aggressive foreign policy to relieve internal tensions, Turkish rulers down to the mid-twentieth century almost invariably recognized the primacy of foreign over domestic policy. The major reform proclamations of the nineteenth century—the edicts of 1839 and 1856 and the constitution of 1876—were all timed or even conceived so as to gain maximum support from Europe at times of major foreign crisis. A temporary departure from this responsible tradition, it is true, came during the Young Turk period from 1908 to 1918—particularly in the headlong rush into World War I as late as October 1914, when German hopes for early victory had already been checked on the Marne. Yet could anything short of such recklessness have liberated Turkey from the incubus of empire and thus cleared the way for Kemal's retrenchment and reconstruction? [2]

---

[1] Gotthard Jäschke and Erich Pritsch, *Die Türkei seit dem Weltkriege* (Berlin, 1929); idem, *Die Welt des Islams*, 10, p. 131 ff.

[2] That this question does not just arise from long hindsight becomes clear from

The War of Independence restored foreign policy to its old primacy. Mustafa Kemal resolutely postponed all internal differences while rallying Westernizers and traditionalists, conservatives and radicals to the defense of the country. In the face of the Greek attack, he protested his loyalty to the very sultan who was declaring him an outlaw and a rebel. Only after victory did he declare the sultanate abolished—timing that measure so as to prevent the sending of a rival delegation from Istanbul to the peace conference. Only after signing the peace at Lausanne did the Kemalists proclaim a republic, draft a new constitution, and abolish the caliphate. In 1925 the impending Mosul conflict provided one motive for suppressing the Progressive opposition. Later, Ismet Inönü (President 1938-50) interrupted his measures for liberalization of the political regime until the end of World War II. In 1945 his desire for Western support against Russian demands strongly influenced his decision to promote the transition to truly democratic elections. It was not until the eruption of the Cyprus conflict in the mid-fifties and until Menderes' appeals for additional American aid in 1957 and 1958 that the effect of domestic tension began to be felt in foreign relations.

The rewards of this responsible course are evident. Having been a helpless victim of the rivalries among the major powers in the 1830's and 40's, the Ottoman Empire became a partner in a grand European alliance against Russia in 1854-56 and an ally of Germany and Austria in 1914. Above all, Turkey in 1923 achieved what neither Germany nor Austria could remotely hope for: she became the only defeated power of the World War to obtain a bilateral, negotiated peace. The new Turkey bordered on British, French, Italian, and Russian territories; yet, midway between two of the most notoriously unstable regions of the world —the Balkans and the Middle East—she has consistently maintained both her territorial integrity and full independence.

The most remarkable result of the responsible subordination of internal to foreign policies was the rapid transition between 1919 and 1923 from an imperial to a national consciousness. Herein, without doubt, lies Mustafa Kemal's most original and most durable contribution—a contribution all the more courageous since it involved accepting the surrender of Macedonia where he himself and most of his closest associates were born. One of the most arduous political tasks for most modernizing peoples is the redefinition of the effective unit of politics—the substitution of closely knit, medium-size nation-states for diffuse empires on the one

---

Cemal Pasha's defense of Turkey's entry into the War, in Djemal Pasha, *Memories of a Turkish statesman* (London, 1922), pp. 125 ff.

hand and petty principalities, tribes, and villages on the other. Atatürk ranks with Bismarck and Cavour as a farsighted statesman who found a viable solution to a highly complex version of that problem. Indeed, he ranks ahead of those two, for his was not a task of expanding a smaller core area (such as Prussia or Piedmont) into a larger nation state, but the far more exacting one of retrenchment and abnegation. The beneficial effects of his policy are plain. Ninety-three percent of Turkey's population today speak Turkish and ninety-eight percent are Muslims. This makes Turkey one of the most homogeneous countries in the non-Western world, one of the very few where national and political boundaries coincide. And whereas in most other countries in this small category—Japan, Burma, Thailand, Cambodia, and others—this coincidence is part of the historic heritage, in Turkey it was the fruit of conscious and deliberate choice.

The Turkish talent for political organization has been a second item in the Ottoman legacy. Next to India, Turkey has developed one of the most elaborate and durable party systems of any non-Western country. The Indian National Congress was founded in 1885, the Society for Union and Progress in 1889; and the latter became the lineal ancestor of the Society for the Defense of Rights of 1919, the People's Party of 1923, and through it of the Democratic Party of 1946 and the Justice Party of 1961. Both in India and in Turkey party organization emerged as the by-product of educational and administrative reforms launched a half century before: the Macàuley Report issued in 1835, the Rescript of Gülhane in 1839. But whereas India benefited from the most intensive administrative and educational efforts of the foremost imperial power of Europe, Turkey developed its modern administration and education primarily out of her own resources supplemented by a host of foreign schools, most of which closed down after World War I.

This tradition of party organization not only facilitated the transition from empire to republic, it also enabled Turkey in the 1920's to overcome the affliction of militarism. The combination of soldierly intervention in politics and political intrigue in the armed forces is one of the commonest phenomena in Latin America, Asia, and more recently in Africa. In Turkey this militarist pattern was evident in 1876 and again from 1908 to 1918; and the reestablishment of a clear distinction between military and civilian affairs may be considered Atatürk's second most important accomplishment (although by 1960 it proved less durable than the first). The Turkish record in this respect is surpassed only by that of Mexico. For Mustafa Kemal commanded an army that even in defeat had preserved its hierarchical discipline, and inherited the remnants of a party organization that ever since 1889 and 1906 had combined civilian and military elements. By contrast, Mexican presidents from Alvaro Obregón and Plutarco Elias Calles to Lázaro Cárdenas (1920-1940) had to create anew a unified, disciplined officer corps and a nationwide party organization. [1]

It is no coincidence that Mexico and Turkey became the first one-party systems in the world to achieve peaceful solutions to the problem of dictatorial succession—Turkey once in 1938 and Mexico no less than six times at regular intervals since 1934. (Since 1964, Russia may perhaps be added as the third country to that list.) And Turkey, unlike Mexico, attempted the unique achievement in 1945 of an orderly transition from one-party dictatorship to multiparty democracy. Even though Turkey's first experiment by 1960 turned out to have miscarried, she remains (along with Israel, Japan, the Philippines, India, Ceylon, and some of the Latin American countries) one of the few non-Western states to have engaged seriously in such an experiment. And Ismet Inönü retains the singular honor of being the world's only statesman who voluntarily abdicated his dictatorial powers so as to promote the introduction of democracy. The renewed trend toward a two-party system after the adoption in 1961 of proportional representation may be considered further evidence of Turkish organizational realism and political maturity.

Every modernizing society confronts three major political problems, which may be called the growth of authority and public service, the search for national identity and unity, and the demand for political equality and participation. Although all three must be resolved before a society may be said to be fully modernized, each presents a different set of difficulties and opportunities and calls to the arena different groups of supporters and opponents. Commonly, therefore, a modernizing society will tend to concentrate on one task at a time, and the sequence in which the tasks are undertaken thus becomes the distinguishing criterion among several alternative strategies of modernization. The most advantageous sequence would appear to be: identity; authority; equality. But this is a sequence available only to the rare societies, such as Japan, where

---

[1] For an elaboration of the themes of this section see Rustow, *World of Nations*. On Kemal's role in overcoming militarism see Rustow "The Army and the Founding of the Turkish Republic," *World Politics*, II (1959), pp. 513-552, especially pp. 543 ff.; and for a more detailed and more critical account, George S. Harris, "The Role of the Military in Turkish Politics," part I, *Middle East Journal*, 19, (Winter 1965), pp. 54-66.

ethnic-cultural identity was securely established in the premodern, traditional era. Turkey, like most European countries, followed what may be considered the second-best sequence : authority; identity; equality. In countries like Britain and France a feeling of modern national identity grew up almost imperceptibly in territories that had been united under a traditional dynasty during the late medieval and early modern periods. In Germany, Italy, and Turkey (as we have seen), national identity resulted from a deliberate policy of either unification or retrenchment. In all five countries the movement toward political equality and participation, the conferral of political rights on the lower classes, came only after the other two tasks were accomplished. (By contrast, the Mexican revolution of 1910 may be cited as an attempt to attain political equality before governmental authority and modern public services were securely established, and before a common feeling of national identity had linked the Spanish-speaking upper class to Mestizos and Indians; the immediate result was two decades of chaotic civil war and near anarchy.) The sultans from Selim III to Abdülhamid II concentrated on the elaborations of authority, on the expansion of public services in education, in finance, in public works, in military conscription. The Young Turk period brought to a head the enormously complex problem of national identity, which was resolved negatively through defeat in World War I and positively through the Kemalist program of national reconstruction within realistic boundaries. Not until 1945 was there any serious move toward political equality and mass participation by the urban lower classes and the peasantry.

Within the Kemalist revolution, too, the orderly timing or major tasks provided the secret of ultimate success. Kemal's program of Westernization had been anticipated by many previous reformers. Abullah Cevdet, for example, in a tract on a political utopia published in 1912, listed almost every single item of reform carried out in the 1920's except for the establishment of a republic.[1] But Cevdet's was only one voice among conflicting counsels of Ottomanism, of Islamism, of Westernization, and of Turkish nationalism that were all equally vociferous during the same Young Turk period. Kemal concentrated first on defending Turkish sovereignty (1919-22), then on erecting the institutions of his new state (1922-24), then on cultural-legal reforms (1924-28), and finally on education and industrialization, leaving matters of social equalization and of agricultural development to a later generation.[2] This orderly

---

[1] The Utopia is summarized in Lewis, *Modern Turkey*, pp. 231 ff.

[2] Kemal himself was fully aware of the importance of timing, of devising an orderly

phasing of the major tasks of modernization, both in the entire course of Turkish reforms from the late eighteenth to the early twentieth centuries and in the foreshortened Kemalist transformation, may be considered the third and final benefit that Turkey derived from its Ottoman heritage of political maturity.

V

The bulk of this paper has turned out to be a celebration of the virtues of Ottoman and Turkish modernization enlivened by favorable comparisons with similar programs elsewhere. But I said initially that the Turks were not the world's most successful modernizers, and it is appropriate to look at the liability side of the ledger. These liabilities have become prominent in recent years, they are felt strongly in the current political and social situation to which other papers in this volume are devoted, and they may be expected to trouble the next several generations of Turkish modernizers.

The Ottoman Empire was located in the world's most strategic region, where parts of three continents are intersected by branches of two oceans. Long before the rise of the Ottomans, Anatolia, the Balkans, and the Middle East had been a historic passageway for invading armies and for migrating peoples. The Ottoman Empire from 1450 to 1918 was at war for an average of 30.5 years out of every half century,[1] and it came to rule over a greater variety of nationalities and cultural groups than most states of similar extent. Ottoman military and educational organization was admirably suited to imposing a modicum of political order on this ethnic mosaic. The empire's soldiers and administrators were recruited at an early age from Balkan subjects and Caucasian prisoners, and the palace schools turned them into a Muslim ruling class devoted

---

sequence of tasks within the overall program. In the monumental account of his leadership, the Six-Day Speech of 1927, he said: "It was necessary to divide the execution into certain phases, to prepare the thoughts and feelings of the nation by taking advantage of events and circumstances, and to advance rung by rung so as to attain the ultimate goal. Yet if our deeds and performance of the last nine years are considered as a chain of logical propositions, it became clear that the general direction we have pursued from the first day to this day did not in any way diverge from the line drawn and the goal envisaged by that first resolution." (Atatürk, *Nutuk* Ankara 1934 p. 11). It may be added that Atatürk's resourcefulness in detouring around political obstacles in pursuit of the same ultimate goal was even greater than for tactical reasons he felt free to acknowledge so soon after the event.

[1] Ward and Rustow, *Political Modernization* p. 439, n. 1.

to the sultan's service and detached from any of the ethnic cultures of the subject non-Muslim population. Outside of this ruling class, the prevailing principle was diversity rather than assimilation. Although the ruling class was recruited by selective cooptation rather than heredity, the dividing line between rulers and subjects thus remained strict and impermeable. The only educational institutions outside the imperial training centers were the religious schools of mosque and church. The function of education, in any case, was differentiation rather than equalization among classes and nationalities.

This traditional political system of education, military organization, and administration was supported by an economy based on an ethnic division of labor. The function of the ruling class was to fight, to administer, and to train future soldiers, administrators, and rulers. The economic functions of society—agriculture, animal husbandry, the crafts, and trade—were left to the various subject nationalities. Balkan Christians, Anatolian Turks, and sedentary Arab Muslims tilled the soil; Albanians, Kurds, Turkomans, and nomadic Arabs raised livestock; and Greeks, Armenians, and Arab Christians specialized in commerce.

The classic recruitment system for the Ottoman ruling class had broken down by the seventeenth and eighteenth centuries. The new bureaucracy and the modernized officer corps of the nineteenth century were drawn entirely from Muslims and predominantly from the Balkans and from Anatolia. The strict distinction between rulers and subjects, however, was maintained, and education continued as the chief instrument of distinction. The new, European-style schools were devoted entirely to the training of officers and administrators, and attendance at these schools remained the only entrance ticket to the ruling class. The gap between rulers and traders, moreover, was widened by the so-called capitulations, a set of commercial agreements with European powers which, by the nineteenth century, had turned into a system of privilege by which long-distance trade and banking, manufacture and remunerative public works became a near monopoly of resident Europeans (known to Europeans as Levantines and to Turks as Sweet-Water Franks) and their local Christian and Jewish protégés.

The social system inherited from the classical Ottoman period and accentuated by nineteenth century developments had important consequences for the modernization program. There was no serious attempt to fuse the diverse nationalities and religions of the empire into a single, culturally homogeneous citizenry. Although the ruling class steadily expanded in size, there were no attempts until well into the twentieth century to bridge the enormous social gap between educated rulers and illiterate subjects. And aside from public works in transport and communications, there was virtually no attempt until the Young Turk and Kemalist periods to supply any economic base for modernization. Reform in military affairs, in administration, and in education, rather than improvement of agriculture of the growth or industry, remained the prime ambition of the modernizers.

Since modernization started with military reform, it was in this sphere that limitations became first apparent. Conscription was enacted in the 1840's, but provision was made for an exemption fee which was set at a higher rate for Muslims, and at a lower rate for Christians and Jews. In practice the new conscript army therefore consisted entirely of Muslims and mostly of Anatolian Turks and Albanians. Only Muslims, moreover, attended the officer training schools, and again natives of Istanbul, Anatolia, and the Balkans predominated. Although Arabs constituted roughly one-fourth to one-third of the late Empire's Muslim population, the proportion of Syrians and Iraqis among the general staff officers was only 5 percent before 1900 and still as low as 14 percent between 1900 and 1914.[1] The officer corps was recruited almost entirely from the Harbiye and other military schools; promotion from the ranks occurred only exceptionally during the Hamidian period and rarely during the Young Turk and Kemalist eras. Finally, while the training of officers and privates was modernized by foreign and later by native instructors, the new army continued to rely on foreign weapons. Ethnic exclusiveness, education for the upper class only, an almost unbridgeable gap between the upper and lower classes, and a sovereign disregard for economics—these were the limitations upon nineteenth century military reform that foreshadowed the political patterns and problems of the early twentieth century.

A comparative perspective can indicate more sharply how serious these limitations were. R. P. Dore has estimated that at the beginning of the Meiji period as many as half the Japanese adult population were literate;[2] in Turkey the proportion of literates among those over seven years of age was only 20.4 percent in 1935 and 39.5 percent in 1960. Defensive modernization in Japan in the late nineteenth century was supported by a major effort of commercial and industrial development;

---

[1] See Dankwart A. Rustow, "Harbiye," *Encyclopaedia of Islam*, 2d ed.
[2] Ward and Rustow, *Political Modernization*, p. 117.

in Turkey, the commercial convention of 1838-1840 [1] guaranteed the earlier European privileges and postponed such a possibility for ninety years. In Russia, nineteenth century writers and political thinkers were animated by a desire for social justice through reform or revolution, a yearning for reconciliation between upper class and peasantry; in Turkish literature such populist themes do not appear until the twentieth century—and works from Yakub Kadri's novel *Yaban* or *The Stranger* (1932) to Mahmud Makal's *A Village in Anatolia* (1950) illustrate the sullen hostility with which Anatolian villagers received the well-meant overtures of their city cousins. The Mexican revolution of 1910-17 proclaimed a long list of ideals of social justice and economic equality; in Turkey such proclamations had to wait until 1961.

The Kemalist revolution, I have suggested earlier, was the culmination of the modernization efforts that began with Selim III and Mahmud II, with the Tanzimat reformers, and with Şinasi. Like the New Ottomans of 1865 and the Young Turks of 1889 and 1908, Kemal and those who rallied around him in 1919 were members of the Ottoman upper class, mainly educated in the new, European way. They were army officers, civil servants, teachers, and journalists who wielded the powerful instruments of political organization and of modern communication. Like their predecessors they worked where possible with the sultan and where necessary against him. And they accomplished the heroic task that had eluded reforming sultans and revolutionary Young Turks: the transformation of a decadent empire into a homogeneous state that could take its respected place in a modern world of nations.

Kemalism also was the first movement that tried to transcend the limitations of the earlier modernization effort; it thus became the prologue to a further transformation, the completion of which still lies in the future. It proclaimed the ideals of popular sovereignty and civic participation by the masses, of concerted economic development and material progress, of science, not religion, as the guide to social action. But the Kemalists, for all their populist convictions and professions, were in fact a small urban, ruling elite, and, as we have seen, they pursued their ideals largely with methods true to the classic Ottoman tradition. Frederick W. Frey has observed that even under Kemal, "Turkish education was unabashedly elitist," and that this policy continued to be justified by the metaphor of the *tuba ağacı*—"a tree which supposedly had its roots in heaven

---

[1] One of these conventions, that with Britain of 1838, is reprinted and the diplomatic context explained in J.C. Hurewitz, ed., *Diplomacy in the Near and Middle East*, I (Princeton, 1956), pp. 110 ffff.

but which lent its delightful shade and its fruits to mankind."[1] And Mustafa Kemal, in one of the most significant speeches of his career, on first arriving in Ankara in December 1919, intimated his own view of his Society for the Defense of Rights as a link between elitist past and populist future :

> If a nation does not become concerned about its existence and its rights with its entire strength, with all its spiritual and material powers, if a nation does not rely on its own strength to secure its existence and independence, then it cannot be rescued from becoming this person's or that person's puppet. Our national life, our history, and our system of administration in the last epoch are a perfect demonstration of this. Therefore, within our organization the principle has been adopted that the national forces are supreme and that the national will is paramount. Today the nations of the whole world recognize only one sovereignty : national sovereignty. If we now look at the other details of the organization—we begin our work from the village and the neighborhood and from the people of the neighborhood, that is, from the individual. If the individuals do not do their own thinking, the masses can be led in an arbitrary direction, can be led by anyone in good directions or in bad directions. To be able to save himself, every individual must become personally concerned with his destiny. A structure that in this way rises from below to the top, from the foundation to the roof, will surely be sturdy. Nonetheless, there is need at the beginning of any undertaking to go not from below upward but from above downward.
>
> If the former could be done, all mankind could achieve their hearts' desire. But since no practical and concrete way of doing this has yet been found, certain initiators are providing guidance in giving to nations the directions that they need to be given. In this way, organization can be built from above downward. In my travels in the interior of our country, I have been extremely gratified to observe that our national organization, which naturally began in this same way, has reached down to its true point of origin, to the individual, and that from there the real structuring upward has also begun. Nevertheless, we cannot assert that any degree of perfection has been attained. Therefore it must be considered a national and patriotic duty that we should make great efforts especially to attain the goal of a structuring from below upward.[2]

Reorganization from the top downward was initiated by Selim and Mahmud, elaborated by the Tanzimat ministers and Abdülhamid, taken over by the Young Turks, and spread further downward by the Kemalists. The guidelines and directions for a modernizing nation were explored by intellectuals and statesmen from Şinasi and Midhat Pasha

---

[1] Ward and Rustow, *Political Modernization*, p. 217.

[2] The address is reprinted as document no. 220 in the appendix of Atatürk's Speech (*Nutuk*, III, 252-62 at 258.) and in *Söylev* (cited note 7), II, 4-5 at 11. For a fuller analysis of Atatürk's political aims and style of leadership see my essay, "Atatürk as Founder of a State", in *Philosophers and Kings*, ed. D.A. Rustow (New York : Braziller, 1970), pp. 208-247.

to Küçük Said and Abdullah Cevdet. They were combined into a consistent program and placed on a cogent time schedule by Kemal Atatürk, who thus achieved the transformation of an empire into a nation, of a traditional into a Western cultural image. But the enormous task of spreading the essentials of modernity to the traditional subject classes, to the millions of Anatolian villagers—this reciprocal, responsive movement from the individual upward which Atatürk foresaw—did not begin in earnest until the middle of the twentieth century. It began once the ruling elite, enlarged in numbers and modernized in its ethos, gave up its age-old habit of confronting the rest of the population with a single imperious face and instead divided into competing groups to solicit the villager's support. It began after İnönü's courageous reversal of domestic course in 1945-47 with the formation of rival political parties and with the opening of party branches in every vilayet and most villages.

Inevitably some of the directions earlier formulated have become subject to reexamination and some of the previous achievements have been endangered. In the politically supercharged atmosphere of the 1960's, Kemalist goals such as the secularization of education, the withdrawal of the military from politics, and an independent foreign policy combined with a firm cultural orientation to the West—such goals now must be vigorously reasserted. They also must be boldly supplemented with new policies for social justice and rapid economic development. Above all, on a political stage crowded and noisy as never before, new techniques must be devised to accommodate demands and to conciliate conflict. Yet, despite the frictions and difficulties, such a broadening of the elite movement to embrace the entire citizenry will be an indispensable part of the total process of modernization. The final heirs of the ideology of modernization that in two centuries filtered down from Sultans and vezirs to school teachers and lieutenants will be a socially and politically conscious lower class.

Rousseau said of the founder of a commonwealth that he must be able "to toil in one century and to reap in another." [1] The accomplishments of Mahmud II in rebuilding a Turkish state and of Atatürk in giving it a modern and Western image will not be secure until the Turkish masses of the future have claimed as their own that double inheritance.

---

[1] *Contrat Social*, II, 7. For an account of the political and ideological divisions of the Second Republic see D.A. Rustow, "Politics and Development Policy", in *Four Studies on the Economic Development of Turkey*, ed. F.C. Shorter (London : Cass, 1967), pp. 5-32.

PART II

THE SOCIAL GROUPS
AND CHANGE IN ROLES

CHAPTER THREE

THE MIDDLE CLASSES IN TURKEY *

Nezih Neyzi

Introduction: Historical Development

In Turkey, the most significant alteration in the social structure during recent years has been the acceleration in the development of a new middle class group originating in economic occupations and professions. Identified partly with Western political values and economic approaches, this group appears to give to the general process of transformation a new dimension consonant with the economic and industrial conditions of the age. This is a middle range group which asserts its political claims and demands that government functions be brought into balance with a changing society. Status, power, and control of modern economic forces have been increasingly concentrated in this new middle class. Thus, at the present stage of development it is necessary to consider the new Turkish middle class not only as an entity to be distinguished from other middle class groups on the basis of cultural modernity as opposed to traditionalism, but also in terms of the differentiation that is taking place within the framework of the middle range social groups. The modern Turkish middle class, comprising both economic and bureaucratic groups, is the product of more than a century and a half of social and economic change. During the nineteenth century, the introduction of capitalistic economic relations and the growth of trade gave rise to a new social element composed of commercial groups and landowners dealing in cash crops and oriented towards a market economy. Concurrently with, and in some instances preceding the development of, this propertied group of notables, a new intelligentsia was beginning to emerge in urban bureaucratic enclaves largely as a result of the government's need for trained personnel. Although still shaped to some extent by traditional

---

* The original paper and the data on Turkey were prepared by the author. The rewriting of the paper, the conceptualization of the material and relevant research on various aspects of the middle classes was undertaken under editor's supervision by Mrs. Sally S. Zanjani, a doctoral candidate at NYU, who is doing research on the middle classes in Turkey and Iran. KHK.

influences as far as its concepts of authority were concerned, this bureaucratic group was already acquiring the characteristics of a new social class by developing occupational habits and ways of thinking different from the rest of society.

The rise of these new social elements and the necessity for an altered system of groups relationships were implicit in the decision to convene an Ottoman parliament in 1876.[1] However, although the foundations of the traditional Ottoman political system had already been radically altered, the new social groups were not yet strong enough to enforce their political claims. It was not until the revolution of 1908-1909 that they began to gain ascendance over the ruling dynastic order, and the political sphere became more closely correlated with the changes taking place in society.

With the advent of the republic and the Kemalist reforms, a formative period of key importance in the evolution of the middle class began. The classical process of modernization through bureaucratic innovation gained in tempo, and a period of state control of the economy after 1931 laid the modern economic foundations from which other occupations could later develop on an individualistic basis. The commercial sector increased rapidly, and the ranks of the professionals and other middle class occupational groupings were also enlarged. By the late 1940's, the new managerial skills that had developed from the bureaucratic nucleus and the capital resources acquired primarily through commercial profits permitted a growing number of entrepreneurs to enter various economic fields.[2]

These social and economic changes had a political counterpart, and it is now evident that the increasing power of the new middle class groups was the key factor in the political change in 1950. To the nascent entrepreneurial sector, a role in the political process meant the ability to act on essential matters of capital and property within a stable system which guaranteed their possessions. While both the Democratic and Republican parties agreed in 1947-50 that private enterprise should be fostered and statism should not be further extended, the Democratic Party succeeded in identifying itself with the aspirations of the entrepreneurial and agrarian segments of the middle class and in mobilizing support from

---

[1] Kemal H. Karpat, "The Ottoman Parliament of 1877 and its Social Significance" *art. cit.*

[2] Alec P. Alexander, "Industrial Entrepreneurship in Turkey : Origins and Growth," *Economic Development and Cultural Change* 8 (1960), pp. 355-356, 359.

the worker and peasant sectors. After the Democratic victory in 1950, the government did not, in fact, discontinue its investments in industry or limit its economic interest. Nonetheless, private enterprise burgeoned rapidly under conditions conducive to investment and assuring profits.

The rise of the economic groups in the middle class during this period, in addition to undermining the power of the bureaucratic elite, further accelerated the decline of the remaining Ottoman elite; the descendants of governors and other administrators in the service of the Sultan and the rich *ulema* families. These derived large incomes from pensions and especially from real estate. However, the growth of modern economic forces, and new regulations such as rent controls, undermined their economic position and ultimately forced them to seek closer contact with the new entrepreneurial and commercial groups. Once this historical elite had scorned business activity and rejected intermarriage with the entrepreneurs and business groups. But now even the better educated among them were obliged to undertake an entrepreneurial career or accept a position as an employee in a large firm and marry into the new wealth. However, some of the surviving Ottoman elite, deficient in entrepreneurial skills, dissipated the last of the family wealth, and in a few cases joined the world of art or migrated abroad.

As the ancient traditional elite declined politically and economically, the focus of the power struggle shifted to the new segments of the middle class. The bureaucratic elite which had attained political control in the interwar period, and their supporters among the older bourgeois groups dependent upon state enterprise, were now faced with the political claims and growing economic strength of new groups of entrepreneurs and landlords. Indeed, in large measure, the political evolution of the past decade has reflected the shifting balance and conflict between these two sectors of the middle class. But these conflicts, implicit and explicit, should not obscure the essential fact that it is the broad composite of groups within the middle class range that provided the social foundations for the current political system in Turkey.

A severe crisis in 1959 occasioned by the Democratic regime's attempt to destroy the opposition was followed by a period of military intervention. However, it soon became evident that a simple military dictatorship could no longer deal with the complex pressures of an increasingly differentiated social structure, and the army relinquished its power to civilians. The aspirations of the entrepreneurial sector were reflected in the constitution of 1961, in the acceptance of a parliamentary system, and the limitations on executive power. The coalition between the new business groups and the lower social strata, which seemed to disintegrate in 1957-59 was reconstituted, primarily through the Justice Party in 1961. The bureaucratic elite, politically manifested in the Republican Party, though bent on monopolizing power had to share it eventually with the newer sectors of the middle class and their allies.[1]

Essentially, the above events signify a transitional period which may be the sequel to the classic stage of modernization through bureaucratic innovation that is now so evident in most of the developing world. This latter stage involves the increasing economic and political involvement of new middle-class groups outside the bureaucratic elite. An examination of the present position of the Turkish middle class with particular reference to these two key groups, entrepreneurial and bureaucratic, can provide a conception of the new system of group relationships emerging within the broad framework of the development process.

The New Middle Class: Dimensions and Life Styles

The lack of class consciousness and of parties formed on that basis, the absence of large middle-range groups in the traditional political system, and especially the constant shift in individuals' opinions as to their place in the social order makes the definition of the middle classes in Turkey quite tentative.[2] It is necessary, therefore, to adopt some rather arbitrary criteria in order to define the middle class. While income and style of life are not the only factors that serve to differentiate the middle class from the other strata of the population, these elements can be utilized to provide a conception of the middle class as a whole that may in turn be utilized for a more detailed examination of the two key subgroups. Using income as the criterion, we can place people living in large cities of more than 100,000 and earning between 1,000 and 2,500 lira per month (about 100-250 dollars in gross monthly income) within the middle-class range. In smaller cities this bracket could be reduced to 700-1,500 lira.[3]

---

[1] Kemal H. Karpat, "Recent Political Developments in Turkey and their Social Background," *The Contemporary Middle East*, eds. Benjamin Rivlin and Joseph S. Syliowicz (New York, 1965), pp. 476-488.

[2] The changing understanding of the "middle classes" is evident even in class-conscious England, where according to a study some workers consider themselves middle class and vote for the Labor Party, while other consider themselves working class and vote for the Conservative Party. See Mark Abrams, "Social Class and British Politics," *Public Opinion Quarterly* 25, no. 3 (Fall 1961), pp. 342-50.

[3] These figures are based on market studies conducted by the PEVA (Market

On this basis, it is possible to determine the present size of the Turkish middle class by utilizing the estimated earnings of occupational groupings, as is shown in Table 3.1. This classification would place 1,251,560 heads of families within the middle class. According to general statistical information, an average family consists of five persons; therefore, we may estimate that 6,256,800 people, a figure corresponding to 20.8 percent of the total population, fall within the limits of the middle class. Of course, the middle class has different ramifications in urban and rural areas. The agricultural sector has been included in this table, but it is clear that the bulk of the rural population does not lie within the middle-class range. Of the 2,322,000 agrarian families, 1,686,000 own land, and only 1 percent of these may be placed within the middle class. Thus, it can be estimated that the present Turkish middle class is about 21 percent of the total population; 75 percent are included within the lower class, while the upper class is restricted to 4 percent.[1] This class is concentrated in cities and towns.

While the status group and the economic order are not interchangeable categories, status is intimately associated with a style of life which is ultimately dependent upon economic factors.[2] Studies elsewhere in the world have demonstrated that certain items are the characteristic posessions of the middle and upper social strata and these may be utilized to identify people in varying sectors of a country on a class basis.[3] In Turkey, the amenities associated with middle-class standards in Western Europe and the United States would be the province of a very small, upper group, while a middle-class family could generally be described as one that could afford an apartment, the necessary household appliances, regular meals, and travel for business purposes but not for pleasure.

A study dealing with income levels and the ownership pattern of various household items was recently conducted in Ereğli, a small town on the Black Sea where a steel mill has recently been erected. At Ereğli,

---

Research Office) for several companies in Turkey and a study of the town of Ereğli conducted by the State Planning Organization. They are valid for the years 1960-1966; any subsequent inflation or devaluation may alter the purchasing power of the lira.

[1] Estimates based on Tables 3.1 and 3.7. Total individuals with high income declarations amounted to 131,000; the high income in the salaried group is accepted as the same figure. Total heads of families are 262,000; thus this group includes 1,300,000 people or 4 percent of the population.

[2] Kurt Mayer, "The Theory of Social Classes," *Harvard Educational Review* XXIII (Summer 1953), pp. 162-164.

[3] F. Stuart Chapin, *The Measurement of Social Status by the Use of the Social Status Scale* (Minneapolis, 1933), pp. 3, 9, 14.

Table 3.1

Estimated Number of the Middle Class in Turkey Based on Earnings
(Earning 1,000-2,500 TL)

Commerce and Services	Registered	Percentage considered Middle Class	Number considered Middle Class
Top level administrators and professionals	174,000	10	17,400
Technicians	181,000	50	90,500
White collar employees	669,000	90	602,100
Foremen	25,000	50	12,500
Skilled workers	252,000	10	25,200
Workers	419,000	—	—
	1,720,000		747,700
Industry			
Top level administrators and professionals	38,000	10	3,800
Technicians	27,000	50	13,500
White-collar employees	85,000	90	76,500
Foremen	33,000	50	16,500
Skilled workers	442,000	10	44,200
Workers	563,000	—	—
	1,188,000		154,500
Government Offices			
Civil Servants (Est. 1965)	455,000	50	232,500
Small business and craftsmen (estimated)	500,000	20	100,000
Agricultural sector (families)	1,686,000	1	16,860
Total middle class family heads			1,251,560
Total middle class (5 per family)			6,256,800
Estimated Percentage and total population		20.8	7,857,720

Sources: *Planlâma*, Devlet Plânlama Teşkilatı Dergisi ("Review of State Planning Organization"), vol. 1 (Ankara, 1962), p. 18. Absolute figures are taken from this source, and percentages are estimated on the basis of probable earnings. Estimates on the size of the average family are based on *23 Ekim 1960, Genel Nüfus Sayımı* (October 23, 1960, General Census) and other statistics published by the State Institute of Statistics, and *Toprak Reformu Kanun Tasarısı* ("Land Reform Bill"), Ministry of Agriculture (Ankara, 1960), p. 7.

a monthly income of 600-650 lira was sufficient to provide a middle-class style of life, although this amount would easily support a person in the low-income bracket in Istanbul due to the living conditions and costs of a large city. Most of the population of Ereğli according to our income measurement does not fall within the middle income category; 38.6 percent of the families earn between 250 and 494 lira per month, while the earnings of nearly 20 percent are below this level (table 3.2).

Table 3.2

Income Brackets in Ereğli

Monthly Income Bracket	Percentage of Total
Below 250 TL	15.7
250-499 »	38.6
500-748 »	22.5
750-1000 »	5.2
1001-1500 »	6.4
1500 + »	3.9
No income	3.5
Unknown	4.1
	4.1
	99.9

Table 3.3

Selected Household Items at Ereğli

Items	Percent of ownership (Figures rounded)
Kilim (inexpensive rug)	95
Copper utensils	91
Sedir (divan)	84
Bed	91
Porcelain Dishes	78
Iron	75
Radio	60
Rug	57
Sewing machine	53
Armchair	38
Aluminum pans	22
Icebox	6

Source: Mübeccel Kıray, Ereğli: Ağır Sanayiden Önce bir Sahil Kasabası, Publication of the State Planning Organization, (Ankara, 1964), pp. 89, 91, 1545. The Ereğli sample was based on households having electricity, and 91.9 percent of the 1,400 houses in Ereğli had electricity at the time of the survey. The sample consisted of 486 households selected on a random basis. The total population of Ereğli in 1960 was 8,815 or about 1,700 families on the basis of 5.04 members per family.

Table 3.3 indicates that items such as beds, sofas, and inexpensive rugs are owned by the vast majority of the population. More than half possess radios and sewing machines. However, less than a quarter of the population own aluminum pans, and the refrigerator is a luxury item restricted to 6 percent. Further studies are needed before the items uniquely associated with the middle and upper strata can be identified with precision. Nonetheless, the Ereğli study does indicate that refrigerators and some small appliances might be placed within this category, and it also provides a basic conception of the possessions that are found on all class levels.

The Bureaucratic Order :
Organizational Nucleus of Modernity

Social classes are not horizontally demarcated layers but clusters around central nuclei.[1] The core of the Turkish middle class, when considered within the framework of the developmental process, has been the bureaucratic elite. Bureaucratic systems exist on all levels of organized modern life, but in most of the developing countries the primary locus of the bureaucracy has been the civil service, because government has provided the most fertile field for employment, status, power, and prestige. Operating on a rational basis and according to established routines, organized in a hierarchical system, and relying upon an impersonal decision-making apparatus, it is this group more than any other which embodies values and approaches in terms of the cultural and social features of the new system. These standards historically associated with the middle class would include industry, thrift, long-range goals with deferment of immediate gratification, individual responsibility, [and] effective performance; together they create a rational value complex that may be defined as "a convinced comprehension of the personal responsibilities dictated by organization."[2] However, these standards associated with the middle classes in the West may not be equally accepted by all the segments of the middle classes in developing societies such as Turkey.

Robert Faris has pointed out that the acceptance of these internal conditions of organization and the rational values associated with them is one of the basic distinctions between the middle class and the lower social strata.[3] But the contrast is becoming less sharp as the bureaucratic elite utilizes the power at its disposal to spread rational approaches from the governmental core to all social levels. Operating with the entire country as its field, the bureaucracy has acted to integrate society under

---

[1] G. D. H. Cole, *Studies in Class Structure* (London, 1955), p. 1. For Turkey see a series of studies in *Orta Sınıfların Yeri, Önemi ve Çeşitli Problemleri* (Ankara, 1963).

[2] Robert E. L. Faris, "The Middle Class from a Sociological Viewpoint," *Social Forces* XXXIX (October, 1960), p. 3.

[3] *Ibid.*, pp. 3-5.

its own authority, and through this process it has played a key role in the historic evolution of the middle class on a national basis. Its policies have been reflected in the rapid expansion, as well as the occupational and income differentiation, of the middle class beyond the bureaucratic nucleus.

The bureaucratic order includes both the civil service and the army. The military wing has been considered a significant factor in the modernization of traditional society. Research on the modernist role of the army, however, has dealt mostly with institutional changes, rational use of authority, and identification with certain modern political values, rather than with intergroup relations, social restructuring and the military's role in perpetuating ancient traditions. Army officers in the Middle East were drawn originally from the upper and then the middle class, and, by and large, the officer corps has retained some links to the propertied sector while the rank-and-file soldier came from the lower classes.[1] Yet, still more significant is the fact that since the close of the Ottoman era the army has been a modernizing force in the sense that it used discipline, rational and impersonal procedures, and positive sciences in education in order to strengthen its own organization and disseminate similar attitudes into the other segments of bureaucracy and even society at large. The technological and organizational, modernizing role of the army should not be construed as extending in the same radical fashion into the realm of values and political attitudes, especially toward the lower classes. The army was the microcosm of the modern world only in the organizational and technological sense mentioned above. It is in this context that recruits drawn from all walks of life through universal conscription were indoctrinated in the new way of life, taught specific skills, and mobilized into a new political unit defined by national boundaries. Outside the confines of the military organization, the army's role as a center of leadership capable of disseminating nationalist values and rational organizational attitudes identified with the new middle class has been particularly evident in the era of the Young Turks and the early days of the Republic.

The experience of the industrialized nations has revealed that old social frameworks do not dissolve but remain and decrease in importance as new social structures are superimposed upon them.[2] In the developing world this double process of modernist superimposition and continuation

---

[1] Manfred Halpern, *The Politics of Social Change in the Middle East and North Africa* (Princeton, 1963), pp. 258, 278.

[2] Cole, *Class Structure*, pp. 106-7.

of the old structure is in full force. Thus, the bureaucratic elite's historic role in expanding the economic sections of the middle class though diminishing somewhat has not come to an end. Recent surveys appear to confirm that the contribution of the bureaucratic order is still an important one. Today, as in the past, the civil service remains an outstanding source of managerial skills, as has been corroborated by a study conducted in 1965, which revealed that 35 percent of the managers in the private sector in Turkey are drawn from state enterprise.[1]

In addition, the rapid growth of the civil service and its professionalization and specialization during recent years had undoubtedly contributed to its continuing importance as a center of innovation. During the decade since 1950, the civil service has more than doubled (Table 3.4), and it is at present the second largest single group in the middle class sector (Table 3.1). While the largest percentage of increase has occurred in the sphere of state enterprises, as a result of the incorporation of railroads and the PPT employees into the civil service, the largest in absolute numbers occurred in the central government offices, where the number of employees increased from 173,608 in 1950 to 313,391 in 1960. In the provinces the number of civil servants has declined slightly (Table 3.4) which may be an indication of the expansion of local government and voluntary organizations.

Table 3.4

Increase in the Civil Service

Employment	1950	1955	1960
Central Government Offices	173,608	190,206	313,391
State Economic Enterprises	15,975	40,130	115,582
Provincial Offices of Central Government	14,159	12,409	12,982

Source: Compiled from Cemal Mıhçıoğlu, *The Civil Service in Turkey* (Ankara: School of Political Science, 1963).

Although guaranteed income and retirement benefits place more than half the civil servants within the middle-income range, this does not apply to the entire civil service. Of the fourteen civil service grades, the first seven may be included in the middle-income bracket, and in rural areas this limit can be pushed down to grade eleven. In common with many governmental bureaucracies, pay scales in the Turkish civil service

---

[1] *İş İdaresi Etüdü*, Publication of the Turkish Management Association (Istanbul, 1965).

are not high, and it is difficult to advance beyond the middle-income range within the confines of a system where even the managers of state enterprises remain within this bracket, except in rural areas where middle-income limits are lower. In addition, it should be emphasized that while the government provides additional means of compensation for specialists, most civil servants are working without additional compensation (tables 3.5 and 3.6).

As the development process has extended the limits of organization and nationalization beyond the bureaucratic nucleus and new centers of innovation, such as research outfits and private business enterprises have appeared, there have been inevitable alterations in the relative position of the bureaucracy. Since the Democratic victory in 1950, and the neutralization of the army in 1961, it has been evident that social change has now advanced to a stage where neither the army nor the civil service can monopolize political authority to direct the reform of society as a whole, since political power is exercised on the basis of a new system of group relationships.

In addition, it is interesting to note that the army may now be more isolated from the new centers of innovation than the civil service, because the army officer does not enjoy the same mobility into the bureaucratic structures of private business that seems to exist in the upper echelons of the civil service. The Institute of Business Administration of Istanbul opened a special course for army officers retiring after the 1960 revolution. However, of approximately 5,000 retired officers, 120 entered the course and only 80 graduated. While these graduates proved successful as entrepreneurs or employees in private firms, others who attempted to enter business without preparation quickly exhausted their capital. (Most of this capital resulted from generous severance pay.) The disinterest of some and the failure of others in the business realm may be ascribed in part to the narrow professional orientation of the military as a whole, and to the upper class origin of some officers. The experiment is illustrative, above all, of the increasing specialization of skills and differentiation of Turkish society occurring outside the nuclei of original innovators and modernizers of the bureaucratic elite. Nonetheless, the army remains linked to society at many points, and it has not lost its significance as an instrument of acculturation and modern organization. Joined in the bureaucratic order, both army and civil service embody the rational approaches that serve to define the middle class as a whole as a modern entity, despite conflicts of interest and values among these and the growing economic groups.

Table 3.5

Pay Scale of Civil Servants, 1968, in Turkish Liras

Grade	Gross Salary (TL)	Net Salary (TL)
1	2,700-2,900	1,900.70
2	2,363.50	1,698.01
3	2,025	1,479.58
4	1,687.50	1,248.69
5	1,485	1,116.64
6	1,282.50	877.13
7	1,080	847.13
8	945	744.75
9	810	652.41
10	675	552.03
11	607.50	499.81
12	540	447.14
13	472.50	402.97
14	405	358.56

Table 3.6

Percentage of Civil Servants Receiving No Supplementary Compensation

	%
Ministries:	
Ministry of Education	90
Ministry of Finance	77
Ministry of Justice	76
Ministry of Interior	75
Ministry of Agriculture	56
Ministry of Health	50
Ministry of Settlement	14
Offices:	
Highway administration	21
State Statistics Institute	20
State Hydraulic Works	3.3
State Planning Organization	0

* Officials not possessing technical skills receive only a fixed salary. Those in services requiring special advanced training are paid compensation often three or four times over the normal salary.

THE PRIVATE SECTOR AND THE EMERGENCE OF THE ENTREPRENEUR

In the industrial nations of the West the entrepreneurial middle class has now been partially converted into a salariat, but the process has been quite different in the developing world where the bureaucratic element originally made up the core of the middle class. The Turkish salariat has expanded from the civil service nucleus to the bureaucratic structures of private business and is now undergoing what Berger has termed the transformation from "an administrative-clerical bureaucracy to a managerial-technical one."[1] As a result of these developments, technocrats have multiplied in the upper ranks of the middle class and skilled workers in the lower. The salaried group still comprises the vast majority of the middle class and will no doubt remain the preponderant element. However, the rapid growth of a small private sector within the middle class is a significant new development that deserves further examination.

As Table 3.7 indicates, only 14 percent of the entire middle class may be placed within the nonsalaried category, a group corresponding to 3 percent of the population as a whole and 181,480 in absolute numbers.

Table 3.7

Salaried and Nonsalaried Middle Income Group

Commerce and Services	Total	Percent Working on own Account	Nonsalaried Middle Class
Administrators and Professionals	17,400	90	15,660
Technicians	90,000	30	27,000
Employees	602,000	1	6,020
Foremen	12,500	—	—
Skilled workers	25,200	—	—
Workers	—	—	—
	747,200		48,680
Industry			
Administration and Professionals	3,800	90	3,420
Technicians	13,500	30	4,050
Employees	76,500	10	7,650
Foremen	16,500	10	1,650
Skilled workers	44,200	10	4,420
Workers	—	—	—
	154,500		21,190
Civil Servants	455,000	1	4,550
Small Business and Craftsmen	100,000	90	90,000
Agricultural Sector	16,860	100	16,860
Middle Class nondependent on salaries			181,480
Middle Class dependent on salaries			1,069,860
Total middle class family heads			1,251,560
Percentage nonsalaried middle class			14.4 %
Percentage of total population			3.0 %

---

[1] Morroe Berger, "The Middle Class in the Arab World," *The Middle East in Transition*, ed. Walter Z. Laquer (New York, 1958), p. 71.

Table 3.8
Income Tax Declarations

Income Brackets	1954 Number of tax declarations	1955	1956	1957	1958	1959	1960	1961	1962	1963
1- 2,500	30,339	39,469	46,706	71,432	70,761	77,941	78,910	95,212	129,990	151,947
2,501- 7,500	26,451	31,130	35,963	48,644	52,451	54,915	61,987	69,228	88,719	66,246
7,501- 17,500	14,882	18,739	21,338	26,956	29,579	31,794	35,697	38,421	44,077	65,783
17,501- 37,500	6,891	8,335	10,605	13,270	14,925	17,559	19,653	20,890	21,738	35,132
37,501- 57,500	1,878	2,603	3,208	4,669	4,942	6,250	7,038	7,718	8,727	15,903
57,501- 77,500	942	1,242	1,641	2,205	2,956	3,398	3,891	4,243	4,888	8,137
77,501- 100,000	471	612	1,062	1,319	1,644	2,197	2,607	3,006	2,786	3,446
100,001- 250,000	916	1,112	1,140	1,337	1,711	1,563	1,870	2,042	2,570	1,128
250,001- 500,000	204	261	372	418	719	653	618	778	751	459
500,001-1,000,000	67	99	138	160	183	227	318	360	272	239
1,000,000- +	18	36	43	53	58	86	110	108	83	117
Total	83,059	103,638	122,218	170,373	179,929	196,583	212,699	242,006	304,601	348,537

THE MIDDLE CLASSES IN TURKEY

Table 3.8

Income Tax Declarations

Percentage of increase over previous year versus 1954	Percentage of Total	24.6 % 24.6 %	17.9 47.0	39.4 204.9	5.6 216.4	9.2 236.5	8.2 255.8	13.7 291.1	25.8 366.4	14.4 419.3
1- 2,500	36.57	38.08	38.21	41.88	39.30	39.64	37.09	39.34	42.68	43.58
2,501- 7,500	31.82	30.04	29.43	28.56	29.15	27.94	29.15	18.60	29.12	19.00
7,501- 17,500	17.90	18.08	17.45	15.82	16.45	16.17	16.79	15.88	14.48	18.87
17,501- 37,500	8.29	8.04	8.68	7.79	8.30	8.94	9.24	8.63	7.14	10.07
37,501- 57,500	2.26	2.51	2.26	2.74	2.75	3.17	3.30	3.19	2.86	4.57
57,501- 77,500	1.13	1.20	1.34	1.29	1.64	1.72	1.83	1.75	1.60	2.24
77,501- 100,000	0.58	0.59	0.87	0.77	0.91	1.12	1.23	1.24	0.92	0.99
100,001- 250,000	1.10	1.07	0.94	0.78	0.95	0.79	0.88	0.84	0.85	0.34
250,001- 500,000	0.25	0.25	0.31	0.25	0.40	0.34	0.30	0.32	0.25	0.13
500,001-1,000,000	0.08	0.10	0.11	0.09	0.10	0.12	0.14	0.16	0.08	0.07
1,000,001 +	0.02	0.04	0.04	0.03	0.05	0.05	0.05	0.05	0.02	0.04
	100.00	100.00	100.00	100.00	100.00	100.00	100.00	100.00	100.00	100.00

Source: *Draft Budget Law* (Ankara 1965), pp. 178-182.

Small businessmen, the overwhelming majority of whom are self-employed, comprise half this group. Most administrators or professional people either own their own businesses or hold shares in them. In addition, a technician has a one-third chance to be in charge of his own enterprise. Middle-class farmers are less than one-eighth of the nonsalaried group, but they are nonetheless important as a bridge across the urban-rural gulf that tends to divide Middle Eastern social structures.

Although the entrepreneurial group is by no means a substantial proportion of the middle class, its present size reflects a period of rapid growth during recent years. The records of the Chambers of Commerce may not be considered comprehensive, but the upward trend recorded by the Chamber of Commerce in Istanbul, where more than 50 percent of Turkish industry is located, may be viewed as an indication of development in Turkey as a whole. The relationship between the continuous growth in the registration of new companies and the rising number of middle-range income declarations provides evidence of the increase in the entrepreneurial group.[1] Registration advanced at a galloping tempo during the period when imports were first liberalized (1952-1956). The effects of this advance can be seen in Appendix I; tax revenues rose 204.9 percent in 1957 as compared to 1954. The relative drop in the percentage increase in 1958 was due to the freezing of bank credits and other anti-inflationary measures. However, after this period of stabilization, business began to pick up and continued its upward trend. Subsequently, the impetus obtained by the entrepreneurial group during the mid-fifties continued to make itself felt even after the military revolution of 1960 (Tables 3.8 and 3.9). According to a report prepared in 1962 by a joint committee composed of members of the Ministries of Finance and Commerce, the Central Bank, and the Halk Bankası, there were more than 500,000 small businessmen throughout Turkey. About one-fifth of these could be placed within the middle-income group.

This expansion in the entrepreneurial groups is the product of both economic opportunities and sociological factors. In general, the entrepreneur shares the complex of rational values linked to the acceptance of the organized aspects of modern life that originated with the bureau-

---

[1] Table 3.8 shows the increase in the number of people filing income declarations, in the 1,000-2,500 and 2,500-7,500 lira brackets from 1954 until 1963. It is evident that in 1963 the largest single group of taxpayers, 43.58 percent, is in the 1,000-2,500 lira bracket and 19 percent of the taxprayers are within the 2,500-7,500 lira range. Therefore, we can assume that 62.5 percent of the taxpayers are officially in the middle class bracket.

Table 3.9

Registrants to the Chamber of Commerce of Istanbul

Year	Individuals	Companies	Total	Percentage of increase over previous year	Percentage of Individuals
1943	8,169 +	1,960 =	10,129	—	80.6
1944	9,345 +	2,136 =	11,481	13.34	81.39
1945	9,113 +	2,064 =	11,177	2.73	81.53
1946	8,774 +	1,985 =	10,759	3.73	81.55
1947	8,966 +	2,331 =	11,297	5.00	79.36
1948	9,257 +	2,481 =	11,738	3.90	78.86
1949	9,946 +	2,523 =	12,469	6.22	79.76
1950	10,927 +	2,784 =	13,711	9.96	79.69
1951	11,382 +	2,964 =	14,346	4.63	79.33
1952	12,628 +	3,258 =	15,886	10.73	79.49
1953	14,259 +	3,700 =	17,959	13.04	79.39
1954	16,598 +	4,149 =	20,747	15.52	80.00
1955	18,998 +	4,952 =	23,950	15.43	79.28
1956	20,975 +	5,300 =	26,275	10.97	79.82
1957	22,437 +	5,665 =	28,102	6.95	79.84
1958	23,675 +	6,220 =	29,895	10.63	79.19
1959	24,190 +	6,785 =	30,975	3.60	78.09
1960	25,355 +	7,202 =	32,557	5.10	77.87
1961	26,198 +	7,511 =	33,709	3.53	77.71
1962	26,832 +	7,982 =	34,814	3.27	77.07
1963	27,017 +	8,027 =	35,044	6.60	77.09
1964	27,693 +	8,172 =	35,865	2.34	77.21

Source: Chamber of Commerce, Istanbul.

cratic elite and is now characteristic of the middle class as a modern entity. However, beyond this broad similarity there are significant psychological differences rooted in the upper working and lower middle class origins of the newer business groups. In essence, the men who later became entrepreneurs were initially confronted with the bureaucratic elite order that failed to fulfill their expectations for social justice as they saw it and opportunity in the new national community. This elite had become isolated from the more traditionally oriented groups; contempt was implicit in their authoritarian attitudes towards the lower social strata.[1]

As a result, individuals from the lower middle and upper working classes sought to win through entrepreneurial attainment the status that

---

[1] Karpat, "Political Developments in Turkey," pp. 477-88.

was denied them within the confines of the new social structure.[1] The peaceful social rebellion that was thus channeled into business activity was less the reaction of a traditional order of rapidly diminishing influence than a response to a new order of social stratification associated with the modernization process. The conjunction of this social movement with the widespread economic opportunities of the postwar period resulted in the rapid expansion of the entrepreneurial sector. Ultimately, this group attained a role in the political process commensurate with its new economic position. However, acceptance from the older sectors of the middle class was not easily won. The old surviving aristocrats despised the new wave for their common origins, while the bureaucrats feared them as a threat to the economic and social position of the state-supported sector as well as to the modernization process as a whole. Although that mutual lack of confidence which was the inevitable result of the conditions preceding the rise of the entrepreneurs tended to prevent the new groups from meeting the bureaucratic elite on common ground, there is now far more social concern among the intelligentsia than was the case prior to 1950.[2] Antagonisms have not yet been finally resolved, but the presence of the entrepreneurial sector, identified with social mobility and political democracy, has already radically altered the character of the middle class.

Economic power and close links to the masses have been a source of strength to the new entrepreneurs, but, in addition, organization has augmented their importance. Several studies have suggested that increased membership in voluntary organizations is a distinguishing characteristic of the middle class as contrasted to the lower social strata.[3] Recent evidence indicates that an infrastructure of group organization in conformity with this general pattern is beginning to emerge among the Turkish middle class, especially in the entrepreneurial sector. The middle class has played the key role in political parties, and in social organizations, such as the Parent Teachers Association (PTA), the Red Crescent, and the Turkish Air League. In addition, the middle class is organizing political control through the Craftsmen's Association ("*Esnaf Dernekleri*") and, oddly enough, through the labor trade unions. Despite the fact that the Craftsmen's Association has been used by the political parties in power, particularly during Democratic Party regimes, it has served

---

[1] Everett E. Hagen, "The Entrepreneur as Rebel against Traditional Society," *Human Organization* XIX (Winter, 1960-1961), pp. 185-187.

[2] Karpat, "Political Developments in Turkey," pp. 477-88.

[3] Faris, *The Middle Class*, p. 4; Chapin, *Measurement of Social Status*.

as an instrument of expression for the middle class. The labor unions act as a buffer between the Labor Party and the various parties seeking the labor vote.

Apart from their role in these groups, small businessmen are organized in numerous professional associations, such as the Association of Foundry Operators. The membership of most of these groups is made up of small-scale entrepreneurs owning perhaps one or two lathes, punching presses, or textile looms. In addition, a wide variety of associations have been created to protect the interest and promote the views of businessmen and craftsmen on a particular issue. Although such groups generally fail to establish a permanent basis of common interest and tend to dissolve or become nonfunctional when the crisis which provoked their formation has passed, their existence, however ephemeral, indicates a significant pattern of group formation for political purposes.

In contrast to these smaller associations, the Chamber of Commerce and the Chamber of Industry are predominantly associated with the large-scale entrepreneur and may not be considered as representing solely the new economic middle-class groups.[1] There is an insignificant department for small industrialists at the Chamber of Commerce in Istanbul where those who do not wish to register at the Chamber of Industry are registered. However, it should be noted that registration with the Chamber of Commerce is increasing every year, as table 3.9. demonstrates. The most active period of registration began when foreign trade was liberalized and many businessmen registered in order to secure import licenses. This influx halted when import regulations were severed after the 1956 and 1958 periods. Since then, registration has increased at a slow but steady pace, rising three times over the original number in 1943.

In addition to these organizations, several associations have recently appeared, which are more oriented toward the technocrat. Within this category, the new Turkish Management Association aspires to unite the managerial class. However, membership was still only 309 in 1966 and therefore insignificant for the whole of the country. The Economic

---

[1] The friction that has appeared between the Chambers and the small businessman serves to illustrate the gulf between these organizations and the middle class. For example, during a survey conducted on small foundry operators established in certain known districts of Istanbul, their addresses could only be secured with difficulty because they were not registered with the Chambers, although they had organized their own Association of Foundry Operators. Subsequent interviews disclosed that the Association did not want to reveal members' addresses because of the fear that the Chamber of Commerce would meddle with their activities.

and Social Research Foundation and the Economic and Social Studies Conference Board, both in Istanbul, which attempt to unite various sectors of the economy, including government officials, business, labor, and the universities, are still very new. Probably there will be an increase in associations in all strata of the middle class in the future, and it is possible that organizations of a broader type may unite a wider range of middle-class groups. However, at present organization is most widespread among the entrepreneurial sector, where the new infrastructure of associations has served to integrate business groups and provide an organizational framework for the advancement of entrepreneurial claims.

Thus, several factors have contributed to the present position of the entrepreneur, but in the further expansion and continued upward mobility of the private sector the financial structure of the business sphere, with particular reference to the problem of capital accumulation, is a matter of key importance. When foreign aid is excluded, generation of capital in developing countries usually occurs through savings (often at the price of living below the standards of present earnings) although the development process itself generates some capital gains for property owners when new dams, roads, etc. are built. Generally, it is the low-income groups that consume and those of more substantial means that save and invest. However, the middle class groups engaged in economic occupations have been primarily recruited from the lower middle and upper working strata, and savings have played a part in this process. A recent study conducted in West Germany shows that Turkish laborers working there have a high propensity to save (table 3.10). Their ultimate objective in returning home is to buy land and machinery. In two or three years workers from the Black Sea coast return, purchase land, generally from absentee landlords, and enter a new way of life as independent farmers.

Table 3.10

Savings Pattern of Turkish Laborers in Germany

Savings tendencies	Percent
Those saving	80.2
Not saving	17.0
Still not able to save	1.8
No answer	1.0
	100.0

Source: Nermin Abadan, *Batı Almanya'daki Türk İşçileri ve Sorunları* (Ankara, 1965), p. 94.

For civil service employees and much of the salariat, income is adequate to provide a middle-class style of life but insufficient for substantial savings. In addition, inflation tends to consume small savings. However, among much of the middle class groups and the lower strata, it appears probable that actual personal savings are considerably in excess of bank deposits. Bank officials claim that in rural areas savings are kept in cash form, either "under the mattress" or buried in a *küp* ("earthen jar"). The sale of the Ereğli steel mill shares in a campaign conducted by the mill itself revealed strong potential purchasing power in the smaller towns, and it is possible that the joint-stock enterprise, drawing on this hidden capital, could become an increasingly important form of business activity.

While this may provide a direction for future expansion, large industry in Turkey is not presently organized on a joint-stock basis. During the fifties, profits acquired through commercial activities served as the primary source of capital for industrial enterprise. However, in Turkey, as in the Middle East as a whole, most private capital is still channeled through family relationships, and industry has rarely expanded beyond the limits of the family enterprise. The prevalence of the family company also indicates that the structure of large industry is still diffuse rather than cartelized; therefore the present stage may be conducive to the expansion of entrepreneurial activity on an individualistic basis.

Credit through state banking facilities is another potential source of capital for the creation and expansion of enterprise. An effort has been made to extend credit through state institutions, but these have proved of limited utility to the small businessman. The Industrial Development Bank serves only the large industrialists. The Agricultural Bank, which is the oldest in Turkey and has the greatest number of branch offices, presumably grants loans to farmers, but these credits are so small that they are mostly used for consumption of current needs. Recently, however, a supervised credit program has been introduced. This has tended to stress the loans for tractor, fertilizer, and livestock. Credits granted by the Central Bank to institutions supporting small business, such as banks and cooperatives, have increased but still are not commensurate with the needs of small business (table 3.11). In addition, the Ministry of Finance has undertaken the capitalization of various projects within the field of private enterprise with funds obtained from the Agency for International Development. But, few of these credits have been channeled to small business (table 3.12).

Private commercial banks are another source for providing operating capital to the small businessman.[1] Their interest rates are legally set at 7-10.5 percent, but they often rise to 18 percent with additional charges. Nonetheless, even these rates are preferable to the usurers' charges, which are sometimes as high as 50 percent. A study at the Türk Ticaret Bankası (Turkish Commercial Bank), which is one of the leading medium-sized private banks with a limited amount of government participation, shows that small credits in amounts of less than 10,000 lira granted through their facilities are only 5 percent of total credit. However, small business utilizing these credits constituted 45 percent of the bank's customers.

By and large, these funds are employed to finance expenses, such as renovation or purchase of equipment, for which businessmen cannot obtain credit from suppliers.[2] In this way, small businesses support each other through the use of bank credits at a rate of 18 percent. As table 3.13 suggests, credit granted to small business approximates only 3.7 percent of the total credit extended through private sources in 1963 and 3.8 percent in 1964. In the country as a whole, all credits granted to small business through both private and public institutions approximates only 1.7 percent of total credit in 1962 and 1.8 percent in 1963 and 1964 (table 3.14), although it must be noted that some commercial and agricultural credits are actually utilized in the small-business sector.

As these considerations indicate, there is no organized financial support for small business. Credits are granted by the commercial banks at the discretion of bank managers, who are more disposed to extend loans to the bureaucratic elite as a goodwill gesture than to the businessman. The Halk Bankası is attempting to provide the small credits at low interest rates needed by the small-business sector, but although a recommendation to increase the capitalization of the bank from 200 to 400 million liras has been made,[3] the organization of the Halk Bankası

---

[1] The fact that declared capital does not always correspond with the scope of a registrant's business indicates that the Chamber of Commerce may be considerably less representative of the middle class than the examination of registration figures would suggest.

[2] The usual procedure is to give a promissory note to the supplier with the bank's approval; the supplier then discounts the note at the bank to receive his payment. In three months it is necessary to renew this commercial credit, and after one or two renewals the bank insists on partial payment. In this manner, a credit of 25,000 lira received for three months would be extended once at that level, once as 20,000 lira and once as 15,000 lira. When the debtor has obtained a guarantee from another reliable businessman and repaid 20 percent of the loan at each of these stages, the bank is willing to extend the remaining credit.

[3] Report dated August 29, 1962, prepared by a joint committee composed of mem-

Table 3.11

Credits Granted by Central Bank to Institutions Supporting Small Business (in million TL)

1958	92
1959	104
1960	120
1961	159
1962	179
1963	184

Source: *Central Bank Bulletin* (Ankara, 1963), pp. 63-64.

Table 3.12

Special Funds created by the Ministry of Finance (in Million TL)

Purpose of Fund	Credits Granted	Interest Rates
Tourism	18	5
Tourism Development	25	4
Ereğli Steel Mill	354	5.75
Ereğli Steel Housing	35	5.75
Mining Credit	25	4
Control of Agriculture	11	4
Marshall Aid to Private Sector	75	4
Agriculture	32	5
Small Business ++	8 ++	0.75 ++
Industrial Credits	60	4.5
Bursa Industrial Site	17	5.5
Soil Conservation	18	4
Agricultural Pesticides	12	4
Medical School	12	0.75
Soil Products Office	90	0.75
Total	792	

Source: Compiled from *Draft Budget Law for 1965*.

("People's Bank") is still very limited. Only 78,257 credits amounting to 155,000,000 lira have thus far been extended under its auspices.

In the smaller towns, the Halk Bankası is replaced by the Esnaf Kefalet Koperatifi, (Artisans' Capital Cooperative) and the government has entrusted the mission of granting credit to this network of cooperatives to the Türk Ticaret Bankası (Turkish Commercial Bank). Although

---

bers of the Ministry of Finance, the Ministry of Commerce, the Central Bank, and the Halk Bankası.

Table 3.13

Private Enterprise Credits (in Million TL)

	Oct. 1963	Oct. 1964
Normal commercial credits	211	267
Export credits	115	80
Tobacco financing	215	350
Import financing	13	—
Industrial and Mining notes	84	93
Agricultural credits	362	426
Agricultural sales cooperatives	78	245
Small business and crafts credits	44	59
Credits on bonds	20	25
Total	1,142	1,545

Source: *Draft Budget Law for 1965*, p. 97.

Table 3.14

Credits According to Sectors (in Million TL)

Sectors	1962	1963	1964
Government	1,451	1,549	1,856
Commercial	5,310	5,608	5,960
Agricultural	1,953	2,143	2,210
Housing	1,131	1,184	1,340
Industrial	334	373	463
Small Business	183	204	218
Total	10,362	11,061	12,047

credit can be obtained through these channels, the process is complicated and expensive because two middlemen, the bank and the cooperative, are involved, and the cooperatives are sometimes utilized as political tools by professional organizers. The small businessman in need of funds must join the cooperative, pay an initiation fee, and obtain a membership letter, which must then be presented to the Halk Bankası or its corresponding bank in order to receive credit. The Halk Bankası has divided small business into two categories: the *müstehlik esnaf*, or trades and services group, such as barbers, coffee shop operators, and shoe repairmen; and the *sabit sermayeli esnaf*, or businessmen with fixed capital, such as brick and tile manufacturers and small foundries. Although those in the second category are often nascent industrialists, they are apparently unwilling to comply with these formalities, and the majority of applicants for credit through the cooperatives are from the trades and services category. In any case, these loans are so small that, like the agricultural credit loans, they are quickly dissipated in paying pressing debts or providing for personal needs.

Thus, although an undeniable effort to extend credit to the small-business sector has been undertaken and the funds granted have gradually increased, credits remain far below the requirements of this group and provide little room for capital accumulation. At the same time, it must be recognized that the need for capital increases as a society develops. In Turkey, as in much of the developing world, continued reliance upon state enterprise and central planning reflects an inability or unwillingness to provide lesser financial services through credit.[1] While the problem of capital accumulation does not check the growth of small business in the trades and services category, where little initial capitalization is required, it has produced a static situation which brakes the creation and expansion of middle-range business in the sphere of production.

Conclusions and Future Projections

The advancing processes of social and economic change in postwar Turkey have thus produced a large and increasingly differentiated middle class embracing more than one-fifth of the population. As the modern sector of a developing society, the broad range of middle-class groupings share the values associated with the acceptance of the organized system of modern life and largely control the complex of new economic forces. In addition, a modest but distinctive style of life based upon this economic position is widely shared throughout the spectrum of the middle class.

However, social relations now have a greater complexity than in the intial stages of development, and, to a considerable extent, a unitary social structure within the framework of the national community has been superimposed upon the remnants of the traditional order. Today the bureaucratic elite, that has been the core of the modernization process since the early days of the republic, remains a powerful force in the process of social acculturation, a governing industrial elite in charge of state enteprise, an important source of managerial skills, and numerically a large and growing sector of the middle class. But somewhat paradoxically, as the goals of development have been increasingly trans-

[1] Alexander Eckstein, "Individualism and the Role of the State in Economic Growth," *Economic Development and Cultural Change* VI (January 1958), pp. 84-85.

lated into reality, a new system of group relationships in which the role of the bureaucratic elite is unmistakably altered has been created. The rapid expansion in the dimensions of the middle class in the postwar period has reflected the emergence of new business groups engaged in production, commerce, trades, and services and a salariat of technocrats and skilled workers employed in the private sector rather than state enterprise.

When a new center of innovation, also based upon the new economic forces and adhering to rational values, appeared in the entrepreneurial sector, the significance of the bureaucratic elite as the modernizing center of a developing society was diminished. Economic power, close links to the lower strata, and an organized infrastructure of group associations have enabled the middle-range entrepreneurial sector to win an important role in the political process commensurate with their economic position. Thus, the rise of new groups, through what was in effect a social movement breaching the barriers of the new elite order through entrepreneurial activity, has produced a new system of group relationships in which government is accountable to a wider range of society and the bureaucratic elite are no longer the sole arbiters of the development process. However, at present, a relatively static situation occasioned by the fact that credit has not kept pace with the growing needs of business is hampering the expansion of the private enterprise sector, decreasing social mobility toward the middle range and beyond through the channels associated with entrepreneurial activity, and maximizing tendencies toward the accumulation of wealth in the hands of a few in the sphere of large industry. In the long run, as the need for capital accumulation increases with development, these conditions could brake the evolution of the entrepreneurial sector and thus alter the social balance within the economic groups of the middle class.

Apart from these economic factors, a second contingency that could reshape the middle class involves the ideological evolution of the present system of mixed economy towards a statist one. In the developing world, where class struggle and the dialectic have little meaning, socialism appears as a philosophy of development under central control, and it is linked to emotional attitudes opposing accumulation of wealth in private hands and considering association with outside powers imperialistic. These factors are also present in Turkey, where the problem of social responsibility in private enterprise has been increasingly evident.

At the present juncture, the high income group is engaged in building commercial empires and rejects social welfare activities and constructive involvement in politics. Although the absence of a public philosophy is by no means restricted to the developing countries, these views among the Turkish upper class are further reinforced by the fact that a community and civic consciousness in the Western sense of the word has not yet developed.

These attitudes have engendered an increasing amount of opposition which has manifested itself as an attack on private enterprise and foreign investment, as seen in the vocal socialist press. At the same time, alignments within the middle class have not yet taken firm shape. The upper-income group appears to be unaware that its behavior conforms too closely to the ancient capitalist stereotype and that there may be a crisis on the horizon. However, the foreign companies, no doubt sensitized by experience, are spending a good deal of time and money on public relations, as is illustrated by the Mobil Oil scholarships to technical schools and universities in Turkey. In addition, their investment programs have already been curtailed.

Thus, it is evident that the defense of a mixed economy devolves primarily upon the new middle-class groups, and it is not yet clear whether other sectors can be mobilized behind their aspirations. Much of the salariat feel that they have neither a vested interest in private enterprise nor a residual philosophical commitment to this system. Top-level technocrats tend to become identified with the private enterprise system in which they are employed,[1] but to the average employee the outcome of the controversy would make little difference. As a result of this distinction in the economic positions of entrepreneur and employee, it is by no means certain that the salariat which is now so large a proportion of the middle class will identify itself with the private enterprise system.[2]

Considering nationalization in terms of its probable effect upon the social structure, it must be emphasized that the expansion of the middle class would not be halted. Whether the development process advances in the context of a statist system or of a mixed economy, the technocrat and skilled worker groups will continue to expand; traditional elements will be increasingly mobilized into the new unitary social structure as the relative importance of agriculture in relation to the commercial-industrial sphere declines and the differences between urban and rural

---

[1] This development in the industrialized nations is noted by Cole, *Class Structure*, p. 85.

[2] This division in the industrial world is discussed by Lewis Corey, *The Crisis of the Middle Class* (New York, 1935), pp. 162-165.

areas dissolve; the trades and services category will expand, at least to some extent, when rising income multiplies the demand for consumer goods.

However, the farther statism is expanded to the left, the more the development of certain sectors of the middle class is maximized (technocrats and skilled workers) and that of others is minimized (small business). In addition, wherever socialism is instituted, the entrepreneurial sector is no longer envisaged as a viable and creative social element.[1] The result would be a return to bureaucratic predominance, although perhaps in a more democratic context. Ironically, although the large industrialist is the focal point of the emotional attitudes dubbed as socialism, nationalization, if carried out within the middle class, would be centered upon the entrepreneurial sector which remains linked to the lower strata and closely identified with democratic values.

Thus, a new consensus on the economic order and social policies may determine the political relations among the various segments of the middle class in Turkey. Clearly, if private industry is to have a place in this order, it can only be as a complex of more socially-oriented institutions accepting broader social responsibilities not directly connected to the needs of business.[2] It devolves upon the new middle class groups and the more socially concerned sectors of the intelligentsia as the most politically active elements in the community to build a new arena of consensus in this functionally differentiated and yet strongly interdependent modern society.

---

[1] Cole, *Class Structure*, p. 89.

[2] Edwin J. Cohn, "Social and Cultural Factors Affecting the Emergence and Functioning of Innovators," *Social Aspects of Economic Development* (Istanbul, 1962), pp. 94 ff.

CHAPTER FOUR

LABOR IN TURKEY
AS A NEW SOCIAL AND POLITICAL FORCE *

BÜLENT ECEVIT

One of the characteristics of the period that followed the Revolution of 27 May 1960, in Turkey, is the emergence of labor as a new social and political force attached to the principles of Atatürk and democracy.[1] This is not due to any sudden growth in the size of the labor force, but to the political and economic assessment of earlier developments.

Numerically, organized labor is still a small group, constituting only about 5 percent of the population. This percentage would grow if the agricultural labor force were taken into account. But agricultural workers still retain their peasant characteristics. The great majority are seasonal workers, some of them owning small plots of land. They are only partially covered by labor legislation, and, for the most part, are scarcely, and ineffectively, organized in trade unions. In short, they cannot be considered as an integrated part of either the industrial or the unionized labor force—except, to some extent, in the state sector, where they have been able to sign collective agreements.[2] If agricultural workers are excluded, then the number of workers in Turkey can be estimated at about one and one-half to two million.[3]

Yet, since the Revolution, the effectiveness of industrial and organized

---

* After the original paper was delivered by the author a series of important developments in the labor movement occurred, including the establishment of DİSK. Information on these, an addendum and tables were added by the editor. KHK.

[1] A declaration issued by a joint conference of the Confederation of Turkish Trade Unions epitomizes these principles: "The Confederation of Turkish Trade Unions, which cherishes the ideal of the building up of a democratic, socialistic, and progressive Turkey, committed to Atatürk's principles, is against every kind of dictatorial tendency, against the ideas that promote class domination and against all systems based on the exploitation of man by man" (Press bulletin *Cumhuriyet*, *Vatan*, March 21, 22, 1965).

[2] All agricultural workers have the right to establish trade unions and sign collective agreements, but in practice this is difficult to carry out. Minimum wages have been set for agricultural workers for the first time, and legal steps have been taken to regulate employment exchange in the agricultural sector.

[3] See figures in tables in appendix to this chapter.

labor as a power group has increased substantially. This is an important development for Turkey. Throughout Ottoman history, power rested in the elite, which was composed of the bureaucracy, headed by the Sultan, the military and the religious men or *ilmiye* (*ulema*). During the Republican period, particularly after the introduction of universal suffrage and a multiparty regime in 1945-46, participation in and control over the administration was broadened through a delegation of power—through elected representatives who still belonged to the elite.

Another important change in the pattern of power distribution during the Republic was the replacement of the official religious hierarchy by an intelligentsia, whose unofficial and secular authority was vested in the universities and the press. The influence of the academics, including the students as well as the professors, became particularly marked just before and immediately after the Revolution of 1960. Businessmen and owners of large land estates also acquired growing importance and power as the economy developed. But these again should be considered as part of the elite.

Thus, deprived of an effective organization, the peasants and workers could not exert any direct, day-to-day influence over the political system. The villagers in particular, who, according to the census of 1960, constituted 71.3 percent of the population, remained disorganized and unable to exert the influence their number commanded. Today, the power and the direct political influence of the workers are far greater than those of the peasants. The significance of this development lies in the fact that at least one group of people outside the elite has, for the first time in Turkish history, attained a real position of influence and is now able to balance to some extent the traditional elites' power. This was secured peacefully, without bloodshed, and, in fact, largely through the initiative of at least some of the elite. But it must be added that this "initiative" was very timely, because it anticipated and avoided approaching social strife.

The Revolution of 27 May 1960 first ended the authoritarian rule of the Democratic Party, which seemed to aim toward the destruction of the very democratic regime which had brought it to power. Second, the revolution strove to restore democracy in Turkey. It achieved these purposes and surpassed its immediate objectives, for this was in its nature. The Revolution created an unprecedented awareness of the social and economic problems of the country. There was a growing realization that the economic interests of the majority had been sacrificed to those of a few, and that this could be avoided only if democracy were supplemented with certain social measures and safeguards. The new Constitution of

1961, which declared the Turkish Republic to be a "social state," and particularly "the Social and Economic Rights and Duties" section of the same are the most eloquent proof of this awareness.

The resentment of the social injustice resulting from the inflationary and "liberal" economic policy of the Democratic Party found an outlet for expression with the restored freedom of discussion of economic and social problems. Discontent and restiveness seemed to have begun to replace the Turkish people's traditional patience and satisfaction with their lot. Profound reaction to injustice may be considered a main Turkish characteristic. Whereas in the past the cure of injustice was sought in legal and administrative decisions, now this expectation was replaced with the awareness that injustice may well rest in the economic and social spheres as well, and the remedy may be found in measures related directly to the cause.

The period between the rise of social and economic awareness and discontent and the granting of satisfaction through constitutional and legal means constitutes a most critical period in the history of Turkish labor. Indeed, the turbulent years of 1962 and 1963 crystallized labor's political and cultural attitudes, as well as the direction of their future actions. Initially, the workers organized spontaneous mass meetings without the initiative or participation of any elite group, not even the university students. The workers denounced social and economic injustice in these meetings and demanded the implementation of the social and economic provisions of the new constitution. Barefoot workers marched in Istanbul and Izmir, the industrial and business centers of Turkey. In Ankara, the capital, such a march was stopped just at the steps of the Parliament building while Parliament was in session. Posters, attacking the "greedy boss" or the "dirty capitalist" appeared for the first time in Turkey.

The workers' unrest, protest, and marches were over and a sense of professional pride instilled as soon as Parliament enacted two major labor laws : the Law for Collective Labor Agreements, Strikes and Lockouts, and the new Trade Union Law.

Six months after the passage of these two laws, TÜRK-İŞ (*Türkiye İşçi Sendikaları Konfederasyonu*, ("Confederation of Turkish Trade Unions") had its convention in Bursa. During that convention, a union leader happened to mention casually "the barefoot Turkish worker". All the delegates, including the organizers of the marches in which the barefoot workers participated, rose up in protest. "This is slander," they shouted, "this is an insult to the Turkish worker... he is not barefoot." The astounded speaker apologized saying that he just wanted to say that it was difficult for some workers to buy a pair of shoes rather than describe them as "barefooted poor".

The new laws were then only six months old. Very few collective agreements had been signed yet, and few of the workers had benefited from the material advantages provided by the new rights. But these rights, being officially granted, gave the workers recognition as a group, a sense of pride, self-confidence, and hope for the future. Incorporated in the legal-political system and allowed to share economic benefits, they no longer felt like "the underdog," and gave up the use of violent methods in order to attain their objectives. The following statement by the Executive Committee of TÜRK-İŞ, in a Report to the Fifth Convention of the Confederation held in Bursa in 1964, best expresses this new philosophy :

> Labor union movements have followed two different paths; first, the evolutionary unionism as we see in the free world today, and, second, the revolutionary unionism as opposed to the first one... We, the Executive Committee, inspired by the unionized labor circles of Turkey, consider it our duty to make clear that our path should be the path of evolutionary unionism, and that revolutionary methods cannot be a positive course for us.

This attitude was proved by deeds even before the passage of the laws. Some disgruntled military officers, exploiting the social unrest and discontent among the people, attempted two coups in 1962 and 1963. They claimed that the Turkish parliamentary democracy was ill-founded, immature, and not equipped to solve the country's social and economic problems. Quite a few intellectuals shared this conviction and gave their open or implicit support to these attempted coups. Yet, it is remarkable that workers did not support the revolutionary officers or the intellectuals. They were among the first to condemn such actions in strong terms. Indeed, at open air meetings organized by TÜRK-İŞ on 22 December 1962, about two months before the abortive military coup, the workers took their own "National Oath." Through the Oath, repeated on other occasions, the workers stressed their support for the Constitution and swore allegiance to democracy. The Oath runs as follows :

> We, the sons of a nation which forever has lived in freedom and independence, we who believe in human rights, in the principles of democracy and social justice and in the Atatürk ideals, we, who are convinced that poverty and misery are the chief obstacles to peace and progress, we the Turkish workers, solemnly declare that we are pledged to undertake whatever sacrifice may be

necessary to defend our constitutional regime against all kinds of subversive acts wherever such acts may come from.[1]

A brief survey of the history of labor legislation in Turkey might serve as a background to evaluate these recent developments. Labor rights were rather neglected by the Ottoman Empire. In contrast, the nationalist Republican leaders, however, showed a degree of social-mindedness early, even during the critical stages of the War of Liberation in 1921, by passing a law designated to protect the coal miners of Zonguldak. This law prevented forced labor, limited the working day to eight hours, and provided for accident compensation, medical care, and benefits. It also established a tripartite committee to fix wages and to provide for the training of workers and the prevention of accidents.

After the War of Liberation, Atatürk convened a National Economic Congress in Izmir, in 1923, to which a delegation of workers was also invited, although its role was limited. Later the government took the lead in its own enterprises in improving the workers' welfare. Gradually, certain provisions of the law concerning the coal miners of Zonguldak were extended to cover other categories of workers. The Civil and Obligations Code of 1926 and the Law of General Hygiene (1930) also included provisions regulating working conditions, instituting health protection measures, and safeguarding the workers' rights.

A year after the proclamation of the Republic, in 1923, the workers were granted the right to weekly rest days, and in 1935 the right to rest was extended to cover public holidays. In 1930 child labor was forbidden. A comprehensive Labor Law (*İş Kanunu*, number 3008) was enacted in 1936. Amended a few times, it remained in effect until 1967 when a new law (number 931) replaced it.

The Labor Law of 1936 covered initially establishments with ten or more workers, but later its provisions were extended to some of the smaller workshops. It provided for tripartite boards to set minimum wages, and for compulsory arbitration. The law also limited working hours, regulated the conditions of work for women and young employees, and provided for compensation for jobless workers.

The Ministry of Labor and the Employment Institutions were set up in 1945 and a trade union law granting the right to organize was enacted in 1947. Workers' insurances covering sickness, industrial accidents, occupational diseases, maternity care, old age, disability, and death

---

[1] See final section of *Türkiye İşçi Sendikaları Konfederasyonu, Beşinci Genel Kurula Sunulan İdari ve Mali Raporlar* (Bursa, 1964), p. 5.

were introduced between 1945 and 1950. Finally, in 1950, tripartite labor courts were established.

Thus, by the time the People's Republican Party ended its 27 year term in office it had fulfilled most of the provisions of its program concerning labor. The rights of collective bargaining and strike were not yet included in the party program. It was deemed originally, that with only two or three years of experience, the labor unions were not ready to use these rights.

The Democratic Party, on the other hand, had promised these rights while it was, in oppositon, contesting the People's Republican Party for power. But, although it remained in office for ten years after May 1950, it did not fulfill its promise. The Democratic Party government did, however, attempt to win the workers' sympathy through various material incentives, since the expansion of industrial activity resulted in an increased working class, and augmented the workers' political potential at polls. During the Democratic Party rule laws were enacted for paid rest days and holidays, Seamen's Labor, mining, labor relations in the press, and paid annual leave.

The government which came to power after the Revolution of 1960 resumed the traditional policy of assuming the initiative in introducing labor legislation. The Constitution of 1961 had already paved the way for this endeavor. Article 45 of the Constitution charged the state to "adopt the necessary measures so that workers may earn wages commensurate with the work they perform, and sufficient to maintain a standard of living befitting human dignity." Article 47 provided that "in their relations with their employers, workers are entitled to bargain collectively and to strike with a view to protecting and improving their economic and social status." The resulting labor legislation drew its justification from these Constitutional provisions.

The new Trade Union Act, the Law for Collective Labor Agreements, Strikes and Lockouts, a new Social Insurance Law, providing for substantial increases in pensions and other benefits and extending the coverage of insurance, and the Act for the Reorganization of State Enterprises which introduced a system of comanagement and profit sharing, may be cited among the new legislation enacted between 1961 and 1965. In addition to the Labor Law enacted in 1967, a new Seamen's Labor law was passed in 1966, but a bill on the Regulation of Labor Exchange in the agricultural sector has not been enacted yet (1969).

The labor legislation enacted during the 37-year period that preceded the Revolution of 1960 included some rights that workers could not have possibly obtained if these had depended on their own initiative and pressure, even if the right to collective bargaining and strike had been granted. Economic development had not reached a sufficiently advanced stage and the trade unions did not have the organized strength to secure such rights. Nevertheless, the absence of the right to strike and of collective bargaining reduced the effectiveness of social legislation, no matter how progressive. The arbitration boards and labor courts were heavily loaded with complaints and requests which they could not handle promptly. The courts had to deal individually with the complaints of each worker. Under these circumstances, sanctions against the violations of laws were not sufficiently prohibitive.

It was obvious that without the right to bargain collectively and to strike, workers could not insure for themselves a just share of the increase in national income. Indeed, the first Five-Year Development Plan published in 1963, revealed that the per capita share of workers in the gross national product had declined by 10 percent from 1950 to 1960.[1] The Law on Collective Bargaining, therefore, provided the avenue for the worker to secure an income proportionate to his effort and to his minimum living needs while protecting him against the employer. The latter, for instance, was "not permitted to engage any other worker in a permanent or temporary capacity or to employ any other person in substitution for a worker whose rights and obligations under his contract of employment are suspended" because of a strike.[2]

Without such a provision, the right to strike could not be effective since a large number of unemployed persons would be always available to replace the workers on strike. Moreover,

"If it is established by the final judgement of a court that a lawful lockout has been ordered with the object of permanently closing the establishment or of depriving the workers of their seniority rights, the lockout shall cease as soon as the judgment is communicated."[3]

The new labor laws aimed also at strengthening the trade unions by recognizing the bigger unions as having special competence in collective bargaining and by allowing them to collect special dues from nonunion workers wishing to avail themselves of the benefits of a collective contract. The law permitted the trade unions to engage in special economic activities likely to increase their funds.

[1] *First Five-Year Development Plan, 1963-67*, Publication of the Prime Ministry, State Planning Organization, (Ankara, 1963), p. 46.

[2] See Article 27 (2) of the Law on Collective Labor Agreements, Strikes, and Lockouts. See also International Labor Office Publication, *Legislative Series 1963*, Turkey 2.

[3] *Ibid.*, Article 20.

The Use of the New Rights

Collective bargaining, despite its novelty and complicated procedure, has functioned quite smoothly. For instance, during the first seventeen months after the passage of the law, 824 collective agreements covering 391,838 workers were signed.

There were seventy-seven strikes and two lockouts in the same period. The strikes resulted in the loss of 196,234 workdays and the lockouts of 13,188 workdays. The percentage of workers participating in strikes stands at less than one percent in proportion to the officially recorded numbers of workers. But, considering that only about one-half of the industrial workers are officially recorded, this percentage should, in fact, be much lower.[1] (See statistical tables 4.1, 4.2, 4.3, 4.4, and 4.5 in the appendix.)

Of the 824 collective agreements, 644 signed in the private sector covered 152,848 workers, and 180 agreements signed in the public sector covered 328,990 workers. The two lockouts were both in the private sector. Of the seventy-seven strikes, seventy-five were in the private and only two in the public sector. In many cases, there were long negotiations before the signing of agreements or before the strikes. Some negotiations lasted as long as six or eight months. This may be regarded as a remarkable sign of patience and of the desire to reach agreement before resorting to compulsory action.

The trade unions have indeed shown commendable restraint, despite a few exceptions, before going on strike. Much was due to responsible and reasonable leadership, and timely interventions by the Confederation of Turkish Trade Unions or TÜRK-İŞ. The Confederation subscribed to the principle stated in the first Five-Year Development Plan, that wage increases, except in the case of minimum wages, should depend on increases in productivity. In compliance with this principle, the Confederation advised the unions to press for increases in the minimum wage areas and to try to reduce the gap between the low and high wage scales.

The Confederation and the unions tackled the problem of increasing productivity more vigorously than the average employer, through numerous productivity seminars organized in various parts of the country and

---

[1] The existing Labor Law covers only part of the industrial workers. The exact number of industrial workers will be known only after the newly enacted Labor Bill becomes fully operative.

attended by union leaders and officials. They also showed interest in mixed productivity committees and, in many cases, pressed for the inclusion of provisions for such bodies in collective agreements. Moreover, the Confederation and the trade unions, promoting their educational policy, advised the workers to work harder to increase production and to better its quality if they wished to obtain wage increases and better working conditions in the future.

This constructive attitude of TÜRK-İŞ and the unions stems from the realization that wage increases not backed by greater productivity, more investment, and real growth in national income would lead to inflation and aggravate the situation of the underdog.

Significant to note is the fact that many enterprises which granted substantial wage increases as a result of union pressures and bargaining achieved better profits than ever at the end of the year. For instance, the large state coal mines in Zonguldak had traditionally been in the red. They achieved their first substantial annual profit of 11 million Turkish liras in 1963, after the workers' minimum wages were raised by about 30 percent. By 1964, after the first collective agreement increased the total wages by 40 million liras, the enterprises' annual profit approached 30 million liras. Meanwhile, the output per capita increased by more than 25 percent.

The unions seem to be aware of the identity of interest between the workers and enterprise, as well as between the workers and the nation as a whole. For instance, several labor unions, instead of going on strike, loaned money out of their own strike funds to certain private enterprises which they thought to be in a really difficult position. In exceptional cases, where certain unions, either within or outside TÜRK-İŞ, insisted on unreasonable wage increases likely to destroy an enterprise, or seriously upset the balance of wages in different enterprises or branches of industry, TÜRK-İŞ intervened promptly and effectively. The following passages from a TÜRK-İŞ publication illustrate well the sense of responsibility displayed by this organization:

> TÜRK-İŞ is convinced that the time of "heroic unionism" is over. Unionism has now become a science. The new order [of industrial democracy] established in Turkey, charges as much responsibility as gives new rights to Turkish workers and union leaders. The Turkish trade union movement, while exerting every effort to protect these rights, will never forget its responsibilities. Only such a mentality would assure that the rights now being obtained are long-lasting and worthy. TÜRK-İŞ will handle with utmost care the right to strike, and free unionism [both of] which are considered among the basic rights and freedoms, and will resist every attempt to degenerate them... In all its activities

aimed at raising the living standards of the masses it represents, at finding solutions to social problems, at contributing to the efforts in the field of education, and at securing the development of the Turkish worker in a manner compatible with human rights and freedoms, TÜRK-İŞ has always given utmost consideration to the society's interests. It is the basic principle of all our activities that every project to be launched and every step to be taken should be in the interests of the Turkish nation as well as of the Turkish workers.[1]

The sense of responsibility and restraint displayed by the labor movement in Turkey during the initial period of industrial democracy has surpassed the most optimistic expectations. The following reasons may be cited as being at the root of this constructive attitude :

There is a sense of order and dislike of anarchy inherent in the Turkish people, which is also shared by the workers. This may be attributed to a long period of organized and disciplined life under government authority. The workers also realized that they were not a strong group numerically and that people in general had strong doubts about the consequences of the right to strike. So they felt that they had to handle the new rights "with utmost care" to allay fears and win over public sympathy.

TÜRK-İŞ launched, with the help of several international organizations, an extensive program of education and training in union leadership early in 1962. This program included lectures and seminars not only on the professional and technical aspects of trade unionism and collective bargaining, but also on economic subjects as well, such as development plans, productivity, management, the Common Market, etc. As a result, although the great majority of trade union leaders did not receive formal education beyond elementary school, the average labor leader in Turkey is probably better informed on economic matters than the average educated citizen. He is, therefore, too conscious of the country's economic problems to advance irresponsible demands. Moreover, the new labor rights were granted before social dissatisfaction reached the breaking point, and even before the injustice in the distribution of national income (which became more marked during the inflationary period that preceded the Revolution) had frozen into deep-seated social resentment and class hatred. The workers, therefore, were not irrevocably alienated from the system.

The new Constitution was a great asset for workers. So they felt that they could afford temperance, and even gain by it, as long as the Government and Parliament honored the Constitution as they did. The con-

---

[1] See *Türkiye İşçi Sendikaları Konfederasyonu, Nedir, Ne Yapar, Nasıl Çalışır* TÜRK-İŞ Publication No. 23 (Ankara, 1964), p. 8.

sequence of all these developments was the establishment of good relations between the Government and the trade unions. TÜRK-İŞ was consulted in the preparation of the Five-Year Development Plan, and was actually invited to participate in the preparation of new labor legislation, as was the employers' organization. Experience showed that union leaders had valuable advice to offer for the protection of national industries. These leaders, together with the representatives of the private sector, are part of the committee which advises the government in establishing import and export policies. Quarterly meetings were held after 1962 between the Cabinet Ministers concerned and labor union representatives. Apart from questions of direct interest to workers, general social, economic, and political problems were discussed in these meetings.

A law on the reorganization of the state enterprises passed in 1964 included provisions for the workers' comanagement and profit sharing. According to these provisions, workers would elect their own representatives to the management boards and committees. They would also be entitled to 10 percent of the annual profits and would be given bonuses according to the increase in productivity or the reduction in the cost of production to be achieved through their suggestions or efforts. The managers, even those in the private sector, although the bill concerned only the state enterprises, reacted strongly to the enactment of these provisions. But trade unions gave their solid backing to the bill. Encouraged by the positive results stemming from cooperation and consultation with labor, the Government proposed in February 1965 to set up a permanent committee composed of government, labor, and employers' representatives. The aim of the committee was to harmonize collective agreements with actual economic conditions prevailing in the country and with the social and economic principles of the development plan. It was stressed that this mixed committee should not be empowered to impose restrictions on the lawful rights of the trade unions, of workers, or of employers. The committee was not formally established.

Turkish workers in general may be said to lack class consciousness. They regard themselves as an occupational group rather than a separate class. There are historical and structural reasons for this. Turkish society was never divided by deep-rooted class differences based on wealth. Presumably the idea of a "classless society" was at the root of the populist movement of Atatürk as well. Certain provisions in the new labor legislation, such as comanagement and profit sharing in the state enterprises, or the possibilities given to workers and their unions to become entrepreneurs in their own right, may help to enhance the development of a classless society, or, at least, of a society where class differences do not go beyond the level of occupational differences. Other reasons for the lack of class consciousness among workers may be the survival of the village culture. Many workers are still partly peasants. Quite a large number are seasonal workers and spend a part of the year in rural societies where class distinction or even occupational differences are practically nonexistent. (See addendum, at end of this chapter, on DİSK, a class-oriented trade union opposed to TÜRK-İŞ.)

Recent legislation has given labor unions great power and importance as well as heavy responsibility. Their work and financial means have increased, resulting in the formation of well-rooted professional union leadership. Trade union leaders and officials, in general, are now better paid than the average government official. All these factors have contributed to raise the workers' social status and have had salutary effects on the psychology of workers as well. Seeing their elected representatives mix freely and on an equal footing with managers and high ranking government officials, workers have acquired a greater sense of importance and self-respect.

The law on collective bargaining does not authorize the negotiation of contracts which would take into consideration the categories and ranks of employees. It has also drawn only a vague line of distinction between the employees' and the employers' representatives. Consequently, white-collar workers can benefit from the right of collective agreement only by acting together with the manual workers employed in the same work branch. One can hardly distinguish workers from managers during negotiation sessions. It is for these reasons that feelings of social difference or superiority among the managerial, white-collar, or manual workers have been decreasing considerably.

There is some dissatisfaction on this account among the employees of higher rank in certain branches of employment, such as officers on ships or foremen in the mines. But this is largely due to fear that their authority might be impaired if their employment conditions were subject to the same collective agreements as their subordinates, who, because of their larger number, dominate the unions.

The mobility among social classes is becoming even more marked as a result of Turkish workers' employment in West European countries. The workers abroad have an opportunity to save money and return home within a few years with a small capital of their own. Many a worker has thus achieved radical changes in his social status or occupation. Efforts to incite a class struggle in Turkey are up against this lack of class consciousness rooted in increased social mobility and opportunity for material advancement. There has been ample freedom of expression and discussion, even Marxist propaganda, in recent years, but communism has made very little headway in the Turkish labor movement.

Although the Turkish worker repudiates communism, he is not a champion of free enterprise. In fact, there is considerable pressure coming from labor for more nationalization in the economy. The Executive Committee of TÜRK-İŞ in the report to its Fifth Convention in Bursa in 1964, stated:

> We are against collectivism in the sense of concentrating all the capital in the hands of the State. Yet, it is a fact that private enterprise and the capital movement that it motivates, do not correspond to the requirements necessary for the development of labor life...We, therefore, believe that the sterile economic structure which makes excessive profits possible in a short time out of little money [originally invested] should be changed.[1]

The Confederation and several unions have demanded total or partial nationalization of the oil and mines industries and of foreign trade. In their view, the oil companies prefer to sell their own imported oil rather than discover new deposits in Turkey, while the coal mine operators in particular use wasteful methods in the exploitation of land resources and pay low wages, often after long delays. The pressure for the nationalization of foreign trade reflects a widely shared philosophy among labor leaders that fortunes in foreign trade are made without contributing directly and materially to the development of industry and of the national economy in general.

Labor leaders argue that if foreign trade remains in private hands it would facilitate tax evasion, waste foreign currency, lead to illegal transactions, and lower the value of certain domestic crops in international markets. They claim that private importers bring in goods already manufactured in Turkey, and thus hamper the development of Turkish industry. They also claim that a large share of the export profits should go to the producers rather than to the intermediaries and exporters, and be used for investment at home.

The following excerpt from a speech by Halil Tunç, Secretary-General of TÜRK-İŞ, who launched the campaign for the nationalization of foreign trade, should help to demonstrate the reasoning behind this trend:

---

[1] *Türkiye İşçi Sendikaları Konfederasyonu Beşinci Genel Kurula Sunulan İdari ve Mali Raporlar* (Bursa, 1964), pp. 5-6.

We claim that the foreign trade sector, in its present shape, is a sector that does not serve the interest of the public and hampers our development. The concept of freedom of trade which is not in the interest of the public is incompatible with our Constitution...We claim that we need capital, but our foreign trade regime does not facilitate the accumulation of capital. On the contrary, it provides a channel for smuggling away capital...We claim that the existing foreign trade regime hampers our industrialization. All the measures taken have failed to protect our national industry against the damaging effects of unnecessary imports. Importers have always managed to find ways for bringing in goods which are already manufactured in the country, thus creating hardships for our national industry. We would have hoped to see our industrialists become aware of where their own interests lie and stand forth in defense of their own products...We claim that...since it is obvious [from so many examples] that conditions would force us increasingly towards enlarging the state's role in foreign trade, we should go ahead with the nationalization of this sector in a rational manner, rather than leave it to pressures and coincidences...This would naturally not be a cause for joy for people who earn millions with their investments which consist of a room with a desk and two armchairs.[1]

Such views and reasoning, regardless of whether one approves or disapproves of them, should be considered as proof of the labor leaders' capacity to relate the workers' problems to broader issues and treat them within a broad national context. For instance, although trade union leaders realized that workers faced certain risks in speeding up Turkey's acceptance in the Common Market, TÜRK-İŞ has not only supported this but also exerted special effort to secure the backing of West European labor circles for Turkey's admission into this organisation. During the peak of the Cyprus crisis in 1964, TÜRK-İŞ asked the member unions to suspend all strikes. Allegations of "betrayal of the workers' interests" by extreme leftist circles were disregarded by the Confederation.

The demands for nationalization do not stem from a doctrinaire conviction but rather pragmatic reasoning. Though workers on the whole are much happier with working conditions in the state industries, they have never expressed any wish for a total nationalization of industry. In fact, trade unions even suggested tax exemptions to encourage Turkish or foreign private investment in industry.[2] Workers realize that the limitation imposed on freedom of enterprise beyond a certain point might endanger democracy and that, without democracy, the newly

---

[1] Press bulletin by TÜRK-İŞ (n.d.).

[2] Resolutions to this effect were accepted by the Fifth Congress of TÜRK-İŞ in 1964. *TÜRK-İŞ Information Bulletin* Ankara, February 1965, p. 6.

gained labor rights could not survive. But there is no doubt that labor support for freedom of entreprise in industry is born from pragmatic considerations rather than principles.

The reticence shown by labor toward private enterprises and the preference for state enterprises stem from practical considerations. Working conditions in the state enterprises are generally better than in private establishments. Although wages are not always higher, in fact they are sometimes even lower than in private enterprises, the fringe benefits offered by state enterprises are extensive. Human relations, although not ideal, ar also usually better in the state enterprises. Furthermore, in a democracy such as Turkey's, workers can exert more direct political pressure, through parties and government offices, on the state enterprises than on private establishments.

There is an even deeper reason than all these for the Turkish workers' preference for state enterprises. A long tradition of independence and lack of aristocracy and serfdom and hence class consciousness under Ottoman rule has imbued society with an aversion toward serving others. But, again, because of the absence of a long tradition of nationhood and the customary downgrading of business (this attitude began disappearing only after the Republic), association with the state, even at the lowest level of service, has come to be regarded as dignified.

These attitudes may change gradually as better human relations prevail in private enterprises, and as more joint-stock companies emerge, thus giving the worker the feeling that he is serving an anonymous, but superior, entity rather than just another individual. Comanagement and profit sharing would also help to change the workers' negative attitude toward private enterprise, but, as yet, hardly any Turkish entrepreneur has warmed up to this idea.

TÜRK-İŞ has had an important role in conditioning labor's political attitudes. The organization has adopted as a guiding principle the idea of not becoming involved in party politics. A joint statement by Seyfi Demirsoy, President, and Halil Tunç, Secretary General of TÜRK-İŞ, at a press conference 19 April, 1965, illustrates, partly at least, the pragmatic reasoning behind this principle :

> What line should the labor movement of Turkey follow in the field of politics? We would like to explain the position of TÜRK-İŞ on this matter. There are mainly two views on this subject. According to one, workers cannot obtain the rights they want unless they are represented in the Parliament. Therefore, the labor movement should try to obtain seats in the Parliament either by effectively establishing a party of its own, or by supporting, from

among those that are already established, a party which they regard as the closest to themselves. Those who hold the opposite view claim that, by putting pressure on the governments and the Parliament with the full force of the masses that it represents, the labor movement should try to promote the rights of the workers in the best possible way and to press for such solutions to the problems of the country as would comply with the principles of labor unions. Both views may have advantages and disadvantages. But while discussing this issue, one should keep in mind the structure of the country and of the labor movement. Turkish labor has studied the issue at great length during its convention held in Bursa last year and the conclusion it reached has become part of its Regulations. The second paragraph of Article 3 of our Regulations, concerning "basic aims and principles" states that "Unless a joint decision has been taken by a committee consisting of the Executive Committee, the Management Committee and one representative from every member organization, TÜRK-İŞ is to preserve its full independence and follow a policy above the parties"...It is obvious that if TÜRK-İŞ cooperates at present with any one party in the elections its growth will be slowed down and may even deteriorate. By remaining above parties thus far TÜRK-İŞ has been able to speed up the development of the Turkish labor movement and secured new rights for workers. Its views on national problems have come to be regarded as indispensable...If the opposite course had been followed and TÜRK-İŞ had supported any one party, could the Turkish labor movement have reached its present position of strength and solidarity? [1]

However, the Confederation, under various influences, has thought twice, in 1962 and 1964, about establishing a party of its own, but such a party could not officially be associated with the Confederation, because the Trade Unions Act stipulates in Article 16, under the heading "Prohibition of Carrying on Political Activities," that trade unions

shall not accept any financial aid from any political party, or organization attached to such a party; that they shall not give financial aid to or join such a political party or organization.

The same article adds that a trade union cannot bear the name of a party.

These are the only legal restrictions preventing the trade unions from engaging in political activity.[2] They do not prevent the Confederation or any union from unofficially identifying itself with a political party. Yet, the Confederation has abstained from political activity. The practical reasons for this attitude may be found in a variety of circumstances. Many union members and leaders support different parties. Some of

---

[1] *TÜRK-İŞ Haber Bülteni*, April 19, 1965, pp. 1-2.

[2] The restrictions on this point were much more extensive in the old law that was abolished on July 24, 1963. It prevented the unions from engaging in politics, in political propaganda, or in publications of a political nature (Law No. 5018, Article 5, February 27, 1947).

them are active members of these parties. Efforts to gather them all under one party might result in the disintegration of some unions and even of the Confederation.

Even if many leaders and workers could be enrolled in a new party of their own, political rivalries within the party itself would create factions in the trade unions and endanger labor unity and strength.

Workers are too small a group numerically and thus unable to acquire power through their own party even if that party could draw some support from nonlabor circles. Even if it won power, such a party might soon be controlled by nonlabor elements.

The existing parties tend to compete with each other for the workers' votes. The labor movement has greatly benefited from this competition through the clever tactics and successful lobbying of the Confederation. But if workers had their own party they could no longer rely on such competition since they might then be treated as a rival political group by the other parties. Last, but not least, the top labor leaders, as some of them have openly confessed recently, do not yet have sufficient confidence in the political wisdom of workers in general. Many of them have loyalties divided between their old party and their newly awakening labor consciousness and interest.

Indeed, the majority of workers voted for the Democratic Party in the past, although this party did not grant them the promised rights and freedoms. Even after the Revolution, many workers voted for parties with which the labor movement differed on social and economic matters. But such contradictions between ideology, interest, and allegiance are common in society. Differences between parties on social and economic policy have come to the fore only in recent years. Consequently political attitudes and social and economic convictions and interests have not yet fully coalesced. There seems to be a growing awareness among workers about the contradictions between their political attachments and their social and economic convictions and interests. This is a period of transition. The Confederation believes that at the present time the best political strategy is to loosen the party allegiances of workers by strengthening their attachment to the unions and to union ideals and objectives.

In order to implement this strategy, the Confederation and several affiliated unions and federations have expressed their opinion on social, economic, and political problems not only on matters of direct concern to workers but also on national problems, and have successfully rallied workers around these opinions.

The Confederation has also been tabulating the voting of individual members of Parliament on various matters, and issued its own platform during elections with the implicit purpose of inducting the workers to use their votes to their own advantage. These efforts have increased considerably the trade unions' influence among workers, political parties, and the public in general.

The Turkish labor movements' political thinking has certainly been developing along socialistic lines. But it is not a militant or doctrinaire socialism. It is rational, pragmatic, and democratic. This stands in contrast to the rigid, dogmatic socialism prevailing in some intellectual circles of Turkey. Indeed, these extremist intellectual circles seem to become increasingly disillusioned with labor's conciliatory policies. In a joint press conference held on 19 April 1965, the President and the Secretary General of TÜRK-İŞ, issued the following statement as a reaction to the pressures from these circles:

> There are many people who attack the policy of TÜRK-İŞ. The increasing strength of TÜRK-İŞ, or, to be more exact, of the Turkish labor movement, is a source of anxiety for certain circles. TÜRK-İŞ is subjected to continuous suggestions and provocations to adopt a different policy...to create trouble at the smallest opportunity, to turn incidents into clashes, and to keep tension in the country at a high level. What would such a policy bring to the country and to the Turkish labor movement? It should be admitted that, up to a certain extent, such actions may ostensibly add some strength to the labor movement. But one need not be a prophet to foresee the harm that would be inflicted on the country by living continuously in a state of tension. As a result, the labor movement would be derailed and disintegrated.
>
> Who are the people trying to push TÜRK-İŞ into such a course and for what purpose? These people fall into two categories. On one side, there are the people who believe, in good faith, that such a course of action would strengthen the labor movement, making it more capable to obtain rights ...We are convinced that such people of good faith will eventually subscribe to our policy as they observe its successful results. In the second category there are those who wish to weaken TÜRK-İŞ, to divide the labor movement, and to see the unions become too frail to defend the workers' rights. Their objective is to prepare the ground every day [for their own power, ostensibly by] defending workers' rights and by promising to solve the country's problems. They will fall short of their own objectives. Every new law issued or decision taken, giving added protection to labor's rights, is a source of dismay for them. Only workers witout unions or with weak unions, workers with no rights and defenseless against exploitation, can serve these people's purpose of creating the suitable atmosphere for a revolution.[1]

The labor movement in general, and the Confederation in particular, have been under strong and direct pressure from the Turkish (Workers')

---

[1] *TÜRK-İŞ Haber Bülteni* April 19, 1965, pp. 2-3.

Labor Party. This small party, established in 1961, has a doctrinaire attitude and extreme leftist views, especially on the question of classes, and has more following among intellectuals than among workers. This party's efforts to identify itself with the labor movement and to gain control of the Confederation failed. Consequently, some of the leaders and supporters of this party took an increasingly hostile attitude toward the Confederation, accusing it publicly of betraying the labor cause, of being a stooge of American capitalism or of the Government.[1] (See addendum at end of this chapter on DİSK.) The Confederation usually disregarded such accusations. But recently it retaliated with counteraccusations, particularly on the occasion of incidents at Zonguldak.[2] These were incited by leaders of the Labor Party (including a union leader who was both the Secretary General of the party and a member of the Executive Committee of TÜRK-İŞ) who urged the workers to use force and, if necessary, even to come to blows with the Army. Criticising the Government for its mishandling of the Zonguldak incident, TÜRK-İŞ also attacked the Turkish Labor (Workers') Party :

> Various members of the Turkish Workers' Party have sought to make capital out of the tragic events in the Zonguldak area and have [lowered themselves] to the level of making use of these incidents to promote their own party interests.... TÜRK-İŞ unequivocally states that it will strenuously oppose any political party that attempts to use industrial unrest as a means for achieving political advantage, and gives due warning that any party so inadvised as to pursue such a course will meet the implacable opposition of the Confederation of Turkish Trade Unions.[3]

These counteraccusations have caused a legal investigation into the

---

[1] This accusation alludes to an agreement for technical assistance between TÜRK-İŞ and Agency for International Development (A.I.D.).

[2] In March 1965, soon after a new Government headed by Suat Hayri Ürgüplü and formed jointly by the Justice Party, the Republican National Peasant Party, the Nation Party, and the New Turkey Party had taken over, there was a widespread, unlawful strike in the government operated coal mines of Zonguldak. The authorities panicked and made the mistake of calling in the army. Two workers were killed and several others, as well as some soldiers and engineers, were wounded. It was the first time in the history of the Turkish Republic that blood was shed in the labor movement. The main causes of the unlawful strike were possibly poor human relations, and lack of sufficient communication with workers. Workers were allegedly misinformed about the way a bonus was to be distributed and this was exploited by a small number of provocateurs.

[3] *TÜRK-İŞ Information Bulletin* March 1965. See copy available in English entitled "The Statement of the Confederation of Turkish Trade Unions."

activities of the Turkish Workers' Party, and brought demands from the rightist circles, which were represented in the coalition government at that time, for the suppression of that party.[1] The incident deepened the cleavage between the leftist intellectuals and the labor movement. Many leftist intellectuals do not appreciate that the Turkish Confederation of Labor Unions represents the first leftist movement in Turkey coming directly from the people, and that this movement owes its success, effectiveness, and acceptability to its solidly democratic convictions and methods, to its pragmatic attitude, and its sense of responsibility and restraint.

The Confederation, and the labor unions in general, have played an important part in supporting social reforms and explaining the real nature and need for these reforms to the masses, to the uneducated, to the exploited, and to the poor, who would be the chief beneficiaries.[2]

---

[1] Under the new Constitution (Article 57), however, a party can be closed only by a decision of the Constitutional Court.

[2] The following excerpts from statements or declarations by the President and the responsible bodies of *TÜRK-İŞ* best illustrate these points: "Reforms to be undertaken by the Government should be supported by the Turkish workers. In principle, workers' organizations support progressive movements. The Government's proposal for land reform, for instance, has made us as happy as the Turkish peasants and the landless agricultural workers....It is essential for the future prosperity of Turkey that an equitable system of taxation be introduced and it is for this reason that we, the Turkish trade union movement, wholeheartedly support the tax reforms proposed by the Government. It is our considered opinion that unless these proposed reforms are speedily introduced there is the danger of the 'ship of state' foundering in the economic storms that lie ahead." *TÜRK-İŞ Information Bulletin* February 1965, p. 1.

From a declaration by TÜRK-İŞ, protesting the rejection by the parliamentary majority of a proposal to set up a mixed committee to secure the speedy discussion of the Land Reform Bill: "We strongly protest, in the name of the Turkish workers, this negative attitude on such a vital issue as land reform. As stated in the Development Plan, land reform is one of the prerequisites of our development. The objectives of increasing the productivity of our soil which, at present, fails to feed the people, of enabling the agricultural sector to provide sufficient support to our industrialization, of regulating the anarchic immigration of people to the cities because of hunger, of struggling effectively with the problems of unemployment and underemployment and of realizing social justice, can only be achieved with the speedy application of effective land and agricultural reform. To reject the land reform, therefore, means rejecting the development of the country and the realization of social justice. Those who volunteer for the defense of a handful of big land owners, despising the suffering of the millions who are landless or with too little land, will bear all the responsibility for the restlessness and tension arising from hunger for land...The Turkish workers will be mobilized to make it known to the people that those who oppose land reform

The intellectuals largely failed for four decades to communicate to the masses the philosophy and justification of the reform movement of Atatürk. The Turkish labor organizations have become the spearhead of this movement among the masses. They have helped to demonstrate that the masses, the ordinary and uneducated people in Turkey, were not reactionary and not responsible for retarded progress and social reforms. It showed that the "progressive" intellectuals were unable to establish communication with the masses, that the educated or partly educated reactionary elements and interest groups had deceived and misguided the masses.

The Turkish labor movement may gain new impetus as a social and political force with the return of the workers from Western Europe. Since the Revolution of 1960, people have been allowed to work abroad. More than 200,000 have already taken advantage of this opportunity. This new movement helps to relieve Turkey's problems of unemployment and underemployment and the shortage of foreign exchange.[1] The people and employers of the host countries, in general, are highly satisfied with the honesty, discipline, industriousness, ability to learn, and the adaptability of Turkish workers. The technical ability and the degree of adaptability to a new way of life demonstrated by these workers appears more interesting if one considers the fact that the great majority of them were peasants. They came into contact with technology and urban life for the first time in their lives in the highly industrialized West European countries.

Thus, for the first time, people outside the limited elite circles and the army are coming into direct contact with Western culture and civilization. They have better opportunities than the elite to penetrate and acquire the outlook, the living and working habits of Western societies. For workers share the daily life and labor of ordinary people in those countries, whereas the elite, who have been going abroad mostly as

are the representatives, not of the Turkish Nation, but of a handful of big landowners." *TÜRK-İŞ Haber Bülteni*, (February 1965).

[1] West Germany, Belgium, Holland, Switzerland and Austria are the chief countries that recruit Turkish workers. An agreement has recently been signed with France also. Apart from these countries, some Turkish workers are also employed in Sweden, although there is no official agreement between this country and Turkey on labor exchange. In 1964, the British Railways Hotels started recruiting a small number of Turkish workers. See Nermin Abadan, *Almnaya'da Türk İşçileri* (Ankara, 1965). A small number went to Australia. Presently (1973) the total number of Turkish workers in West Europe is about 600,000. The remittance from abroad has solved Turkey's chronic foreign currency deficit. Early in 1973 the foreign currency reserves of Turkey were close to one billion dollars. KH.K.

tourists, government officials, businessmen, or students, can, as a rule establish only limited contacts and form superficial impressions.

Turks who spend several years abroad as workers learn by firsthand experience that the social, economic, or fiscal measures regarded as radical innovations at home are just part of democratic human rights. They realize, for instance, that taxes are not too high in Turkey, even after the recent reforms; that without a social policy entailing certain sacrifices and limitations the housing problem cannot be solved; that Westernization does not necessarily mean moral debasement; and, although more intensive communist propaganda is directed to them, they became more consciously anticommunist by realizing that labor and human rights and the prosperity of workers can best be promoted in a democracy.

They are also learning the value of big business as opposed to small, individual enterprise. Although the average Turk is rather shy of joining business enterprises or of becoming a shareholder in an enterprise, Turkish workers abroad have already started buying shares in the few large joint-stock companies at home or are pooling their savings to start such companies on their own. A proposal to establish such a company to undertake industrial projects in Turkey, in which the workers abroad could become shareholders and would have priority for enrollment as employers when they return home, has met with great enthusiasm.

Contacts with Western trade unions after 1960 were also conducive to a widening of the outlook of the Turkish labor movement. Although the International Conference of Free Trade Unions (I.C.F.T.U.) had long extended TÜRK-İŞ an invitation to membership, the Democratic Party governments did not permit TÜRK-İŞ to accept this invitation. It was only after the Revolution that permission was granted by the Revolutionary Government and thus TÜRK-İŞ became a member of this international body.

Since then, several national unions and federations have also affiliated themselves with their international counterparts within the I.C.F.T.U. The new Trade Unions Act give the unions the right to join international organizations without prior permission from the Government. The Law states, however, that a Turkish trade union cannot join an international organization whose activities are not compatible with the democratic principles of the Turkish Constitution and the principles of democratic unionism. The Government can annul membership in such an organization. The Turkish union concerned can, in turn, appeal to the independent Council of State against such an annulment.

The new Trade Unions Act also allows trade unions to accept aid from the international organizations to which they are affiliated. They are required to obtain prior permission from the Government only for foreign aid other than that provided by international organizations. Such permissions have been granted to TÜRK-İŞ for receiving aid from the International Labor Organization (I.L.O.), the Organization for Economic Cooperation and Development (O.E.C.D.), and the Agency for International Development (A.I.D.).

Contact and cooperation with various international organizations have provided Turkish trade unions with not only additional financial resources, which are mostly utilized for education, but also with the opportunity to learn from the experiences of others. The impact of contacts with international democratic labor organizations was evident in the political attitude and social and economic thinking of the labor movement in Turkey. The following quotation from the joint press conference of TÜRK-İŞ leaders illustrates it best:

There are two different kinds of unionism in the world. One kind of unionism aims at eradicating capitalism by completely paralyzing the industry and changing the structure of the economy with revolutionary methods. With this aim in mind, it makes use of every opportunity to create clashes between the workers and the security forces or to organize unlawful marches or public meetings. It has been observed that such a policy eventually weakens the trade unions and results in the regression of workers' rights. Such a policy, which always harms the workers, is repudiated by the international movement of free trade unionism. The unions which adhere to the second kind of unionism, try to take a place in the forefront of the forces protecting the democratic order, and to achieve social justice in the full sense of the term by taking a close and active interest in the social and economic life of the country. Every problem concerning social justice is a cause for struggle for such unions. For instance, it is their unflagging objective to secure a fair distribution of the national income, a fair taxation system and the most productive exploitation of the national resources in the interests of the nation. They want to have their word on every subject of interest to the nation, and they want to participate in every effort aiming at the development of the country. These are principles upheld by the international movement of free trade unionism. In developing countries, trade unions have to regard it as their chief duty to be actively interested in the problems of the country, while fulfilling their obligation to struggle for themselves. This is the only way in which they can both serve the country and raise the living standards of the masses which they represent. This is the path that the Turkish trade union movement has chosen—the path upheld by the international movement of free trade unionism.[1]

---

[1] *TÜRK-İŞ Haber Bülteni* April 1 1965, p. 1.

Conclusion

The reestablishment of democracy in Turkey on a sounder basis after the Revolution of 1960, the social rights introduced and guaranteed by the new Constitution, and the new atmosphere of freedom have provided fertile ground for the rapid development of a free and democratic labor movement in Turkey in recent years.

Mr. Omar Becu, Secretary General of the I.C.F.T.U., who visited Turkey in 1965, stated in a lecture delivered in Ankara that nowhere else in the world had free trade unionism developed so rapidly and soundly as in Turkey during these few years. This healthy development in the labor movement made possible by the democratization of Turkey, has contributed, in turn, to the strengthening of democracy in Turkey. Trade unions are now among the chief bulwarks of democracy in Turkey and they enable democracy to function on a broader basis with extensive direct participation of the people.

Developments in the labor field were also enhanced by the growing awareness among citizens of the country's social and economic problems. The labor movement, in turn, played a vital role in harnessing this awareness into a rational and constructive course of action. If it were not for the labor movement's policy of moderation and pragmatic, democratic social welfare, and if it were not for the tangible results that trade unions have obtained through such a policy, extremist ideologies would have swept away Turkish democracy and prevented healthy and promising social and economic development.

Workers in Turkey have become aware that without real democracy free trade unionism cannot exisist and many people have already realized that democracy cannot function properly and cannot be sufficiently secure without a free trade-union movement.

Addendum Concerning Labor Developments in Turkey

DİSK (Devrimci İşçi Sendikaları Konfederasyonu, "Confederation of Revolutionary Trade Unions") a socialist trade union confederation, was established on February 12, 1967, by a group of labor leaders who had resigned from Türk-İş. These represented the left wing of Türk-İş, and many had close ties with the Labor Party. Some of these leaders occupied important positions in the party, until it was abolished in 1971.

DİSK claimed that its parent organization had neglected the workers' rights and interests, had ignored its own by-laws and collaborated with each government in power. It appears that the conflict between Türk-İş and DİSK's founders came into the open after the elections of 1965. A number of trade unionists became candidates for the Justice Party, which won the elections, and subsequently occupied important positions in the administration of Türk-İş. Thus, the conflict between the Labor Party and the Justice Party was reflected in the trade-union movement. Moreover, Türk-İş, according to DİSK, ceased to be a national-minded organization since it depended heavily on U.S. subsidies (AID funds) and promoted American viewpoints. Consequently, in order to protect the workers' rights, DİSK proposed to conduct an independent struggle to end exploitation and to establish social justice through the workers' direct participation in the administration of the country. DİSK placed high priority on economic development to be achieved through industrialization. An organized, united, and politically conscious labor class would assume the leadership in the struggle against backwardness and against those classes which kept society underdeveloped for their own interests.

DİSK aimed at securing the workers, through democratic methods, a share in the conduct of government. Consequently, it proposed to become first, a powerful professional organization, and assume the leadership of the entire labor movement. Then, it proposed to abolish all laws which were against labor interests, to assure the workers' participation in all organizations dealing with labor problems, and to compel these organizations to make decisions in accordance with the principles of DİSK.

Eventually DİSK became the champion of political action. It claimed that the workers' interests would be better protected not through collective contracts but by collective participation in political decisions. In fact, DİSK claimed that the real cause for the break with Türk-İş occurred because of disagreement over the question of participation in political activity. The founders of DİSK, echoing a viewpoint strongly advocated by the Labor Party, claimed that the trade unions could not remain above politics and political parties. Instead of waiting for the government to grant them their rights the workers should take their due by themselves. Consequently, it advocated the workers' direct participation in politics through their own organization, such as DİSK, and possibly through a political party. The basic purpose of DİSK was to assure the highest value for work, to give the workers leadership and political consciousness, and to create a trade union movement based on class consciousness.

The activities of DİSK have remained confined so far to a handful of trade unions, many of which were headed by the founders or by affiliates of the Labor Party. The total membership of DİSK is not known but it may be safely assumed that it has about 15,000 to 20,000 members. Its most powerful trade unions are in İstanbul. In the summer of 1970 DİSK organized a violent demonstration in Istanbul to protest an amendment to the existing legislation which would have undermined its recruitment of members. It created wide disturbances which were quelled only after martial law was established.

The leadership of DİSK derives not only from among trade unions but also intellectuals and professionals long associated with leftist causes and movements. The association with the Labor Party, though not formal, gives DİSK a certain ideological consistency in claiming to combine logically theory with action, but such intellectual subtleties do not seem to impress the pragmatically-oriented rank-and-file workers. Yet, the activities of DİSK, which diminished considerably after an initial upsurge, have forced Türk-İş to review some of its policies and to streamline its own organization and work towards becoming a better spokesman for Turkish labor—through a political revitalization. K.H.K.

Founders of Disk

Name	Birth Date	Trade-Union Affiliation	Party Affiliation
Kemal Türkler	1926	Metal Products Industry	Labor Party
Riza Kuas	1926	Rubber Industry	Labor Party
Mehmet Alpdündar	1928	Miners	Labor Party
Kemal Nebioğlu	1926	Food Industry	Labor Party
İbrahim Güzelce	1922	Press	Labor Party

APPENDIX

Table 4.1.

Number of Workers Affiliated with the Confederation of Trade Unions of Turkey (TÜRK-İŞ), 1960-1968

	IV Session 1960-1962	V Session 1962-1964	VI Session 1964-1966	VII Session 1966-1968
National Unions (*Türkiye tipi*)		138,266	184,264	234,614
Federations :				
DDY İş (Railroads)	15,205	15,337	30,000	30,100
Harb İş (Military installations)		11,157	29,271	17,950
Maden İş (Mining)	40,000	48,088	55,712	58,512
Metal İş (Metal)	3,950	8,545	14,580	14,715
Toleyiş (Hotels, restaurants)	3,950	920 [1]	8,865	7,370
Tes İş (Electric, water, gas)		1,271	7,207	15,064
Müskirat İş (Beverages)	15,763	33,081	41,338	29,532
Ulaş İş (Communication)			10,810	12,889
Yol İş (Roads)		10,100	19,800	34,197
Tif İş (Teksif) (Textile)		6,700		
Yapı İş (Construction)		4,2'0		
Directly affiliated Trade Unions	6,597	17,022		
United Trade Unions			10,028	
Local Unions	33,162			
Other Professional Federations	59,093			
Total [2]	173,770	294,697	411,975	544,943

[1] This figure has not been verified.

[2] This number doesn't include approximately 15,000-20,000 workers affiliated with DİSK (Confederation of Revolutionary Labor Unions), the socialist labor organization.

Sources: The General Reports of TÜRK-İŞ submitted to its General Conventions No. IV, V, VI, and VII.

Table 4.2

Employers' Unions, Workers' Trade Unions and Collective Bargaining Contracts Enacted

Years	Employers				Workers				Collective Contracts Enacted						
										Number of work places			Number of workers covered		
	Unions	Members	Federations	Confederations	Trade Unions	Members	Unions and Federations	Confederations	Number of contracts	State Sector	Private sector	Total	State Sector	Private Sector	Total
1960	33	1,150	—	—	432	282,967	27	1							
1961	35	1,706	1	—	511	299,676	28	1							
1962	47	1,820	1	—	543	307,839	36	1							
1963	78	1,605	2	1	665	295,710	26	1	96	29	127	156	3,494	5,978	9,472
1964	92	1,769	2	1	595	339,769	28	2	1,078	1,435	2,483	3,918	263,836	172,926	436,762
1965	104	1,927	2	1	658	360,285	29	2	871	1,113	1,741	2,854	121,700	49,109	170,809
1966	107	2,073	2	1	724	363,654	24	2	1,130	988	1,532	2,520	146,915	165,315	312,230
1967	104	4,075	3	1	798	834,680	18	3	741	554	607	1,161	45,380	52,461	97,841
1968*	110	6,338	3	1	747	834,580	23	3							

* Tentative, dating to 11/1/68. Some workers covered by contracts were not registered union members.
Source: An unpublished report by the State Statistical Institute.

Table 4.3. Labor Strikes 1963-1967

Industry	1963 No. of strikes	1963 No. of striking workers	1963 Lost working days	1964 No. of strikes	1964 No of striking workers	1964 Lost working days	1965 No. of strikes	1965 No. of striking workers	1965 Lost working days	1966 No. of strikes	1966 No. of striking workers	1966 Lost working days	1967 No. of strikes	1967 No. of striking workers	1967 Lost working days
Agriculture							1	85	1,020				1	86	2,064
Coal and mining							1	364	364	3	426	2,067	2	352	3,184
Petroleum	1	200	4,200										7	569	45,602
Food	1	6	6	49	568	34,511	10	96	7,249	2	208	443	27	140	1,416
Textiles				8	1,962	65,020	3	2,317	201,383				2	126	12,012
Leather							6	336	10,321						
Wood				3	352	9,504	9	44	819				1	60	12,000
Printing							2	94	480				1	7	80
Rubber, plastics	3	1,037	7,097	2	379	20,177	1	9	252	7	3,968	98,732			
Chemicals, drugs							1	1,004	40,160	1	12	12	1	95	1,995
Ceramics				2	300	1,370	1	351	11,020	14	123	492	1	83	10,873
Glass										1	2,400	199,200			
Cement							1	197	4,728				1	219	1,533
Metal products				8	1,810	65,463	1	212	10,812				4	226	9,633
Construction				4	711	22,513	3	326	1,564						
Masonry													6	350	5,529
Power										2	228	5,748			
Land transport													1	32	1,408
Storage													6	801	106,199
General work	1	204	4,080	4	711	22,513	2	206	5,397	1	61	2,318	11	1,532	38,419
Hotels, restaurants	2	53	4,076	1	192	4,032	1	132	132				1	821	7,389
Clerical				2	15	3,831							16	1,875	90,261
Publishing													1	27	5,967
Military installations										2	336	1,320			
Total	8	1,500	19,459	83	7,000	248,934	43	5,773	295,701	33	7,762	310.332	90	7,401	355,564

Source: An unpublished report by the State Statistical Institute.

LABOR IN TURKEY 179

Table 4.4

Average Wages for Workers Covered by Social Security in TL [1]

Work branches (industry)	1958	1959	1960	1961	1962	1963 [2]	1964	1965	1966	1967
Fishing	8.71	15.11	16.29	14.99	14.14	15.30	20.12	15.00	21.99	29.47
Coal mining	8.44	10.10	10.86	10.77	13.54	14.09	15.21	16.45	21.55	22.19
Extraction	8.86	10.93	11.86	13.25	12.82	14.93	16.80	18.22	21.09	22.60
Mining and quarrying	8.33	10.21	11.13	12.63	12.12	13.88	15.57	16.55	19.56	22.99
Manufacturing	10.86	13.17	14.11	14.88	15.73	17.21	19.07	20.66	22.66	24.75
Food industry	9.81	12.29	13.85	13.92	13.76	15.15	17.60	18.91	20.50	21.73
Tobacco	7.03	9.20	9.61	10.25	11.59	12.98	15.96	17.54	20.53	21.92
Textile	11.48	12.66	13.49	14.53	14.70	15.54	16.92	18.23	19.37	21.25
Printing	14.38	19.03	17.79	22.46	24.95	24.35	25.53	28.90	30.23	31.87
Chemicals, drugs	13.66	16.63	18.97	18.74	19.56	20.74	24.15	26.13	27.34	29.61
Metal products	14.36	19.62	18.11	18.39	19.14	20.64	20.73	22.67	23.33	25.31
Machine manufacture and maintenance	11.94	14.65	16.01	18.21	20.88	20.39	23.55	25.94	24.69	27.20
Vehicle industry	11.81	14.98	16.24	17.48	18.13	20.24	22.24	23.98	27.76	31.88
Construction	11.41	13.99	15.35	16.83	16.94	18.61	19.62	21.33	22.83	27.09
Electric, Gas, Water Installations	11.61	14.34	16.08	17.42	18.14	18.70	18.14	19.20	22.12	24.14
Trade	16.08	19.55	21.94	23.59	25.02	25.34	26.74	28.26	29.79	29.53
Communications	11.43	14.76	16.38	18.99	19.42	20.80	21.88	23.79	28.49	31.56
Services	11.84	14.62	16.28	17.86	19.05	20.63	23.25	24.95	25.99	27.57
Total Average	10.86	13.25	14.44	15.59	16.48	17.91	19.50	21.61	23.53	25.83

[1] $ 1 = TL 9. (1965) TL 14 (1973)

[2] Enactment of the Act on Collective Bargaining and Strikes.

Source: An unpublished report by the State Statistical Institute.

Table 4.5

Social Security and Minimum Wage

Years	Social Security Number of work places	Social Security Number of insured	Minimum Wage enforced Number of provinces	Minimum Wage enforced Number of work branches
1951	10,361	348,430	3	5
1952	16,132	384,359	5	7
1953	17,476	432,222	5	7
1954	18,418	449,212	6	7
1955	19,466	466,851	11	8
1956	21,402	506,527	20	15
1957	23,284	530,392	29	18
1958	24,733	550,135	38	33
1959	25,558	555,746	39	37
1960	31,919	778,034	44	41
1961	36,568	611,901	44	45
1962	40,426	639,279	47	49 [1]
1963	46,310	670,196	49	38
1964	51,443	680,074	51	39
1965	73,020	822,686	51	39
1966	127,687	894,529	63	41
1967	171,972	973,055		

[1] Agricultural branches were separately indicated : incorporated in other branches in the following years.

Sources : Unpublished report by the State Statistical Institute.

CHAPTER FIVE

THE INTEGRATION OF THE VILLAGER INTO
THE NATIONAL LIFE OF TURKEY

John Kolars

Introduction

The history of social and economic development in Turkey has been told largely in terms of the urban foci around which the national identity is organized. That this has been the case is logical. Unlike many developing countries Turkey has for centuries contained a great crossroads metropolis, Istanbul, with a resident administrative cadre and intelligentsia. The geographic focus of power has shifted in recent times from Istanbul to Ankara, but without affecting the continuing presence of an urbanite core which has initiated reform movements involving the economy, society, and political structure of the nation. The history of modernization in Turkey has always centered on one or the other of its two major cities with ancillary events occuring in a few other places. The city has led; the country followed.

But any explanation or description of contemporary development in Turkey that confines itself to the limits of the larger cities begs two fundamental questions : what is the nature of the reciprocal relationship between the urbanized minority and the vast, rural proletariat? And what is the role of the villager in the changes which have and are taking place? When faced with such questions, observers hardly know where to begin. Each discusses those aspects of the problem which interest him most, the result being phrased in economic or sociological or political terms relating to the country as a whole. Meanwhile, the historian points out that the political territory recognized by the Ottomans of Istanbul was far different areally and ethnically from that important to contemporary Ankara Turks. The peasants of Anatolia who are the majority of today's Turkish citizens were but one group among many during the Empire. A problem of comparability thus arises which can be avoided only in part by the approach one selects. The choice of the "contemporary Turkish villager" as the topic for this discussion eliminates the other subjects of the Ottomans, but the question of the relationship between Anatolian peasant and Istanbul or Ankara cosmopolite remains.

One may even ask if before Atatürk such a relationship existed. It is in reference to this point that we may gain new insight concerning the nature of development in Turkey. Originally, participation in the effective social and political (if not economic) community of the Empire required in almost all cases residence in Istanbul. Those with origins beyond the great city had little chance of entering elite society as representatives of their particular regions. In some special cases the sons of country folk educated in the military, administrative, or religious establishments in the city found success and high position among the Ottomans. But they were grafts on the trunk of the body politic and never served as representatives of constituencies back home. To be a peasant was to remain anonymous.

Since the foundation of the First Republic, qualification for participation in the affairs of the nation-state has been defined increasingly by Turkish citizenship. Thus men of humble background and provincial residence can aspire to elected and appointed government positions. Similarly, the state has more and more concerned itself with the total population, both urban and rural. It is this increasing integration of government and populace that differentiates Turkey from the Ottoman Empire.

The Development of the Nation-State in Turkey as the Growth of Effective Space

Modern societies concentrate themselves in cities, but even in cities the geometry of life demands some distribution of people. Man's space-occupying characteristics become even more apparent when rural populations engaged in the manipulation of soil, water, and biotic resources are considered. Such phenomena are distributed across wide areas, and an essentially rural, agricultural society such as Turkey's must live in patterns of dispersed settlement in order to optimize their access to the resources upon which they depend. Thus, when urban and rural populations are plotted on maps at scales capable of showing entire nations, cities with their political, administrative, economic, and esthetic functions and the groups of people responsible for them appear as points, while agrarian elements of the society occupy wide areas.

The problem of development can thus be stated in topological terms involving the effective arrangement, integration, and interaction of these point and area elements in spatial systems. A third element in such systems is the various lines of communication linking the first two. The more complete and efficient the linkages and the greater the integrated area, the more modern the character of the nation. The integration of the villager into the national life of Turkey when discussed in these terms is more easily comprehended and, in turn, the growth of Turkey as an effective nation-state becomes more clear.

This idea, which may be thought of as the growth of "effective space" [1] within the political boundaries of a nation, warrants a brief review before making use of such an approach in the remainder of the discussion. John Friedmann, a major proponent of this idea, describes it as an approach to the study of developing nations based upon the morphology of growth. Development implies not only the breakdown of traditional patterns of behavior but the creation of new systems which through their increased efficiency allow the release of latent energy and the attainment of new goals.

This simple fact of social dynamics is clearly perceived by the great national leaders of today whose countries are submerged in just such a process of disruption through forces both from outside and within. These leaders are facing up to the immensely difficult task of welding a diversity of limited interests into a national whole. They have to struggle with problems of language, custom, value-orientation, political structure, economic dualism, and the like. By comparison, and we mention this only parenthetically, the problems of savings and capital formation appear to be of relative minor importance, to belong rather to a sub-category of problems than to the core of the problem itself. For to a considerable extent, the solution of economic problems is dependent upon the simultaneous if not prior solution of the general problem of social integration.[2]

Traditional societies are integrated at the family or village level; developed nations are integrated socially, politically, and economically at the national level. Wherever development occurs, the pattern of change brings about a shift from integrated areas bounded by village or regional limits to those encompassed by the boundaries of the nation. Dualism, so common to the developing world, is overcome and national values are substituted for regional preferences. In this manner, larger and larger portions of the national area are eventually drawn into a single system with the development of the state.

---

[1] John Friedmann, "Integration of the Social System: An Approach to the Study of Economic Growth," *Diogenes* 36 (Spring 1961), pp. 75-97.
Ibid., "Cities in Social Transformation," *Regional Development and Planning*, J. Friedmann and Wm. Alonso, eds. (Cambridge: 1964), pp. 343-60.

[2] Friedmann, "Integration," p. 79.

Four kinds of space may be considered as subject to the integrative processes of development. These are social, political, economic, and geographic in character. While the first three spaces are abstract in nature, they find expression in the fourth. Cities initiate development and act as foci of control while serving as well as the transformers by which external influences are interpreted and eventually channeled into rural areas. Thus, development begins both in time and space at the center and spreads outward to the provinces. It is this outward movement of new ideas, new technology, and new systems of organization from urban core areas where interaction and integration are greatest that epitomizes the process of development.

When the concept of effective space is combined with the idea of urban foci linked to rural areas by various communication media, a systematic analysis of the integration of the villager into the national life of Turkey becomes possible. A well developed "hierarchy of urban places represents the ultimate means of organizing a geographic area into its component social, political-administrative, and economic spaces." [1]

Such an analysis for Turkey can be divided into two parts. The first deals with the growth of effective space as it reflects increasing control and integration of the Turkish hinterland by city-centered elements of change. The second approaches the same process from the point of view of the villager, and considers what changes have been wrought in his life by his increasing integration into a single, national unity. That such changes have been and are taking place has been well established,[2] but until the present time there has been little success in combining existing knowledge of the diverse elements of change in rural areas with the more complete and traditional analyses and descriptions of economic development in the Turkish nation as a whole. The remainder of this discussion will attempt such an integrative approach.

In order to state more clearly the argument presented herein, and because of the lack of specific and pertinent data relating to life in rural areas in Ottoman times, the period considered in this text will be limited to the twentieth century and in most part to the years following the War of Independence. The three aspects of Turkish development to be considered systematically are : 1) administrative-political; 2) social; and 3) economic.

---

[1] Friedmann, "Cities," p. 349.

[2] John Kolars, "Types of Rural Development in Turkey," *Four Studies on the Economic Development of Turkey*, Frederic Shorter, contributing ed. (London, 1967), pp. 42-63.

The Growth of Administrative-Political Spacial Relationships

As Halil Inalcık has shown,[1] the majority of the population which would today be described as the Turkish electorate (particularly Anatolian Turks) well into the nineteenth century had no direct contact with the Istanbul government. Leaders at the local level (*ayan, ağa,* "cleric") worked, instead, to maintain traditional institutions within which the peasant had as little contact with the central government as possible. Rural areas spawned no popular demands for reform, and the small group responsible for the Tanzimat were city Turks exposed to European ideas, sometimes to travel abroad or responding to changes from the interior. In the same way, the minorities of Anatolia lived under the *millet* system and were responsible to their own leaders who, in turn, dealt with the agents of Istanbul. Isolation was the mode of village life and provincialism that of the towns.[2]

Only with the collapse of the Ottoman Empire following World War I did town-dwellers in the Anatolian hinterland wake to political activity which expressed a "nationalist" viewpoint. This took place when the Association for the Defense of Rights of Anatolia and Rumelia headed by Mustafa Kemal was formed from smaller, local organizations. Although this organ of the new republic met in the interior through necessity, its early meetings at Erzurum and Sivas marked a shifting of the seat of government nearer to the center of gravity of today's Turkish population. The establishment of the capital at Ankara shortly thereafter was the dramatic expression of Kemal's insight into the problem of communication and the growing move to reach the masses.

The initial resolutions concerning the nature of the new nation which were announced by Mustafa Kemal in July 1919 emphasized his appreciation of the need to consolidate the country both geographically and politically. Independence, geographic unity, "the will of the nation as the sovereign power," and equal rights for all citizens were the key elements of that pronouncement.[3] But not only did Kemal recognize the need to integrate the territory under his control by demanding the alle-

---

[1] Halil Inalcık, "The Nature of Traditional Society," *Political Modernization in Japan and Turkey*, Robert E. Ward and Dankwart A. Rustow, eds. (Princeton, 1964).

[2] Richard D. Robinson, *The First Turkish Republic* (Cambridge, Mass., 1963), pp. 39-64. A reconstruction of village and town conditions is found in the above pages.

[3] *Ibid.*, pp. 65-76.

giance of the military and civilian authorities remaining in Asia Minor, he also gained control of the telegraph system, thus assuring control of the only communication network which at that time integrated, however imperfectly, the geographic space of Anatolia.

The subsequent tours through Anatolia made by Mustafa Kemal and those of the ill-starred first opposition party's leader, Fethi Okyar, in 1930, further extended effective political space by introducing a new geography to Turkish politics : the grass-roots campaign trail. In much the same way, although the reforms of the first years of the Turkish Republic were least effective in the villages, they dramatized the changes which were occuring, and news of them, filtering out and down to the peasants, helped prepare the rural population for what was inevitably to follow. People's Houses (*Halk Evleri*) and People's Rooms (*Halk Odalarc*), established from 1932 to 1940, were another direct effort to reach the majority of the population and until their end in 1951 marked a new focusing of the central government's attention on small towns and villages.

It is necessary, however, to consider carefully the type and degree of expression given these political-administrative developments after their conception and/or legislative enactment. Once given formal expression or made into law, some received little or no application while others were implemented in such a way that their influence spread outward from the point of legislation (i.e. the city) to the widely scattered agrarian population. Thus, the Village Law of March 8, 1924, incorporated a wide range of goals but failed to put most of them into practice. The effort of writing such a law may have served to educate the legislators to the desirable amenities of rural life, but not the peasants.[1] The most effective aspect of this law undoubteldy was its giving legal and administrative entity to the Turkish village, but its effect on social and economic conditions was negligible.[2] On the other hand, efforts like the People's Rooms, however imperfect, extended tangibly across physical and political space, thus involving more and more people. This phenomenon has been repeated many times, and the question must be asked, "Which is more effective, the fine phrase uttered at the center, or the imperfect action on the periphery?"

The development of political and administrative functions during the

---

[1] Donald Everett Webster, *The Turkey of Atatürk* (Philadelphia : 1939), pp. 263-68.

[2] Joseph S. Szyliowicz, "Erdemli : A Case Study in the Political Integration of the Turkish Villager" (Ph.D diss., Columbia University, 1961), pp. 40-52. Also see Joseph

thirties was in the hands of a single group, the People's Republican Party. It was this organization which dominated and was responsible for the People's Rooms and the reforms directed at the villages. But as Weiker indicates,[1] the decade preceding World War II was one devoted essentially to creating among Turkey's elite the attitudes and skills necessary for modern government as opposed to those of the traditional Ottoman hierarchy. This elite was concentrated in urban centers, and reform at the village level as well as integration of the villager through the extension of a political-administrative network throughout the countryside remained incomplete.

World War II extended this period of one-party control well after Atatürk's death, but by 1946 growing urban-centered pressure for a multiparty system resulted in opposition groups being permitted to organize. When this took place, the need to court the electorate became very real. The Democratic Party responded immediately and was closely followed by the People's Republican Party, both of which established widespread grass-roots organizations with branches in nearly every rural community. By 1960, when the National Unity Committee suspended political activity and eventually banned the Democratic Party, the two major parties plus the Republican Peasants' Nation Party maintained about 140,000 local and 14,000 county branches.[2] The geographical extent of these offices and their organization into a hierarchical system assured that nearly every villager in the country was exposed to the influence of party politics.

The Revolution of May 27, 1960, slowed but did not irrevocably alter the development of local politics, and the appearance of the Justice Party in place of the outlawed Democratic Party organization (plus a spate of smaller groups) continued to involve the peasantry in national politics.[3] Even during the period of military control following the revolution, efforts were made to influence the rural population. The National Unity Committee sent speakers the length and breadth of the country explaining the revolution to the people. A Reserve Officer Teacher Program was instituted by means of which lycée graduates became village schoolteachers rather than army officers, and a campaign to send news-

---

S. Szyliowicz, *Political Change in Rural Turkey : Erdemli* (The Hague and Paris : 1966), pp. 37-49.

[1] Walter F. Weiker, *The Turkish Revolution : 1960-1961* (Washington, D.C. 1963), pp. 3-6.

[2] *Cumhuriyet*, June 24, 1960, as reported in Weiker, *Turkish Revolution*, p. 8.

[3] Szyliowicz, "Erdemli," pp. 236-242.

papers to the villages was begun.[1] Though each of these, and many other similar actions, has been less than totally effective, the sum of such influences resulted in the deeper involvement in politics of more and more people. The proliferation of small parties and the need for coalition government in the second Turkish Republic after the May 27 Revolution often has been cited as evidence of political instability, but it may be argued that such conditions represent instead a period of transition needed by a more fully involved electorate in order to work out inevitable problems of identification and organization. As the integration of political space in Turkey has steadily progressed, it has been paralleled first by the misleading tranquility of a one-party system acting and reacting in terms of seemingly simple political alternatives and, at present, by a multiplicity of political choices facing a growing number of selectors. The information overload experienced by a young housewife in an American supermarket presents an analogy. Confrontation for the first time with a wide choice of commodities—be they groceries or governments—results in inevitable but resolvable confusion; as experience increases so does selectivity.

The Growth of Economic Space and Exchange

It is not the purpose of this discussion to recapitulate the many studies of Turkish economic growth.[2] Rather, the point to be emphasized here is again the geographical spread of economic change into rural areas where the majority of the population is domiciled. Three types of economic development have been felt beyond the cities and towns. These center about the growth of government agencies and the services which they provide, about the development of urban-centered industries which serve as magnets for excess rural labor, and about the parallel development of an improved transportation/marketing system. These three elements have contributed not only to increases in the Turkish gross national product but also to the integration of the countryside into the nation-state.

Along with increasing political awareness and the corollary organization of political space has come significant articulation of the service agencies of the Turkish government which perform technical rather than

---

[1] Weiker, *Turkish Revolution*, pp. 143-46.

[2] Z. Y. Herschlag, *Turkey: The Challenge of Growth* (Leiden 1968), p. 406; Malcom D. Rivkin, *Area Development for National Growth: The Turkish Precedent* (New York, 1965), pp. 228.

political functions. As extensions of the central government which represent and implement its policies, success or failure of their technological programs has significant political implications, but such agencies have so changed the economic condition of the countryside that their role in the development of Turkey and the integration of its peasantry is economic as much as administrative in significance.

Thus, agencies of the central government such as the Directorate of Hydraulic Works (*Devlet Su İşleri*), The Farm Irrigation and Conservation Service (Toprak Su), and many others have not only swelled the Ankara-centered bureaucracy but also have sent their agents and engineers into the hinterland. The hierarchy represented by their branch offices now stretches across the country, and policy derived in Ankara is given tangible expression throughout the nation. The works performed there have not always succeeded or produced optimum results, though many have, but one aspect of these programs is undeniable: the presence of educated technicians is no longer thought unusual by most villagers, whose exposure to new ideas, however imperfectly or unpersuasively presented, continues and increases daily.

A case in point is the growing influence of the Ministry of Agriculture upon the rural population. This Ministry, created by Law 3203 dated June 4, 1937, has been in existence less than forty years. In this short period of time it has organized departments of agriculture, veterinary services, forestry, agricultural supply, meteorology, soil conservation and farm irrigation, cotton production, plant protection, and animal quarantine, as well as state breeding farms and a special show place, the Atatürk Farm. In 1960 it incorporated four regional agricultural schools, four technical agricultural schools, fifteen agricultural experimental stations, fourteen sugar factories, and has placed fifty-four home economics workers in the field.[1] Such a list, incomplete as it is, becomes more impressive when the areal extent of these services is also considered. Illustrative of this is the Ministry's "4-K" program (similar to the American 4-H Farm Youth Program) which in 1960 had chapters in 210 villages in forty-seven provinces.[2]

The construction of public works and the introduction of improved seed, livestock, equipment, and farming techniques have had an inevitable effect on rural life. The quantitative differences which have occurred

---

[1] E. N. Holmgreen, "Agricultural Extension in Turkey," Publication of the United States International Cooperation Administration (Ankara, 1960).
[2] *Ibid.*

are difficult to evaluate,[1] but beyond the question of per capita change in productivity is the more basic issue of the villager's incorporation into the national life. The expansion of government agencies has undoubtedly accomplished this, if little else. Keleş and Türkay in their study of change in Turkish villages found that, from forty-four villages examined with regard to the causes of change in agricultural practices, seventeen of the twenty-four villages which replied cited government sources of stimulation as most important.[2]

The questions of urbanization, industrialization, and population growth again emphasize the incorporation of rural peoples into the national milieu. A population growth rate of nearly 3.0 percent after 1950 has created great pressure upon available land resources and a subsequent increasing demand for nonagricultural jobs.[3] The inability of rural areas to absorb surplus labor has resulted in cityward migration and urban growth which exceeds that of the nation as a whole. For all of Turkey, cities with more than 50,000 population numbered five in 1927, eleven in 1950, and twenty-seven in 1960.[4] At the same time, industrial production though plagued with a variety of troubles has continued to grow and to provide more jobs for migrant labor.[5] This activity in the urban centers of the country at first might be thought to have little influence upon modes of rural existence, but strong kinship ties link villagers with their relatives working in the cities. The feedback of urban-generated capital and ideas to rural areas has a definite effect upon village communities. Money and goods find their way to the hinterland, and returning migrants leaven the loaf of village tradition. Even more dramatic may be the eventual effect on village life of those workers drawn to jobs in West Germany. A sample of 494 Turks employed in West Germany showed 18.2 percent had come directly from villages of less than 2,000. More significant is the fact that of the 200 workers who before departing for Germany had lived in Istanbul vilayet only 86 had

---

[1] Abraham and Eva Hirsch, "Changes in Agricultural Output Per Capita of Rural Population in Turkey, 1927-60," *Economic Development and Cultural Change*, XI, 4 (July, 1963), pp. 372-94.

[2] Ruşen Keleş and Orhan Türkay, *Köylü Gözü ile Türk Köylerinde Iktisadi ve Toplumsal Değişme* (Ankara, 1962), pp. 24-25.

[3] Ömer Sarç, "Population Trends in Turkey and Their Economic Consequences," *Capital Formation and Investment in Industry*, Publication of the Economic and Social Studies Conference Board (Istanbul, 1962).

[4] Fehmi Yavuz, *Şehircilik*, (Ankara, 1962).

[5] Herschlag, *Turkey*, chap. 18.

been born there.[1] The city thus prepares the villager for further experiences which in turn will be transmitted back to rural areas.

The growth of urban markets resulting from city development and increases in both the level of living and the number of people in non-agricultural activities has been matched by the development of wholesale markets in localities which produce specialized commercial crops such as citrus.[2] Parallel to these developments has been a significant expansion of the transportation network within the country. Railroads have been improved and expanded since the War of Independence,[3] but the major change in Turkish transportation facilities has centered around improvements in the highway system. Highway building began in earnest in 1948 after two years of initial planning by the central government. Actual construction was implemented through cooperation with the Public Roads Group of the American Aid Mission in Turkey. Stabilized all-weather roads increased from 9,000 kilometers at the beginning of World War II, to 15,000 kilometers in 1950, and to 33,000 in 1966.[4] Gross ton-kilometers of railroad freight increased 87 percent in the decade following 1948 while similar haulage by motor trucks increased 600 percent during the same period.[5] Here was a materially effective binding of Turkey's urban centers to the hinterland, and a significant increase in the peasant's access to the outer world.

The Growth of Social Space and Breakdown of Rural Isolation

The effective integration of Turkey's rural society into a single, national grouping is inextricably intertwined with the developments discussed in the preceding pages. Political-administrative and economic expansion outward from the cities to the hinterland has inevitably brought social

---

[1] Nermin Abadan, *Batı Almanya'daki Türk İşçileri ve Sorunları* (Ankara, 1964), pp. 49-50.

[2] John Kolars, *Tradition, Season, and Change in a Turkish Village*, Department of Geography Research Publication No. 82 (Chicago, 1963), pp. 184-87.

[3] Webster, *Turkey of Atatürk*, pp. 135-37, 258-60. Herschlag, *Turkey*, p. 303.

[4] Organization for European Economic Cooperation, *1955 Economic Conditions in Turkey* (Paris, 1956), p. 8; and T.C., The Minister of Finance, Board of Financial Research (Ankara, 1957); English ed., p. 63. Also see *Second Five-Year Development Plan: 1968-1972*, Publication of the State Planning Organization (Ankara, 1967); Table 375.

[5] James A. Morris, "Recent Problems of Economic Development in Turkey,' *The Middle East Journal*, XIV, 1. (Winter, 1960), p. 5.

change into the life of every villager. A reorienting of Turkish popular thought basic to most societal change was the switch in ideological loyalty (if such loyalty existed at all in pre-Republican times) from empire to nation and from the concept of a Muslim commonweal to that of the citizen Turk who follows Islam. In this respect, the nation-state represents a shrinking rather than expansion of social space. But pan-Islamic or Ottoman loyalties were at best poorly defined in political terms for the rural population and seldom effectively articulated.

The War of Independence introduced a new era. Atatürk's emphasis upon a territorially cohesive nation centered upon Anatolia brought rural allegiances to a focus which has strengthened in the following decades. Party loyalties may vary, friends and allies may change, but for the Anatolian Turk the concept of the motherland remains. Minorities were at first expected to share in this new allegiance, but the exchange of populations with Greece, the removal of the Armenians, and the suppression of the Kurds' revolts (due in large part to these groups' own reluctance to accept the new order) has created in large part a homogeneous linguistic and religious citizenry.

This image in the Turk's mind of his membership in a uniform group sharing a common language as well as common aspirations and loyalties has been enhanced by the expansion of the primary school system with a single curriculum emphasizing Turkish history, geography, and language in addition to the three R's.

The news media of the country also help to create unanimity of opinion, or more accurately, to transcend regional issues by presenting the population with questions of national scope (e.g., planning) or of international importance (e.g., the Korean war and the Cyprus question). The important thing is that while the electorate may disagree about the best responses to these issues, there is common subject matter for discussion.

Newspaper circulation has increased and even at the village level helps to form public opinion. Every coffeehouse usually has at least one person, literate and willing, who will read to those assembled. Similarly, in such a semi-literate nation the spread of ideas and opinion by radio assumes important dimensions, and the increase in radio receiver ownership, particularly of transistorized, battery-operated models, has brought an amazing variety of opinion into remote villages. *Bizim Radyo* from eastern Europe, the Voice of America in Turkish, Cypriot, Israeli, Arab, and Greek broadcasts vie with local stations for their audiences. However, official Turkish radio dominates the country, though in some instances it achieves unanticipated results. Certainly, broadcasting the

Yassıada trials of deposed Democratic Party leaders disillusioned many villagers, who, at first willing to entertain doubts concerning their deposed leaders, were unconvinced by broadcasts from the courtroom.

The army and the *jandarma* are further means by which the Turkish people find uniformity of thought. This occurs in three ways. The first is through the common experience of every draftee, and includes for those who enter the ranks without adequate education an additional six month period for literacy training. The second is the wrenching of the individual from the context of his extended family and placing him among strangers. The third is the policy by which *jandarma* recruits are stationed in areas other than their home territories. This latter practice is intended to avoid favoritism but has the same effect as the army in exposing the individual to other parts of his country and to other Turks. The common experience of every draftee helps to create the strong sense of identification with the military that became evident immediately following the 1960 Revolution. The soldier's removal from the protection of his family results in his seeking a special friend, his "army brother" (*ordu kardeşi*), with whom tenuous contact may be maintained after his enlistment is terminated. Army travel expands the horizons of the villager and facilitates his identification with places and people that may be mentioned by the press or radio. In all these ways, the common Turkish experience is strengthened, though beyond the formal structuring of the army itself no regular spatial pattern of relationships results.

Like the army, political parties have helped lift the villager's eyes from his ancestral soil. Not only have the parties through their elaborate hierarchical organization added structure to the Turkish ecumene but they have also facilitated the transfer of individual loyalties from the extended family or similar kin-groups to larger configurations. Extended family structures such as the agnatic kin-group, the *kabile*, may eventually assume local identification with political parties; neighborhoods (*mahalle*), once associated with territories dominated by family groups, can become fervently partisan in their politics while their local opponents remain the same as those formerly engaged in feuds overtly based on land or honor. Once local identification has been established between the villager and his party, political machinations at the national level—little though they personally involve him—engage his attention. Certainly, the favors received for party loyalty and for voting on the winning side are enough to convince the villagers of the efficiency of the system.

Political and economic success has helped to create a "new" middle class which appeared in the nineteenth and early twentieth century.[1] Whereas the "old" middle class consisted of the intelligentsia, the military, and the bureaucracy, the new is derived from the ranks of artisans, entrepreneurs, and contractors. These people may be relative newcomers to the life of the cities and still retain village connections, but their locus of existence is predominantly urban. And yet, within the villages a similar phenomenon is occurring. Daniel Lerner has pointed out the role of the "transitional" type in Turkish society.[2] These are the people who are willing to learn and to abandon the ties of tradition. But whereas Lerner epitomizes this group by its ability to *empathize* and its *desire* to participate, part of this middle stratum of village society is more action-oriented and serves as "transformer" between the forces of modernization and integration and those of tradition and isolation. In other words, there is not only the group which is willing to change, but also one which has already experimented and experienced new ways, and which serves to instruct the more passive transitionalists.

Here the question of scale once more becomes important. When viewed from the national level, the social structure in a single village or group of Turkish villages may appear homogeneous because of the economic and technological gap which separates such places from the cities. But if the village microcosm is examined closely, and its economy and society viewed in enough detail, there appears a stratification of rural society similar to that described for the nation as a whole. Within these rural strata traditional groups continue to play a predominant role, and yet there can be found in nearly every village some representative of a rural "middle class," neither poor nor rich, belonging to neither the privileged traditionalists nor to the impoverished majority. Little is known about this group, but it seems likely that these are the families which are most ambitious and which seek to improve their positions by sending sons to lycées or setting them up in apprenticeships. In the same way it is this group which is most effective in initiating change at the village level.

The processes of change occurring in rural Turkish society are mainly due to the shattering of the small community's spatial isolation. New experiences and skills, new sources of income, and new crises born of demographic pressures and the disruption of the traditional pattern of

---

[1] Kemal H. Karpat, "Society, Economics, and Politics in Contemporary Turkey," *World Politics*, XVII, no. 1 (October, 1964), pp. 59-60.

[2] Daniel Lerner, *The Passing of Traditional Society* (Glencoe, Ill. 1958), pp. 69-75, 141-146.

life have all resulted from the increasing interconnection of the population and territory within the boundaries of the country. These linkages are generated in the cities and extend outward into rural areas to include greater and greater segments of the population. Since the population being impinged upon is mostly concerned with the exploitation of agricultural resources, it is a scattered one. In order to contact and influence a widely dispersed people, communication networks and movement along them have become increasingly matched by the incorporation of rural products into the national market system and rural people into urban activities. There is no simple way to describe this phenomenon. It can be compared to the growth of an organism—though this analogy should be used with caution—for the character of the nation-state involves not only spatial structure but the articulation and expansion of that structure into increasingly complex forms. In the preceding pages this expansion has been described as the increasing organization of several kinds of space and the areal integration of a previously isolated and independent population into a more highly articulated and interdependent whole. The effect has been to describe, however imperfectly, the process as it applies to the entire nation. To the specific villager the pattern has been much less clear. The remainder of this discussion will attempt to describe the situation from a rural point of view and will draw heavily upon the author's own observation in a number of villages.

The Village Viewpoint Broadens

It is difficult for the western urbanite to imagine himself in the village context of modern Turkey and nearly impossible to create in his imagination the narrow world encompassed by the village mind on the eve of World War I. Ignorance, self-sufficiency, and xenophobia were scarcely leavened by rare travelers and infrequent trips to nearby towns. Government officials were tax collectors and army recruiters, and a combination of fear plus the routines of traditional hospitality left little room for establishing educative contacts with such visitors. Deference to authority was extreme and the feedback of opinion from village to city was lacking and unwanted. This was the context of World War I for the villagers, and comments of those surviving from that period indicate their lack of identification with the issues which led to the end of the Ottoman Empire. Recruits taken from the village were unlikely to return, and only the relatively well-to-do could make the pilgrimage to Mecca which was long, difficult, and expensive. Thus, knowledge of the outside world remained negligible.

The response generated among the countryfolk by Atatürk's call to arms at the beginning of the War of Independence is difficult to understand when considered in the context of traditional apathy to Ottoman affairs. Perhaps the foreign invasion, the impending destruction of the motherland itself, was considered also an imminent threat to Islam and sparked the people's effort; undoubtedly Atatürk's charismatic appeal to the peasantry helped break their isolation. In any event, his effort succeeded and the successful War of Independence left the rural population with a sense of victory and accomplishment that, however slight, helped provide a proper climate for what followed.

This is not to say that villagers expected or even wanted revolutionary change. Rather, it seems that they hoped for a less involved life in which they might consolidate a way of living already familiar to them and alleviate some immediate pressures. Thus, when the People's Republican Party was established it largely inherited the role abdicated by the Ottomans. A one-party system, however much it differed from that which came before, created for the villagers none of the dilemmas of choice stemming from multiparty organization. The establishment of villages as legal entities and the reforms of the twenties were interpreted very much as were the orders sent from above in times past. They were to be obeyed to the letter whenever authority was present to enforce them; they were to be interpreted in village terms and finissed or ignored whenever opportunity allowed. It might be said that the success of those early measures, although limited, was because there were no alternatives offered the villagers. Similarly, the villagers' slowness to change was due to their lack of integration into the national whole, or more accurately, the incompleteness of the national structure. Education to new ways requires repeated contacts and close supervision, and both these qualities were, at first, lacking in the Republic.

Because of this, change occurred slowly and officials of the new government tended to perform their duties in the manner to which they were accustomed. Local officials expected and demanded deference from villagers, and villagers in turn, anticipated no new attitudes on the part of government representatives. Such stereotyped responses continue to the present time and find expression in the persistence of traditional village attitudes in contemporary situations. For example, village patriarchy still survives and the author has observed the heads of extended families answering census questionnaires for their grown and married sons and supervising the casting of family ballots en bloc.

On the other hand, the growth of the multiparty system has helped bring about new patterns of political behavior. The basic facts of campaigning pertain in Turkey as in the United States and the success of the defunct Democratic Party, built as it was upon appeal to the villagers, has induced a certain politeness on the part of many officials toward the people whom they serve. Conversely, this growing opportunity for political choice by the villagers has created new tensions within the rural milieu. Not only may villages be divided along party lines so that one neighborhood votes predominantly contrary to another, but individual grudges may find expression at the ballot box. This raises an important and as yet unanswered question as to the voting pattern within rural communities. Do traditional village leaders, the old men, *imams*, and titular *ağas*, disproportionately influence the electorate, or do nonconformists—be they individuals or families—find it possible to cast unpopular votes in otherwise homogeneous neighborhoods?

Traditional patterns of village leadership continue to prevail and in many instances the *muhtar* may be an older, influential man or conversely some literate near-youth who serves only in a clerical capacity while true leadership remains vested elsewhere. Nevertheless, the growth of the government hierachy of offices combined with increasing involvement of central agencies in rural affairs means that someone in each village must more and more represent it before officialdom. Since such contacts, if successful, may result in better roads, an increased water supply, or a variety of other benefits, the role of the village representative is of necessity changing and becoming more important. Literacy becomes essential as does a certain ability to dress in city clothes and to conduct oneself with the proper combination of deference and persistence. Certainly as urban/rural contacts continue to increase, knowledgeable younger men who have traveled beyond their own home territory and who can attain a certain success when dealing with the bureaucracy are beginning to assume importance disproportionate with the role assigned their age-group within traditional society. Here again the role of the "transformer" becomes important; that is, a person in and of the village who can successfully act as interpreter between representatives of the urban elite and the rural milieu.

The importance of such people is increasing yearly, for new laws and new development programs create conflicts between the rural populace and the state. Forest conservation laws, for example, have closed the woods more and more to traditional exploitation by villagers, and in some areas scarcely a grown man can be found who has not paid a fine or served a jail term for violating forest closures. Situations like this are indicative of a lack of fit between the desires of the state and the realities of the countryside. Only through an exchange of ideas between the governed and the governors can equitable solutions be found and only the "transformers" in village society can facilitate such a rapprochement. In the same way, possibly necessary but unpopular changes must be considered for implementation at the village level. Among these are the questions of initiating a personal income tax and adjustments in the head tax (*salma*) which no longer realistically reflects the value of the lira. Here are issues which are unpopular with the people and yet which must be faced before the nation can become truly developed.

Economic and social changes at the village level are inevitable concomitants of political and administrative development. Perhaps the greatest difference between the village viewpoint and that of the urban administrators is in the timescale at which such changes take place. The administrator, located as he is near the functional center of government, is in a position to perceive and appreciate annual increments of change for the nation as a whole. For example, each year mileage is added to the nation's road network; each year new schools are opened; and each year the national ledgers are summed up. Sometimes there are reverses, and sometimes the rate of progress is unacceptably slow, but the overall effect is one of gradual and steady alteration of past conditions. To the villager, change appears very differently, as a series of quantum jumps often separated by long periods when nothing new happens. Examples of this are numerous; the government in a single year may build an all-weather road through or near a previously isolated village; or a small community, without its inhabitants being consulted, may be singled out as the site of some agricultural development scheme. Thus, what appears from above as a gradual process of development and expansion throughout the nation comes as a series of often precipitous events or shocks to the structure of a given village. As more developments take place in a specific area their effect is cumulative and with experience the ability of the villagers to interpret, integrate, and accept continuing change improves. However, it is this difference between the administrator's implementing the familiar in yet another place, and the villager's abrupt plunge into the waters of change that accounts for much of the misunderstanding between the two groups.

In many ways, economic developments are most spectacular and the yearly increment of equipment and material goods most often catches the observer's attention. Certainly this has been the case with farm machinery,[1] but the effect of such acquisitions upon the villager who finally obtains such mechanical aids may be unexpected. The efficacy of equipment in better meeting the needs of the agricultural year is well known, but the freedom from the exhaustion induced by man-handled, animal-drawn equipment and the subsequent improved health of farmers lucky enough to own tractors is seldom discussed, though it is well appreciated by those concerned. This spotlights a difference in opinion between older and younger generations of Turkish farmers concerning the nature of contemporary developments. While those born within the past twenty-five years may complain that life is hard, such comments by members of the older generation will upon closer questioning often give way to the admission that, regardless of difficulties, times are better now than in the twenties and thirties. Evidence by Keleş and Türkay indicates that 1950 marks the turning point for most villagers.[2]

This does not mean that the decisions that villagers must make or the situations to which they must relate are becoming easier. On the contrary, these are times when the old, time-proven responses provided by tradition no longer apply. Richard Robinson has commented on the new tensions between father and son upon the youth's return from the army.[3] Now out of necessity or desire more and more villagers travel to the cities to seek their fortunes, and exposure to urban ways further widens the gap between the traditional patriarchy and new generations. For example, when the author visited Alişar Village in 1963,[4] the refusal of the son of a prominent villager to return home from Istanbul to be married had precipitated a crisis in his household.

Material change within the boundaries of the village also creates new potential for failure as well as for success. Where cash cropping has been substituted for subsistence agriculture incomes have risen dramatically, but overdependence upon a single crop, however profitable, may hold unforeseen disaster if climatic conditions or markets fail. This has been the case in the citrus-raising villages of the Antalya region,[5] which have enjoyed an unprecedented prosperity but which have also ex-

---

[1] Charles D. Busch, "Agricultural Mechanization in Turkey," Publication of the United States Operations Mission—Turkey, Food and Agriculture Division (Ankara, 1960).

[2] Keleş and Türkay, *Köylü Gözüile*.

[3] Robinson, *First Turkish Republic*, pp. 249-50.

[4] John A. Morrison, *Alişar; A Unit of Land Occupance in the Kanık Su Basin of Central Anatolia*, (Chicago, private ed. 1939).

[5] Kolars, *Tradition, Season, and Change*, pp. 142-43.

perienced new problems because of the strain placed upon limited supplies of irrigation water. Bitter intervillage litigation over limited water resources offers no easy solution. Nor is this case unusual, for it is a rule that villagers think primarily in terms of their own settlement and usually lack the attitudes and social organization essential for cooperative efforts on an intervillage or regional basis.

At this point, the coordinating activities of the central government play an important role as does arbitration by local courts,[1] but too often the villager fails to find common purpose with government officials. This is due in large part to the continuation of traditional bureaucratic attitudes and can present a serious check to planned economic development.

The success of economic development projects in rural areas depends upon village cooperation at all stages of execution. Interviews indicate that villagers often feel a sense of estrangement from the government agencies involved in the projects. Although the aim of a project may have been explained to the the villagers, they are often left in the dark about the various steps to be taken, and about the phases of execution of a project. Thus the villager sees the stages of a project as rather mysterious and arbitrary actions by strangers, and consequently he does not co-operate as required for success. Impediments faced by agents of development when working in the village are often not caused by a lack of desire by the villagers to improve themselves, but rather a lack of understanding, and by the traditional mistrust of villagers towards government officials.[2]

The response of village society to the many new experiences of the last half century has been most selective. Where government fiat has made change inevitable the villagers have accepted the new rules but as much as possible in their own terms. Thus, education may be intended for boys and girls, but the former still predominate in primary schools. Women as well as men may be allowed the vote, but the patriarch still can determine how his household's ballots will be cast. Where change is effected by material improvements which allow a freedom of response such as new roads or the extension of credit to small holders, the villagers have reacted cautiously but with increasing commitment. There is nothing to indicate that the average farmer will reject the means to a higher level of living. Rather, he is a careful person who by following the examples set by the successful innovators within his community slowly takes advantage of the opportunities presented him. Mean-

---

[1] The troubled history of the recently established *Köy İşleri Bakanlığı* ("Ministry of Village Affairs") indicates similar problems of coordination at the summit.

[2] T.C./F.A.O., "Pre-Investment Survey of the Antalya Region," *Third Interim Report* (Antalya, Turkey : December, 1964), pp. 4-11.

while, his life has become politically and administratively more complex. His range of political choice has increased, but with this increase have come new tensions. Officialdom's attitude toward him is in many ways more deferential, but, simultaneously, he finds his life increasingly controlled and under the scrutiny of the central administration. Conflicts with unrealistic or misunderstood laws continue to occur, but at the same time much more seems possible than before and the attaining of new goals places greater importance upon those villagers with experience of the world beyond. Thus tradition, while still strong, increasingly defers to the rules and laws of a more completely integrated society and to those people who are learning to operate within it. In the same way, as the horizon of the villager's world shifts outward from his hearth, the urban-centered state extends to meet him.

CHAPTER SIX

THE FREE BOARDING (LEYLI MECCANI) SCHOOLS *

İLHAN BAŞGÖZ

INTRODUCTION

The free boarding schools in Republican Turkey appear, in the broader context of general education, as a specific channel of upward social mobility by means of education, professional training, and subsequent recruitment into the government service. These schools are in part the sources of bureaucratic elites who gained social status based on educational achievement and possible identification with government policies, ideologies, and goals. Finally, the schools represent the adaptation of traditional methods of recruitment into government services to the specialized, technological needs of contemporary society. The remarks above apply especially to boarding schools at the university level and to a special category of professional schools at the secondary educational level. They do not apply to elementary boarding schools. This study deals only with specific characteristics of one segment of the Turkish educational system and not with its total transformation. It offers also an insight into the problems of technical and professional specialization in a developing society. Finally, when related to overall political development in society, the study relates the transformation in the educational system as a whole to the structural functional changes in society.

The free boarding schools offer free education to highly qualified students, usually from the lower income groups. The costs of education, including food, clothing, and even pocket money is provided by the government, which in turn expects the student attending a university or a professional school to work in an assigned place for a period of time

---

* The main research for the paper was carried out by the author. Professor Kemal Karpat contributed in reorganizing and giving an interpretive socio-political orientation to the original paper. Some of the information contained in this article appeared in a different context in I. Başgöz and H. E. Wilson, *Educational Problems in Turkey, 1920-1940* (Bloomington, Ind., 1968).

calculated in proportion to the legnth of subsidized education received. The basic purpose of this education is to train people for specialized government jobs and positions in education.

The extent of the government's need for skilled personnel, its basic political philosophy, the general level of education and income distribution among the population, as well as the availability of other outlets for education determine the role of such boarding schools. This system, still in existence in Turkey, played a crucial role in the early decades of the Republic in training sorely needed personnel in medicine, education, engineering, civil administration, law, and other fields. It recruited students on a competitive basis, usually from Anatolian towns and cities and even villages. In practice, however, the system was often limited to the urban middle classes since they could acquire the minimum formal education necessary for gaining entrance into these boarding schools. The chief requirement for admission was a high scholastic record, insufficient income, and commitment to work for the government. This system increased the number of skilled professionals and indirectly helped create an elite corps whose status derived essentially from educational achievement and professional association with the government.

Many of the individuals trained by the government became free professionals at the end of their compulsory government service. Others reimbursed the government for their educational expenses after graduation and joined the ranks of the ever-growing liberal professionals. The latter group grew in size after the 1940's by acquiring higher education at their own expense. The boarding schools must not be confused with the various government scholarship programs in Republican Turkey. The recipients of small scholarships were usually free of obligation, whereas those receiving full aid for the duration of their education still undertook service obligations.

Historically, the origins of the free boarding schools (the Turkish terms *leyli meccani, parasız yatılı,* or *parasız leyli* have the same meaning) can be traced to the *Enderun* or Palace School of the Ottoman Empire in the fifteenth century. The Palace School, recruiting its students from the *devshirme* youth tribute system and the slave military establishments (the *ocaks* of Janissaries), and occasionally from other sources, trained personnel for many of the highest administrative positions. It functioned, however, strictly for bureaucratic purposes, since, ideally, the graduates were permanently devoted to government service and had no interest in relations with the lower social groups. A similar pattern of education, although totally different in purpose and methods, existed in the *medrese,* the religious schools supported by the *wakfs* or religious endowments.[1] The idea of providing board to students as practiced in the Palace School was adapted to the modern schools established in the eighteenth and especially nineteenth century after the Ottoman government began to centralize and modernize the bureaucracy. The educational efforts after the Tanzimat Reorganization in 1839 led to the enlargement of existing schools or the establishment of new ones. The Military Medical School, School for Civil Administrators, Harbiye (War College) at higher levels, and the *Rüştiye* and the technical schools at lower levels are among the best known. The principle applied here, with some exception for the lower-level schools, was essentially the same as in the modern, free boarding schools.[2] However, the service requirements were less stringent than in Republican Turkey, when competition for modern education increased, since this was the surest avenue to higher social status. Yet the "modern" schools established after 1839 were in some respect less pratically oriented than the old Palace Schools. For instance, the training in practical skills and the physical education which occupied an important place in the curriculum of Palace Schools was not found in the "modern" ones of the nineteenth century reform era.

---

[1] In a way the religious schools had a broader popular basis of recruitment and thus closer contact with the masses. Thousands of children, those of poor farmers, tribesmen, and even government clerks, as well as of slaves could join the *ulema* ("learned religious men") class as a result of education received in the *medrese*, and could eventually reach high positions in the Empire (Bernard Lewis, *Istanbul and the Civilization of the Ottoman Empire*. [Norman, Oklahoma, 1951], p. 151).

[2] The Tanzimat reformers had resorted to this relatively expensive educational system in order to compete with the free education offered by the *Medrese* ("religious school") and thus attract students to the new and unpopular Western-type schools. For a traditional society in which the education offered to the people had consisted merely of religious teaching, the new schools appeared extremely strange. They were accused of being the source of heresy ("*küfr*") and were attacked and even destroyed by angry mobs. People refused to send their children to these new schools. The War College ("*Harbiye*") could not find at the beginning enough students to justify its existence, so the school administration drafted orphans from the Istanbul streets. There were no registration prerequisites for admission to the military medical school— only the name of the nominee needed to be registered. Osman Ergin, *Türk Maarif Tarihi* I (Istanbul, 1939), pp. 286, 312, 362. For a general treatment see Andreas M. Kazamias, *Education and the Quest for Modernity in Turkey* (London, 1966), p. 31. See also Barnette Miller, *The Palace School of Muhammad the Conqueror* (Cambridge, Mass., 1941).

The New Education and Populism

The views on education of the leaders of the Republic (1923) were shaped on one hand by a newly emerging socio-political outlook which regarded the education of the people as an essential condition of modernization, and on the other by the government's pressing need for trained personnel. Added to these there was the practical need to consolidate the new political system by enlisting the support of large popular groups and by indoctrinating them with the Republican philosphy.

The new ideas on education had their roots in a new and broad philosophy of man and life often echoing the ideas of the French Enlightenment. Man was considered to be born free and equal in potential but still in need of developing his intellectual faculties. But the idea that education was a basic condition for a civilized modern man rather than existing merely to meet the government's need for personnel began to be expressed openly only at the beginning of the twentieth century as part of the general philosophy of populism. The latter idea appeared originally as a reaction to the cultural and political dichotomy caused by modernization. In its more idealistic forms, populism championed the cause of the masses against the elitist philosophy deeply entrenched in the minds and habits of the ruling bureaucracy. Populism in education, however, as in other fields did not promote political mass movements from below against the established order but aimed at finding an ideational formula which would bridge the gap between the masses and the ruling bureaucratic intellectual groups. Consequently, it did not envisage a violent radical change in the social and political institutions but hoped to reshape government functions in accordance with the society's felt needs, and its modern cultural and political aspirations. It failed, therefore, to deal with the causes of the contradiction which created tension between the masses and political leadership. Education was carried out chiefly through government-sponsored institutions. The lack of nationally organized and financially independent educational organizations or other civic establishments placed the government in the unique position of assuming the task of providing schooling. It had the organization, a relatively trained staff, and the basic financial resources.

The need to educate people by using government resources was voiced throughout the early stages of modernization. Ziya Gökalp (d. 1924) the nationalist ideologue of the Young Turks and later of Republican Turkey, wrote :

No child should enter this world as a slave. No child should be without proper care or diet in the first part of his life, or without school and education in the latter. Who knows how many children, born into poor families could, with proper education, become geniuses in the future? Society has been deprived of these talents because of economic inequalities. The prime purpose of populism should be to rear children under equal conditions and to provide them with sufficient diet and equal educational opportunities.[1]

As early as 1914, Ismail Mahir Efendi declared in the Ottoman House of Deputies :

At this slow pace, our educational system will not be established even within the next 150 years. We have 70 provinces; we can create 70 educational districts. Let us build in each province either on established farms or on government-owned land, two large elementary boarding schools, one for girls and one for boys. We can then recruit as pupils boys and girls from the villages, according to their population...[2]

The same views were expressed at the Economic Congress which met at Izmir in 1923 :

The State should undertake to establish in every district of the country boarding schools at the primary level which could serve groups of villages situated near each other. It would allot a suitably large plot of land to each of these schools, whose curriculum would include, alongside the primary program of courses, elementary agricultural instruction, both theoretical and applied.[3]

The compelling moral force behind these utterences was the grim reality of a huge number of uneducated peasantry who had lived for centuries abandoned to the whims of fate. In 1927-28 the percentage of literates, concentrated mostly in towns and cities, was only 10.6, in 1935-36 it went up to 20.4, then gradually to about 40 percent by 1950, and then remained fairly stable at 40 percent thereafter. The very structure of Turkish villages created from the beginning insurmountable technical and financial difficulties. In 1927 more than 12.4 million people, of a total of 16.2 million, lived in about 40,000 villages. More than 32,000 villages

---

[1] Ziya Gokalp, *Yeni Türkiye'nin Hedefleri*, Hikmet Tanju ed. (Ankara, 1956), pp. 46-50.

[2] Rauf Inan, "Ismail Mahir Efendinin Fikirleri," *Köy ve Eğitim*, no. 10-11 (1955), p. 12.

[3] Ahmet Hamdi Başar, "Izmir Iktisat Kongresi," *Türk Iktisat Mecmuası*, no. 12-13 (1923), p. 324.

had a population of less than 400 people.[1] Most of these villages, poor as they were, did not have schools. Neither could they build one or support its teacher despite an educational law enacted by the Young Turks (1908-18) as early as 1913, which placed the responsibility for local education on the villagers.

The Republican government, on the other hand, caught in its own struggle for power and beset by dissension among its ranks between 1924 and 1930, failed to materialize the populist, progressive educational hopes present at its inception. The financial burden necessarily resulting from these projects (besides the government gradually began to rely more on its bureaucratic apparatus than on popular support and participation to maintain itself in power and protect the interest of its associates) restricted the education program greatly. By 1933, only 2,600 elementary schools had been built, mostly in villages with a population of over 800. Thus, without the support of a strong elementary education system, the upper training schools were deprived of a broad recruiting base and eventually were forced to draw their students from the narrow circle of cities and towns. These were already privileged to have schools and living standards far better than those relatively few villages lucky enough to have schools.

Social Philosophy and the Boarding Schools

The government boarding schools were plagued persistently by their relatively low prestige and by a long-standing tradition which favored the children of urban dwellers and government officials. In order to find a remedy to the situation educational problems were discussed in the Republic as early as 1921, but without any decisive conclusion being reached. Attempts were made to increase the number of students in some of the existing boarding schools inherited from the Young Turks, especially the teacher-training schools. Steps were also taken such as building a central elementary school in order to service five to ten villages,

---

[1]

Group	Village Population	Number of Villages
I	over 1,200	514
II	801-1,200	1,427
III	401-800	5,505
IV	151-400	16,305
V	1-150	16,052

See İsmail Hakkı Tonguç, *İlk Öğretim Kavramı* (Istanbul, 1947), p. 214.

and relieve the shortage of teachers.[1] However, these educational and vocational schools offering free education did not attract many students at least at the beginning. As late as 1932, the Minister of Education reported to the National Assembly:

> We have enlarged the free boarding student quota at Gazi Teacher Training Institute, but we have attracted only twenty-six students. The situation is similar in the case of the High Teacher Training School (*Yüksek Muallim Mektebi*); we expected forty-five students to attend but only thirty registered.[2]

Actually the negative attitudes shown toward the boarding schools resulted from the cultural and social values of the towns people and their economic status, all of which was reflected in Turkish educational philosophy.

To the relatively educated and well-to-do town pupils the boarding schools had limited appeal, especially in view of the hardship in the *taşra* (back country) where they would perform their government services. Moreover, since many of the vocational boarding schools had been established in the past for orphans and the children of the poor, especially during Mithat Pasha's premiership in the 1870's, these still had low prestige. Indeed, as late as 1926, some trade schools' boarding facilities were opened as charities to those "without father or mother and property."[3] One must also mention a certain odd division of labor resulting from imbalanced social and economic development and social differentiation. The regular (nonboarding) schools training men and women for higher administrative jobs were filled by the children of the upper classes, whose families often were already in the government service. These were less interested in entering the technical and vocational schools, which trained personnel for practical jobs considered not to be mental. Indeed, those graduating from vocational schools, although often employed by the government, received low salaries and

---

[1] Publication of the Ministry of Education, *Cumhurbaşkanları, Başbakanlar ve Milli Eğitim Bakanlarının Milli Eğitimle Ilgili Söylev ve Demeçleri*, I (Ankara, 1946), p. 360.

[2] *Ibid.*, p. 182.

[3] The boarding schools were long associated with the idea that they were for the lower classes. In 1926 Mustafa Necati, of the Ministry of Education, emphasized the fact for a free boarding system in *lise* and other middle schools was established to provide educational opportunities for underprivileged children. He said, "Most fathers cannot bear the financial burden of providing education of their children for as much as ten to fifteen years. This is why we have to undertake the education of those children. Only those to whom we give free room and board are able to pursue their education to the end." *Cumhurbaşkanları*, I p. 357-358.

were relegated to third-rate jobs without policymaking authority. Consequently, the schools which offered free board as an incentive were attractive mainly to the children of the poor who could thus continue their education beyond elementary school and acquire a modestly better position, but still below that of the elite.[1] The Health Officers' Schools (*Sağlık Memurları Okulu*), Finance Schools (*Maliye Meslek Okulu*), School of Land Registration (*Tapu ve Kadastro Okulu*), Police Schools (*Polis Okulu*), Mining School (*Maden Okulu*),[2] and others of the same category, although modified greatly to provide further advancement to their graduates, have retained even today some of their original tendency to be filled with children of the low income group.

The graduates of vocational schools could not enter the university directly. This right was reserved only to the graduates of theory-oriented *lise* (upper secondary schools) attended usually by children of higher income groups. According to a quota, the Schools of Medicine, Law, and Engineering offered free education only to *lise* graduates on the limited quota basis. As *lises* were located mainly in provincial capitals, they mainly trained the children of local people, mostly government officials, and of relatively wealthy men who lived nearby or who could afford to support their children in the city.

There were a number of *lises* with boarding facilities where one year of service was required for each school year. However, most of the *lise* graduates tended to enter the university until well into the early 1950's. Those who did not or could not usually served as school teachers, or in a few cases entered the army. (Public law of 1926, number 362, had abolished the fees at all educational levels.)

---

[1] In 1935-36 only 7 percent of the graduates of elementary schools were able to continue their education beyond that level. This figure was not more than 10 percent in 1940. We do not know how many of these students were from villages which had elementary schools, but answers from a sample survey made among village school teachers may give an idea. "The number of pupils at my school is 78," one teacher declared, "but only five graduate each year, and these five are not able to pursue their studies elsewhere." "The number of school-age children in our village is 100," said another, "but never more than ten graduate, and even these remain in the village plowing the land. Only one student was able to go on with his studies, entering the Faculty of Medicine, because his father had money. Other families are not in a position to finance any kind of education for their children." Namık Ayaz, "Zivarik köyü" ("Village of Zivarik"), *Ülkü* 27 (1934), p. 230. Nuri Osman, "Ahırlı köyü" ("Village of Ahırlı") *Ülkü* 15 (1932), p. 397.

[2] For a list of twenty-one Technical Schools opened between 1869 and 1923, see *Political Modernization in Japan and Turkey*, Robert Ward and Dankwart A. Rustow, eds. (Princeton, 1964), p. 215.

The subtle discriminatory policy towards the children of the lower classes, that is to say, providing expenses for the relatively inexpensive middle level education in exchange for long years of service, and not permitting them to enter universities, can be seen easily from a comparison with students at the university boarding schools. The service requirement for the university graduate was originally two years for one year of schooling but this was eventually equalized year per year.[1] (A law enacted in 1930, requiring two years of government service from all graduates of the Medical School was found undemocratic and abrogated in 1932.) On the other hand, the graduates of the Village Institutes established in 1941 were asked to teach twenty years in villages at pitiful salary levels (20 liras or 11 dollars a month according to the rate of exchange at the time) for the five years of schooling. The Village Institute students were recruited originally and primarily from villages. These examples illustrate the serious disadvantages faced by these higher secondary boarding schools.

Free Boarding Schools in Elementary Education

The first elementary boarding schools were set up in 1924, altogether thirty-four in number. Fourteen were located in Eastern Anatolia. Another fourteen were orphanages partly open for more than 30,000 orphans who had lost their fathers in the War of Independence. The government undertook the responsibility of educating them freely from elementary school to university. The average number of students per year attending free boarding elementary schools from 1924 to 1939 was 2,500 of a total of 37,500 students (table 6.1). There was no obligation to serve the government for the boarding education provided at this level.

The gradual decrease in the number of elementary boarding schools must be attributed to their high costs. The Minister of Education stated in 1925 that one elementary boarding school cost from 15,000 to 20,000 Turkish liras. If 200 such schools were set up half of the education budget would have to be spent only for that purpose. The cost of educating one student in such a school was as much as that in a teacher-training

---

[1] A similar system was established for the training of students abroad. The government paid all transporttaion expenses, school fees and maintenance for the length of study in the Western countries. However many of the students thus trained, especially engineers in the U.S.A., found lucrative positions, paid off their debts to the Turkish government, and stayed on.

Table 6.1

Students attending Free Boarding Elementary Schools, 1924-39.[1]

Year	Boarding Schools	Students	Total of Elementary Students	Percentage of Boarding Students
1924-25	30	4,000	300,000	1.2
1925-26	49	7,760	302,500	2.0
1926-27	—	3,870	458,000	.84
1931-32	19	4,208	487,911	.84
1932-33	15	3,074	536,123	.56
1933-34	14	2,066	563,718	.36
1934-35	9	2,940	623,977	.46
1935-36	6	1,186	667,091	.46
1936-37	5	833	714,178	.1
1937-38	4	637	764,691	—
1938-39	4	613	813,636	—

institute.[2] Kühne, the German educational adviser, suggested that the Turkish government close the free boarding schools in order to reduce educational costs.[3] The Turkish government, of course, did not close all the schools at once as this would have eliminated the only possible means of educating thousands of orphans who otherwise could not afford their own educational expenses. It tried, unsuccessfully, to lessen the high cost of free boarding schools. The *Köy Yatı Mektepleri* (Village Boarding Schools) program was one of these experimental projects. They began in 1933, while Reşit Galip was the Minister of Education. The students of surrounding villages were brought to a central village which had a school and lodging facilities. Every week the students' parents brought them food for the coming week to be prepared by village women (yati anasi). The woman also undertook the housework and care of the students. The project was abandoned in 1936, because of lack of adequate transportation between villages, especially during the winter. The free boarding schools at the elementary level were finally abandoned after 1940. The task of educating village children was given to the Village Institutes and to the instructors trained in the *Eğitmen Projesi* (Project for training instructors). These projects enabled some

---

[1] Sources: *Cumhurbaşkanları*, I, p. 391. *T.C. Istatistik Yıllığı, 1942-1943*, (Ankara, 1944), p. 393. *Milli Egitim Bakanliği Ilk Öğretim Istatistikleri, 1944-45*, (Ankara, 1946), p. 8.

[2] *Cumhurbaşkanları*, I, p. 290.

[3] Kühne, *Mesleki Tebiyenin İnkisafina Dair Rapor*, (Istanbul, 1939), 0p. 6.

village children to receive education near their homes. However, some free elementary boarding schools were reopened in Turkey after 1961, at the beginning of the Second Republic. Unfortunately, no exact figures are available regarding the location and student body of these schools. According to newspaper reports, most of them operate in East Anatolia.

THE FREE BOARDING SYSTEM IN SECONDARY EDUCATION

Public Law No. 915, of 1927, reorganized the free boarding system in *lises* and some junior middle schools (Orta Okul). Most of the *lises* already possessed boarding facilities. All but four of the existing twenty-five *lises* provided board in 1925. The law charged the Ministry of Education with the responsibility of establishing dormitories (*"pensions"*) in major cities for the *lise* and *orta okul* students. The "pensions" for dormitories were financed in large measure by the Ministry of Education with funds allocated from the national budget. The day-to-day administration was left to the directors of the schools to which the boarding facilities were attached.

Two types of students were admitted. The first group consisted of those who could pay the expenses of their education, but had no relatives or friends who could provide living facilities in the city. These paid for their board and room according to a standard schedule. The second group consisted of students who could not afford the cost of education beyond the elementary level. Ultimately these received education and boarding free of obligation. The former group found shelter, proper food, and necessary supervision in the lodging houses, whereas those in the latter group could complete their education with their expenses paid by the Ministry of Education. A student applying for admission to these free boarding schools needed, according to Public Law No. 409 of 1926, "a very high credit from the elementary school, had to pass a qualifying examination, and be unable financially to afford the expense of his education. Orphans, and the children of those who have lost their lives in the War of Independence are given preference." [1]

Another important category of middle level schools based exclusively on the principle of free boarding were the Village Institutes mentioned earlier. Their establishment was consistent both with the modern educational philosophy and the technique envisaged for attaining this goal. It was a new approach devised to finance education at the lowest possible cost for the government. This movement produced a dynamic

---
[1] Hasan Ali Yücel, *Türkiye'de Orta Öğretim*, (Istanbul, 1939), p. 390.

new group of village teachers and leading writers, scientists, and painters. It also eventually gave rise to a significant and controversial social and political debate influencing not only education in Turkey but also village planning and the administrative, legal, and political systems of Turkey.[1] Although the movement lost its original character after 1947, it nevertheless provided valuable experience and insight into some of the educational problems of Turkey. Only village children with elementary education were accepted in the Institutes. They were trained for five years to become village teachers and health officers. The students worked tracts of land owned by the Institutes and studied irrigation, well digging, pest eradication, planting, poultry raising, and handicrafts. Theoretical instruction was only a part of this broader education. Students were required to learn pratical skills useful in the villages, such as carpentry, fishing, farming, bookkeeping, etc., not only for imparting these skills to villagers but also to utilize them in supplementing their inadequate pay. The government provided the necessary tools, equipment, and land for this purpose when graduates returned to their villages as teachers. The Village Institutes were converted after 1947 and 1950 into general teacher training schools and students were recruited from both villages and town dwellers. But their coeducationall free boarding character was preserved. Tables 6.2, 6.3, 6.4, 6.5, and 6.6 indicate the fluctuations in types of schools and numbers of students during some two to three decades.

Table 6.2
Free Boarding Students in Lises [2]

Years	Number of boarding Students	Total Number of Students	Percentage of Boarding Students
1924-25	1,116	2,234	50
1926-27	630	3,152	20
1927-28	933	7,482	12.4
1930-31	1,213	8,109	14.8
1934-35	904	7,697	11.7
1937-38	756	10,358	7

(The figures below include also students in special private *lises* where boarding was paid. These serviced higher income groups.)

1939-40	1,669	9,707	10.7
1944-45	1,669	27,734	6.3
1948-49	1,553	22,100	7
1959-60	1,245	58,945	2

[1] See Kemal H. Karpat, *Turkey's Politics* (Princeton, 1959), pp. 377-80, and Fay Kirby, *Turkiye'de Köy Enstitüleri*, (Ankara, 1962).

[2] Publication of the Ministry of Education, *Milli Eğitim Bakanlığı Orta Öğretim*

Table 6.3

Free Boarding Students in Trade Schools [1]

Year	Number of Trade Schools	Number of Boarding Students	Total Students in Trade Schools	Percentage of Boarding Students
1927-28	9	940	1,098	85
1930-31	9	1,166	1,334	86
1935-36	9	1,385	1,847	77.5
1940-41	9	1,256	3,879	33
1945-46	55	2,303	18,948	12
1950-51	81	485	17,750	2.7
1954-55	79	260	23,414	1.1

* The sudden increase in the number of trade schools and the drop in the number of boarding students was due to the fact that these were recognized as equivalent to other middle schools and their graduates had ample employment possibilities in industry and various enterprises. Demand for admission increased as many pupils interested in studying in *lises* could enter the trade schools whose status had greatly improved. Meanwhile economic activity intensified and GNP began to rise. Private enterprise also expanded.

Table 6.4

Boarding Students in Teacher Training Schools [2]

Year	Number of Boarding Students	Total Number of Students in Teacher Training Schools	Percentage of Boarding Students
1927-28	4,761	5,022	95
1931-32	4,246	5,535	77
1935-36	2,477	2,657	93
1939-40	2,696	2,930	92
1946-47	1,034	1,395	74
1948-49	1,104	1,132	91

Istatistikleri, 1944-1945 (Ankara), p. 166; *1945-1946*, p. 78; Kemal Kurdas, "Egitim Sistemimiz ve Soyalist Düşünce" ("Social Thought and Our Educational System") Lecture given at Sosyalist Kültür Derneği, Ankara, 1963). Kurdaş was then President of the Middle East Technical University in Ankara.

[1] Reşat Özalp, *Rakamlarla Türkiye'de Mesleki ve Teknik Öğretim* (Ankara, 1956), p. 56.

[2] Yücel, *Türkiye'de*, p. 114. *Istatistik Yıllığı : 1949* (Ankara, 1950), p. 130.

Table 6.5

Students in the Village Institutes.[1]

Year	Number of Institutes	Number of Students Boys	Girls	Number of Graduates Boys	Girls
1940-41	14	1,074	107	—	—
1941-42	17	4,933	438	103	—
1942-43	18	8,834	837	230	24
1943-44	18	11,563	1,276	1,787	124
1944-45	20	12,593	1,432	1,621	207
1945-46	20	13,068	1,396	1,284	176
1946-47	20	12,822	1,336	1,945	145
1947-48	20	11,814	1,078	1,926	236

(All received free boarding, clothing and school supplies.)

Table 6.6

Boarding Students in other Vocational Secondary Schools, 1946-47 [2]

School	Number of Boarding Students	Total Number of Students
Agricultural Schools (Ziraat Okulları)	3,379	3,543
Health Schools (Sağlık Memurları Okulları)	1,226	1,299
Istanbul Technical Schools (Istanbul Teknik Okkulları)	107	111
Ankara Conservatory	103	103
Finance Schools (Maliye Meslek Okulu)	178	178
School of Land Registration (Tapu-Kadastro Okulu)	77	77
Police College	127	127
Vocational School of State Railways (Devlet Demiroylları Meslek Okulu)	235	235

Free Boarding Students in Universities

The situation of a boarding students in universities is basically different from those in primary and secondary levels. The question here is to train

---

[1] Fay Kirby, *The Village Institute Movement in Turkey* (Ph.D. diss., Columbia University, New York, 1960), p. 906.

[2] Publication of the Ministry of Education, *Milli Egitim Bakanlığı Meslek Teknik ve Yüksek Öğretim Istatistikleri*, Ankara 1947, pp. 80-90.

individuals for more highly-skilled jobs mostly in accordance with the government's own needs and countrywide estimates of needed personnel. Differing from the second two levels which are administered almost exclusively by the Ministry of Education, board and lodging in universities is financed and supervised jointly by this Ministry and that concerned with the specific field, e.g., the Ministry of Health for students in Medicine. The obligation to serve for set periods in areas designated by the government is general for students enjoying university boarding.

University education provides the major avenue to high income and superior social status. Therefore, the boarding privilege, covering usually all living and school expenses, guarantees both university education and assures social mobility. It is free of the stigma of "charity" associated with some of the boarding schools at lower levels. Increasing competition for admission to universities was the main factor in greatly raising the standard of admission to boarding schools. The number of boarding students in universities in 1939-40 rose to 2,422 or 19 percent of the total number of students. In 1949 the total decreased to 17 percent, and in 1960 it was down to only 4 percent or altogether 2,000 students out of a total student body of 59,000.[1] This decrease was caused in part by the expansion of general educational facilities as well as the number of universities, the rapid rate of urbanization, growth of the middle classes, and a relative increase in living standards, all of which reduced the demand for government support for university boarding facilities. Thus the government could now staff its administrative apparatus without having to spend money to both board and train its own personnel at all educational levels.

The ideological orientation of the groups in power was also responsible for this decrease in the number of university students wholly supported directly by the government or by its economic enterprises. (The latter had special budgetary allocations for training their personnel at home or abroad). The "liberalism" of the Democratic Party after taking power in 1950, coupled with its opposition to the state bureaucracy (chiefly because the latter tended to support the Republican Party) resulted in a de-emphasis of education schemes likely to strengthen the bureaucratic orientation of the elites. This policy although offset partly through the granting of scholarships free of obligation, was nevertheless detrimental to the children of lower classes. The military revolution of 1960, and the outburst of social demands thereafter reversed this trend.

---

[1] Kurdaş, "Socialist Thought."

The Constitution of 1961 (Article 50) gave to the state the main responsibility for educating the people, and charged it specifically to provide the "capable students deprived of material possibilities with scholarships and other necessary means to enable them to reach the highest levels of education." Though the social aims of the Constitution have not been fully reflected in education philosophy, nevertheless some intellectuals began to envisage education within the framework of a broader social democratic orientation, absent in the early decades of the Republic. The immediate impact of these developments was the strengthening of the scholarships program at middle and university levels. Thus, in 1962 4,041 university students, or 5.7 percent of a total of 69,798, received scholarships or were boarding students.[1]

Table 6.7 gives the main schools in universities and the independent institutions of higher learning, and the number of boarding an non-boarding students:

Table 6.7

Boarding Students at Universities in 1939-40 and 1943-44 [2]

University Schools	Year	Number of Boarding Students	Total Number of Students
School of Language, History, and Geography	1939-40	23	249
(Dil-Tarih-Coğrafya Fakültesi)	1943-44	101	699
Gazi Institute of Education [3]	1939-40	317	377
(Gazi Eğitim)	1943-44	466	490
Ankara School of Law [4]	1939-40	180	3,067
(Hukuk Fakültesi)	1943-44	397	1,363
Ankara School of Science (Ankara Fen Fakültesi)	1943-44	14	33
School of Political Science	1939-40	382	398
(Siyasal Bilgiler Fakültesi or Mülkiye) [5]	1943-44	389	429
School of Agriculture	1939-40	616	620
(Yüksek Ziraat Fakültesi)	1943-44	637	803
Istanbul School of Literature	1939-40	102	584
(Istanbul Edebiyat Fakültesi)	1943-44	658	1,457
Istanbul School of Medicine	1939-40	379	838
(Istanbul Tıp Fakültesi)	1943-44	756	3,232
School of Dentistry	1939-40	4	61
(Dişçilik Fakültesi)	1943-44	16	82
School of Navigation	1939-40	112	112
(Yüksek Deniz Ticaret Okulu)	1943-44	187	187
Istanbul Technical University	1943-44	395	792
Yıldız Engineering School [6]	1943-44	199	252

(Notes on next page)

Number of Girls in the Teacher Training Schools

Year	Number of Girls	Number of Boys
1942-43	1,576	1,030
1945-46	1,219	921
1950-51	754	1,457
1955-56	2,712	12,523
1959-60	5,401	15,605

Istatistik Yıllığı : 1959-1960 (Ankara, 1961), p. 171. The table does not include the students (officers) in military academies either. A limited number of cadets were trained in various University schools in specialized fields such as law, medicine, engineering, and even the Schools of Language and History in order to replenish the ranks of the military bureaucracy. The table does not include the students trained abroad either. Their number between 1935 and 1962 was as follows :

Year	Number of students abroad supported by the state	Number of students at their own expense
1935-36	224	—
1940-41	81	—
1945-46	47	—
1948-49	28	898
1955-56	155	1,311
1959-60	364	3,017
1961-62	477	

Istatistik Yıllığı : 1959 (Ankara, 1961), p. 177; *1960-62*, p. 173.

[1] *Ibid.*

[2] *Istatistik Yıllığı : 1939-40* (Ankara 1941), p. 214. The table above does not indicate the number of girls. However, their number in boarding schools, especially in teacher training schools, tends to be relatively high. This is due in part to restrictive social customs as well as to the parents' desire to secure regular protective care for their daughters.

[3] This school has usually reflected the government's viewpont on educational policy. It is the major educational institution of Turkey, located in Ankara; it trains mainly teachers.

[4] The chief, original purpose of this institution was to provide a modern, legal, political background for the men needed by the Republic. It was established by Atatürk. Different from a similar school in Istanbul, its graduates joined the civil service rather than the bar associations.

[5] This institution trains top-ranking civil administrators, foreign service officers and finance personnel. It has remained closely attached to the government and is still a major source of statist minded political leaders. It is considered along with the Harbiye ("War College") a basic source of elitist philosophy and of the men aspiring to top leadership in Turkey.

[6] This is essentially a technical school whose students have fought vigorously for equality with their privileged colleagues the *yüksek mühendis* ("high engineers") graduated from engineering schools.

Conclusions

The free boarding school program in Turkey is an inherent part of the modernization process. It embodies the political philosophies of the social groups leading the modernization drive and offers training for specialized functions expected to be performed by the government. The scope of the boarding schools varied in accordance with the ideology of the regime, the growth of new social groups and the availability of personnel capable of undertaking technically specialized jobs. Modernization during the first three decades of the Republic was generated and implemented by a small group of intellectuals and civilian and military bureaucrats. The secular-modernist-minded political regime established by the group, despite various democratic populist undercurrents, remained confined to the upper layers of society. The boarding schools consequently were concentrated at the middle and higher levels and served as a means of recruitment for the ruling elite. The schools were geared to disseminate the ideology of the Republican regime, and train the intelligentsia accordingly. The gradual shrinking in the number of boarding schools at the elementary level, due in part to high costs, proves also that the regime relied chiefly on the middle and upper urban groups to carry out its modernization program.

The emergence of new social groups in urban areas, such as industrial workers, entrepreneurial, business groups and lower class intellectuals was stimulated by economic development but also by the very educational system itself. The middle classes increased in size and diversified. Eventually the entrepreneurial groups, the free professionals such as lawyers, doctors, engineers, etc., who had good incomes, became interested in vocational, technical, and liberal education, which they provided to their children without incurring obligations to the government. Education remained relatively free of tuition but this apparently democratic measure worked to the benefit of the upper groups in cities, that could take advantage of the existing facilities supported by the taxes collected from the general public. Yet, one must not overlook the essential fact that in numerous cases these very professionals came from families of modest origin educated originally in boarding schools. Thus, the boarding schools fulfilled an essential role in facilitating social mobility, although this remained primarily confined at the beginning to the urban middle classes and especially bureaucratic groups.

The institutions training teachers for elementary and middle level schools as distinct from universities used the boarding incentives extensively to attract students from the lower classes. The modest social origin of teachers, their relatively low salaries and dependence on the government, both for education and employment, is evident in their statist-socialist political orientation, as well as in an advanced degree of group consciousness and cohesion lacking among other professionals. [1]

The relation between the political regime and education in Turkey is clearly demonstrated by the increase of boarding schools during statist-minded regimes (1923-50) and relative stagnation under government with a "liberal" orientation (1950-60). However, statism and liberalism in Turkey, as in most other developing states, were not determined by exclusive loyalty to an ideology but by immediate practical needs arising from the necessity of rapid modernization. Modernism in Turkey was originally envisaged as consisting primarily of a modern political system. This system, once established, stimulated social growth but without being able—in part due to the very lack of firm commitment to an ideology—to control and channel this growth according to a scheme devised in advance. Thus, the boarding schools, while reflecting the social philosophy of groups controlling the government, basically reflect the internal social transformation of Turkey and the power shifts among various social groups.

The future of the boarding schools may be determined by the very fate of the political regime. In the present circumstances, however, one may expect the further decline of boarding schools at the university level, and a further increase at middle and lower levels, especially in the training of teachers. This development in turn may further widen the differences between the liberal professions and the government personnel, and increase social tensions. The following case study dramatizes the opportunities for upward mobility offered by the government boarding school programs.

CASE HISTORY OF SOCIAL MOBILITY IN A FAMILY EDUCATED IN BOARDING SCHOOLS

The original family consisting of parents, two daughters, and two sons lived in a small village near the town of Gemerek in Sivas province, a

---

[1] Peasant children who graduated from Village Institutes are at present (1966) very active in social and political movements. The National Federation of Turkish Teachers Unions is under their control. Seventeen of the twenty-four members of the administrative body of the Federation, including the Secretary General, were educated in the Village Institutes.

relatively poor area. The father owned at the turn of the century a small piece of land which provided for his subsistence. The two boys (the daughters did not pursue education and were married) after somehow attending the newly-opened elementary school in Gemerek went to the teachers' school, opened in Sivas in about 1896, chiefly because of free boarding. Both became teachers, but the older son lost his life in World War I. The surviving son, whom we shall call Ahmet, was appointed to teach in the elementary school in Gemerek. Eventually Ahmet married and had first a daughter whom he wanted to educate in a *lise*, probably as preparation to enter the university since only the graduates of *lises* could enter the university. However, unable to support her independently in a *lise* he asked to be transferred to teach in an elementary school in a city where the daughter could attend school (no tuition was necessary) and live at home. Ahmet's request for transfer to a city being rejected, the daughter entered the Teachers' School in Edirne which offered free boarding in 1934. She eventually became a teacher.

Ahmet had, in addition to the daughter, three sons. When the oldest son reached middle school age, Ahmet asked once more to be transferred to a city so that he could send his sons to a *lise*. He was eventually transferred to Kayseri where his three sons graduated successfully from the *lise*. The children wanted to attend a university. Consequently, Ahmet asked once more to be transferred to Ankara where a university had recently been opened but he was not successful. Subsequently the eldest son, whom we shall call Sabri, taking the father's meagre savings, went to Ankara in 1939, in the hope of entering the School of Dentistry. Since this school had no boarding quota, Sabri, after a lengthy search, joined the Military Veterinary School which offered free boarding to one hundred competent *lise* graduates. Sabri graduated in 1943. He then served as a veterinarian in the army for eight years in Erzurum, an eastern city considered at the time a hardship area. In 1951 he was transferred to Istanbul and was able to attend the Dentistry School while still serving in the army. At the time Sabri graduated from Dentistry School, he had completed his service obligation to the government. Consequently, he resigned his commission in the army and opened a dentistry office in Istanbul where he is still practicing as an independent professional.

The careers of Ahmet's other two sons (Sabri's brothers) were also determined by education through boarding schools. The second son graduated form the *lise* in 1952, at a time when the boarding schools, relatively in disfavor, were accepting only a limited number of students. Consequently, unable to gain admission to a professional boarding school, he entered the War College (Harbiye), which offered board, and became an officer. The youngest son Davud was also unable to enter a boarding school and consequently joined the army in 1954, and became a reserve officer like all other *lise* graduates. This special social distinction offered privileges which were finally abolished a few years ago. Davud had hoped to save some money to continue his higher education. However, at the end of his service the Ministry of Defense, hard pressed by a shortage of army officers trained in military schools, appealed to *lise* graduates and reserve officers to become permanent members of the officers corps. Davud consequently became a career army officer. Thus, all three sons of Ahmet, although trained in *lises* and wishing for careers in civilian professions, used the boarding facilities offered by military schools to attain a higher social status. Their children, however, should be able to attend the university and become professionals without resorting to government support.

The two daughters of Ahmet had similar experiences. The elder daughter Fatma's husband, a farmer, died in the War of Liberation (1919-1922). He left two sons. The first finished elementary school in Gemerek and then entered the military school in Erzincan to become an officer. He is now a colonel. After graduating from elementary school the second son entered the Teachers' School in Sivas, which had free boarding facilities. He served six years as a teacher in an elementary school in order to fulfill his obligation toward the government. Afterwards, he enrolled in the university and became a geography teacher for the *lise*. When this was written he was director of Basic Education (Halk Eğitimi) in Izmir.

Ahmet's second daughter—Hatija—married a teacher in elementary school and had 12 children of whom only six (five girls and a son) survived. Hatija's husband taught in Gemerek and then after retirement in 1932 moved to Sivas to educate his children. However, being conservative, he did not approve of coeducational schools. Consequently in 1934, after the junior high school in Sivas became coeducational, he stopped the girls' education. The son pursued his education in the *lise* in Sivas, then received a scholarship to attend the university and eventually became a professor. This case study documents how one family benefitted greatly from free boarding school programs leading to substantial professional and social advancement otherwise hardly accessible to its members.

PART III

THE POLITICS AND IDEOLOGY
OF SOCIAL GROUPS

CHAPTER SEVEN

SOCIAL GROUPS AND THE POLITICAL SYSTEM AFTER 1960

KEMAL H. KARPAT

INTRODUCTION

This study is an attempt to analyze empirically the process of internal conversion and adaptation of the Turkish political system to an interest oriented rational pattern of political recruitment, and to the representation of the social groups capable of articulating and defending their demands. The analysis, though comprising references to the historical origin of various social groups and their political subculture, is confined essentially to the developments in two periods, first that between 1945 and 1960 and then mainly to that after the revolution of May 27, 1960. The focus of analysis is directed upon the ideological and power struggles between the statist and economic groups, described further below, in order to secure an influential role in decision-making at the national level. Furthermore, the analysis is based on the assumption that the rise and the competition for power of the two groups was preceded by economic change and structural differentiation which had the effect of intensifying social mobility, sharpening group consciousness, and raising the idea of group and individual interest to a rational and hence articulable level. In other words this is the segmental or micro-analysis of the historical or macro-survey present ed in Chapter I.

Two groups with different social origins and different cultural-behavioral attitudes determined Turkey's politics after 1945 and especially after 1960. The first group which can be called *statist, directing*, or *administrative* was made up of the intellegentsia-bureaucracy including the military and their subgroups. These in their contemporary form had emerged as the product of modernization of the government apparatus which had begun in the nineteenth century. The statist group therefore owed its existence primarily to the government's need for men with the skills and attitudes necessary to perform the specialized functions in a society whose structure was differentiating. This group performed also a symbolic representative function as the agent of "modernity" which carried with it the implicit mark of superiority, thus giving to the intelligentsia the position of "elite" on behalf of a new and in some ways alien pattern of life. The ways and methods, the internal and external political-cultural pressures through which the intelligentsia was induced to develop its "modernist" philosophy and policy do not concern us here. However, the success of this elite in making itself acceptable to the society at large depended in the long run not only on authority but also on the practical usefulness of its modern training and ability to legitimize its role.

The second group, which can be called *economic* or *productive*, comprised most of the commercial, agrarian, entrepreneurial, and labor groups. These, though different in composition, interest, and somewhat in mentality, were rooted in the basic process of production either as employee or employer, or in villages as self-sustaining units. Their economic relations, conflicting as they might have been at times, were superseded by the fact that this group as a whole was confronted by a ruling elite which had a limited role in production. The government apparatus and the statist groups were still the carriers of traditional practices contributing little directly to economic life but benefiting greatly from it. In the latter centuries of the Ottoman Empire, economic life had remained largely outside the sphere of government authority. Through centralization and subsequent expansion of authority in the twentieth century the economic sector was brought under government authority but without the intelligentsia-bureaucracy developing the economic know-how to become a organic part of the process of production. It is true that some of the commercial and entrepreneurial groups came into existence largely as the government's effort to create a sustaining national economic basis for its ever-expanding bureaucratic order. But these groups were not officially recognized as participants in the decision-making process despite their indirect influence upon the government.

The question of legitimization of authority, however, brought about a different type of alignment. The statist elite and the upper segments of the agrarian commercial and entrepreneurial groups were in implicit agreement as to the traditional views of authority rooted in history, culture, and religion. These leading groups had a rational, interest-oriented understanding of their position in the social body, whereas the supporting lower groups, peasants and industrial workers in the early days of the Republic, accepted the existing power structure as natural, and almost predestined. There was, however, the possibility that one of the groups, that is either the statist or the upper segments of the economic groups, would try to enlist mass support in order to assert its own power when threatened by the other. There was a precedent. We know, for instance, that one of the reasons for the proclamation of the Tanzimat in 1839 was partly the Sultan's and the new bureaucracy's search for support among broader segments of the population in order to break the power of the country gentry, the *ayans*. In the War of Liberation (1919-1922) the leaders secured mass support not only by appeals to nationalist-religious sentiments but also by promises of social and economic liberation from the imperial bureaucracy and the Sultan. This coalition between the military and the intelligentsia on one hand and the masses through their religious, communal leaders on the other was replaced later by the realignment of the nationalist-secularist bureaucratic-intelligentsia with the powerful socially conservative but secularist country groups.

The lack of a clearly defined social ideology in the ruling statist group, as well as the absence of immediate challenges to its power left it largely unaware of the structural differentiation, inequality, and pressures developing in the social body between 1923 and 1945. It became aware of this only at the end of World War II when it attempted to enact a rather extensive land reform law but was thwarted in implementing it by the agrarian interests in Parliament. The government through its statist policy, had exploited agriculture in order to build up industry and to create a relatively high standard of life in urban areas. All this made the statist group lose its appeal to the masses. It was, in fact, the upper segment of the rural groups, which had deep roots in the local communities and controlled the wealth, that won the support of the masses, and through them, eventually achieved control of government in 1945-50, when it brought the Democratic Party to power.

The structural differentiation and the political changes mentioned briefly also affected the lower classes. Their political reaction was expressed first, in the form of association with any movement which demanded change, manifested in the form of government criticism. Later the reaction appeared as concrete demands. These demands may be defined roughly as being material betterment, regulation and definition of state authority (expressed usually in bitter complaints against the pressure and inefficiency of the bureaucracy), and recognition of society's own values and cultural identity. The next step in the involvement of the masses in the political-social-cultural life of their own society was the acquisition of an intellectual awareness that neither the social nor the political order, including the ruling groups, was an arrangement ordained by divine will but decided by human beings and motivations. Thus, the involvement and participation of the masses in politics, and their subsequent political awareness, though hardly complete or perfect, forced a change in the very pattern of relations between the masses and the elites, as clearly demonstrated by the ideological development in Turkey since 1950 and especially after 1960.[1] Consequently, ideological development in Turkey, as elsewhere in the third world, is far more significant than the "end of ideology" school, based on the experience of the West, can perceive.

The relations between the masses and the elites after the period 1946 to 1950 began to be based on consensus and persuasion and affected life at all levels of activity. This idea of consensus in turn provided the philosophical basis for a new form of group differentiation and for the use of political means to attain goals according to new socio-economic conditions.

Thus, following the theories of Max Weber and Karl Mannheim concerning the origin of ideas and ideology in general, we may say that social differentiation caused by modernization in Turkey gave to individuals a new sense of group identity based on their interests, which manifested itself in the form of political demands and new ideologies. A degree of cultural-educational preparation in turn enabled the individuals belonging to one group or another to promote their own interest-oriented ideology in the guise of general policies and justify it as beneficial to the public as a whole. The above view, while helpful in defining the ideological position of some social groups, nevertheless fails to explain satisfactorily the reasons why some social groups in Turkey did not engage in struggle against their economic opponents (worker against the private entrepreneurs) as the classical interest theories predict, but opposed the groups in control of the government. Obviously there could be many ingenious explanations to the claim that the social groups in Turkey actually would have conformed to the classical doctrine of class conflict if it had not been for the impediment of various temporary causes, such as the lack of class-oriented political leadership and insufficient class consciousness. Yet, the truth remains that, in twenty years of accelerated change and agitated political activity in Turkey since 1946, the economic groups, including peasants and workers, have invariably united and supported the parties opposed to the rule of a bureaucratic intellectual elite. The paradox of the situation also lies in

---

[1] These problems have been studied in detail in Kemal H. Karpat, *Political and Social Thought in the Contemporary Middle East* (New York, 1968), especially in the section "Ideology in Turkey After the Revolution of 1960." See also chapter IX.

the fact that the economic groups have integrated themselves in the political system and adopted the social ideas promoted by that very statist-bureaucratic elite.

Fundamental questions suggested by the Turkish political experiment still remain to be explored. The first basic question is to determine how a Middle Eastern society changes in practice by incorporating into the modernized system its traditional culture, customs, and political habits, and resolves new conflicts arising from all these. We know how the statist groups emerged but possess little insight into the manner in which the society interpreted and assimilated the changes brought about by these elites. The second question is to determine whether the instrumental role played by the bureaucracy and the intelligentsia in the establishment of a modern state endows them with a permanent elite philosophy that transforms itself eventually into a statist, and then a socialist, ideology aimed at preserving their own power.

These are theoretical questions the partial answer to which may transpire from our empirical analysis of the struggle between statist and economic groups in Turkey after 1960. We should note at the very beginning that the leadership for the opposition from 1945 to 1950, and for the Democratic Party government from 1950 to 1960, came from a new provincial elite consisting chiefly of professionals and agrarian groups and that the rise to power of these groups was one of the chief causes that prepared the ground for the military revolution in 1960. After the Revolution of 1960 the professionals, technicians, and business groups gained political power to the detriment of the agrarian segments while society underwent further group differentiation and specialization. This was accompanied by a definite sharpening of interest conflicts among these groups. However, these conflicts, instead of merging groups with similar interests into a single political class, e.g., workers and peasants, prompted them to seek economic advantages through action as pressure groups. In fact, industrialists, skilled and unskilled labor groups, managers and capital owners, as well as some professional sections of the intelligentsia and bureaucracy, seemed to have begun to transform themselves into interest and pressure groups. The transformation of social groups into interest and pressure groups, if achieved fully, could, in fact, supersede the differences dividing the economic and statist groups. It is for this reason that we have chosen to emphasize the economic or interest factor, not as a collective but as an individual search for material betterment, as the dynamic force in Turkish politics after 1960.

Economic issues, indeed, have become the dominant theme in Turkish politics. The preoccupation with economic matters since the revolution has been responsible, in part at least, for developing a rational, objective view of society and the world in general. This objective view has been also instrumental in reshaping the new constitution, the government, and the course of politics in general in the light of a concrete understanding of human beings, society, and of man's motives and aspirations. Meanwhile, a raging ideological battle has developed between the vanguards of the statist and entrepreneurial groups : the first embraced socialism and statism (the terms are often used as synonymous) while the latter espoused liberalism. Both concepts, however, have little in common with their Western meaning since they stem not from philosophical commitment to a given school of thought but from conditions specific to Turkey (See Chapter IX).

The Revolution of May 27, 1960, clarified the issues in Turkish politics and indirectly enabled various social forces to produce a potentially broad, representative, political order. It also helped to replace the old pyramidal, hierarchical power organization with a horizontal system based on the balance of social groups. Finally, it ended the last vestiges of a moral concept of government rooted in traditional notions of authority, and for better or worse, plunged the country fully into the age of power politics.

The Revolution of May 27 and its Social and Economic Causes

Social and economic factors motivated the revolution as well as the policy of the military after the take-over on May 27, 1960. The military justified their action as intended to save democracy and to prevent internal strife. The revolution in their view "was not against any individual or any group... every citizen regardless of his identity and party affiliation shall be treated in accordance with law and the principles of justice." Elections were to be held soon. But subsequent measures and declarations indicated that the revolution was, in fact, directed against certain groups. A committee of university professors, charged by the military to draft a new Constitution, legitimized the coup by condemning the Democratic government as having degenerated into a power tool in the hands of an interest group. It would be wrong, the committee declared,

To view the situation in which we find ourselves today as an ordinary political *coup*. It is regrettable that, for many months and even years now, the political power that should have been the guardian of civil rights and that symbolized the principles of state, law, justice, ethics, public interest, and public service has lost this quality; it has become instead a materialistic force representative of personal influence and ambition and class privilege. Whereas the power wielded by the state would represent a social capacity that derives its vigor from the law to which it is attached, this power was transformed into the means of achieving personal influence and ambition. That is why political power ended up by losing all spiritual bonds with the true sources of state power, which reside in its army, its courts of justice and bar associations, its civil servants...its universities...the press...and the basic and essential institutions of a true state... No clique that caused acts so totally devoid of any connection with the true concepts of right, law, and state could continue to be looked upon as a social institution... This particular deed stripped every semblance of a social or national institution from the government and showed it up for what it had become, namely, a means and a tool for the realization of personal power and ambitions. [1]

The committee described the ousted government as having deviated from Atatürk's reforms and indicated that the new Constitution would establish the proper moral and social order by paying due attention to the existing forces in society and preventing the supremacy of any special group.

It is necessary at this point to outline the socio-political background of the above developments. The ousted Democratic Party government, whatever its faults, was the first truly civilian authority in the entire history of Turkey. It represented those groups whose direct influence in the government had been negligible until 1950, such as business groups, landowners, and contractors, and courted the peasants and workers with material incentive. The Democrats were backed originally by the military and the intelligentsia until about 1953. After this date their economic policy swung openly to the support of entrepreneurs, landowners, and commercial groups. Meanwhile inflation hit hard at salaried groups, especially the military and the bureaucracy and lowered their living standards. The new elite of the politician-entrepreneur-business groups

---

[1] For the text of the first declaration by the military announcing the overthrow of the Democratic Party government see Sabahat Erdemir (ed.), *Milli Birliğe Doğru* (Ankara, 1960), p. 293. For the professors' declaration see Karpat, *Political and Social Thought*, pp. 307-9. The declaration resembles the *mufti*'s *fetva* deposing the ruling sultan. For additional information see Kemal H. Karpat, "Society, Economics, and Politics in Contemporary Turkey," *World Politics*, October, 1964, pp. 50-74; also Walter F. Weiker, *The Turkish Revolution: 1960-1961* (Washington, D. C., 1963); Ali Fuad Başgil, *La révolution militaire de 1960 en Turquie: ses origines* (Geneva, 1963); and George S. Harris, "The Role of the Military in Turkish Politics," *Middle East Journal*, Winter 1965, pp. 54-66, Spring 1965, 169-176. See also Kemal H. Karpat, "The Military and Politics in Turkey, 1960-64; the Socio-Cultural Analysis of a Revolution", *American Historical Review*, October 1970.

acquired social and political power and prestige. Thus the revolution in part expressed the social and economic resentment of the adversely affected statist elite against the new power group, but also a yearning for a new balanced system of power capable of preventing power abuses and inequitable distribution of income. The military government, following the advice of some university professors, arrested all the Democratic Party deputies. It also interned in a camp at Sivas some 220 landlords from East Anatolia, and established special committees to investigate the fortunes of some individuals enriched under the Democrats' rule.

The Cabinet formed under the military was composed mainly of civilians, but these were mere executive agents of the *Milli Birlik Komitesi*, "National Unity Committee," henceforth NUC, the sole decision-making body. The Committee consisted of thirty-eight officers representing all branches of the armed forces. Actually the ground forces outnumbered the others. The government, thus established, immediately launched an economic program intended to check inflation and restore financial stability. The Minister of Finance in a nationally broadcast speech revealed dramatically the country's dismal financial situation. The foreign debt, according to the Minister, was 1,345 million dollars, while gold reserves had declined from 118 tons to 16 tons, and the foreign currency reserve stood at a bare 16 million dollars. The domestic banks had a credit balance of 1,120 million dollars, one-quarter of which was loaned to agriculture and the rest to commercial and industrial enterprises.[1]

The Minister of State, Şefik Inan, declared that 33 percent of the foreign debt was owed to private firms abroad dealing mainly with local commercial enterprises, and that easy bank credits and import licences had enriched certain commercial groups which in turn had provided ample funds for the Democratic Party.[2] The taxes paid by these groups were minimal. For instance, 1,300 companies out of the 3,850 declared in 1959 that they made profits of less than 2,500 liras or only about 260 dollars. Forty percent of the businessmen showed profits of only about 2,500 liras, and thirty percent of 7,500 liras. But private

---

[1] See speech in *Büyük Kurtuluş* (n.p., n.d.), pp. 120-28; and *Cumhuriyet*, June 18, 1960.

[2] The enterprises politically favored secured bank loans at low interest rates while small businessmen and craftsmen paid up to 20 percent interest on their own borrowing. See lists of firms contributing funds to the Democratic Party, *Cumhuriyet*, August 11, 1960.

capital was accumulated at a rapid pace. The reported individual earnings of over a million liras was the following : in 1953, 11; 1955, 36; 1957, 53; and 1959, 86. The number of half-million lira earnings, was the following : in 1953, 40; 1957, 160; and 1959, 227.[1] In view of the loose Turkish tax system, the unreported number of earnings above a million was probably at least six or seven times higher than the above figures, indicating the existence of a rather disturbing imbalance of wealth.

The economic measures following the above declarations were stern. Bank operations and a number of personal accounts were frozen, certain construction projects were stopped, loans were suspended (later a high interest rate of 10-12 percent was charged), government bonds at 6 percent interest were compulsorily sold—and still are in 1971—to all wage and salary earners. Middlemen were subjected to rigorous controls. Subsequently, the prices of fruit and vegetables, which are among the major items of consumption, fell considerably, causing delight in cities but plain despair among villagers who had to purchase manufactured goods at the same old prices. Other measures had social and political implications. The craftsmen's associations were forced by law to reelect new executive boards since the old ones were deemed "corrupt" through associations with the old regime. The Trade and Industrial Chambers, the chief business associations of the entrepreneurial groups, were asked to disband their administrative boards in order to hold new elections "in accordance with the integrity of the profession and the need for solidarity." [2] Later the tax on land was increased ten times and the one on buildings two to six times, causing profound reactions among the affected parties. Income tax law Number 193 of December 13, 1960, imposed on all those subject to annual income declaration, that is, chiefly private enterprises, the obligation to submit an additional declaration (Art. 114-6) listing all their assets. This was called *servet beyanı* or wealth declaration, and although intended to help assess taxes correctly, it carried with it ominous, far-reaching political implications. The press in turn, taking courage from the declarations of some members of NUC, published lengthy reports about the corrupt dealings and illegitimate profits of various entrepreneurial and commercial groups, while depicting pathetically the poverty of lower classes in order to dramatize the need for social justice.

---

[1] *Cumhuriyet*, December 16, 1963.

[2] Law Number 2 of June 14, 1960. This was the second law adopted by the military following the enactment of the Provisional Constitution two days earlier. The craftsmen held elections under Law Number 39 of July 29, 1960.

Yet, despite the unfavorable political atmosphere, the business and entrepreneurial groups vigorously defended their own position. Some considered the "declarations on social reforms by members of NUC as the expression of their negative attitude toward property, profits and wealth" and asked for assurance that this was not the prelude to nationalization and socialism.[1] Bankers, business groups, and landlords began to press the government to rescind the economic restrictions in order to end business lethargy and unemployment. About six months after the revolution, President Cemal Gürsel apologetically confessed that there had been some "extreme and unbalanced actions" in the economic field and assured the business world " as the head of the government that events up to now are past and ended. Henceforth the defense of your rights is as important as our own. Believe in these words and decide your future actions accordingly." [2] He also advised them not to smuggle their money abroad but invest it at home. Meanwhile, in 1960 and 1961, the salaries of military personnel were increased and special fringe benefits offered to officers, such as an orderly, or 200 liras a month, housing credits, et cetera. Eventually the military's salary rose to 60 percent above that of their corresponding ranks in the civil service.

Over seven thousand officers were retired in August 1960. These received, besides generous severance pay, high pension salaries and housing credits to become thus a new middle class group; some engaged in politics or business while others occupied government jobs in administration and security. The salaries of civil servants were to be gradually increased 35 percent by 1963.[3] (Salaries of government personnel increased three and one-half times between 1939 and 1960, while the gross price index went up eleven times). Thus, the dissatisfied salaried groups were economically vindicated and inadvertently, perhaps, made to develop an interest in the emerging political system. A new personnel payment scale introduced as a sweeping measure in 1970 met resistance from various bureaucratic groups.

The first six months of military rule, until the ousting of the "fourteen"

---

[1] From a private report submitted to Iş Bank in 1960.

[2] *Cumhuriyet*, October 7, 1960. A similar declaration was also issued by the military governor of Istanbul.

[3] The number of regular government officials was placed at 312,088 in 1960, although a variety of additional groups falling under special categories raised the total number to over half a million (*Ulus*, August 18, 1960). About 81.5 percent received salaries of between 277 and 503 liras or an average of about 427 liras a month, while 679 liras a month was considered the minimum income for modest living. See also chap. III.

officers from the NUC on November 13, 1960, brought into the open the economic grievances of Turkey and laid the bases of future developments. The ousting of the "fourteen" who advocated continuous strong rule by an elite, represented a victory for those military favoring an early return to civilian rule through the adoption of a new constitution and representative institutions. It also delayed the implementation of some pressing social reforms. The following period lasting roughly from November 1960 until the appointment of the first elected civilian cabinet in November 1961 encompassed the basic constitutional changes which resulted in the Second Turkish Republic. This constitution, besides establishing a horizontal balance of power, incorporated the major groups into the political system.

The Constituent Assembly and the Constitution of 1961
Structure and Philosophy

The National Unity Committee, in a document entitled "Basic views on national problems," indicated its desire to "insure the reorganization of a democratic order of state and law based on national... foundations, and to balance it with a virtuous administration through... a constitution conforming to our [social] structure."[1] It pointed out specifically the need for economic and social measures related to the military, workers, and villagers and called for cooperation between private and state enterprises seeking common goals beneficial to the public. The final objective of this document was to grant political recognition to all social groups and balance them with each other within the framework of a new constitutional system. It is with this new idea of extending recognition to every force in society that the military, although firmly committed to secularism, declared in the document that "the place and value of men of religion in *our social structure* [italics added] should be properly determined." But supposedly the "fourteen" had delayed the implementation of this document. Indeed, almost immediately after the ousting of the "fourteen," President Cemal Gürsel announced that work on the constitution would proceed rapidly. Consequently Turhan Feyzioğlu of the Republican Party, and a former professor at the Faculty of Political Science in Ankara, drafted the law for the election and the convening of a Constituent Assembly.[2] (Some

---

[1] *Official Gazette*, no. 10605 (September 16, 1960).

[2] Laws Number 157 and 158 of Dec. 13, 1960. Later Feyzioğlu in a dispute with the socialist wing in PRP resigned and established the *Güven Partisi* in 1967.

claimed that the junta planned to use the Constituent Assembly chiefly as an advisory body,[1] but eventually the organization acquired some legislative powers, although most of its time was taken up with the debates on the Constitution).

The members of the Constituent Assembly were selected in the following manner : The President appointed 10 and the National Unity Committee 18, while all members of the Cabinet became ex-officio members. The provinces elected 75 representatives, the People's Republican Party 49, the Republican National Peasant Party 25, the bar associations 6, the press 12, the veterans' union 2, professions (crafts) 6, youth organizations 1, Trade Unions 6, Chambers of Trade and Industry 10, teachers' associations 6, agricultural organizations 6, university representatives 12, and justice courts 12 members.[2] The Assembly adopted the idea of "professional representation" in part as a reaction to the system of general representation implemented in the 1946-60 period, which had favored the Democratic Party, and in part to give political recognition to occupational groups. In fact, the Committee drafting the Constitution in Istanbul was already on record with a proposal to make the Senate a professional chamber and thus exclude political parties. This view was defeated through the politicians' efforts, and arguments put forth by the younger Faculty of Political Science in Ankara. The latter viewed political parties as means of social mobility, political education, and as the only effective weapons for preventing the establishment of dictatorial regimes. This Faculty was in agreement with modern notions of politics while its august counterpart, the Law Faculty at Istanbul University, remained immersed in the nineteenth century state theories of European legists. The Istanbul Committee prepared a draft constitution but without preventing the Faculty of Political Science from drafting a Constitution of its own.[3] This draft, along with the one prepared by the Istanbul Committee, was accepted for debate in the Constituent Assembly. It may be said that ultimately the constitutional philosophy embodied in the draft of the Political Science Faculty prevailed. The latter insisted that the political and social organizations should "provide provisions for

[1] *Vatan*, November 12, 1960. See also C. H. Dodd, *Politics and Government in Turkey*, (Manchester, 1969).

[2] Art. 2, of election law Number 158 of Dec. 13, 1960, *Official Gazette*, no. 10682 (1960). The texts may be found also in Server Feridun, *Anayasalar ve Siyasi Belgeler* (Istanbul, 1962), pp. 91-107. One should note the large number of representatives elected by the press and universities in comparison with agriculture and crafts.

[3] *Siyasal Bilgiler Fakültesi Idari Ilimler Entstitüsünün Gerekçeli Anayasa Tasarısı* (Ankara, 1960), p. 46.

enabling the nation to organize itself freely in every field [of activity] and to arouse the interest of popular masses in politics." The fact that the Faculty of Political Science became closely associated with the military government (three of its members became ministers and several others occupied high positions), had considerable impact in making their views accepted. This Faculty, together with the military, formed the backbone of the modernizing elite group and played decisive political roles in the modern history of Turkey.

The majority of the members in the Constituent Assembly belonged to the Republican Party or were its sympathizers, since Article 18.4 of the election law forbade the election of those who "had supported until the Revolution of May 27, through their activities, publications and attitudes the policy and the acts contrary to the Constitution and human rights." This provision left out the former Democrats. But it did not prevent sharp ideological conflicts stemming from the Constituent members' different occupational and educational backgrounds and interests, even though outwardly their party sympathies were similar.

These differences led eventually to the formation of two groups in the Constituent Assembly : a social-minded statist group comprising all shades of opinion from center to extreme left, and a liberal group which included all opinions from center to extreme right. The first group, usually in the minority but backed by the military, represented chiefly the urban, intellectual sections of the population. The second group, much larger but less articulate, represented a conglomeration of agrarian, commercial, and local interests. In a way the "liberal" group spoke on behalf of rural interests and local government while the "statist" one upheld the ideals of an integrated and centralized modern state in which they would have the upper hand. The differences in political philosophy became evident during the debates on the final form of the Constitution, especially on the articles dealing with property, rights, free enterprise, the government's role in the economy, local government, and nationalization. The business and agrarian groups claimed that the ultimate shape of the regime would be determined by the extent of the rights accorded to private property, and rejected the view that socialism would achieve balanced economic development. Eventually the government's right to nationalize private property and enterprise was considerably narrowed, and its enforcement rigidly defined. Large land estates, if nationalized, were to be indemnified in ten years at the most, while small farmers would be paid immediately. [1]

---
[1] The nationalization clause was accepted with 81 votes against 73 (*Tanin*, April

The report of the Constitutional Committee in the Constituent Assembly provides basic insights into the social and political philosophy of the new Constitution.[1] The report began with a historical survey of constitutional movements in Turkey. It described the Constitution of 1924 of Atatürk as having established the supremacy of the Assembly based on a doctrine of unity of powers, which was not suitable to the majority election system used after 1946, for it rendered public opinion ineffective. Consequently, the power of any majority in the Assembly became absolute, and political parties could not properly voice the opinion of various social groups. The report emphatically stated that the following needs had become evident before the revolution of 1960: to update the concepts of representation and of political power by relating them as closely as possible to the basic purpose or the idea of popular mandate embodied in the idea of elections and harmonize all these ideas with the need for economic and social development. It proposed a parliamentary regime based on a mild separation of powers in which public opinion and political parties would play essential roles. Full freedom, according to the report, could be attained if those groups and individuals that were socially and economically weak were to be protected and given the opportunity to develop morally and materially through state support, and in accordance with the principle of social justice. Consequently, individuals, either as persons or as members of a group, were entitled to a job and profession, and an opportunity to advance therein.

The Constitution as a whole may be described as consisting of a series of compromises between the statist and the economic groups. It was quite liberal with respect to human rights and freedoms, and extremely generous with promises of economic and social welfare. These goals were stated in terms of future ideals rather than current possibilities. Yet, in its social philosophy and concept of power the new Constitution was closer to the realities of Turkey than that of 1924. Society was regarded as a composite of groups, the totality of which formed the nation and the state, rather than being an amorphous conglomeration of individuals gathered around an ideal represented by an

---

25, 1961). An English translation of the Constitution of 1961 by Kemal H. Karpat and associates appeared in the *Middle East Journal*, Spring 1962, pp. 215-38.

[1] See text in Feridun, *Anayasalar.*, pp. 205 ff. This report, although dated March 9, 1961, adopts a classical, chronological view of constitutionalism very important in indicating the evolution from a monolithic and totalitarian concept of society and government to a pluralist one.

elite. Some of the framers of the Constitution, that is the social minded statist group, saw some groups in society as being socially and economically underprivileged. They sought to redress the social imbalance by strengthening these groups economically through government support. The peasants were described as being in need of land, and consequently land reform (Art. 37) was made mandatory. It has not been enacted yet (1973). The workers were also recognized as entitled to the right to organize trade unions freely, to engage in collective bargaining, and if necessary to strike. (Art. 46-47).[1]

The Constitution guaranteed private property and inheritance rights, provided that these were not used in a manner detrimental to public interest in which case such rights would be limited by law. The state was to draw plans for economic, social, and cultural development through democratic means (Art. 41) and to undertake measures for assuring the dignity of labor. However, the state role in economic and social fields was to be proportionate (Art. 53) to the availability of financial resources and the rate of development. This was an important provision, for it prohibited the state from using political means, that is to say, forced measures, to achieve economic development. Theoretically at least, the government was to seek and utilize purely economic means to reach its social and economic ends.

The power of the local government, an issue of vital significance for the local groups in their continuous struggle against central authority, was recognized through a provision which accepted the autonomy of locally elected bodies and expressly forbade the dismissal of elected local officials by the central government. Only the courts could decide their dismissal (Art. 116). The Constitution provided also "whether in power or in opposition political parties are indispensable entities for a democratic political life." (Art. 56-57). The Constitution introduced a bicameral system, a House of Deputies with fixed membership of 450 members serving for four years and a Senate for six years. The President was to be elected by both houses for a term of seven years. He could use a limited veto power, and could, under special conditions,

---

[1] The debates in the Constituent Assembly on the budget for 1961 indicated the regime's forthcoming political orientation. The propertied, business and agrarian groups demanded the repeal of declarations of capital assets and a revision of the tax measures adopted by the military. The pressure of these groups and the organized activities of the Trade and Industrial Chamber led to the formation of a Tax Reform Commission. The latter recommended a reduction in land and building taxes, and fiscal exemption for investments (*Cumhuriyet*, April 2, 1961; *Tanin*, April 12, 1961).

dissolve the Parliament. The Constitution established a system of checks and balances aimed at restricting the Executive's power. The members of the National Unity Committee—all former officers—became lifetime senators, in addition to the regular membership. They functioned in part as spokesmen for the armed forces and guardians of the measures enacted by the military in 1960-61.

The Constitution was submitted to popular referendum on July 9, 1961, and was approved by 6,348,191 voters against 3,934,370. The referendum vote was actually conditioned by widespread desires for a rapid return to civilian rule rather than an objective appraisal of the Constitution itself. Indeed, the return to civilian rule was dependent on free elections which in turn were tied to the ratification of the Constitution.

The other important factor affecting the constitutional referendum was the reemergence of political parties on the national scene in 1961. This shifted the center of political activity once more into the countryside, broadening the debate of old issues and especially of the new problems created by the military administration since May 1960.

Ekrem Alican, an economist representing a new group of leaders, established the New Turkey Party early in 1961. This party adopted a rational approach to economic development and hoped to attract the former members of the Democratic Party. But the latter, chastised and occasionally persecuted by the military government at the revengeful instigation of their personal enemies in the Republican Party, had been isolated and waited for a voice and a leader. Soon these expectations materialized. The Justice Party, established in 1961 by the late Ragip Gümüşpala, a disgruntled general who had been made Chief of Staff by the junta and then summarily retired, provided the true rallying organization for the former Democrats. Despite public declarations in support of the revolution of May 27 and of the Constitution, the original aim of the Justice Party was to annul some of the measures initiated by the military and return to the economic policies prevailing before the revolution. Thus the Justice Party better represented the mood of the former supporters of the Democratic Party and soon became their chief representative.

The Justice and New Turkey parties, backed by their own newspapers and a growing number of sympathizers, including large numbers of professionals, concentrated their activities in the countryside. In the main urban centers, however, the Revolution of May 27, and its vague reform plans had already become a symbol of progress among the statist intelligentsia. The concept of *zinde kuvvetler* ("energetic forces") was born among these circumstances. It was used to define in the main the military, the intelligentsia, and the press, or the groups we defined as "statist".

The Republican Party of Ismet Inönü, which had associated itself with the military and the intelligentsia in their common opposition to the Democrats, became eventually heir and defender of the measures known as the *Reforms of May 27*. This party had identified itself further with revolution by assuming major responsibilities under the military including the establishment of the Constituent Assembly. The Republican Party hoped to win the forthcoming elections, and prove its claim to be a modernizing force by fulfilling the social aims of the Constitution, although in reality it still preserved archaic oligarchic features.

Paradoxically a group of young intellectuals, catapulted to power and fame by the revolution, came to associate themselves closely with the Republican Party in the hope of implementing social and economic reforms and, incidentally, consolidating themselves in power. It was, however, the authoritarian-minded Old Guard in the Republican Party which took over the leading positions. Outwardly the Old Guard seemed to agree with the younger group on the extensive use of state authority, but proposed a conservative social and economic policy. A third liberal wing of the party, headed by former Secretary General Kasim Gülek, was opposed by Ismet Inönü himself and defeated. The Republicans entered the elections of 1961, under the domination of the Old Guard in the rural branches and of the new statist groups in the central urban bodies.[1]

The Elections of 1961 and the Parliamentary Structure

The election campaign began in a tense and confused atmosphere caused by the harsh sentences imposed on former Democratic Party leaders and deputies at the Yassıada trials.[2] Fifteen persons were con-

---

[1] These developments occurred at the Republican Party convention of August 1961. The writer followed all the proceedings.

[2] The Justice and the New Turkey parties declared publicly that they formed a powerful group to be reckoned with and asked that their wishes and thoughts be properly considered. The declarations actually had another purpose, namely to impress upon the military leaders the danger likely to arise from dealing harshly with the former leaders and deputies of the Democratic Party (*Ulus*, September 9-12, 1961).

demned to death (only Adnan Menderes, Hasan Polatkan, and Fatin R. Zorlu were executed) and several hundred sentenced to various terms in jail. The purpose of the elections was to establish a civilian government which would preserve the measures adopted by the military and enforce the Yassıada sentences.

The Republicans entered the elections with a detailed program embodying the social provisions of the new Constitution: land reform, the right to strike, welfare measures, housing credits, reforms in the educational system and the civil service, and more. The Republicans proposed to give free enterprise the same possibilities offered to state enterprises.[1]

The Justice Party promised to reform the income and corporate taxes, to abolish the declaration of capital assets and the compulsory buying of saving bonds. To farmers it promised a financial and economic policy likely to increase production. The Justice Party proposed to introduce land reform which would respect the specific features of each region and consider properly the costs of operation so as to make each farmer a producer.[2] It also proposed to reform the civil service, reorganize the villages, and grant new rights to the workers.

The New Turkey Party accepted private enterprise and industrialization as the basis of economic development and proposed to use government facilities to promote these goals. Proper balance between production costs and investment was to be established. Education in the broadest sense was considered an essential requisite for any kind of development. Both the New Turkey and Justice Parties considered religious freedom a natural human right and supported the idea of impartial religious education within the framework of secular principles.[3]

The Republican National Peasant Party placed priority on political rights rather than on economic and social ones. Yet, the Secretary General of this party, in one of his speeches over the radio, described the differences of wealth and opportunity as causing social tensions.[4] The industrial revolution in the West, according to the speaker, had created a new economic and social system and new currents of thought. Turkey was undergoing a similar transformation, and consequently the government had to provide employment opportunities to all individuals according to their needs and capabilities, for equality of opportunity was a basic feature of democracy.

---

[1] *Ulus*, September 24, 1961.

[2] *Cumhuriyet* and *Yeni Sabah*, October 1, 1961.

[3] *Milliyet*, September 30, 1961.

[4] *Kudret*, October 6, 1961.

The reform of the civil service proposed by the Justice and Republican parties, despite their different views of the government's social and economic roles, indicated the fundamental evolution occurring in the concept of authority and administration. The social system had evolved to the point where it was felt that an efficient, well-organized and professionally competent bureaucracy was an absolute condition for further progress. In other words, the bureaucracy had to place priority on its professional functions rather than its social position as the symbol and the representative of modernization. The bureaucracy was to make rational use of resources. (This development supports fully Max Weber's conclusions regarding the close connection between the rise of a rational economic order, that is capitalism, and the emergence of a professional, impartial modern bureaucracy).

The election campaign conducted in absolute freedom appeared at first sight fairly similar to the previous ones.[1] However, the issues discussed and the general tone of the debates differed markedly from the past. The solution of economic and social problems, envisaged primarily in the light of group interests, was requested as a matter of right and not as a favor as in the past. The press, which had covered the entire countryside for *nabız yoklaması* ("pulse control"), a kind of informal opinion poll, denounced the *şeyhs*, *ağas*, and landlords for using traditional communal loyalties to control the local vote. But often the accused leaders explained that their title was mostly an echo of past social arrangements for in reality their roles and functions had changed drastically. They still wielded power but not as religious leaders or tribal chiefs but as party leaders, employers, or landlords, who sought support by satisfying the demands of their constituencies rather than merely appealing to their traditional kinship or religious ties.[2]

---

[1] The campaign, although taking place in a tense atmosphere, was free of interference from above. Consequently, relatively few incidents resulted. For instance, in the period between September 24 and October 8, 1961, there were only 150 election offenses of which, notwithstanding 69 pending cases, only 9 cases drew court sentences. Most of these offenses resulted from technical violation of the law: early or late meetings, improper formalities, and the like. During this period a total of 2018 political meetings were held (*Cumhuriyet*, October 10, 1961).

[2] As usual, local issues weighed heavily in determining the citizens' vote. For instance in Merzifon, a town with an illustrious cultural past, the main issues concerned the construction of a high school, the development of roads and the recognition of the town as the provincial capital. In Burdur, a province with one of the highest per capita incomes in Turkey and a center for the carpet industry, the campaign revolved around local economic issues. Konya, regarded as a conservative Muslim town,

The elections gave the Justice Party 158 seats in the Assembly and 70 in the Senate; the Republican Party won 173 and 36; the New Turkey Party 65 and 28; and the Republican National Peasant Party 54 and 16 seats respectively.[1] The Republicans won as usual in the Eastern provinces. The stronghold provinces of the former Democratic Party in the West were won partly by the Justice Party, and partly by the National Peasant Party largely because of its brash antimilitarist stand. The New Turkey Party won heavily in the Eastern provinces simply because its organization was established first. In the East, a new group of local professionals assumed the leadership of the opposition immediately after the Democratic Party leaders had been arrested or deported by the military. In

---

actually was concerned more with the slowdown in business activity than religious issues. Konya is an important supply center of finished goods for the surrounding agricultural areas. Eventually the province of Konya elected six deputies for the Republican Party against ten for the other three parties combined. In the town itself the shoemakers' association, resembling the old Ahi guilds, appeared as a strong organized force. In 1961 it had a membership of 581 benches (each shop registers according to the number of working cobbler's benches) and indirectly controlled 300-325 unregistered benches representing not less than 2,000 people. Konya had three groups claiming some sort of cultural leadership : the modern enlightened intellectuals, the *şeyh* of the *mevlevi* dervish order representing the upper stratum of the old order, and the orthodox conservatives who were influential among the town population and the craftsmen, although the latter two were also fond of the Mevlevi. However, the differences in mentality between these culture groups were superseded by pride in local history and common civic interests as well as family ties. The Republican Party chairman of Konya Province, when interviewed by this writer, claimed that his party made no concession to religion. This attitude is usually the posture the Republicans adopt with outsiders, notably toward intellectuals. However, the Republican district leader from Seydişehir (Konya Province) described to this writer, after the province chairman left the room, how he had persuaded an *imam* and his village, all of whom had unanimously supported Democratic Party until 1957, to vote for his own party. He showed the *imam* a picture of Celal Bayar, the then President, embracing the Ecumenical Patriarch Athenagoras.

[1] Party affiliations varied greatly between 1961 and 1965. At one time the number of independents increased. Then the New Turkey and National Peasant Party deputies began to join the Justice Party. The 450 seats in the National Assembly in April 1965 were divided among parties as follows : Justice, 168; Republican, 190; Peasant 20; National, 13; New Turkey, 29; independent, 18; vacant, 12. Senate seats were distributed as follows : Justice, 77; Republican, 43; Peasant, 3; Labor, 1; National, 3; New Turkey, 9; independents, 11; vacant, 1. There were 15 Senators appointed by the President and 20 lifetime Senators, of a total of 185 (*TBMM Albümü*, Ankara, 1964, pp. 170, 190). After the 1969 elections, the Justice Party had 256 seats in the National Assembly; the Peoples Republican Party, 143; the New Turkey Party, 6; the Reliance Party, 15; the National Action Party, 1; the Union Party, 8; and independents, 13. See Walter F. Weiker, "Turkey's Election May Bode Ills," *Mid East*, December, 1969, p. 11.

fact, the deportations were considered a form of discrimination and therefore the local leaders were eager to express their discontent by joining the first opposition party. This happened to be the New Turkey Party.

The elected Parliament appeared as a whole to be dominated by professionals, the overwhelming majority being lawyers. The distribution of professions among the major parties appeared to be rather similar. However, an appraisal of professionals based on prima facia evidence would lead to erroneous conclusions, since many of the deputies had additional occupations or listed only the profession which implied intellectual achievement, such as doctor or lawyer (See Chapter I tables 1.17-1.19).

Several Republican deputies and senators had been ministers and members of previous Assemblies. About one-third, although elected from provinces, were residents of Ankara or Istanbul, and some made politics their full-time occupation. On the other hand, the deputies and senators of the Justice and New Turkey parties came primarily from small towns. Few had been elected to the Assembly in the past or played a major role in national politics, though many had been active in local politics. The Democratic Party leaders were in jail and their close associates and relatives, with some notable exceptions, were too intimidated to enter politics openly at this early stage. Thus, the deputies and senators of the Justice and New Turkey parties represented the provincial elites, usually the professionals, entrepreneurs, and businessmen. These replaced in good measure the established families of the landed gentry who had held leading positions in the Democratic Party. The businessmen, contractors, and engineers in the Justice Party, therefore, represented the new entrepreneurial groups in the countryside. Thus the elections of 1961 helped bring to power the professional-entrepreneurial segments of the new economic middle classes. Some of these were definitely achievement-oriented. This was a truly fundamental development in the context of Turkish social history. The Republican Party had its own business groups, but these represented mostly the old interests, usually the bigger capitalists or the privileged groups created and nurtured by state capitalism in the past.

The large number of administrators in the Justice Party included a few who had been retired by the military for their partisan attitude under the Democrats' rule. Many, however, rose to prominence in local towns and provinces through their own abilities and were interested in practical matters. The percentage of former army officers was relatively high among the parliamentarians of the Justice Party. Most of these officers belonged to the *Eminsu* (Retired Revolutionary Officers) organization, and generally supported the Revolution of May 27, but opposed the National Unity Committee for its decision to retire them in August 1960. These officers provided at times useful contacts with their former colleagues still active in the army and assured them that the military's problems could find a sympathetic understanding in the Justice Party as well. They also worked to bring the Justice Party closer to the ideas of the military.

The Republican Party comprised almost twice as many landlords as the Justice Party. Indeed the Republican Party, despite its progressive image on the national front, was often supported in the countryside by the established families, notably in the less developed Eastern sections, and by local dynasties which had acquired control of party organizations during the period of one-party rule. They preserved their "aristocratic" pretenses and oligarchic attitudes, which in the countryside were considered to be evidence of the Republicans' inability to "descend to the level of the people and be like them." [1] The party's critics in the countryside complained that the military Revolution of May 27 had brought back to power the same established families which had lost their social and political positions between 1946 and 1950. Parliament, despite differences among political parties, was a civilian force. It represented the new and some old elites from the countryside but also some urban groups, such as newsmen, former officers, and a few university professors. The latter groups were rather articulate in their avowed allegiance to high moral virtues but disorganized and without well-defined, central political ideas or practical proposals. The entrepreneurial groups, on the other hand, were oriented toward the defense of their interest and seemed to have more precision in their political pursuits. The structure of Parliament and the diversity of opinions prevailing there became evident in the latter part of 1961 and 1962, after this body began its regular legislative

---

[1] Throughout the country this writer was told over and over again by simple men that they distrusted the Republicans chiefly because of their superior attitudes, disdain of ordinary men, failure to understand local problems, and reliance on authority. Indeed, in several places, I have witnessed the cold formality prevailing in the Republican Party organizations, and the almost arrogant attitude of local leaders long accustomed to treat their fellow men as inherently inferior. In contrast, the meetings of the other parties were animated with free talk, unrestricted movement, and a feeling of community; leaders could hardly be distinguished from followers. There was also evidence of independent thought. In more than one instance spokesmen for the Justice and New Turkey parties, in private, criticized Adnan Menderes' policies and especially the fact that a clique emerging after 1954 in the Democratic Party had greatly restricted the freedom of local organizations.

work. Before this development, however, there was a far more difficult and vital task to perform : to establish a truly civilian government and to take over power from the military.

THE MILITARY AND PARTY POLITICS

From the military's viewpoint the elections initially appeared to have created the least desired situation. The former Democrats and their sympathizers, grouped around parties with different party labels (in reality these parties in terms of leadership were different from the Democrats), had secured a majority in both the Senate and Assembly. The military and many intellectuals regarded the election results as a reactionary affront which could lead to revengeful action against the revolutionaries and the possible loss of a variety of benefits secured after 1960.[1] On October 21, 1961, thirty-eight officers (eight generals, two admirals, and twenty-eight colonels) and a number of university professors, always ready to provide guidance but never to take risks, met at the War Academy in Istanbul and reached a series of decisions to be enforced not later than October 25, 1961 : to intervene and dissolve Parliament before it con-

---

[1] A Military Council composed of active officers emerged as the spokesman of the armed forces as early as August, 1960. It was, in fact, a pressure group expressing the military's viewpoint. The attempt by the ruling junta (NUC) to disperse this group failed when the Air Force flew its jets over Ankara on June 2, 1961, and forced the government to rescind the appointment of Irfan Tansel, the Chief of the Air Force and one of the group leaders, to a post abroad. However, this open defiance of the military government created negative reactions both among civilians and officers. Consequently, the commanders of the armed forces issued a declaration through Cevdet Sunay, then Chief of Staff and then the President of Turkey, promising to support a civilian government, to oppose any political activity in the armed forces, and to fully withdraw from politics on the day Parliament convened. However, soon afterward, according to Avni Doğan, a disgruntled old-guard Republican, Cevdet Sunay had a talk with İnönü and decided on behalf of the military commanders to support the Republican Party. But the younger officers, who did not share the loyalty of their seniors to İnönü, opposed this partisan position and eventually the commanders decided to stay out of politics. See *Türkiye Yıllığı 1962* (İstanbul, 1962) for the names of the Council. Avni Doğan, *Kurtuluş, Kuruluş ve Sonrası*, İstanbul, 1964, p. 308. But Doğan himself, along with three other Republican Party members, was accused of having entered into dealings with the military and was suspended from party membership. The background of these developments with occasional new insights is given in the memoirs of Metin Toker, İnönü's son-in-law, published in installments in *Milliyet*, February 1969.

vened, to inactivate all political parties, and to turn over the revolution to the "nation's real and competent representatives." [1]

These decisions were communicated to General Cevdet Sunay, the Chief of Staff, who conveyed them to Cemal Gürsel, the President and head of the National Unity Committee. The Committee, whose members were due to become lifetime senators, alarmed by these developments, appealed to the army and the public in general through a series of public proclamations. They even attempted to organize demonstrations in defense of the army's political neutrality, and historical role of establishing the bases for modernism and democracy, and stressed emphatically the validity of the interparty agreements concluded before the elections to safeguard the reforms of May 27. "The Turkish army, youth, intellectuals and the press upon whom you [the people] relied to achieve the revolution and perpetuate it," declared the NUC, "are bound permanently by their oath to restore the democratic order of law in the shortest time." It asserted that national sovereignty belonged unconditionally to the nation and described it as a permanent principle of Turkish life and state and consistent with the spirit of Atatürk's reforms. "The army," affirmed the NUC, "will fulfill its duties as one of the bodies [charged] to carry out the policy of the State within the limits of a Constitutional regime by remaining faithful to its historical tradition [noninvolvement in politics] and Atatürk's principles." [2] Sunay personally argued against forceful intervention and convinced the signatories that the forthcoming government would be acceptable to the military.

Meanwhile, after intensive talks, the representatives of the political parties and the army commanders reached a series of agreements. First, they agreed to nominate General Cemal Gürsel as the presidential candidate. Subsequently Ali Fuad Başgil, the senator-elect from Samsun, nominated as a presidential candidate by the Justice Party, withdrew from the race, and the Senate. Second, they agreed to enforce the sentences passed upon the Democrats by the court at Yassıada. Third, they pledged to keep the military out of politics, and safeguard the officers' rights secured after 1960. "Our main goal" declared the parties to the agreement, "is to see that the army carries out its duties in moral and material security. We envisage all issues related to the military in this

---

[1] Doğan, *Kurtuluş.*, p. 310; Can Kaya İsen, *Geliyorum Diyen İhtilâl* (Istanbul, 1964), p. 19. For a general view, see Ergun Özbudun, *The Role of the Military in Recent Turkish Politics*, Publication of the Center for International Affairs, Harvard University, Cambridge, 1966.

[2] Texts in *Cumhuriyet*, October 24, 1961.

frame [of mind] and do not approve the revoking of any rights granted to the military." With the military's interests thus assured, the Chief of Staff issued a declaration stating that "the army and the political parties have absolutely no difference of opinion. The are in perfect agreement concerning the existence of the democratic regime within the framework of the existing and valid Constitution." [1] The Chief of Staff expressed the hope that with God's will good intentions would prevail over all difficulties.

The agreements had saved the parliamentary regime by incorporating the military into the new order both as supporters and beneficiaries. The military, in turn agreed to look upon itself as the "executive organ of the state" instead of identifying itself with the state as the foundation of the entire political and social order. The military thus became not *the Group* but one of the many groups which made up the Second Turkish Republic. This new outlook coupled with the general differentiation and professionalization in society turned the military into a kind of pressure group whose economic and professional motives were as evident and valid as those of any other social group.

The political parties, and through them the Parliament, were compelled to accept the new ideas and forces unleashed by the Revolution of May 27 as the permanent features of the Turkish political and social system. They recognized that a mere victory at the polls was not an absolute mandate to power. Other forces, not formally represented in the Legislature, could exercise considerable influence, and even compel Parliament to take a course of action contrary to the group interests of its members. The agreements between the military and political parties were not concessions resulting from weakness but comprised of mutual interests and therefore had excellent chances of survival.

A few days after these events, the "fourteen" officers ousted in November 1960, and assigned to diplomatic posts abroad, met in Paris and, hoping for a comeback, declared that "the election results proved that we were right in our thoughts of not going to elections so soon after the revolution." [2] They claimed that political democracy should have been preceded by social democracy and that the Parliament could not solve the existing economic problems. However, Senator Sıtkı Ulay, a former member of NUC, insisted that the Constitution was suited to the solution of all problems, and that the military's return to power through a new

---

[1] Text in *Ulus*, October 25, 1961.
[2] *Ulus*, October 31, 1961.

revolution as desired by the "fourteeen" was no longer possible. Henceforth, according to Ulay, there was need for an intellectual revolution to manifest itself through political parties and programs. Cevdet Sunay in turn declared that the "military are out of politics because the revolutionary period is over" and that the "fourteen" were no longer members of the armed forces. "The Second Republic," declared Sunay, "is established. What can [the "fourteen" ask for]. To use the army for any political purpose is a betrayal... Besides, the army personnel is not so naïve and unrealistic as to become a tool for others. NUC is part of history now."[1] Indeed, following the agreement between the army commanders and the political parties, Parliament finally convened on October 26, 1961. Cemal Gürsel was elected *de jure* President. Hayri Ürgüplü (an independent elected on the Justice Party slate) was elected President of the Senate by defeating Kazim Orbay, a former general proposed by lifetime senators. Fuad Sirmen of the Republican Party was elected chairman of the Assembly. The memory of recent events had led to a quick compromise, which was to be forgotten soon in the controversy over the formation of a government. (General Cevdet Sunay was elected President after a stoke incapacitated and then caused the death of General Gürsel in 1966. His term ended in 1973, and he was replaced by Fahri Korutürk, a former admiral.)

Struggle and Compromise in Parliament

Parliamentary activity began amid a set of unusual circumstances. First, there was the constant danger of military intervention under the pretext of defending the reforms of May 27. Second, the legislature was divided into a series of groups with conflicting views on economic planning, trade, taxation, centralization, population control, land reform, and social justice. Moreover, outside Parliament there were a number of groups with radical ideas. Parliament was immediately deadlocked in disagreement over the formation of a government. Since no party had an absolute majority, a coalition seemed the only possible solution. Indeed, a coalition government consisting of the Republican and Justice parties, the two supposedly implacable enemies, was formed on November 20, after a month of hard bargaining.[2] The Justice Party

---

[1] Text of declaration in *Ulus*, October 31, 1961; and *Son Havadis*, November 3, 1961. For a general background survey see Dankwart A. Rustow, "Turkey's Second Try at Democracy," *Yale Review*, Summer 1963, pp. 518-38.

[2] The Justice Party joined the coalition through the decision of its General Committee and not of its parliamentary group after four days of continuous debate and

demanded amnesty for the jailed Democrats, the elimination of wealth declarations, the abolition of compulsory savings bonds, and the revision of the tax system, including the agricultural tax. It also demanded a variety of other measures intended to alleviate the economic pressure on the propertied groups. The Justice Party eventually toned down its demands, not only because of pressure from the military but also from the business groups interested in political stability and peace.

The powerful Trade and Industrial Chambers and representatives of the entrepreneurial groups warned all deputies and senators that their uncompromising political attitudes caused further stagnation in economy and urged them to place priority on the solution of the economic problems.[1] The two parties consequently regarded their coalition agreement as a step toward the normalization of political life which was a prerequisite condition for economic development.[2] Eventually taxes were revised in favor of small business, handicrafts, and wage earners, the wealth declarations were eliminated as a basis for taxation, and tax exemptions were adopted for investments.[3] Despite these measures, the Justice Party still felt that it was compelled to support an essentially statist government program, while its own campaign platform and the voters' expectations, supposedly favoring a liberal economic policy, remained unfulfilled. Moreover, the party found it difficult to abide by

---

bitter clashes between its extremist and moderate wings. The extremists were bitterly opposed to the Republican Party and to the military. These represented the urbanite, semiintellectual, nationalist groups which had begun to rise to power during the latter part of Menderes' rule. The moderates represented the newcomers to politics, the professionals with well-defined interests, and a variety of other countryside groups interested in maintaining a civilian parliamentary regime. See, for instance, the speech of Saim Sarıgüllü, a Senator from Aydın (the constituency of Menderes), who accused the extremists in his own party of endangering the regime and of placing their personal feelings and interests above those of the party (*Cumhuriyet*, November 13, 1961).

[1] The Chamber of Marmara and the Thrace region declared that "economic issues constituted the most important national problem...above parties. Political parties should, therefore, arrive together at a common understanding and formulate a policy. We need a national economic charter." Political security, according to the national Chairman of the Chambers, was a prerequisite to economic development. Some deputies from the eastern regions in which landlords were arrested and forced to settle in the western section of the country (only 55 landlords were settled) described Settlement Law Number 105 as utterly undemocratic and asked for its abolition. See *Milliyet*, *Yeni Sabah*, November 11, 1961; *Hür Vatan*, November 18, 1961; *Milliyet*, November 7, 1961 (See declaration by Talat Oğuz of Mardin).

[2] *Ulus, Cumhuriyet*, November 17, 1961.

[3] *Büyük Zafer*, March 28, 1962; *Hür Vatan, Dünya*, April 9, 12, 1962.

its original commitment to respect the Yassıada trial sentences. An extremist group in the Party and relatives of the jailed Democrats demanded amnesty for the revolution and for the proposed social and economic reforms.[1] The controversy over amnesty was actually a useful device to defend group interests and acquired privileges. Those clamoring for amnesty included rightist elements who extolled the virtues of nationalism and past glories while condemning social legislation, taxation, and planning as leading to socialism and communism.

At this stage political ideologies began to be identified with economic issues. Economic and social conservatism was defined as nationalism by rightists, while social and economic planning began to be referred to as socialism.[2] Thus the split of Turkey's political elites into two groups —statist and economic (entrepreneurial-commercial)—which was already an acknowledged fact, received ideological recognition, and even a label. The first, which had a secular socialist orientation, comprised the youth groups and the military, that is to say, the intelligentsia. These referred to themselves as *zinde kuvvetler* ("energetic forces"). These declared that their intention was to defend by force the reforms undertaken by the military government. The civil bureaucracy, although not specifically called a *zinde* force, was part of it. The "reforms" often mentioned by this group were deemed to be inherent in the spirit of the revolution and could be materialized only by a progressive government. The *zinde* forces, instrumental in carrying out the revolution of 1960, were still indirectly in control of the means of violence (the army) and the press, and retained much political initiative. The second group, as one may well expect, united around the Justice Party. But the Justice Party, even though in the government, had no command over the army, or the

---

[1] Immediately after the establishment of the coalition government some groups in the Justice Party while agitating in favor of amnesty demanded also the abolition of Law Number 45 of August 8, 1960. This law had decreed that former general secretaries of the National Assembly, Presidency and Foreign Affairs, deputy ministers and their assistants, governors, director generals, mayors, chairmen of state enterprises, directors of factories, and the like, would be questioned and tried for crimes of "mismanagement" committed between May 22, 1950, and May 27, 1960 (the term of the Democrats) and thereafter. Actually, mismanagement meant favoritism to various business groups. The inquiry committees established under the law could investigate any commercial dealings of the past and probe into the transactions of contractors and businessmen. It was reported that 33,000 files had been assembled for investigation.

[2] See Kemal H. Karpat, "The Turkish Left," *Journal of Contemporary History* 2, (1966), pp. 169-86, and chap. IX.

police, or influence over the press, a good part of which was turning rapidly socialistic. Consequently it resorted to moral pressure by stressing the supremacy of national will and its representative, the Parliament. Party meetings, held throughout the country in order to dramatize the party's popular backing, ended with the chant "sovereignty belongs to the nation." This campaign was also an answer to some former army officers who claimed that the revolution had set limits to legislative authority. Indeed, a senator, a former member of the NUC, declared publicly that "the revolution is still continuing," that the military would intervene to keep it alive while others demanded a regime with a strong executive headed by a man like de Gaulle in France.[1] The Justice Party in turn declared through a deputy that "we are facing many situations which are likely to throw a shadow on our democracy. We are forced to compromise in every direction, though we are the representatives of the national will. I believe it is about time to call our system by its right name," [2] that is to say, a civilian parliamentary democracy run by the military.

The Justice Party delivered antimilitarist speeches in the countryside and some deputies even urged the population to rise in revolt if the military took over power. But the Justice Party deputies had not overlooked the economic consequence of political unrest. "The newspapers which talk about the continuing revolution," declared one, "are frightening away the capital," while another one described the currents against the Parliament as being "purposely instigated... The instigators," he stated, "know what kind of regime they want to bring to Turkey. It is laughable to declare that social justice can be achieved only through socialism... we shall not accept to live under tutorship." [3] The military eventually compiled a list of deputies whom they accused of insulting the army and asked that they be tried. But Parliament defied the request and refused to lift the parliamentary immunity of these deputies.

The abortive *coup* of Colonel Talat Aydemir occurred on February 22, 1962, amid these circumstances. It appeared at first sight as the army's reaction to the Justice Party's anti-militarism.[4] In reality it was the work

---

[1] *Yeni Sabah*, November 15, 1961.

[2] *Cumhuriyet*, December 23, 1961.

[3] *Dünya*, December 22, 1961; see also *Cumhuriyet*, March 6 and April 30, 1962.

[4] Already before the coup the government and the army commanders proved that they had the situation in hand when they retired a number of officers suspected of revolutionary activities. Aydemir was described by some intellectuals as being a socialist. However there is little evidence to prove that he had any social program.

of a small group of dissatisfied officers who wanted to replace the existing regime with a rightist dictatorship in the hope that the army and intellectuals would support them. But the overwhelming majority of the armed forces, the press, and the intelligentsia, while bitterly critical of the existing Parliament, were not yet prepared to dismiss the regime as a whole. The coup collapsed but its authors were pardoned and left free until the next round in May 1963, when after another unsuccessful *coup* they were arrested, tried and sentenced; two were executed.

The coups of 1962 and 1963 proved to be turning points in the civilian-military relationship. The army's interference in politics raised serious dangers of civil war since the country as a whole, and Parliament in particular, appeared firmly opposed to military rule however benevolent it might be. The competition for power also created friction and jealousy among officers and threatened the very reforms of the 27 May revolution with which the military were identified and which they were committed to defend. Finally, involvement in active politics seemed to deteriorate the military's own professional standards and undermine the traditional public confidence in the army as a national, impartial institution. In the NATO exercises held that year, for instance, the Turkish officers, usually rated among the best in the post, ranked at the bottom of the performance list.

The Justice Party, realized that politics was not only a question of abstract principles but also an interplay of active forces. It appeared obvious that each group had to take into consideration and respect the interest, power, and ideals of the other if the new system were to survive at all.

"The political parties and the Parliament are not the sole powers in which the national will is embodied," declared a realistic Justice Party deputy. "Power and the national will [may] be represented also by the press, the army and intellectuals. The Justice Party claims power by describing itself as the sole [organization] created by national will. This contention has ulterior motives and intensifies political tension. The Justice Party together with some forces outside the Parliament are leading the country to disaster." [1]

A month after the attempted coup of 1962 the Justice Party's General

---

On the contrary, he seemed to be under the influence of Colonel Alparslan Turkeş's nationalist views (Isen, *Geliyorum.*, pp. 13 ff). See also Walter F. Weiker, "The Aydemir Case and Turkey's Political Dilemma," *Middle Eastern Affairs*, XIV (November 1963), p. 261 ff.

[1] *Milliyet*, June 18, 1962.

Committee and representatives from forty-four provinces held a meeting. They decided to stay in the coalition government and expressed gratitude "to the glorious army for its patriotic attitude and for its attachment to the Grand National Assembly and its government." [1] Later, answering charges that their party yearned for a return to the Democratic Party's policies, a spokesman for the Justice Party declared that their party was a new political organization committed to the rule of law and the democratic ideas of the Revolution of May 27. Other deputies conceded the officers' right to follow political developments as a matter of right and interest, but opposed their active participation in politics. They also protested against those politicians who tried to promote their own ambition under the pretext that "it was the army's wish." [2] The latter point was aimed at Inönü who, according to the Justice Party, used the threat of potential army interference in order to enforce the views prevailing in his own party.

The above developments brought quiet only for a short time. The law introduced to pardon the military involved in the coup of February 1962 was criticized as condoning an open attempt to abolish the new constitution, while the Democrats were being kept in jail merely for having violated the previous one.[3] This issue, together with a variety of attacks by intellectuals on the parliamentary regime, despite the *Tedbirler Kanunu* (this law enacted on March 5, 1962, aimed at protecting the sanctity of the Revolution of May 27 and the parliamentary regime), obscured the significant struggle developing with the Justice Party. The moderates, who reflected more accurately the party's general spirit, denounced militancy and proposed concrete action for social and economic development and better working relations with their Republican coalition partners. But the extremists in the Justice Party, led by a small group of nationalists and advocates of liberal free enterprise, opposed the proposals and finally Inönü resigned as Premier on May 30, 1962.

The causes leading to the collapse of the first coalition offer basic insights into the foundations of contemporary Turkish politics. Inönü refers rather casually to the disagreement over Democrats' amnesty at the very end of his letter of resignation.[4] The main sections of the letter

---

[1] *Büyük Zafer*, March 21, 1962.

[2] Burhan Apaydın, "Ordu ve Huzur," *Büyük Zafer*, March 4, 1962.

[3] *Zafer Demokrasinindir*, June 22, 1962. At this time Colonel Talat Aydemir, who had been pardoned, declared publicly that his attempted coup was right and justified.

[4] *Yeni Sabah*, June 1, 1962. Actually there was a tacit agreement between the Republican and Justice parties to release the jailed Democrats gradually but the

discuss the disagreements over economic policy and the role of the State Planning Organization (SPO). Indeed, the philosophy and methods envisaged for economic development had the potential to determine the basic orientation of Turkey's political regime, and these were the real causes that undermined the coalition.

The SPO was established by the military on September 30, 1960 (Laws Number 91, 99, 340), as an advisory body to the government. Soon it attracted a number of young economists and administrators who idealized SPO as the most suitable means for rapid economic development and social justice and issued a series of sensational statistics aimed at dramatizing the lack of social justice in Turkey. The group in charge of SPO, lacking experience though not enthusiasm, had been catapulted to fame and power by the revolution. It became overnight the nucleus of a power elite which strove to preserve its newly won status by idealizing the role of authoritarian planning as vital for economic development. Central state planning and executive authority above Parliament, entrusted to SPO, were to be the methods of this economic development. This statist social view prevailing among a small group in the Republican Party conflicted violently with the "liberal" views of the Justice Party although both parties, as mentioned, were in the coalition government. A good number of deputies and senators in the Justice Party favored planning but were against the excessive reliance on state and authority from the top. A small minority, however, opposed vehemently any kind of planning, and one of them bluntly declared that Europe progressed without plan or state economic organization.[1] When Inönü refused to compromise on the statist economic policy and the supreme economic authority demanded for SPO by the small group in the Republican Party the coalition fell apart.

Inönü was entrusted to form a new coalition. After twenty days of negotiations with the New Turkey and Republican National Peasant parties, Inönü confessed that his attempts were unsuccessful due to the "misconceptions and unwillingness of other parties" to enter into a coalition with the Republicans, that is to say, to agree on the priority of statism and centralized planning.[2] "The source of disagreement,"

extremists wanted immediate and absolute pardon. In any case, by October, 1965, all the detained Democrats were released.

[1] *Yeni Istanbul*, March 1962.

[2] It was said that the difficulty in arriving at an agreement was due to the ambition of Ekrem Alican, the leader of the New Turkey Party, to become Deputy Premier. This indicates that personal motives are still erroneously regarded as the main force of politics in Turkey.

wrote Abdi Ipekçi, the perceptive editorialist of *Milliyet*, "lies not actually in the allocation of [Ministerial] seats but in the different economic views of the parties involved in the coalition talks. The importance [attached to the position] of the Deputy Prime Ministry is rooted in these differences and this is why it causes so much discussion. The State Planning Organization, which prepares long-range plans for economic development, shall work under the Deputy Prime-Minister... This indicates that political parties with basically different economic and political views cannot become partners in a common cabinet. Even though its establishment may be formally possible such a partnership cannot last long, because it is unrealistic." [1]

Meanwhile the Trade and Industrial Chambers urged all political parties to reach agreement and again stressed the importance of economic and social matters. They also urged any government to accept in theory and practice the possible contribution of the private sector to economic development and promised that this sector would do its best to achieve such development.[2] Finally a new coalition was formed, and Ekrem Alican, the Chairman of the New Turkey Party, became Deputy Prime Minister. The vital position of Minister of Finance was filled by a Republican, Ferit Melen, known as a liberal in his economic views. The interparty agreement accepted Atatürk's reforms and those of May 27 and described the new constitution as "having embodied the new world view and the economic, cultural and social aspirations of the Turkish society." It defined the democratic ways as the only mode of life acceptable to society and as the only philosophy of economic development. The private sector was assured of constitutional protection and urged to work in peace and in cooperation with state enterprises. The agreement proposed also to develop the remote regions in the East, to accord new benefits to labor, to revise the tax system, and to replace the wealth declarations taken in 1961 and 1962 with a new one. Membership in the

---

[1] *Milliyet*, June 20, 1962.

[2] The Chambers had been active throughout 1961 and 1962 in enlisting support for private enterprise and in expressing the views of this group. In a memorable radio program, the wealthiest man of Turkey, Vebhi Koç, expressed his own views. He urged all political parties to dedicate their energies to economic development and leave aside political debate. In fact, he condemned political activity and demanded government support for free enterprise which he believed performed social functions as though it were national property. Public addresses in favor of private enterprise by the top representatives of the business community were a new experience and helped considerably to project to the public a new image of the private sector. See text of speech in *Hür Vatan*, March 28, 1962 and *Yeni Sabah*, June 19, 1962.

Common Market was considered essential in view "of unity of destiny with the Western World."[1]

The program of the second coalition government, following these views, departed drastically from that of the first one. It abandoned a good part of the statist measures in favor of the private sector, but without adopting a laissez faire view. The second coalition represents a turning point in Turkey's economic and political life. It accepted planning and an organized rational economic life not as matters of ideology but as basic conditions for a modern society. The private sector secured a victory, not in gaining absolute control over government but in asserting its power in open competition with the superior, organized forces of the traditional ruling groups.[2]

The coalition compromise also created deep dissatisfaction within the Republican party. A group known as the "63," claimed that the statist features of their party were a natural response to the economic and social transformation of Turkey occurring from 1950 to 1960, and in 1961-1962, and criticized the party for abandoning its traditional statist philosophy. Turhan Feyzioğlu, the Republican Minister in the coalition, found it necessary to declare that "PRP has not renounced statism. It is statist but it is against doctrinaire and revolutionary socialism."[3] Later, in 1967, Feyzioğlu, concerned over the drift of his party to the left, resigned with a group of followers and formed his own *Güven* ("Reliance")

---

[1] Text in *Hür Vatan*, June 20, 1962. For the specific views of the Republican National Peasant Party, the third coalition partner, see *Cumhuriyet*, June 17, 1962. The coalition agreement also provided for the gradual amnesty of the jailed Democrats, the abolition of the High Justice Court established in 1960 to try the Democrats, and the end of forced settlements. These views have been formulated jointly by the coalition partners, not as vindication of the Democrats but as a logical consequence of the new democratic constitutional order. Alican accepted 7 percent annual growth of GNP as an optimum rate of development but disagreed with the heads of the State Planning Organization on the method to achieve it. He believed that the 7 percent growth could be attained through better tax incentives and investment by private enterprises and less by reliance on state authority. It was this difference of opinion which led to the resignation of various heads of SPO. Eventually SPO became an advisory body to the government on economic policy. See *Dünya*, July 22, 1962.

[2] Mehmet Ali Aybar, the leader of the leftist Labor Party at that time, denounced the coalition as having "recognized extensive privileges to private enterprise. Taxes, financial policy, credits are to be planned in accordance with the needs of the private enterprises. A capital market will be established and technical assistance to private enterprises provided" (*Milliyet*, July 31, 1962). A conference on capital market met in Istanbul in December, 1964, but without visible results.

[3] See declaration in *Hür Vatan*, June 4 and July 23, 1962.

Party. It has a middle-of-the-road philosophy. İnönü himself agreed that cooperation between private and public enterprise was essential. He urged the citizens to follow his own example by adapting themselves to new conditions of life, and to think in terms of social growth. The changes in society were continuous and forced one to reconsider his own ideas. İnönü conceded candidly that workers in private enterprises were better paid than in most state enterprises and urged them to rid themselves of noneconomic considerations.[1] Behind these compromises lay also the pressure of labor unrest, yet to be studied.

The developments after the summer of 1962 followed basically the above agreements. The first Five-Year economic plan was amended in favor of free enterprise and finally accepted by Parliament in 1963. Meanwhile the Trade and Industrial Chambers, emboldened by the recognition accorded to the private sector, demanded a stable economic policy, a friendly attitude toward foreign capital, and intensive private investment in the East, including the Kurdish areas. They even asked for the abolition of the Exporter's Unions in the hope of assuming their functions.[2] (The Unions had been established in 1941 in order to facilitate exports and to control their quality, under government supervision.) The second coalition survived several crises largely because of a certain spirit of compromise developed between İnönü and Alican.[3] The latter, after an initial success in asserting his own views, eventually followed İnönü's views and was accused in the countryside of identifying himself with the ruling statist groups and undermining its prestige.

The Municipal elections of November 17, 1963, dealt a heavy blow to the coalition parties. The Justice Party received 46.2 percent of the votes, the Republicans 37.5 percent and New Turkey Party only 6.5 percent. The Republican National Peasant Party received 2.6 percent. Thus, the latter two members of the coalition had lost almost half of the votes they had received in the general elections of 1961. The election results were a heavy blow to the New Turkey and National Peasant parties. Both resigned from the government and the coalition fell disinte-

---

[1] *Dünya*, August 8, 1962. The government enterprises according to one survey employed 167, 864 workers and 118,053 officials or 12 officials for 17 workers. In private enterprises the ratio was 2 to 13. The per capita production for one official in State enterprises was only TL. 73. *Cumhuriyet*, July 29, 1962.

[2] *Yeni Istanbul*, November 19, 1962; *Cumhuriyet*, February 7 and August 16, 1963.

[3] The Justice Party began to agitate again for amnesty although in 1963-1964 most of the jailed Democrats had been liberated.

grated. A third coalition between the Republican Party and the Independents was a caretaker government which finally fell on a vote of no-confidence. Finally the Justice Party formed the fourth coalition with the other minor parties early in 1965, and left the Republicans out. This was natural and expected.

The ability of the Justice Party to form the coalition proved that the military had developed confidence in this party, largely due to the fact the moderates finally took over the power in the party convention of November 1964. At this time the delegates brought Süleyman Demirel to chairmanship by a large margin of votes, in open defiance of the extremists. Demirel, an engineer with considerable experience in administration, represented the professional groups in his party and advocated economic planning, not as a political means but as a modern, scientific approach to development. The ascendancy of the Justice Party to government power was facilitated also by apprehension among some of the military that discussions on social justice and economic planning had strengthened the position of the leftists. In fact, President Gürsel, who said originally that socialism might have some good effects in Turkey, was reported to have accused the Republicans of having supported the leftists. Indeed, Turkey's rapprochement to the Soviet Union, caused by the failure of the United States to support the Turkish cause in the Cyprus dispute, had opened a unique possibility for the rise of the left. The internal politics of Turkey had reached a synthesis; its stability was tested in the general elections in October 1965. The election issues in 1965 revolved around liberalism and statism-socialism, the latter being represented by the Republican party and the marxist Labor Party established in 1961. The Justice Party emerged victorious with a clear majority in the Assembly, winning 239 seats out of a total of 450, despite incredible legal tangles and plots to prevent its victory. Unfortunately a detailed analysis of the period after 1965, however tantalizing it may be, falls beyond the scope of this study.[1]

---

[1] For elections see Nermin Abadan, *Türkiyede 1965 Seçimleri ve Neticeleri* (Ankara, 1966). The release of Celal Bayar, the former President, in March 1963, was accompanied by bellicose mass meetings in which some rank-and-file soldiers apparently participated. Bayar made a few declarations hostile to the revolution and was promptly returned to jail while student groups demolished the Justice Party headquarters in Ankara. Eventually Bayar was quietly released. İnönü's appointment and talks with army commanders without consulting the other parties in the coalition caused another crisis which led to a new agreement. During this period the politicians objected to the fact that one ex-general was appointed Minister of Communications and another Director of the State Airways. The correspondent of *Cumhuriyet* expressed the situation as

The Politics of Social Groups Outside Parliament : the Intelligentsia, Labor and Peasants

In the preceding sections we have studied the political activities of the main groups represented in the Parliament or capable of exerting direct pressure on the government : the entrepreneurial groups, the professionals, and the military. The intelligentsia, labor, and peasants had no formal parliamentary representation although the programs of the political parties contained provisions deemed to appeal to each of them. Following the prerevolution practice the concept of general and not class representation prevailed. However, the general pattern of economic and social differentiation before the revolution, and the political-intellectual rationalization of this differentiation created, as mentioned before, an interest-oriented, group consciousness. Consequently, the groups without direct formal representation in Parliament began to organize and demand a constitutional order and a parliamentary action according to their own historical background, political experience, occupational outlook, and expectation.

The secular-socialist intelligentsia developed an increasingly negative attitude toward the parliamentary regime but without convincing the workers and peasants to share its views, despite promises of social measures. The intelligentsia has failed so far to integrate itself politically with the lower classes, even in the face of consistent efforts by the leftist Labor Party to form a populist front headed by a socialist elite. These efforts, nevertheless, sharpened the political consciousness of each major social group. This consciousness enhanced further the sense of professional identity and the ideas of group interest and group power. A general analysis of three major groups not formally represented in Parliament may better illustrate the above points.

The Intelligentsia

This group, essentially a by-product of the initial efforts to create a modern bureaucratic system in the Ottoman Empire, derived its claim to status and power on the basis of formal education, still a valid but

---

follows : "According to them a small-town politician can become a deputy or a Minister but an engineer and a general cannot be appointed to head a Ministry connected with his profession." (*Cumhuriyet*, June 27, 1962).

diminishing foundation for elitism.[1] This claim was further reinforced in the period from 1923 to 1945 by a monolithic view of state and society hardly compatible with the developing, pluralist social order. The intelligentsia, conscious of its role in modernization, regarded itself as the symbol and agent of change but also as its beneficiary. It dominated all social and political organizations and considered the state as a private institution of its own.

The intelligentsia, coming from the lower urban groups, was instrumental in mobilizing public opinion and articulating liberal political demands from 1945 to 1950. It seemed that the intelligentsia viewed its own role in party politics after 1950 as dominant and privileged as before. But soon it found itself isolated and politically neutralized. The emergence of new political parties and a competitive election system changed the pattern of political recruitment and the means for attaining power and status. The Democratic Party won the elections in 1950 and came to power. After a period of confusion the power in the Democratic Party was assumed by the upper agrarian group and later by the professionals and entrepreneurs, as mentioned before. Gradually, afterwards, wealth and party position became the bases for power, prestige, and status. After 1953, the unplanned economic development and an overall empirical orientation, coupled with various compromises on secularism, appeared to intellectuals to be undermining the social order and to be contradictory to Atatürk's reforms. The need for planning, system, organization, and the defense of secularism seemed to provide legitimate grounds for the intelligentsia's new claim to leadership.

The revolution skyrocketed the intelligentsia's prestige along with that of the military and the press, since these were the main forces which had fought to overthrow the Menderes government. The military consulted with the university professors and were associated with them in key decisions such as the drafting of a new constitution and the trial of Democratic deputies. Some intellectual groups even advised the military

---

[1] The ideal approach to the study of Turkish intelligentsia would be a comparative one. The important studies on the intellectuals and the ideology of developing countries provide excellent insights into their modernizing roles. We believe that the modernizing role of the Turkish intelligentsia today is markedly different from that of similar groups in Africa and Asia. Turkey is presently at a more advanced level of social and political development. The works of Edward Shils, Raymond Aron, and such classics as Max Weber, Karl Mannheim, Pareto, and Ortego y Gasset have provided much of the background for our treatment of the problem in the Turkish context. See also Frederick W. Frey, *The Turkish Political Elites* (Cambridge, Mass., 1965) which shows certain changes in the structure of Turkish elites.

to establish a strong regime and leave power to them. But the dismissal of 147 university faculty by the military government for a variety of professional and ideological reasons indicated that the military did not share the civil intelligentsia's high opinion of its own abilities. Consequently the intelligentsia, especially the socialists, turned against the military and indirectly began to advance their own political claims.

The defense of secularism became the first issue—a true group ideology on which the intelligentsia based its claim to power. The bigoted *imams* and *tarikats* ("religious orders") were denounced, and the involvement of religion in politics forbidden through the Constitution and a variety of legal measures. The press reported fully the activities of religious conservatives but without arousing much reaction beyond the small circle of dedicated secularists. The countryside seemed to pay little attention to the intellectuals' secularist outcry, chiefly because economic issues there had acquired vital priority. Politicians found quickly that villagers and small town dwellers were not interested in scientific explanations of the origin of mankind or the universe but in current matters.[1] As long as the virtues of Islam were not challenged directly, the citizen would not be drawn into religious controversy or rely on religion to solve all his problems. The fact remained that the basic reforms were deeply rooted in the social body and no group challenged the secular character of the regime.

Several developments had brought about a changed attitude toward religion. First, the military, although opposed to the use of religion for political purposes, regarded Islam as a source of spiritual nourishment, cultural identity, and loyalty to their country. Second, large sections of the middle classes looked upon religion as a natural element of life, a useful means of education, an outlet for spiritual expression, and a possible means of social reconciliation. Third, some intellectual groups, deeply torn by spritual crisis, came reluctantly to the conclusion that an excessive implementation of secularism had led to the rejection of all religion and hence the spiritual values of life. The question was no longer one of religion versus secularism, but of spirituality. Actually, the entire issue of secularism in Turkey was intimately connected with the establishment

---

[1] These observations are based on my own field investigations in about 40 provinces in 1961-62, 1964, and 1965. On the question of secularism I have been often contradicted by various intellectuals who claimed that religion was the most powerful issue in Turkey although few of these intellectuals ever visited the countryside. Even when they did so many acted subjectively, based on their preaccepted ideological view rather than on an objective evaluation of facts.

of a modern state and its institutions. After the attainment of these goals secularism was bound to be viewed not as a political problem but a cultural one. In fact, religion had become a subculture of the political system and was desacralized in the areas related to the existential order.

The intelligentsia's interest in social and economic problems eventually eclipsed in part its preoccupation with secularism, expecially after the ban on political parties was lifted and Parliament convened in 1961. A new ideological alignment replaced secularism. The liberalism or anti-statism promoted by the entrepreneurial, business, and agrarian groups was, in fact, an ideology designated to safeguard and promote their own interest. The intelligentsia, in turn, adopted statism and a hybrid form of socialism as its own ideology, supposedly on behalf of underprivileged social groups. In addition to the socialists there was a nationalist intelligentsia but its importance was limited.[1]

The statist-socialist intelligentsia, mainly composed of teachers, journalists, and academicians, eventually came to condemn the political parties and Parliament as being tools of privileged groups and therefore hostile to the establishment of a true democracy.[2] It described the peasant and the worker as being exploited by landlords and business groups because of ignorance. A true democracy, the intelligentsia claimed, could be established only by ending exploitation and illiteracy under its own enlightened guidance.[3] The real motives behind the intelligentsia's claims were accurately described by Turan Güneş, a professor of political science and an influential member of the Republican Party:

"In Turkey the masses have not reached the desired economic and cultural level," wrote Güneş. "They say that the dictatorship of the enlightened is necessary to develop the masses and enrich them with the values of the West and of modernity. I do not believe in the sincerity of many advocates of this idea. Actually, perhaps without realizing it, they [intellectuals] seem to me to defend their own group interests. In order to become a Western type of society, Turkey has accomplished many reforms which we call Atatürk's reforms...In Turkey our intellectuals were called middle class and have benefitted from the blessing of these reforms and of Western civilization. But the large masses

---

[1] This situation is notably different from Apter's view that socialism in developing countries is used as a weapon against traditionalism, colonialism, and against the nationalists who had entrenched themselves in power after winning independence. See David Apter, *Ideology and Discontent* (London, 1964), pp. 23 ff.

[2] See the first open ideological dispute in *Basın*, January 11, 1961.

[3] The Turkish word for intelligentsia is *aydın* which can be literally translated as "enlightened." The earlier term *münevver* derived from *nur* ("ray") had a similar meaning.

did not benefit from these reforms, yet, as much as we want them to because the reforms stand out as our own, that is to say, as the result of the middle class [intelligentsia's] view of the world. Before the advent of democracy and general suffrage, this middle class lived well. Frankly stated the state worked for us...With the general suffrage this way of life which entailed no responsibility was endangered. The masses have revolted. As a result of this revolt, we shall either make the masses like ourselves or the masses will crush us...The attempts to quell the revolt of the masses undertaken after the revolution of May 27 are worthy of attention [the proposal to deprive the illiterates of the right to vote]. For me the dictatorship of the enlightened means the dictatorship of a middle class. This would be a regime which will work for the benefit of a group self-defined as enlightened...This [regime] entails the supremacy of a class over the others; a self-proclamation [to assert] tutorship and mastery over the large masses. The name of this regime is not progressivism but fascism and reaction." [1]

The leftist-statist intelligentsia was subjected to criticism also by rightists and the spokesmen for the Justice Party. Mehmet Turgut, a champion of liberalism, who later became a minister in the Justice Party government, attacked some university professors who had proposed four votes for each intellectual in order to offset the peasants' numerical superiority. He asked the professors (one of whom proposed surgery in order to control birth) whether they knew anything about the peasant's life or had studied any of his problems. "Well, efendis," he concluded, "you may remain if you wish in your ivory towers but do not calumniate the peasant. Do not act on his behalf. If you nurture such an ambition then first learn how to know him and love him." [2]

There was also self-criticism among intellectuals. This was expressed liberally both by leftists and rightists, usually under the title of "What is a true intellectual?" or "What are the duties of an intellectual?" The immediate purpose of this criticism was to convert the undecided intellectuals to a particular viewpoint and induce them to engage in some action accordingly. Basically, however, these writings echoed the very transformation in the social structure; the emerging new balance among social groups, the obsolescence of the old elitist concepts, and the acceptance of achievement as the basis for social status. It was abundantly clear that one's intellectual achievement lay not in pompous titles and symbolic diplomas but in concrete practical deeds. In the new social setting every individual would have an economic, administrative, or other functional role and would be conferred social recognition on the basis of his practical performance. The society had become "modern" through change

---

[1] Turan Güneş, "Aydınların Diktatörlüğü," *Hür Vatan*, February 20, 1962.
[2] Mehmet Turgut, "Köylü ve Profesörler," *Düşünen Adam*, March 10, 1961.

from inside, and pursued its own course of development regardless of the intellectual's opinion. In this transformed social system formal education, ideally speaking, was no longer the mark of superiority and the criterium deciding social status but a preparation for assuming civic and professional responsibility. Indeed, the leaders with a sense of social responsibility who rose from among labor, merchant, and peasant groups proved to be far more resourceful than those who wasted their life acquiring useless diplomas in high institutions.

The growing importance acquired by professionals, such as engineers, doctors, and architects, pointed to the increasing need for practical education.[1] Many of these professionals became identified in interest and thought with various economic groups and formed, in fact, their upper intellectual stratum. It is, therefore, understandable that free enterprise, liberalism, and constitutionalism were promoted mainly by these high-income and other self-employed professionals. About 70 percent of the deputies, and all senators had a university education and profession falling in the above categories. This situation in turn acted as an ideological catalyst upon other groups of intellectuals, such as school teachers, journalists, students, and above all the civil servants, whose income consisted of fixed salaries. The overwhelming majority of these depended upon the government for a living and became natural supporters of of statism and socialism. These sought—unsuccessfully—to assume the leadership of workers and peasants by redefining their role in the changed social environment of Turkey. Social reviews, such as *Yön* (Direction), and *Eylem* (Action), and the Labor Party were born out of these considerations.[2] However, on practical matters the salaried intellectuals kept in step with other groups' interest-orientation. They staged meetings and demonstrations with the purpose of pressing the government and Parliament to accept their own demands. The teachers' associations, riddled with ideological disputes as they were, gradually became pressure and interest groups. For instance, the Teachers' Federation, a part of which later became a union—*Türkiye Öğretmenler Sendikası*

---

[1] Pressure on universities and on the educational system to adopt a practical philosophy has increased since 1961. Students have protested the teacher's formal, impractical preparation and indifference to research and to the country's practical needs. The student revolts in 1968-69 began in large part as a consequence of the demands for better education. They degenerated into terrorist violence and assassinations, especially among extreme leftist and rightist groups.

[2] These problems have been studied in Kemal H. Karpat, "Socialism and the Labor Party of Turkey," *Middle East Journal*, Spring 1967, pp. 157-172; idem, *Political and Social Thought in the Contemporary Middle East* (New York, 1968).

(TOS)—organized a meeting and selected delegates to meet the President and the Parliamentary leaders in order to ask that a decision denying payment to teachers who had seniority but no promotion be reconsidered. If the demands were refused the teachers threatened to organize "silent marches and to hold meetings throughout the country." [1] Meanwhile a series of other developments, such as the teacher training program which compelled thousands of city intellectuals to teach in villages during their military service, and the abolition of the right to become reserve officers (a status symbol) conferred to high school graduates, further removed the social barriers between village and city and permitted the intellectuals to become identified with the country's problems. Thus, while the intelligentsia continued to preserve the appearance of a social group, in reality it was integrating itself into other social groups which had a true economic basis, and at times provided them with much-needed intellectual stimulus.

The intelligentsia, while struggling to acquire power, also played a vital role in exposing the political parties, Parliament, and the public to new social and political ideas. It reminded them that the legitimacy of authority did not depend solely on the manner of its acquisition but also on the ability to exercise it according to the needs and ideas of the age. The Turkish intelligentsia will bear for generations to come the marks of its own history and experience. It may still play an important part in politics but, short of a dictatorial regime with elite conceptions, it may never resume its traditional political and social supremacy.

Industrial Workers

The workers constitute the largest organized group, created almost exclusively during the Republic. The number of industrial workers rose from about 35,000 in 1923, to over 1.5 million in 1962, while the number of agricultural workers was estimated to be as high as 2 to 3 million. The number of unemployed or semiemployed workers in villages was estimated to be about 3.5 million.[2] The fastest rate of increase among workers occurred during the Democrats' rule through the expansion of private enterprise and industrialization. Thousands of villagers moved into cities, hoping to find employment, and when they found it, they

---

[1] *Milliyet*, September 16, 1963. It was estimated that 300 individual teacher associations were represented in the Federation.

[2] *Hür Vatan*, May 6, 1962. Declaration by former Labor Minister, Bülent Ecevit, See his article chap. IV.

showed their gratitude by voting for the incumbent Democratic government. The group consciousness and the idea of organized defense of labor rights, evident among some workers in older establishments, were hardly noticeable among the newcomers. These viewed the government with distrust based largely on their sad experience with government controls imposed on rural areas during World War II.

The intelligentsia and the bureaucracy, on the other hand, showed little interest in labor problems almost until the Revolution of 1960. This left the workers relatively free of ideological commitment or association with political parties. Some labor legislation was passed after 1947, and insurance, paid holidays, and trade unions were the result of government intitiative rather than direct pressure by labor. The right to strike, although promised as early as 1946, was not accorded until 1963, chiefly for lack of workers' pressure, abundance of manpower, and, paradoxically enough, because of some competition for skilled labor in a few areas which pushed wages up in certain private enterprises.

Liberalization after 1946 led political parties to seek labor votes, and this had a certain beneficial impact on workers' moral and material status. Some labor organizations were established between 1946 and 1950, under the Trade Union Law of 1947. The *Türk-İş* ("Labor Confederation") emerged eventually as the central national body of labor. It functioned under the vigilant supervision of the government. But whenever expedient, the politicians in government did not hesitate to confer with labor leaders and even meet some of their demands, in exchange for votes but also to prevent labor from deviating to the left. This paternalistic interest shown in labor resulted, among other things, in the expansion of the Workers' Insurance Organization ("*İşçi Sigortaları Kurumu*"), established in the late 1940's. This mammoth organization, with considerable material assets, built a large number of income-producing buildings and also initiated housing projects; a total of 13,401 workers' dwellings were thus financed up to 1960. By 1958 labor had enrolled about 200,000 of its members in trade unions. Inarticulate and powerless in their dealings with employers, the trade unions nevertheless became the training ground for a group of leaders whose organizational ability and political flair appeared outstanding. The trade-union leaders from 1946 to 1960 seemed interested in occupational-vocational problems, which in turn created a degree of professional consciousness. These leaders regarded the trade unions chiefly as a means of material betterment rather than as a political weapon, a viewpoint shaped in part by generous Western technical assistance and advice.

Thus, on the eve of the Revolution of 1960, Turkey had a large group of workers who were not fully integrated as participants in the existing political system. The revolution brought no immediate relief to labor, although the military government did lift some of the Democrats' restrictive measures. On the contrary, the military government hurt labor by dismissing thousands of workers for their support of the Democratic Party, and left many others jobless by suspending work on projects deemed uneconomical. The intelligentsia and the military as usual disregarded the workers' opinion, even in matters of economic development, as evident in the establishment of the State Planning Organization when labor leaders were hardly consulted. The Five-Year Plan also was drafted chiefly by a handful of economists with only a scant labor contribution. The Constituent Assembly itself, which opened in early January, 1961, included only six workers' representatives, while the universities had twelve representatives. Meanwhile, the workers' financial situation immediately after the revolution worsened, first, because of the mandatory sale of state savings bonds, and second, from the freezing of wages at their existing level in order to check inflation. The Minister of Finance, while defending the salary increases accorded to the bureaucracy, explained that the workers' wages would not be raised since these had followed the increase in living costs, while the salaries of the civil service had remained stagnant.[1]

Labor was quick to react to this situation. A letter written on behalf of workers in an ammunition factory expressed best the workers' feelings:

The problems of every social group are being considered one by one and solutions searched. The workers' problems are totally disregarded.... The fact that the politicians and the press did not intervene [on our behalf] has left us, the labor group, totally without hope. In each phase of history and of humanity, men have discovered that every virtue lay in science, culture, technology and justice [that is] in work, and in paying respect to the working man... If a [social] group is not incorporated into the state [social] structure or its needs are not attended [the state cannot function]. If we are to give evidence of foresight... and establish a stable life based on the principles of justice and law, and if our purpose is to advance by relying on our will and power, we must think that there is need to place power next to science, the worker next to the official and the man with less culture, even the ignorant, next to the scholar. We are not asking the government for plenty of money or for rights which do not belong to us. We are demanding that a group of people should not be rewarded while another group is oppressed as during the past era. We are asking for social

---

[1] The average worker's monthly wage in 1960 was T.L. 168 or about 18 dollars at the official rate prevailing then. The currency was devalued in 1970 from nine to fifteen liras per dollar.

justice, for rights to be accorded to each person according to his contribution, and that the workers should not be oppressed in establishments... We are asking that in the future, democracy, which is the method of government of the people by the people should be allowed to emerge with its true identity.[1]

The Trade Union Confederation, consequently, began an organized drive to press the Constituent Assembly debating the Constitution to give proper recognition to workers' rights. The six labor representatives in the Assembly were asked to resign for being too passive, while the Istanbul Federation of Labor, in association with the National Confederation, decided to hold a public meeting and press for the inclusion of specific workers' rights in the Constitution. Labor leaders insisted that workers should be considered a social group as entitled to claim its own rights as any other group, and declared that, if necessary, they would secure by force the right to strike.[2] The martial-law authorities in Istanbul questioned the Labor leaders about these declarations but, apparently satisfied with their explanations, promised to convey the workers' demands to the higher authorities in Ankara. Eventually the Constituent Assembly incorporated in the Constitution the workers' rights to strike and to collective bargaining, and recognized the freedom of their extensive organization. The Trade Union Confederation, thereafter, decided to support the Constitution and thus identified itself with the Revolution of May 27.[3]

The leftist sections of the intelligentsia, which had ulterior motives, did not fail to include labor among the *zinde*, or energetic forces of progress. It had hoped to take over power from the military and establish a social regime in which all productive groups would subordinate themselves to the elite's rule. This hope vanished in 1961 after the establishment of Parliament. Nevertheless, these groups in their drive for power began to look upon labor as a potential source of organized support. Their political calculations materialized in a stream of propaganda leaflets in which class struggle and revolution and the workers' role in them were romantically glorified.[4]

The attempt to establish a *Çalışanlar Partisi* ("Workingmen's Party") by some trade union leaders in association with the pro-Republican

---

[1] *Öncü*, February 14, 1961. For related declarations see *Cumhuriyet*, February 4, 1961; *Öncü*, February 21, 1961.

[2] *Vatan, Tanin*, March 3, 13, 1961.

[3] *Vatan*, April 22, 1961.

[4] See a series of articles, "Türk Işçisi Ne Istiyor?" *Cumhuriyet*, November 29, December 1, 1961.

Party intellectuals failed. The trade union leaders conducted a series of intensive talks in 1961-62 with the purpose of organizing themselves for political activity, namely to secure representation in Parliament, but decided against it lest it create dissension and weaken labor's professional organizations.[1]

The constitutional rights granted to labor, the sympathetic intellectual interest in the workers' problems, the regime of freedom after the elections of 1961, and the weak coalition governments from 1961 to 1965 created favorable conditions for labor activities. The economic stagnation and the sharp rise of unemployment, on the other hand, created hardship among workers while Parliament squabbled over partisan issues. Meanwhile, the entrepreneurial groups advocating speedy accumulation of capital through low labor costs seemed to oppose the workers' demands for higher wages, the right to strike, and collective contracts. Consequently, trade-union leaders insisted that they would use the workers' constitutional right to strike regardless of the absence of regulatory statutes. Indeed, strikes and protest meetings took place throughout the country and the government proved unable to prevent them. For instance, on the last day of December 1961, one hundred thousand workers defying an official ban held a gigantic but orderly meeting in Istanbul demanding official recognition for the right to strike and collective bargaining.[2] But Parliament, dominated by small-town professionals caught in their own struggle for power, failed to grasp the significance of these meetings until faced with a dramatic and ominous show of force. On May 3, 1962, just a few days after a Justice Party minister declared that Turkey had no problem of unemployment, about 5,000 unemployed workers in Ankara met in an orderly fashion. The governor tried to soothe the demonstrators with unconvincing promises and the customary parental advice. This angered the workers who decided to present their demands directly to Parliament. They broke through several police barricades and after an awe-inspiring stampede through the fashionable districts of Ankara reached the gate of the Grand National Assembly, where they were barely stopped by military units. The demonstrators refused to disperse even after a delegation was allowed to present petitions to Parliament asking for employment.[3] Similar meetings were held throughout the country in order to demand higher wages, em-

---

[1] The establishment and activities of the Labor Party mentioned in chap. IX must be viewed as the intellectuals' attempt to seize control of labor.

[2] For details see the Istanbul press of January 1, 1962.

[3] See *Türkiye Birlik*, *Ulus*, May 4, 5, 1962.

ployment, welfare rights, and economic development. Workers in the Aegean region gave the government ten days to initiate measures likely to create new jobs, while a trade union delegation visiting the Premier openly accused Parliament of inactivity.[1] "We address you," a labor leader told Parliament. "Wake up, time is passing by. The unemployed worker who cries for bread is providing salary for you. You should come among the jobless instead of driving your Cadillacs to your clubs... and ask the worker if he has a job or any money. We too have come into this world to live like human beings."[2] Some labor leaders saw the end of unemployment in intensive investment which in turn could come, as Ismail Topkar, the representative of the first district (Istanbul) put it, from "parliamentary action capable of inspiring confidence to the private sector," along with other measures.[3] Parliament finally began to devote closer attention to the workers' demands, and even the most conservative groups acknowledged the importance of labor problems but not without accusing the left-wing intellectuals of inciting the workers against established authority.

The chief labor agitation occurred during the coalition crisis in the summer of 1962 and compelled the leaders of political parties to compromise on economic policy with a view to intensifying investments and creating employment.[4] Thus labor, acting to meet its own immediate economic needs, helped speed up the political synthesis. Labor's right

---

[1] See details in *Milliyet*, June 4, 1962.

[2] *Ibid.*

[3] *Zafer Demokrasinindir*, June 17, 1962. The press favoring the private sector reported mostly speeches by labor leaders, which upheld the right of free enterprise, while the socialist press gave extensive coverage to those speeches which praised the social role of the government (*Yeni Istanbul*, May 7, 1962). A labor leader best epitomized the situation : "It is painful [to say it] but we are defending the private sector [enterprise]. Believe me it is right. But the private sector is not aware of it. It is ignoring its own security and is endangering its own existence. I have told the representatives of the private sector in one of the meetings of the Work Council that poverty in a country places them in danger above anyone else...and I told them, God forbid, if they cause a social disaster [change of regime] in Turkey, we, the workers, have nothing to lose. But you [employers] would lose a great deal." (Speech by Halil Tunç, Secretary General of the Workers' Confederation, *Türk İş*, April 1966, p. 15. Labor leaders indeed refused to associate themselves with the statist intellectuals and instead supported the parliamentary regime which supposedly favored the entrepreneurial groups.

[4] The main compromise, as mentioned before, came from the Republican Party which amended its statist policy in favor of private enterprise in order to expand economic activity.

to strike and to engage in collective bargaining was legally granted on July 23, 1963. Since then a series of strikes, some rather violent, have occurred in support of labor claims but the collective contracts reached through bargaining outnumber those secured through strikes. The full emergence of labor as an interest and pressure group aware of its power resulted from the workers' own efforts, although the impact of other internal and external developments, which are not dealt with in this paper, should not be overlooked.

The main body of workers, despite its harsh criticism of Parliament and insistent instigations from the extreme left, did not advocate the abolition of this institution or propose to replace the democratic regime with a dictatorial order. Labor secured welfare legislation, the right to strike, and other benefits by exercising pressure on the legislature based on its constitutional rights. The economic and professional motives of labor remained above political preoccupations; the right to strike was regarded as a means to secure economic gains and not as a political power. Some private employers, heartened by this attitude, began to envisage labor as a potential partner, since a "balanced power [structure] necessitated the establishment of free associations by workers and employers" to discuss the modes of cooperation, as stated by Şahap Kocatopçuoğlu, a high-ranking entrepreneur, in a meeting of the employers.[1]

The future of labor relations in Turkey is not yet clear. But past developments indicate that labor has taken its place in the new social and political setup and, in fact, has become one of its bases. The rapid changes in the public attitude toward labor and the increasing role assumed by trade unions in matters of economic and social planning are optimistic indications for Turkey's political future.

The Villagers

The villagers' group consciousness and the vital changes in their political mentality since 1960 deserve extended treatment. We shall, however, limit our observations to a few points related to the villagers' group consciousness and interest orientation within the framework of the changes brought by the revolution of 1960.[2] The villager was in

---

[1] *Cumhuriyet*, August 17, 1963.
[2] See Chap. V.

many ways treated with generosity and consideration by the Democratic administration. Certainly this was a calculated effort to secure votes but it produced some beneficial results. The villager discovered between 1946 and 1960 that his vote was greatly valued by all politicians. The bargaining with political parties on behalf of the peasants was carried out by rural leaders who found in this position an ideal opportunity to assert their own power. The overwhelming majority of villagers' demands concerned local needs such as roads, bridges, drinkable water, and the elimination of the endless bureaucratic formalities ranging from complicated marriage licenses to the sale of land. A series of intermediaries, beginning with the local party head and ending with the elected deputy in Ankara, exercised continuous pressure upon government officials on behalf of these demands. A survey found that 97 percent of the *kaymakams* ("district prefects") were subject to political pressure, and that 81 percent of those exercising pressure in districts (*"kaza"*) and 56 percent in provinces (*"vilayets"*) were local party leaders.[1]

The heads of village and neighborhood precincts, that is of *ocak* and *bucak*, formed the largest and the most important rural pressure group. The total number of rural party precincts in Turkey probably reached 80,000 units (some places it is as high as 140,000) each one headed by a chairman and an executive board and involving a total of about 350,000 people. Having mainly rural origin and enjoying some status in their communities, these village and town precinct leaders consolidated further their position by assuming party leadership in their respective localities. One may well regard this group as being the most important source of power, propaganda, and action in rural areas, and capable of reaching individual peasants within a matter of hours. The intelligentsia and the urbanites, imbedded in their traditional postures of superiority, originally dismissed the villagers' political and social roles as well as the power and influence of village leaders.

The Revolution of 1960, as mentioned before, took place in Istanbul and Ankara without the villagers' support. All at once the villager found himself cut off totally from the decision-making bodies at the national level since the political parties, his main channel of demand and communication, were banned. Moreover, the villagers were accused of having supported Menderes in exchange for material benefits. In fact, some felt that it was Menderes and the peasants who, teamed up in the

---

[1] *Kaza ve Vilayet Idaresi Üzerinde bir Araştırma*, Prepared by the School of Political Science (Ankara, 1957).

Democratic Party, had taken the country nearly to the brink of disaster, although about thirty-five percent of the rural vote went to the Republican Party.

The measures initiated by the military government in order to stabilize the economy and to prevent political unrest affected mostly the peasants. Credit facilities were curtailed drastically and left rural producers to the mercy of town usurers. The agricultural subsidies were abolished and the prices of farm products, instead of being determined by market forces, were arbitrarily set by the government or by municipal authorities, all of which were controlled by officers. The military director of the fruit and vegetable market of Istanbul, praised as a hero by the city dweller as the man "who provided us with fruit and vegetables at low prices" was a villain in the eyes of both the producers and the intermediaries, though for different reasons. Many tobacco and cotton fields were not harvested since the price offered for such products did not meet even the production costs. This inept economic policy estranged the peasant from the military.

Meanwhile, the military and the intelligentsia began to attack the *şeyhs* and *ağas*—most of whom were in the East—who supposedly oppressed and exploited the ignorant peasants.[1] These denunciations together with other measures, such as the arrest of landlords, undermined the traditional social organization in the rural East and paved the way there for a more dynamic and individualized form of social and political life. However, the Western section of the country had an advanced economic and social structure. Here the villager dealt directly with the commercial enterprises, the banks, and the cooperatives in town and not with the *şeyhs* or *ağas*, who did not exist for the most part. Consequently the Western, Central, and North Anatolian regions were economically crippled by the measures taken by the military and showed readiness to support any party promising to eliminate these measures.

The military abolished all the village and neighborhood political precincts, the famous *ocak* and *bucak* mentioned before, and thus antagonized from the beginning hundreds of thousands of people, regardless of their party affiliation, by threatening their local political position and status. The heads of the *ocak* and *bucak* were attacked in the press as ignorant but shrewd, selfish individuals who exploited the peasants and used the deputies in Ankara to put pressure on government

---

[1] The *şeyhs* and *ağas* of the East often changed party loyalties for personal gain. They also identified themselves with some local group problem, such as dispute over pasture lands.

officials. This attitude was in a way a thinly disguised attempt to reassert the city's traditional domination over the village and the elite's over the masses. A professor expressed best this state of mind :

"In a city like Istanbul with many intellectuals," he wrote, "personalities slated as independent candidates in one election did not win....The precinct leaders who are the true masters of the political party, while selecting candidates, instead of choosing those who would look after the nation's interests are searching for men to serve them and protect their own interests. In one word these [candidates] become the spokesmen...of an interest group...The deputies who are thus elected to the Assembly become subject to the wishes of [local] party leaders who hold the government in their hands. Consequently, a second interest group emerges in the Assembly...Without the divine intervention of the Turkish army we would have faced these power hungry men seeking benefits and positions and would have been deprived of expressing openly the present thoughts. The precinct organization facilitates the emergence of an interest network [supposedly] on behalf of national will and destroys the faith and confidence in democracy." [1]

Thus, looked at from the villager's viewpoint, the revolution appeared as the urbanites' effort to reestablish their traditional political and social supremacy; indeed, the Constituent Assembly had no peasant representatives. Other measures, such as the prohibition to visit field administrative officers, even on business, the imposition of land taxes and the reinforcement of the military police authority ("*jandarma*") in villages, however justified, seemed to support the peasants' suspicion that the "good times" were over and the return to "old unhappy days" imminent. [2]

The villager's group consciousness began to emerge amid these circumstances as a self-defense reaction. The *ocak* and *bucak* leaders, leaving aside their petty feuds and party differences, quickly united and formed an informal rural front against all outside dangers. Consequently, as soon as the ban on political parties was lifted early in 1961, the New

---

[1] Cahit Tanyol, "Parti Teşkilatı ve Halk Hakimiyeti", *Cumhuriyet*, July 16, 1960.

[2] Fevzi Lütfü Karaosmanoğlu, scion of a leading aristocratic family in Western Anatolia, approved of the closure of the precinct party organizations and cited convincingly a series of incidents to back this measure. He also mentioned a villager party leader who refused to let the Minister of Health enter his village because the Minister refused to see him in his office in Ankara (*Öncü*, July 25, 1960). This was possibly Karaosmanoğlu's reaction for he was not reelected in 1957 when he ran on the Freedom Party ticket. There were, however, a number of realistic men, including Ismet Inönü, who regarded the closure of precincts as enhancing the power of the middle classes while limiting the direct participation of the lower classes in active politics. See also Kemal Sarıibrahimoğlu, "Partilerin Ocak ve Bucaklarının Kaldırılmasının Mahzurları," *Ulus*, July 6, 1960.

Turkey and Justice parties could establish their countryside organizations overnight, thanks to these local precinct leaders. Their organizations immediately spread into the provinces and districts and once more the *ocak* and *bucak* leaders found themselves in the leadership seat, though the local party precincts remained formally closed. It is obvious that a political system based on extensive mass participation called for elements capable of communicating with and mobilizing the peasants. Consequently, the *ocak* and *bucak* leaders were bound to retain their importance as indispensable channels of communication as long as the party system survived. This system could potentially strengthen local interests and groups and thus provide arguments enabling statist urban groups to criticize the existing political regime.

The Justice and New Turkey parties were the natural favorites among villagers, although it would be a gross error to assume that other parties had no rural backing. The villager's return to politics was evident in the parliamentary activity of the Justice Party. Prodded by a continuous series of village delegations (deputies of all parties complain that their honorarium is spent on entertaining village delegations) headed by some local leader, the party began to define its position in accordance with the peasants' demands. For instance, a cabinet decree,—a useful one—charging the peasants to maintain village roads was promptly denounced by the Justice Party as being a return to strong rule and forced labor.

Yet, the revolution forced the peasant to realize first that numerical superiority alone did not assure him permanent power, and second, that he was not immune to the developments occurring at the national level. Moreover, the intensive press coverage of conditions in villages exposed all the backwardness and ignorance prevailing there, and had the effect of making the peasant aware of his own situation. Thus, while the peasants became better aware of their status and interest as a rural group, they were forced to think of themselves also as a part of larger economic and political units.

We have studied in the preceding pages the group politics from 1960 to 1965. This was a crucial period for social realignment and political adjustment as well as compromise, temporary as they were, among the old and new elites. In other words, it was a period in which a new system of balance among the most active groups emerged. The Constitution of 1961 provided the basic legal framework to establish such a balance. The question was whether the new political elites in actual control of power could achieve in practice a working solution by incorporating into the system the representatives of all the major social groups, or at least the views and policies demanded by them. The parliamentary representation, though more broadly based than in the past, gave to the middle class groups far greater legislative representation than their number would warrant, while the peasants and workers remained underrepresented. Nevertheless, the press as well as various social-minded groups defending the rights of the underdog compelled the government and the political parties to acknowledge and meet the social and economic demands of the underrepresented groups. The intensive ideological debates added new social and intellectual dimensions to the contemporary Turkish political culture and provided political education for all, including the workers and the peasants. Thus, one may say that Turkey has adapted herself with relative success to the exigencies of a more democratic and social-minded political life. Yet, this political stability looked not like a permanent solution but instead the result of short-range compromises designated to meet emergency situations. The relative stability which prevailed from 1965 to 1970, may be attributed in good measure to such adjustments and political-ideological compromises worked out earlier, between 1960 and 1965. The Justice Party won the confidence of the military largely by promises to abide by the reformist principles of the Republic and to prevent vengeful reaction to the authors of the military coup of 1960. The fact that a social-minded group in the Justice Party, originating in the large urban centers and whose political philosophy was close to the intellectual-bureaucratic elites, waged a constant struggle against the conservative, rightist wing in their own party helped soothe further the military's apprehension. The representatives of the rightist wing were eliminated from government position after the election of 1969, and eventually dismissed from the Justice Party. This group formed the Demokratik Party.

The Republican Party, on the other hand, misjudged the power of the new middle class groups, which incidentally are the backbone of its own countryside organizations, and drifted more in theory than in practice toward the left in order to marshal the intelligentsia's loyalty. But the repeated failure to increase its electoral votes seemed to have persuaded the party to view more realistically the interests and philosophies of its constituency. During the election of 1969 the Republicans adopted a more moderate stand on social issues. Thus, this party also adopted compromises which did not suit its structure.

The economic development between 1963 and 1970, which achieved a real growth of 6 to 7 percent annually, was another major factor in helping to consolidate the existing system and, incidentally, to secure another electoral victory for the Justice Party. Indeed, the last national elections, held on October 12, 1969, after the cumulative vote was eliminated gave the Justice Party a comfortable majority in Parliament but also increased the Republicans' parliamentary representation at the expense of the smaller parties. Thus, the minor middle-of-the-road, small parties, such as the New Turkey and Nation, as well as the radical right—the National Action Party—and the radical left—the Labor Party—were practically eliminated from Parliament. Yet, the two major parties, the Justice and the Republican, lost some popular votes.

The loss of popular votes by the major parties was due in part to the lowest voting participation since 1950. It may be considered, in fact, the symptom of a major qualitative transformation occurring presently in the thinking of the Turkish electorate. Succinctly, it may indicate that many of the issues which formed the backbone of Turkish politics from 1960 to 1969, are exhausted and that a new political era is about to commence. It remains to be seen whether the Turkish political system will show the same resilience and adaptability when faced with demands stemming from a complex and sophisticated society as it did during the transition from the semirural order to the current semiindustrial and semiurban life. For all practical purposes the expedient measures, the temporary compromises which were rooted in the situation created by the military take-over in 1960 have outlived their usefulness. Something more basic and permanent is needed to base the Turkish Democracy on solid foundations. The recent developments in Turkey, if carried to their logical conclusion, may in fact achieve it (see Preface).

CHAPTER EIGHT

TURKISH PROVINCIAL PARTY POLITICS [1]

Frank Tachau

One of the hallmarks of the present stage of Turkish development is the emergence of new groups to positions of power and influence. These groups—merchants and entrepreneurs, small town professionals, gentlemen farmers, and local notables—are new in the sense that their overt bid for national power and influence is of recent origin. It began with the inauguration of multiparty politics in the late 1940's, suffered a setback with the military coup of 1960, and reemerged with the resumption of civilian government in 1961.

These groups are not all "new"; many are, in fact, quite traditional. The interaction of these traditional elements with more typically modern institutions gives rise to combinations which have been described as "amalgamate patterns".[2] But the means they utilize in their quest for power and influence are rather modern.

One of these modern instruments is the political party. The political party may be regarded as 1) a "relatively stable and enduring" organization whose basic aim is 2) the attainment of political power by means of 3) an appeal for mass support. Officially at least, the party is 4) dedicated to the promotion of the public interest rather than private gain. Finally, in a competitive system, the party is 5) a voluntary association.[3] The

---

[1] The basic research for this study was done in 1964 and was made possible by grants awarded under the Fulbright-Hays program and by the Joint Committee on the Near and Middle East of the American Council of Learned Societies and the Social Science Research Council. Both grants are gratefully acknowledged. I wish particularly to thank the members of the Fulbright Commission in Ankara, and its former executive secretary, Mr. Omer Mart, and his staff, for their generous patience and cooperation. The views expressed here belong entirely to the author.

[2] See Dankwart A. Rustow, *Politics and Westernization in the Near East* (Princeton University, Center of International Studies, 1956); also reprinted in R. H. Nolte, ed., *The Modern Middle East* (New York, 1963).

[3] This formulation is based partly on the exposition of Nobutaka Ike in Robert E. Ward and Dankwart A. Rustow, eds., *Political Modernization in Japan and Turkey* (Princeton, 1964), pp. 389-90; and partly on Max Weber, *Wirschaft und Gesellschaft*, Vol. I, *Begriff und Wesen der Partien*. It is subject to qualification. For example, all parties are not equally interested in the attainment of political power, nor in appealing for mass support.

party can perform the function of elite recruitment on a rational and competitive basis only in a modern social and political context. It is certainly not compatible with such traditional principles of elite recruitment as kinship, heredity, and even charisma in its strictly traditional, religious form. Perhaps the most distinctly modern trait of the party is its appeal for mass support. Popular partcipation in national politics is a unique feature of modernity, whether of the competitive or autocratic pattern.[1] Finally, the precise character and role of specific parties depends on the particular cultural, social, and political context in which they must operate. They may use traditional loyalties to acquire power but may also use them in maintaining social cohesion while formal institutions of the past are disintegrating.[2]

The precise form assumed by the political party is conditioned by the environment in which it exists. Consequently, a study of individual parties or party systems with due regard to their social background should provide many key, analytical insights into their modern roles and the remoulding of the social, cultural environment in which they operate.

These general considerations apply with particular force in the case of Turkey. The major Turkish political parties are essentially modern in structure and form; in other words, they conform to the five features listed earlier. The Turkish party system is one of the few which has made the transition from dictatorial, one-party rule to a competitive system dominated by pragmatic parties.[3] What is more, we now know that

---

[1] Neil McDonald defines the function of a party as "a unique role in reconciling and making congruent the impulsive and uncalculated elements in a society in order that calculated control be made possible." Conversely, he suggests that "party is best regarded as the entity, process, or formation which emerges out of the more immediate impulse to control government." Either way, the notion of party is intimately connected with the idea of popular control of political or governmental power (*The Study of Political Parties* [New York, 1955], pp. 84-85). Gabriel Almond identifies the party system as "the distinctively modern structure of political aggregation" (G. A. Almond and J. S. Coleman, eds., *The Politics of the Developing Areas* [Princeton, 1960], p. 40). These views may be compared with those expressed by Robert Michels, *Political Parties* (New York, 1962); M. Ostrogorski, *Democracy and the Organization of Political Parties*, 2 vols. (New York, 1964); and M. Duverger, *Political Parties*, 2nd ed., rev. (New York, 1963).

[2] See Myron Weiner, *Party Politics in India* (Princeton, 1957). An excellent example of such "amalgamate patterns" in a working party system is the case of Lebanon as described by Labib Zuwiyya-Yamak, "Party Politics in the Lebanese Political System," *Politics in Lebanon* ed., Leonard Binder (New York, 1966).

[3] The terminology is that of Almond and Coleman as applied by Rustow, *The Politics of the Developing Areas*, pp. 391 ff.

major changes in the party system during the period of the Republic reflected important social and economic developments.[1]

In this paper, we seek to examine empirically the political parties in their current provincial setting with the purpose of testing the hypotheses just stated. The study consists of two parts. First we shall analyze the personnel in the provincial party organizations, their social and political backgrounds, and the resulting patterns or trends of action. Second, two specific cases are analyzed to determine the relationship between the parties and local social and economic structures, the functions played by parties in the local environment, and the relation between the provincial party units and the national center.

The personnel in the provincial executive committees represent the highest level below the national organization and are the formal link between the local party organizations and the national center. They oversee the local organizations and exercise control over election activities. (Political parties in Turkey tend to mirror governmental administrative structure from the center through the province to the sub-province. Since 1961, however, party organizations below provincial level have been outlawed.) Second, these committees provide a stepping-stone for individuals with political ambitions. Some current members of these committees may be the potential political leaders of the future. Third, membership on these committees may be an indication of interest in politics, which in turn should serve as an index of a more general involvement and thus of social and political dynamics. Finally, the provincial committees are relatively easy to identify and to reach, as contrasted with county executive committees, financial supporters of the party, or rank-and-file members.

What types of persons are active in the provincial organizations of the major parties? The data for selected provincial committees across the country cover four items which are related to the overall process of political development or modernization. These are : 1) age, providing insight into the process of recruitment as well as social change between generations; 2) place of birth, an index of horizontal social mobility; 3) occupation, providing an index of social diversification (the

---

[1] For historical background see Dankwart A. Rustow, "Development of Parties in Turkey," *Political Parties and Political Development* eds., J. LaPalombara and M. Weiner (Princeton, 1966), pp. 112-13. See also Kemal H. Karpat, *Turkey's Politics* (Princeton, 1959); and Frederick W. Frey, *The Turkish Political Elite* (Cambridge, Mass., 1965).

Table 8.1

Members of Provincial Executive Committees *

Age	Percent	Place of Birth	Percent
Over 45	37	Same province or Region	87
35 - 44	43	Elsewhere in Turkey	11
Under 35	20	Outside Turkey	2
Not Available	—		—
Total	100		100
Occupation		*Education*	
Professionals (doctor, laywer, engineer)	29	No formal schooling	2
Public Service (military, teacher, civil service)	6	Primary School	17
Industry or commerce	47	Intermediate	24
Artisan	6	High school	13
Farming	7	University	41
Other	5	Other	3
Total	100		100

* Some individuals reported more than one occupation. Thus in a total of 306 individuals there were 318 occupations. Educational background was indicated by 266 people.

professions, public service, and certain types of commerce and industry are relatively more modern than artisanship, small-scale commerce or farming; while large-scale land ownership or industrial enterprise may indicate elite status and vice versa); and 4) education as a general condition of modernization.

The data are derived from a sample of approximately 300 members of provincial executive committees representing fifteen provinces in all parts of the country except the Southeast.[1] Table 8.1 indicates that these

[1] See legend for Table 2. Several provinces were incompletely covered (e.g.: Kayseri, İçel) and therefore not included in Table 2. The data summarized here were gathered in two different ways. Where time permitted, as many as possible of the members of party provincial executive committees were interviewed extensively regarding both their personal background and political experience. Where time did not permit (i.e., in all but two provinces) only one or at most two committee members from each party were intensively interviewed. Additional basic information, summarized in Table 2, was collected on the remaining members of the committees. Some of this information

members are a relatively young group, their average age being in the early 40's. An overwhelming majority, amounting to almost 90 percent, were locally born if locality is defined in terms of geographic region. Over half were engaged in industry and commerce or were skilled artisans, while about 30 percent were professionals, chiefly lawyers, but including a number of doctors and a few engineers. There were very few public servants or farmers among them, although many who were primarily engaged in nonfarming activities shared in the ownership and management of family lands. Finally, over 40 percent had a university degree or its equivalent; better than half had completed a minimum of twelve years of schooling (high school or *lise*); and only 2 percent had apparently no formal education at all. In short, the provincial political party organizations were staffed by relatively young, educated, local professionals and businessmen. Notably, farmers, landowners, and public servants were not well represented.

The educational background of another group of local and provincial politicians, i.e., candidates for mayor in provincial capitals and towns, was similar in general to that of the local party executives. However, the mayoral candidates tended to have a more pronounced tendency toward higher education.[1] Although there is no firm evidence, these differences probably reflect the higher expectancy of leadership and ability inherent in the office of mayor. The office may be used by locally ambitious politicians to reach national office. It follows that the mayoralty would attract persons of relatively high prestige, which in the Turkish context means professionals, certain types of public servants, and generally anyone with a modern education or with skills acquired as the result of specialized training not widely available.

---

may be approximate since official records were rarely consulted by informants (usually the provincial chairman, vice-chairman, or secretary). There may thus be inaccuracies in the data presented here. However, any distortion is unlikely to be important in the case of age and occupation, since the former can be quite accurately estimated, especially by long-standing acquaintances, and the latter must be obvious. The relatively high proportion of those who have allegedly completed intermediate school, relative to those who did not go beyond primary school, may well be explained by the importance attached to education. Consequently the answers may reflect the respondents' desire to appear well educated.

[1] The results of the survey of mayoral candidates in the 1963 election have been reported in my "Local Politicians in Turkey," in *Regional Planning, Local Government and Community Development in Turkey*, papers of the Eighth Seminar on Housing and Planning (Ankara, 1966).

There is, in fact, some overlap between activity in the party organization and candidacy for elective office. However, not all organization men can expect to run for such prominent offices as mayor or a seat in Parliament. Most of them perform inconspicuously more specific and mundane functions, such as liaison with nonparty groups, associations, and interests, soliciting financial support and marshalling support for the party in a variety of other ways.

The political party, like any other association or social institution, ought to reflect the environment in which it operates. It follows that the provincial party organizations should show variations according to the level of social and economic development, the historical background, the peculiar interrelation with the rest of the country, and other specific characteristics related to a particular province. This simple hypothesis can be easily tested by classifying our data on a provincial basis. Table 8.2 gives the resulting breakdown for twelve selected provinces representing virtually every geographical region and different levels of economic and social development. All but one of the four indicators (age, place of birth, occupation, education) show clear variations among the twelve selected provinces. First, the more populous and well-developed provinces of the West and South have lower proportions of locally born politicians than the other provinces. To some extent, this is undoubtedly due to the dislocation following World War I, such as internal migration, exchange of population with Greece (1924) and inflow of Turks from the Balkans. The point is substantiated by the appearance on these committees of individuals born outside the present boundaries of Turkey.

In the more developed provinces (Izmir, Bursa, Adana, Aydın) a substantially higher number of politicians are engaged in the professions while a smaller number work in commerce, industry, and skilled crafts. On the other hand, the least developed provinces tend to have the lowest proportion of professionals (particularly Ağrı) and the highest proportion of agriculturists.[1] The highest proportion of those engaged in commerce, industry, and skilled crafts are in the eastern Black Sea provinces of Trabzon and Rize. In no case is the proportion of former public servants (military officers, teachers, and civil servants) very high. Where they appear, they are usually retired military officers, some former judges and prosecutors, and even a retired *vali* or provincial governor.

---

[1] The proportion of those engaged in farming or agriculture may be understated if we consider the fact that many members of these committees maintain an interest —often an active interest—in inherited family lands. During interviews, this information was usually elicited only after some probing.

Table 8.2
Members of Provincial Executive Committees from Twelve Selected Provinces

Province	1	2	3	4	5	6	7 A %	7 B %	7 C %	8 A %	8 B %	8 C %	8 D %	8 E %	8 F %	9 A %	9 B %	9 C %	9 D %	9 E %
İzmir	3	592	1	Aegean	26	43	N.A.			47	4	42	—	—	8	8	4	15	73	
Bursa	8	441	1	Marmara	21	45	57	29	14	43	14	33	—	—	10	—	19	19	62	
Adana	9	380	1	South	17	43	73	27	—	63	6	19	—	13	—	7	13	—	80	
Aydın	12	352	3	Aegean	19	39	73	15	10	45	—	40	—	15	—	16	10	5	68	
Balıkesir	15	325	2	Marmara	21	41	90	10	—	19	14	59	9	—	—	5	5	27	29	33*
Trabzon	17	311	2	North	28	39	97	—	3	12	—	69	19	—	—	36	25	14	25	
Erzurum	37	234	2	East	21	44	94	5	—	24	—	76	—	—	—	19	48	10	24	
Malatya	40	231	2	East-Central	16	45	94	—	6*	38	6	38	—	19	—	6	19	13	62	
Rize	44	224	4	North	21	41	100	—	—	10	5	62	19	5	—	33	14	14	14	24*
Sıvas	46	218	2	Central	24	43	88	12	—	32	16	44	4	—	4	8	20	20	52	—
Kars	55	198	3	East	20	54	85	15	—	26	—	53	—	21	—	16	32	10	26	5*
Ağrı	56	195	4	East	24	43	87	8	5	8	—	67	4	21	—	42	50	—	8	10*

See next page for legend.

Legend for Table 8.2

Column 1: Rank order on 1964 State Planning Organization, Index of economic and social development, incorporating data on social services and economic facilities. Of the sixty-seven provinces, the highest index is for Istanbul (1,218) and the lowest for Hakkâri (110). The median is Afyon (245). It will be noted that half of the twelve provinces are above the median, and half below. For a description of the S.P.O. index system, see Rüşen Y. Keleş, "Regional Disparities in Turkey," *Ekistics* 15, No. 91 (June 1963), pp. 331-34.

Column 2: 1964 S.P.O. Economic and Social Index number.

Column 3: Population grouping for provincial capital, as follows:
    1 - Over 100,000   3 - 25 to 50,000
    2 - 50 to 100,000   4 - 10 to 25,000
Figures are based on 1960 census; see *Census of Population, 23 October 1960*; *Population of Turkey* (Republic of Turkey, Prime Ministry, State Institute of Statistics, Publication No. 452, Ankara [1965]).

Column 4: Geographical region, based on the classification developed by Hamit Sadi Selen, University of Istanbul, and used by Rüşen Keleş *Türkiyede Şehirleşme Hareketleri 1927-1960* (Ankara: Faculty of Political Science, Institute of Public Finance, mimeographed; 1961). See also M. D. Rivkin, *Area Development for National Growth; the Turkish Precedent* (New York, 1965), Appendix, pp. 203-4.

Column 5: Total number of committee members surveyed in each province.

Column 6: Average age of committee members.

Column 7: Place of birth:
Sub-column A: Same geographical region.
Sub-column B: Elsewhere in Turkey
Sub-column C: Outside Turkey.

Column 8: Occupations:
Sub-column A: Professions (medicine, law, engineering).
Sub-column B: Public service (civil service, military, teaching).
Sub-column C: Commerce and Industry.
Sub-column D: Artisanship or craftsmanship.
Sub-column E: Farming
Sub-column F: Other.

Column 9: Education:
Sub-column A: Primary.
Sub-column B: Intermediate.
Sub-column C: High school.
Sub column D: University or equivalent.
Sub-column E*: Data not avialable.
          **: No formal education, but literate.

Percentages in columns 7, 8, and 9 should total within a point or two of 100 reading across in each case.

In educational level, once again the more developed provinces (Izmir, Bursa, Adana, Aydın, Malatya, Sıvas) tend to stand out with the highest proportions of university-educated politicians. Here, too, the least developed province (Ağrı) shows the lowest educational level.

Age is the one indicator which shows no clear pattern of variation. In all but three provinces the average age falls between a lower figure of 41 and an upper limit of 45. There is no apparent reason why the committees in the eastern border province of Kars should be substantially older, but it is notable that the age distribution there is similar for the two parties. The same is true for the two provinces that fall below the lower age limit of 41. Moreover, these two provinces, Aydın, in the Aegean area, and Trabzon, on the Black Sea, are not only geographically remote from each other, but dissimilar in most other respects as well.

In short, the members of provincial party organizations in more highly developed areas tend to differ significantly from those in lesser developed parts of the country. The former show a higher degree of mobility, a greater tendency toward professional rather than commercial occupations, and a higher level of education. But there are also exceptions. Two of our lesser developed provinces (Malatya and Sivas) resemble the more highly developed areas in terms of the variables under consideration here. These two provinces share certain common features. Both have large capital cities which are located in relative isolation from other urban centers, and both are pockets of strength for the Republican Party. Conversely, one prosperous province, Balıkesir (the capital city has about 60,000 people), which ranks high on the index of social and economic development and is close to two major urban centers, Izmir and Bursa, resembles the lesser developed provinces in terms of our variables. Moreover, this province appears to have a long history of opposition to the government, at least during the Republican era, and has been a stronghold of the Democratic and Justice parties.[1]

---

[1] Malatya is Ismet Inönü's constituency. In the case of Sıvas, PRP strength can be explained partially by its symbolical historical significance—the convention of 1919, defining the goals of the Liberation War, was held here—which made the Republicans give it special treatment during their term in office. Sivas also has a large group of Shi'ite (Alevis) who supposedly regard PRP's advocacy of secularism as a bulwark against oppression by the Sunni majority. Kemal Karpat, on the other hand, based on his study of Balıkesir province, told the writer that certain sections, particularly the mountainous and the tobacco-growing areas, are under the control of local

Table 8.3.

Members of Provincial Executive Committees, by party, from Twelve Selected Provinces in 1964
(all figures in percentages except for N)

Age	JP	PRP	RPNP	Place of Birth	JP	PRP	RPNP
Over 45	35	43	29	Same region	83	75	96
35 - 44	43	45	29	Elsewhere in Turkey	3	13	—
Under 35	11	11	42	Outside Turkey	3	2	—
No infor.	11	—	—	No information	12	10	4
N	100	148	24	N	99	148	24
Occupation				*Education*			
Professions	24	39	8	No formal schooling	6	1	—
Public Service	4	6	—	Primary school	13	15	38
Commerce, Industry	67	38	46	Intermediate	14	19	29
Artisans	2	5	23	High school	18	11	8
Farming	3	9	23	University	39	46	25
				No information	—	7	—
N	99	160	26	N	90	149	24

The differences among members of provincial organizations is significant in comparing the major parties. Table 8.3 summarizes the data in this respect. It appears that of the three parties surveyed the People's Republican Party (PRP) exhibits the greatest degree of physical mobility, the Justice Party (JP) somewhat less, and the Republican Peasant's National Party (RPNP) least of all.[1] Similarly, the Republican Party seems to be staffed by a larger percentage of professionals, the Justice Party more by businessmen, merchants, and industrialists. The high percentage of farmers and artisans among members of the RPNP should perhaps be discounted in view of the small size of the sample, but it does confirm the generally conservative and traditionalist character of the party, at least prior to its take-over by former Colonel Alparslan Türkeş.[2]

---

gentry. This reduces social mobility greatly and, despite the favorable location, makes this province resemble the East. The tobacco-growing gentry in the country —especially in Sındırğı—supported the Republicans in the early 1960ies, whereas the professionals and businesses concentrated in the city and the West backed the Democratic and Justice parties.

[1] Expressed in terms of "localism," this tendency confirms the findings of Frederick Frey, which distinctly reflect the closer ties of the Democratic Party to localities and regions in comparison with the Republican Party (*Turkish Political Elite*, pp. 188-89).

[2] It should be noted that this survey was undertaken more than a year before the

PRP personnel seem to be only slightly better educated than their JP counterparts. The age difference between the two major parties does not appear significant. The RPNP, on the other hand, appears to be staffed by younger and less well-educated men.

The data reviewed above suggest some tentative conclusions. In gross terms, we noted that the personnel of the major political parties at the provincial level were relatively young and well-educated local professionals and businessmen.[1] A breakdown by province suggested that with the exception of local origin, these tendencies were more pronounced in the more highly developed parts of the country. Finally, comparison of the major parties indicated that the Republican Party was slightly closer to the more developed or modern pattern in terms of mobility and education. Most significantly, the Republican Party was staffed more generally by professionals and public servants, the Justice Party by merchants and traders. In terms of the hypothesis set forth in other chapters of this book, we have here an indication of the political inclination of the "new" middle class in favor of the Justice Party and the "old" middle class toward the Republican Party.

Important questions remain, some of general scope, others of a more specific nature. What is the relationship between the social tendencies we have noted among local politicians and the general process of modernization? What is the relationship between the parties and the social groups represented in the local organizations? What is the role of the party organization in the local communities? Are the tendencies we have noted within the parties indicative of tendencies in the communities? In short, why have these groups rather than others, such as farmers, artisans, or landowners, staffed the parties? These are substantive questions the answers to which are best sought in a closer examination of several individual cases : the provinces of Adana in the south and Aydin in the Aegean area.

---

change in RPNP leadership which brought Colonel Turkeş to the helm in the summer of 1965. There were, however, evidences of the impending move by Türkeş at the time of this survey.

[1] We should emphasize the word "relatively" here. One might question the apparent absence of even younger men among these local politicians. Does this indicate inability of the parties to attract new blood? A firm answer to this question would require further examination of local party organizations, including their youth branches. There are occasional signs of disillusionment with partisan politics. On the other hand, deference to age is a traditional value which has not yet been completely undermined.

Politics in Adana

Adana is one of Turkey's largest, most populous, and most rapidly developing provinces. It is situated in the large, flat, and fertile plain of the Çukurova, thrusting in the shape of a wedge from the Mediterranean Sea north-eastward toward the Taurus Mountains. This area has been a crossroad between Europe and the Orient since ancient times, situated as it is on one of the few routes that permit easy passage through the Taurus Mountains via the Cilician Gate to the Fertile Crescent. After World War I, Adana was temporarily occupied by the French but not without opposition from the nationalist resistance groups organized in the mountains above the plain.[1]

Adana is blessed with a subtropical climate and rich soil, producing cotton, citrus and other fruits, vegetables, some grains, and considerable rice. Industrial development has made headway, chiefly in the textile field. Wealthy landowners, whose income is derived primarily from cotton, rice, or citrus products dominate Adana both economically and socially. Some of them have also invested in manufacturing and commercial enterprises. Significantly, however, land ownership is a symbol of prestige and status. Those who have acuired wealth or status by other means are thus apt to purchase, say, 1,000 *dönüm* (about 200 acres) of land as a a sign that they have "arrived," while those who possess nonagrarian sources of income will still retain ownership and management of their land. Some of these wealthy families have deep roots in the region. Others have risen to wealth and prominence more recently, particularly since the phenomenal development of cotton as a commercial crop and the improvement of health conditions. It is the prominence of these families and their occasional feuding, as well as the unplanned growth of the city, that has led some to describe Adana as an overgrown village. The development of industry has been accompanied by the growth of

---

[1] The local chapter of the Society for Defense of Rights was organized by Ahmet Remzi Yüregir, a landowner and newspaper publisher. Mustafa Kemal authorized the formation of the chapter by telegram on November 3, 1335 (= 1919). Yüregir's account of his experiences as a leading participant in the events of these turbulent years "Milli Mücadelede Çukurova" ("The Cukurova during the National Struggle") was published in *Yeni Adana*, the newspaper he founded in 1918, in installments beginning with the issue of December 25, 1952. The account depicts the formation of an antinationalist front by the French and local Armenians with the cooperation of a faction of Turks apparently led by a prominent member of the local branch of the *Hürriyet ve Itilâf* ("Freedom and Alliance"), the major opposition to the ruling Union and Progress ("Ittihad ve Terakki") Party.

labor organizations. The Turkish Labor Confederation maintains a regional office in the city of Adana representing at least 25,000 union members in the immediate area. The left-wing Labor Party also had an active organization in the area.

Politically, the province of Adana has been split fairly evenly between the two major parties. Until 1965 the Republican share of the vote fluctuated between 43 percent and 55 percent.[1] In 1965 the PRP vote dropped to 35 percent, while minor parties, particularly the Labor Party, picked up about 7 percent.

In 1964 only three parties had active committees at the provincial level in Adana, and two of these had a full complement of subprovincial or county committees as well; the Labor Party had only a provincial committee. The RPNP had an organizational structure on paper, but it was evident that the party was in fact moribund.

The biographical data relating to members of the provincial committees in Adana may be concisely summarized. The average age of committee members was 43 (see Table 2), conforming to the national pattern. There was no great age differential between the two major parties. Horizontal mobility was comparatively high, with better than one quarter of the politicians surveyed beying born outside the region. All of these belonged to the PRP.[2]

---

[1] Voter participation tended to follow national trends, starting from a figure of 89.5 percent in 1950, rising to a high of over 95 percent in 1954, then dropping to a low of 76.5 percent in 1957. The corresponding figures for the general election of 1961 and the provincial and local elections of 1963 were 85 percent and 77.5 percent respectively (data made available by the Research Bureau of the Republican People's Party in Ankara). Adana is thus a swing district. In the 1969 elections the JP won 6, the PRP 5, the Reliance Party 1, and the National Action Party 1 of the 13 seats of Adana Province in Parliament. In neighboring İçel Province 4 of the 7 parliamentary seats were won by the JP and the remainder by the PRP (*Yeni Gazete*, October 14, 1969).

[2] Interestingly, the number of fathers of PRP members who were locally born was slightly higher than for the members themselves. This is indicative of a tendency for some provincial and small-town professionals to return to their ancestral homes upon completion of their education, although they were not born there, and may not have lived there at all. Often these men are sons of public servants who served in various parts of the country during their careers and were thus exposed to intensive physical mobility. These figures should be treated with caution since the PRP sample was larger than the JP sample. This in itself may be significant, since PRP members were more accessible to the interviewer and seemed to understand more readily the nature and significance of the questions being asked. We should also recall that at the time of this survey, the PRP was in power and the JP in opposition. With the roles reversed, it would not be surprising if reticence of this sort shifted from one party to the other.

The educational background of JP members was somewhat higher. Knowledge of foreign languages seemed to be evenly distributed, but a considerably larger proportion of JP members had travelled outside Turkey. All of the JP members interviewed were professionals, but only slightly more than half the Republicans; the rest were businessmen and/or landowners (middle-scale farmers or participants in large-scale agricultural operations). A few of the professionals in the PRP doubled as middle-to large-scale landowners (owning approximately 1,000 *dönüms*, or about 200 acres each). Half of the fathers on both sides were or had been farmers. These were most probably small- to medium-scale farmers, for the indications are that the number of medium- or large-scale landowners among the active party members who inherited their properties is quite low. As noted below, some of these owners acquired their lands through purchase rather than inheritance. On the JP side, the remaining fathers were engaged in business or commerce.

The PRP fathers, by contrast, represented not only business but also the legal profession, engineering, and public service. In view of the relative scarcity and consequently higher status of such professions in the fathers' generation, this suggests a significant socio-economic contrast between the parties. The Republicans represented the professional intelligentsia created in the early days of the Republic whereas the Justice Party represented the upcoming groups from a more diversified social and occupational group. Very few of the fathers on either side could claim a university education. A few had no formal schooling at all.

The Adana party executive committees of the two major parties thus appear to follow a national pattern in that they represent a rising new type of middle class consisting chiefly of professionals and entrepreneurs whose occupational background placed them in a different category than the elite which ruled Turkey in the early stages of modernization. The clearest evidence of this upward mobility lies in the differences in occupational distribution and educational level between fathers and sons. Clearly, however, the fathers were not of the lowest social standing, if the low number of illiterates among them can be taken as an index.

Past political experience represents another significant conditioning factor of local committee members. The data for the Çukurova, gathered from interviews with individual members, suggest a high degree of political continuity and stability which is reflected in the national party organizations. On the PRP side, no member had ever belonged to another party, a mark of the exceptionally high degree of loyalty characteristic of this party. The date of first membership in the party tends to fall into three categories representing three distinct elements. The first, and the largest group, consists of those who joined the party prior to its first ouster from power in 1950. The second group represents those who joined it during the 1950's. These are generally individuals who became increasingly disillusioned with the Democrats' rule and found in the PRP the best means of expressing their disillusionment. Some of them were civil servants who either lost their jobs because of Democratic partisanship or resigned under various pressures. Others were former supporters or active members of the Democratic Party who made the transition in stages, first joining the Freedom Party led by a Democratic splinter group in 1955, and then merging with the PRP in 1958. A similar pattern appears in the province of İçel, also in the Çukurova, to the west of Adana, where the entire PRP organization seems to have fallen under the influence of a group of former Democratic-Freedom Party members for a number of years, particularly in the towns of Mersin and Tarsus.[1] In most cases the defense of Atatürk's reforms was a major reason given for joining the PRP.

The third group of PRP members is made up of those who joined the party after the military coup of May 27, 1960. These generally include retired army officers and civil servants as well as younger men entering politics for the first time.

Among Adana PRP executive committee members, the first group —which we might call the Old Guard—dominates the scene. The Old Guard's power was enhanced by the adherence to the party of a somewhat younger age group with apparent long-standing loyalty to the party (possibly for reasons of family and convictions) who reached the requisite age only during these later years.[2] The small number who joined the

---

[1] In Adana Province the Freedom Party apparently failed to establish a foothold. Dissident Democrats there broke away earlier and formed the Peasants' Party ("*Köylü Partisi*") under the leadership of the late Professor Remzi Oğuz Arık, a native of Kozan. The party's strength, such as it was, seems to have been concentrated in the vicinity of that town. This party merged with the conservative Nation Party in the late 1950's. As of 1964 it was moribund in the entire area. Unlike the Freedom Party group in İçel, the former members of this dissident group have scattered somewhat. Some of them joined the Justice Party and achieved temporary position of influence there. Almost none seem to have moved over to the PRP, however.

[2] One member of this group in the Adana region stands out. He worked extremely hard on behalf of the party during the late fifties and early sixties, and claims to have swung a number of solidly Democratic villages into the Republican column. His father was a *mufti*—religious leader—and he himself is a schoolteacher with a

party after 1960 also fall in this category. As a whole, however, the PRP in Adana appears to have been rather unsuccessful in attracting new blood.

On the JP side, the element of continuity obviously must be sought in former membership and activity in the Democratic Party (DP). In many areas, the local organizations are staffed either by former members of the DP or by their relatives and friends. This is clearly the pattern in İçel Province where some of the local JP organizations are manned by the same people who formerly ran the DP organization. The pattern in Adana is somewhat different. Here the identification of the JP with the DP is not so clear (although in terms of electoral support it certainly is). In fact, there are a small number of former dissident Democrats who came to the JP via the National Republican Peasants' Party, as contrasted with the dissident Freedom Party (ex-Democrats) in İçel who ultimately took over the local PRP.

The explanation for the disparate background of JP members in Adana in comparison with their counterparts in İçel may be explained by the undisputed domination of the latter province by the Democrats during the entire period of the Menderes regime. This rigid domination was managed by a highly cohesive organization, in spite of the Freedom Party splinter in the mid-fifties. The town of Tarsus, for example, gives the impression of being tightly controlled by a highly efficient political machine. The leaders of this machine were jailed following the military coup of 1960, but the organization appears to have survived almost unscathed. Adana, by contrast, was lost to the Republicans in 1957. Other than the mayor of the city, few dominant Democrats held office and therefore could not be imprisoned after the revolution.[1] This may well explain the fact that the level of partisan animosity was somewhat lower in Adana than in İçel after the reinstatement of civilian government.

---

decidedly reformist bent. After his retirement from active politics in 1961, he published a study of electoral trends and their relation to social structure in rural villages, based on a statistical sample of villages in the Tarsus and Mersin area. He stoutly maintains that the military coup of 1960 prevented a potential peaceful return to power of the PRP via the ballot box. See M. Altın, *Türkiye'de Siyasi Hareketler ve Sosyal Yapı* ("Political Movements and Social Structure in Turkey") (Ankara, 1961).

[1] The personalities of the military governors who took over these two provinces may also have had some effect. It was alleged, for example, that the governor in İçel acted in a highly vengeful manner, while his counterpart in Adana was more moderate. The resentment of pro-Democratic voters was thus likely to be higher in İçel, with the result that the newly formed Justice Party probably had greater sympathy and support. İçel, incidentally, was the constituency of Refik Koraltan, one of the founders of the DP.

The majority of members of the executive committee of both parties had been candidates for elective office, most for seats in the provincial or municipal councils. A few had also run for Parliament. Each of the two major parties had for a few months in 1963-64 a former deputy as its provincial chairman. There were altogether only three local organization members who became deputies. These appear to have been exceptions to the rule that provincial organizations are staffed by men on the way up rather than down.[1]

In sum, the provincial executive committees of the two major parties in Adana consisted of middle level politicians representing a provincial or local middle class of professionals and businessmen, some of whom probably entertained greater political ambitions. Notably none of these people were themselves members of the established local socio-economic elite. This raises the question of the relation between that elite and the political parties, both locally and nationally.

It has been suggested that Atatürk organized the Republican Party by relying on the twin pillars of the civil bureaucracy at the national level, and local notables in the provinces.[2] This alliance between the local notables and the Republican Party endured as long as the national leadership did not threaten the social and economic position of their local allies. Significantly, the first successful opposition, the Democratic Party, split off from the Republicans precisely on the issue of agricultural reform, and at least one of its founders, Menderes, was a large landowner.

This alliance was apparently very strong in the Çukurova, and it has partially survived to the present day. For example, of twelve deputies and four senators representing Adana from 1961 to 1965, at least seven could be identified as members of large landowning families. Four of them

---

[1] This point is confirmed by the fact that two of the members of the JP provincial executive committee in 1963-64 became candidates for Parliament in 1965, occupying the eight and ninth spots on the ticket; but only six JP candidates were elected. On the PRP side, the list of candidates included a committee member in 1964, who had been an unsuccessful candidate for mayor in 1963. Also nominated were several prominent members of subprovincial committees from the towns of Ceyhan and Osmaniye. The PRP elected four candidates (*Cumhuriyet*, September 4, 1965 for list of candidates; *Yeni Adana*, October 13, 1965 for election results).

[2] See Kemal H. Karpat, "Society, Economics and Politics in Contemporary Turkey", *World Politics* 17 no. 1 (October 1964), pp. 55 ff; Turan Güneş, "CHP Halktan Nasıl Uzaklaştı?" ("How Has the PRP Removed Itself from the People?"), *Yön*, December 20, 1961, p. 14, cited in A. H. Ulman and F. Tachau, "Turkish Politics: The Attempt to Reconcile Rapid Modernization with Democracy," *Middle East Journal* 19, no. 2 (Spring 1965), p. 159.

were elected on the PRP ticket. One of these switched to the JP in 1964. The 1965 list of nominees of the two parties included a similar sampling. Furthermore, the PRP's greatest strength in the province of Adana, aside from several small mountain districts, seems to lie in plains areas strongly dominated by wealthy landlords, some of whom have achieved national prominence. One Adana landowner became one of the three most powerful men in the country as a member of the three-man national party executive which included then-President İnönü. Another (Kasım Gülek) became Secretary General of the PRP during the years of opposition in the 1950's. Other landowners have achieved prominence through the Democratic and/or Justice parties. One of these (Ahmet Topaloğlu) was Minister of Defense from 1965 to 1970. Another (Cavit Oral) switched from the PRP to the DP in the later forties, then back to the PRP in 1961, and in 1962 to the JP.[1]

What determines the party affiliation of these landowning individuals and families? Why have some remained loyal to the PRP while others went over to the opposition? One possible basis of explanation lies in the aforementioned alliance between the PRP and the local elites established early in the Republican era. If we assume that those socially and economically prominent in the late 1920's would become the natural partners in this alliance, it follows that they would identity with the regime and the party. On the other hand, those who rose to political prominence and/or wealth later would be inclined to join a new opposition party in order to gain power and prestige.[2] In short, one might expect to find new wealth concentrated in the Democratic Party, older wealth in the Republican Party. This pattern seems to hold generally in Adana, where the industrialists, most of whom favor the JP, have acquired their wealth relatively more recently than those landowners who remained loyal to the PRP. This point is most dramatically illustrated in two smaller towns of the Çukurova : Kadirli and Tarsus.

In Kadirli, according to the testimony of one of the landowners, this pattern had fairly deep historical roots. Kadirli had two kinds of landowners : the first descended from the traditional *ayan* ("notables") or *derebeys* ("lords of the valley") of the area, the second from a group

---

[1] Of the seven major families of Kozan whose genealogies Wolfram Eberhard has described, at least four have now or have had representatives in Parliament (the Kutuk or Bozdoğan, Akçalı—who also held the mayoralty of Kozan and a seat on the municipal council in Ceyhan—Arıkoğullar, and the Yeğenoğullar). See "Nomads and Farmers in Southeastern Turkey," *Oriens* 6 (1953), pp. 42-44.

[2] The point is also true for party attitudes at the national level.

of rebellious *yörük* ("nomads") who were settled by the central government during the second half of the nineteenth century. Today the former appear to fully control the local organization of the PRP; the latter are more closely identified with the JP, but with one exception.[1] It is said that when their interests are at stake, the landowners are able to cooperate without regard for party affiliation. Thus, a member of one of the older families became a vociferous spokesman in defense of property rights in the debates of the Constituent Assembly in 1961. He was opposed by prosocialist intellectuals, although both sat as representatives of the PRP. This points up the two-sided character of the party itself.

In the case of Tarsus, the split between new and old wealth is even more striking. The traditional group of *eşraf* ("notables") is represented here by an industrialist who belongs to the aristocratic Ramazanoğlu family which had a long tradition of land wealth and social position. His father was politically identified with the Young Turks, having served as a deputy in Istanbul from 1914 to 1919. He later acquired a textile plant from an emigrating Greek entrepreneur. The younger Ramazanoğlu had stuck with the PRP until near the bitter end in 1960, when apparently irresistible pressures persuaded him to join the Menderes-sponsored *Vatan Cephesi* ("Fatherland Front"). He abhorred the "bureaucratic mentality" and argued that neither of the two major parties could

---

[1] This historical analysis is persuasive but not completely documented. It is significant, however, that my informer made such a distinction. For further details of a similar nature on the neighboring town of Kozan, see Eberhard, "*Nomads and Farmers*", pp. 42-44. Kadirli is an unusual town in other respects. Five representatives of the local landowning families sat in the national Parliament between 1961 and 1965. Two were affiliated with the PRP and three with the JP. Moreover, Kadirli has produced one of the outstanding novelists of contemporary Turkey, Yaşar Kemal. Two of his novels, dealing in part with land rivalries and the struggle of former nomads with town people, have been translated into English under the titles *Memed My Hawk* and *The Wind from the Plain*. Early in 1962, Kadirli became the focus of national controversy when an action-minded young *kaymakan* ("prefect"), who had supported some of the villagers in their attempts to gain legal control over water sources that had been preempted by rice-cultivating landowners, was peremptorily transferred to a remote and desolate county on the Russian border. The government was then a PRP-JP coalition, and the Minister of the Interior who had authority over the transfer was Ahmet Topaloğlu, one of the five Kadirli Deputies. Later he became the Minister of Defense in the First and Second Cabinets of Süleyman Demiral, from 1965 to 1970. On the latter controversy, see *Yeni Adana*, March 22, 1962, *et. seq.*; *Cumhuriyet*, March 23, 26, 27, and 28, 1962. For evidence of the potential reemergence of the dispute over water rights, see *Yeni Adana*, February 28 and March 1, 1966.

effectively overcome this incubus, which he felt was the greatest obstacle to the economic development of Turkey.[1]

By contrast, the owner and operator of the other large textile plant in Tarsus was a simple cotton farmer and cotton gin operator who happened to be the leader of the local Democratic organization when that party came to power in 1950. Allegedly he was able to acquire the wherewithal to build his textile plant as a result of his position in the party. Unlike his more artistocratic counterpart, this entrepreneur has had little formal education, and probably enjoyed little social prestige prior to his acquisition of political power.[2] This case suggests another facet of the relation between new wealth and the DP-JP, i.e., the use of political ties for the aggrandizement of an individual or a group.

Our analysis so far suggests that although the local socio-economic elite in the Çukurova has not assumed a direct role in the staffing of the provincial executive committees of the major parties, it has shown some interest in gaining elective offices at the national level, i.e., membership in Paliament. In fact, the picture is not quite so simple. In the first place, it goes almost without saying that access to Parliament is related to influence in the provincial party organization.

The central party leadership at one time exercised complete control over the nominating process, but its direct influence in this field has been curtailed. Indeed, under the system prevailing since 1961, the parties conduct something on the order of a nominating convention. The national leadership still retains the nominating privilege for a certain quota on the ballot, and often exercises this right to preempt the first or second slot. Moreover, the system of proportional representation now in effect means that in provinces where the party is weak this power is tantamount to nullification of local nominations altogether. Below a certain point, and this varies with relative party electoral strength, it is immaterial who gets which place on the ballot.

---

[1] In view of the marked identification of other industrialists with the Justice Party, this attitude is notable. It is reflected in interviews with others of similar background and interest elsewhere in the country. It has been suggested that the reason for the pro-DP tendencies of the industrialists was their dependence on the government for import licences, allocations of materials in short supply, etc. It may be that ideological considerations are now also beginning to have an impact.

[2] Although he now professes no further interest in politics—and was reluctant to be interviewed—the fact is that one of his nephews was the local JP chairman in 1964 and was elected Deputy in 1965. He operated under the watchful eye of an older brother who was a DP deputy from 1954 to 1960.

Yet, if an aspiring politician has firm control of the local organization he may prevail over the national organization's scheme in his locality. It is significant that both in 1961 and 1965, the top spot on the Adana PRP ballot was occupied by Kasım Gülek, whose unsuccessful bid for Secretary General of the party had put him completely at odds with the national leadership. Indeed, he was expelled from the party for several years but was readmitted preceding the elections of 1965. Gülek's control of the Adana organization in 1961 appears to have been so strong that several other nationally prominent natives of Adana, including the then Secretary General and his deputy, Kemal Satır and Suphi Baykam, were forced to seek candidacy in other provinces. The central organization, however, with the support of a local anti-Gülek faction, made at least a partial comeback in the period 1961 to 1965. It dissolved the Gülek-dominated provincial executive committee in 1963, and appointed a new anti-Gülek committee. In the provincial party congress of March 1964, a compromise was struck between the two embittered factions, though both sides claimed majority support within the Congress. Similarly, the 1965 slate of Parliamentary candidates shows evidence of compromise. The salient fact in this situation was the staunch support given to Gülek's faction by the traditional elite landowning groups, while the new elite composed of middle-class, professional groups looked to Ankara for support. On the Justice Party side, neither factional strife nor conflict between locally dominant groups and national leadership was evident. Landowning interests were also represented, but did not seem as prominent as in the PRP. Nor were the industrialists much in evidence.

The factionalism within the Adana PRP is important. It suggests that, although the long-standing landowning elite remained powerful, it no longer completely dominated the scene. It now faced not only the central organization controlled by bureaucratic and socialist minded intellectuals but also the rising provincial middle class as well.

The existence in Adana of a Farmer's union ("*Çiftçi Birliği*") is significant in this respect. This is a private organization which speaks for prosperous large-scale famers. It was founded over thirty years ago in Adana, and appears to have remained primarily a local organization until quite recently, when new chapters began springing up in various provincial centers in the more prosperous parts of the country. In Adana, this organization was dominated by a locally prominent member of the PRP. Significantly, this gentleman now professed reticence toward the PRP. The organization, not to be confused with the quasi-official

Chamber of Agriculture, is a strictly privately organized and financed pressure group. Its major national activity in the early 1960's appears to have been its campagin against land reform. The growth and development of this organization is a clear sign of the new interest-bound ideological orientation of Turkish politics.

The two major parties in Adana tend to be staffed at least partly by relatively young and well-educated businessmen and professionals. But it would be misleading to assume that these parties have uniform internal solidarity or are identical images of one another, either in socio-economic or other terms. Our discussion of the influence of large landowners in the PRP is only one illustration of this. Thus, in contrast to the old elite faction within the party the younger PRP members favor social reform, staunchly advocate secularism, and voice support for the statist or socialist policies pursued by the national leadership.[1]

Such a split did not seem to exist within the JP in 1964. That party seemed firmly united in favor of economic liberalism, and antisecularism.

Correspondingly, the younger professionals who staff the JP appear less sophisticated and refined than most of their PRP counterparts. It will be recalled that background data on fathers of committee members indicated some social differentiation between the PRP and the JP, the former representing a somewhat higher social stratum than the latter. Many of them are also newer to politics, and their feelings of hostility toward the PRP are often very intense.[2]

---

[1] Nowhere is the Jekyll-and-Hyde character of this party more sharply revealed than on the first of these points, particularly with reference to the proposals for land reform, which included provisions for limitations on size of landholdings. One prominent member of the PRP Adana executive committee, for example, strongly supported the land reform proposals in public, while in private he consulted a wealthy farmer for advice as to how he could himself evade the allegedly stringent provisions of the bill. This politician was keenly aware of the potential harm the party might suffer on this issue, since the wealthy landowners had been a prime source of finance. For similar reactions among industrialists on the issue of socialism, see the description of the Tarsus textile manufacturer, and a similar case in Aydın discussed below.

[2] These tendencies are probably more clearly apparent at the sub-provincial level. The sub-provincial chairman for the city of Adana in 1964 may be a leading case. He was entirely new to politics, never before having served in any party or run for elective office. He was engaged in retail carpet sales, but also qualified as an *imam*. He was a graduate of the School of Divinity in Ankara, and served for six years as teacher and director of the *Imam-Hatib Okulu* ("Preacher Training School") in Adana. His father, a native of Isparta, was also a preacher and merchant. This young man declared that he had joined the party in order to save the country from atheistic communism, which, he declared, was entering the country under the aegis of the PRP.

Three other minor factors have played a role in regional and local politics in the Çukurova. The first of these was evident in the mayoralty race in the city of Adana in 1963. The PRP candidate was a young lawyer of "Arabic" origin, i.e., a member of the local Arabic-speaking minority. The party chairman referred to "his" candidate as "the Kennedy of Adana." The idea was that the "Arab" vote had split in the past. His strategy was to use the candidate to draw the bulk of Arab votes to the PRP and thus to win the election. The strategy was unsuccessful, but it is nonetheless significant that it was consciously employed.[1]

The second factor was historical. It consisted of citing previous opposition to the Republic, or collaboration with the enemy during the War of Liberation, so as to lower a candidate's prestige. For instance, one candidate in the municipal elections of Antakya ("Antioch"), the capital of Hatay Province, was accused of belonging to a family which had allegedly cooperated with the French when the territory was part of Syria, and opposed the cession of the area to Turkey in 1939. Other individuals and families in the Çukurova were exiled during Atatürk's lifetime for similar pro-French activities or for oppositionism; these quite naturally would gravitate toward an anti-PRP party. On the other hand, many of those who participated in and supported Atatürk's nationalist resistance movement also joined the Democratic Party in the forties and fifties.[2]

Finally, interparty rivalry in Adana also appears in the form of a "relentless effort of the parties to infiltrate associations and institutions of every sort."[3] In Adana, this endeavor assumed extreme forms, resulting in bitterly fought contests in several associations, particularly certain cooperatives and the Chamber of Commerce. In the latter

---

The most representative version of what the JP stands for came from an Adana lawyer, member of a prominent landowning family long active in politics, first in the PRP, later in the DP. This gentleman saw the JP as a conservative and nationalist party, as anticommunist but not antisocialist or antistatist, favoring an "activist" economic policy, respectful of religion, and, above all, as a party that had won the confidence of the people.

[1] This candidate occupied seventh place among the twelve candidates for Parliament in 1965. Only four were elected.

[2] See Yüregir, "Milli Mücadelede Çukurova."

[3] Ward and Rustow, *Political Modernization*, p. 424. In June of 1964, the entire JP slate was elected to the executive board of the national Municipalities Association, much to the dismay of some observers. Powerful figures in the JP indicated that control of this voluntary association was to be used in the future to facilitate pressure in favor of greater local autonomy, a point strongly favored by some JP leaders.

case, the election of the executive board was, in fact, declared invalid several times because of evidences of unlawful partisan activity. Even the local chapter of the Turkish-American Association, a bland and nonpartisan organization, fell victim to this type of partisan conflict. In most of these cases the JP won resounding victories.

Only the labor unions appear to have escaped infiltration by the parties. This reflects the determination of Labor Confederation leadership to avoid involvement in party politics. Adana labor leaders seemed to pursue specific demands and interests related to their industries and union members. On the other hand, the Labor Party, promoting the workers' active involvement in politics based on Marxist socialism, polled about 8,000 votes (3 percent) in the 1965 election. This represented a fourfold increase over its showing in the 1963 provincial elections. The latter attract fewer voters than national elections. The Labor Party, despite the hostility of the Labor Confederation, seemed to enjoy the support of several union leaders in Adana. But its link with organized labor is not nearly so strong or effective as it is rumored to be in Istanbul. Not even in neighboring Mersin, where the Labor Party is led by the highly skilled employees of the foreign-owned oil refinery (ATAŞ), does it show much strength. Initially an engineer of ATAŞ was elected a deputy from the Labor Party but his votes were added to the national contingent in 1965 and his election nullified. In Adana, by contrast, the party leaders appear to be mostly workers and artisans.

Politics in Aydın

The province of Aydın resembles Adana in many respects. It is located in a fertile coastal area and derives its wealth mostly from cotton but also from figs, olives, and tobacco. The province centers around the Menderes ("Meander") River, which provides a fairly steady supply of water for irrigation. The valley is also a rich storehouse of historical memories. The ruins of Greek and Roman cities (e.g., Ephesus, Miletus, Priene, Dydima) are being turned into an economic asset, as are the magnificent beaches on parts of the Aegean shore.[1] International cruise ships docking at Izmir call regularly to permit passengers to tour the nearby ruins of Ephesus. Clearly, if the anticipated influx of international tourists from Europe and America materializes, this area will be one of the prime beneficiaries.

---

[1] The charming small coastal town of Kuşadası has been declared a pilot area for the development of the tourist industry.

Large-scale industries in the area are less well developed than in Adana : a cement factory, a 100-year-old English owned licorice processing plant in Söke, and textile plants in the towns of Aydın and Nazilli are the main enterprises. There are also numerous smaller industries, such as cotton ginning and olive oil processing, as well as soap manufacturing.

Aydın differs in two important respects from Adana. First, it is not a major regional center. It is, in fact, a satellite of a neighboring center, the city of Izmir, the third largest in the country. Consequently, the economic, social, and political life of Aydın is dominated by Izmir. Some of the leading citizens of Aydın, for example, maintain permanent residences in Izmir and stay only part of the time in their own town. Izmir is easily accessible via a modern asphalt road over a distance of approximately seventy miles and a rail line with daily services.

A second major difference between Aydın and Adana is political in nature. Whereas Adana is a "swing" district, Aydın has been firmly in the hands of the Democratic and Justice Parties almost from their inception.[1] The fact that the leader of the Democratic Party, Adnan Menderes, was a popular citizen of Aydın may partly explain this pattern, but not entirely. It should be recalled that this was also a center of great strength for the Free Party in 1930. Menderes, in fact, had been active in that short-lived effort at establishing an opposition party. The more proper and basic question, then, should be why a man like Menderes chose the path of opposition in the first place, and why he was eminently successful at it. Our analysis may give some insights in addition to known facts, even though we do not address ourselves specifically to these questions.

Only the PRP and JP were actively organized in Aydın Province in 1964. The New Turkey Party was active at one time but its efforts were minimal and short lived. The Labor Party, active in Izmir, had just established a branch in the town of Söke at the time of this survey. It was far too early to tell how effective it would be, but indications were not favorable.[2]

Our survey of the parties' provincial executive committees in Aydın

---

[1] Election statistics show the PRP to be strongest in three counties : Kuşadası, where it has never fallen below 40 percent; Karacasu, where it dropped from a high of 52 percent in 1950 to a low of 31 percent in 1961; and Sultanhisar, a new county for which the 1961 returns show the two parties running equal.

[2] In 1965, for the province as a whole, the Labor Party polled over 6,700 votes out of a total of 180,000 votes cast or about 3.5 percent.

shows the JP members to be somewhat younger than their counterparts in PRP. About three out of four members on each side were locally born; only one member of each was born outside Turkey.[1]

Family backgound suggests a fair degree of mobility; only about half of the fathers were born locally. This is undoubtedly a result of the upheaval following World War I, when the entire province came under Greek occupation and much of the population fled eastward.[2] Fathers' occupational distribution revealed some variation between the parties; the majority of the JP appeared as small farmers. Only two out of eight of the JP fathers were in commerce or industry, while an equal number were listed as teachers. One reported a lawyer father.[3] Almost half of the PRP fathers were either professionals or public servants (most of these being lawyers). Close to 40 percent were listed as farmers. Somewhat smaller numbers were in commerce or industry. There was one artisan, and one lawyer-judge who also trained *imams*. A higher percentage of the PRP fathers were university graduates than on the JP side. On the other hand, half the JP fathers had completed high school or better, as against just over one-third for the PRP. Only one JP father had no formal education. PRP fathers thus seem to have a slightly higher socio-economic status than JP fathers, but, as in Adana, neither executive committee included a representative of the local traditional elite.

The occupational differences between fathers and sons noted in Adana were also evident in Aydın. Thus, half the JP members were in commerce or industry (more than half if we include one pharmacist); only two of the eight committee members were engaged in farming, while three were lawyers. The more specific businesses of those engaged in commerce are worth noting. The list includes : ownership of a large

[1] For Aydın, statistics on county executive committees are also available. These show almost identical age distributions for the two parties. About 90 percent on both sides were born locally, but on the JP side the remainder were all born outside Turkey, while on the PRP side they were evenly split between those born elsewhere in Turkey and those born outside.

[2] The Greek occupation of Aydın was undoubtedly a far more violent interlude than the French occupation of Adana. Not only did it last longer, but it brought the Greek ethnic minority into a position of dominance. In Adana, the Armenians may have benefitted from French occupation, but they were clearly subordinate to the foreign power. A mark of the intensity of the upheaval is the fact that while a large proportion of the Turkish population of Aydın fled the Greeks, no such migration seems to have occurred in Adana. Moreover, the town of Aydın was largely in ruins when the Greeks retreated in 1922.

[3] Note again that some reported more than one occupation; in this case the lawyer father and one of the teacher fathers were also listed as farmers.

number of shares in the Aydın textile factory; retail sale of agricultural chemical products (fertilizers and pesticides); wholesale olive oil, and sale of cotton and building materials; and retail sale of medicines. It is notable that only two of these businesses are directly related to agriculture, and one of these deals with modern products. There were no artisans among the JP members.

On the PRP side, the occupational differences between fathers and sons were not so marked. The committee was dominated by lawyers (six out of eleven members). This situation is reflected in the political alignment of the local Bar Association. The organization's members were pro-Republican and formed the only significant island of party strength in an anti-PRP sea. Only three of the PRP committee members were engaged in commerce or industry: auto parts dealership, soap manufacturing, and insurance. There was also one farmer and one artisan on the PRP committee.

Both parties had a majority of university-educated committee members, with the PRP majority somewhat greater: eight out of eleven versus five out of eight. All members in both parties appear to have had some formal schooling. A majority of the members of both parties were familiar with at least one foreign language, but a slightly smaller number than those in Adana had traveled abroad, most of them in Europe.

The political background of the Aydın committee members showed greater homogeneity than those in Adana. Thus, all but one of the JP members reported previous affiliation with the DP, including active responsibilities in the organization. Moreover, since the establishment of the JP in 1961, the committee itself appeared to have remained quite stable in its membership. There was no evidence of factionalism. The only changes that took place appear to have occurred with the elevation of members to full-time public office.[1]

On the Republican side, also, there was not a single report of previous membership in another party. Thus the continuity of the DP and the JP had an identical counterpart in the Republican Party. Moreover, 75 percent of the Republican committee members had previously served the party in one capacity or another. Over 80 percent had joined the party prior to 1960, in fact more than half prior to 1950. Thus, as in Adana,

---

[1] The subsequent career of three successive JP provincial chairmen is instructive. The first, who was mayor before 1960, was elected to Parliament in 1961. The second became mayor in 1963. The third was elected to Parliament in 1965. Another member of the 1964 provincial executive committe was also elected to Parliament in 1965. Three of these four men were lawyers.

the party in Aydın does not appear to have attracted much new blood recently. The introduction of proportional representation might be expected to favor a minority party in Aydın but current electoral statistics do not yet indicate any variation from the pre-1960 pattern. The PRP did win two out of the eight parliamentary seats at stake in 1961, and again in 1965 and 1969, but these went to nominees placed at the head of the ticket by the national organization. No local candidate was in fact elected, thus reflecting the relative weakness of the local organization of the PRP.

A slight majority of both committees had been candidates for elective office. On the JP side, only one of these had run for Parliament; the rest were elected to provincial and municipal councils in 1963. None were candidates in any pre-1960 election. It should be recalled that the parliamentary delegation of Aydın prior to 1960 included some of the best-known members of the DP. On the PRP side, the provincial chairman was a candidate for Parliament in 1954, 1957, and 1961. As noted above, he was placed on the list after the nominees of the central organization and thus narrowly missed being elected deputy. (The chairman was a lawyer in his early forties, apparently well respected in the town, and favored the "reformist" wing of the party. He was not a candidate in 1965). Four other members of the PRP committee were elected to the municipal council in 1963.

In sum, the members of the executive committees in Aydın resemble their counterparts in Adana, although they are slightly younger in age, and form a more homogeneous political group. Perhaps because of special historical circumstances, they also show a somewhat greater degree of mobility. Membership on the executive committees in Aydın has been a surer stepping-stone to elective office, at least on the JP side. In neither province was the local elite directly represented on the party executive committees. In terms of occupational structure, the fathers of the PRP committee members in both provinces appear to have belonged to a somewhat higher social stratum than fathers of the JP committee members. The committee members of the JP in Adana include many more professionals than their counterpart in Aydın, while the PRP does not show much variation in this respect. Similarly on educational level, the JP in Adana ranked somewhat higher than in Aydın, but not the PRP. It may thus be surmised that interparty differences in social and occupational status are less notable in Adana than in Aydın.

The Adana parliamentary delegation, it will be recalled, included some prominent landowners. In Aydın the Menderes family provides the clearest parallel, though the late Prime Minister moved his candidacy elsewhere soon after the founding of the party. In 1965, however, his son Yüksel Menderes headed the JP slate. Six of the total of eight deputies and three senators elected by the PRP and the JP from Aydın in 1961 were lawyers, one of them the widow of Namık Gedik, the Minister of the Interior of the Menderes regime. Of the remaining five, one was a teacher and journalist, a product of the Village Institutes now prominently identified with the socialist faction in the national teachers' federation.[1] The second was an engineer, the third a former mayor of Aydın, the fourth a retired colonel, and the fifth a former official.

The elite of Aydın is comparable to its counterpart in Adana; its primary economic base is land; a secondary base is industry. The town of Aydın being smaller than Adana and not a regional center, its elite group is less extensive and more easily identifiable. Moreover, in Aydın there is no clear split between old and new wealth. In fact, much of the wealth of Aydın generally seems to be quite new, deriving from cotton cultivation which came into prominence during the 1940's. This development favored the old landed families. Thus unlike Adana, where new wealth seems to have created a new elite rooted in industry, the new material wealth of Aydın remained rather confined to the established landowning elite.

One leading family in Aydın claiming to have historical roots is a good example of the political attitudes of the provincial Turkish elite. A member of this family was considered the pace-setting farmer of the area in terms of cultivated acreage and the scientific manner in which he managed his land, almost all of which was given over to cotton. He was also reputedly one of the wealthiest men in the town though not in the province. He also possessed a fine modern apartment building in Izmir. Politically, this gentleman was definitely behind the reformist wing of the Republican Party, in spite of the rather negative attitude of his class toward land reform. He was undoubtedly a contributor to the local PRP organization.

Another member of the same family was a Democratic deputy prior to 1960. After his release from prison he took up residence in Istanbul and left the management of the family's cotton land to his son, a young English-educated gentleman. Since he was not directly involved in the feuds of the pre-1960 period, this young man maintained a certain degree

---

[1] The teacher, Şükrü Koç, was placed at the head of the PRP list by the central organization. He is a native of Aydın. He again headed the list in 1965.

of political impartiality, though he seems to lean slightly to the JP side. The oldest living member of the same family is also considered the leading citizen of the town. He has recently devoted more attention to his industrial interests than to his land. Aside from a block of shares in the local textile plant, which entitled him to a seat on the board of directors, these industrial interests are relatively small : cotton ginning and olive oil processing. He is also a member of the executive board of the local chapter of the Aegean Chamber of Industry.

This gentleman's social position and views are highly reminiscent of the Tarsus industrialist of the Ramazanoğlu family described earlier. Both men have aristocratic backgrounds and initially dereived their wealth from the land, but later shifted their interest to industry. Both were once closely identified with the PRP—so closely, in fact, that they ran for Parliament in 1950 on its slate only to be ignominiously defeated. Finally both recently developed serious second thoughts about the PRP. The gentleman from Aydın cited socialist trends in the party and the the country as the source of his concern. Apparently he cut off his financial support to the local organization in the mid-1960's.

Aydın Province has a country that resembles Kadırlı. This is the county of Söke, which includes the wide plain of the lower Menderes River and its estuary. Large land holdings cultivating primarily cotton are far more prominent here than farther upstream. Söke also has a small group of wealthy, landed families whose dominance of the area is more pronounced than in the provincial capital. Some of these families support the PRP, others are split between the two major parties, and at least one favors the JP.[1] Moreover, like their counterparts in Kadırlı, members of these families command some national influence : one was Secretary General of the PRP and another one a national vice-president of the Chambers of Agriculture. These families appear generally to have adjusted remarkably well to the forces governing Turkish politics and economics and to have used new opportunities successfully. Söke is further similar to Kadırlı in that tension between the wealthy and the poor is quite evident. The man who is reputed to be the largest landlord has opposed land reform—especially the limitations on size of holdings. He has conducted an almost personal crusade by utilizing his position as a leader in the national federation of farmers' unions originally based in Adana. He insisted that Turkish agriculture could develop only if

---

[1] There is even one individual identified with the Labor Party in Izmir. It also happens that the former *kaymakam* ("district prefect") of Kadirli was appointed in 1964 to the county of Söke!

fragmented land holdings were consolidated so that large-scale economic operation with modern equipment and techniques might be applied. This attitude is a clear example of the kind of interest-articulation that is now occurring in Turkey.

Labor unions are also operative in Söke, as in Aydın and Nazilli, but they seem to lack strong leadership and do not appear to exert much influence locally. In this field, too, the center of gravity appears to lie in Izmir.

The above information does not explain fully the tremendous strength of the DP-JP in Aydın and the Aegean area. The idea that this strength derives from new wealth is weakened when one recalls that this area was the center of greatest strength of the abortive opposition Free Party as long ago as 1930. However, if the rise of the new middle class is traced to the economic and social transformation which occurred at the end of the nineteenth and beginning of the twentieth centuries and which was not different in essence from current development, the liberal political orientation of the new wealth, both in 1930 and between 1950 and 1970, appears to follow a consistent line. The relative level of sophistication that seems to prevail in the Aegean region and the replacement of Greeks by Turkish immigrants from the Balkans after 1924 may be cited as additional educational, social, and economic factors which contributed to political mobilization in Aydın. Moreover, the relatively intensive economic organization and activity have long been characteristic of this part of the country, and this could have caused dislike of governmental dictation and red tape, and bred an inclination toward greater individual economic freedom. It has also been suggested that important industrial and export crops, such as tobacco, produced large-scale government involvement in the economy of this area, and consequently caused frustration and ultimately opposition among the farmers. Religious traditionalism is probably not as important as some claim it to be. There was less evidence of this among the politicians in Aydın Province than there was in Adana.[1]

Our analysis suggests one major conclusion as well as some questions for further analysis. In both provinces political and social influence and power is being diffused to larger groups. The local elite still exercises influence at the national and local levels, but their position is no longer unchallenged. The political challenge to the elite is manifested in the form of interparty struggle and factional strife within the PRP organization as

---

[1] Nevertheless, several informants insisted that religious reaction was rife. With regard to the history of the Free party, see Walter Weiker, "The Free Party of 1930", Ph.D. diss., Princeton University, 1962.

evident in Adana. The central national party organization seems to have been the strongest force resisting the domination of the local party organization by the local landowning elite of Adana. The fact that the attitude of the central organization was determined by the feud between Kasım Gülek and Ismet Inönü, resulting in the temporary expulsion of the former from the party, does not alter the fact that the beneficiaries of this feud were primarily the nonelite members of the local party organization of Adana. The restiveness of some younger members of the local elites imbued with reformist ideas evident on the national scene may presage at least a partial political realignment.

Another piece of evidence suggesting greater diffusion of influence and power is the growth of voluntary associations, some of which are in fact interest groups. The remarkable development of labor unions and the farmers' unions, the latter appealing to the large landowners, indicates the use of organizations for interest-articulation. It is unlikely that the need for such a shift would have been felt if the formerly dominating groups had preserved their undisputed control. Whether this development will be beneficial or harmful to the political parties remains to be seen. Insofar as the energies of the locally prominent landowners are siphoned off into interest groups, it may leave the other members of the party more freedom for maneuver. It may also force the parties to bargain more extensively for support on the basis of differentiated interests and views of social groups.

Further evidence indicating broader diffusion of power, is related to the personnel staffing the provincial party organizations, not only in Adana and Aydın, but also in the other ten provinces cited in the first section. There can be little doubt that the results reported here may be indicative for the whole country.

The provincial party organizations are being staffed by middle-class professionals and entrepreneurs, not by members of the local elite groups. It would be significant if further research were to establish that this had not always been the case. It would be even more significant if the time of change could be defined more precisely. F. W. Frey's work on members of Parliament between 1920 and 1960 has already provided evidence of similar changes at the national level. There is every indication that many of the members of Parliament included in his survey served their political apprenticeships as members of local and provincial party organizations. No doubt these organizations served as steps on the ladder to political fame and fortune.[1]

---

[1] Preliminary analysis of the political backgrounds of members of Parliament

To be sure, the evidence is far from conclusive. It could be argued, for example, that local party organizations do not play a very important role in their provincial context. Power within the parties is still concentrated at the national center in Ankara, and the provincial arms may appear as mere appendages of the central organizations. However, if political trends in Turkey were analyzed in a dialectical fashion and compared with earlier periods, it would be evident that local and provincial groups have been gaining in relative power and influence, not only at the local and provincial but also at the national level. Moreover, the parties have served as a means of influence and power outside bureaucratic channels and often in opposition to officialdom. This becomes quickly apparent to the most casual observer of the provincial scene. He will hear countless stories of how civil servants have been either harrassed or circumvented by the chief of the local party branch. He may even witness occasional instances where party functionaries are called on to assist citizens caught in the meshes of bureaucratic red tape. This type of function was assumed mostly by the Democratic organizations during the 1950's. Presently, all parties are conscious of the citizens' need for this kind of service and seek to provide it insofar as they are able.

The causes of the apparently increasing diffusion of power and influence in the Turkish provinces may lie beyond the scope of this study. It is appropriate, however, to cite one or two factors. The existence of several competing political parties means that opportunities for exerting influence—or escaping the influence of others—are multiplied. This tendency is enhanced by the current system of proportional representation which, unlike the majority-list system of the First Republic, guarantees all major parties some representation in each province if they can win the minimum number of votes. It remains to be seen how this system will

---

during the First Republic reveals an increasing number of deputies with past experience at the local and/or provincial level. Elective office appears to have been a somewhat more effective path to Parliament, judging from these figures, though the comparative advantage declined, particularly in the 1950's. An interesting additional point is that the number of those with elective experience dropped sharply, though only temporarily, in 1950 when the Democrats took over, while the number with experience in the party organizations continued to increase without reference to the change in regime. By contrast, the number of those who came to Parliament with appointive experience as governors or prefects declined fairly steadily both in terms of numbers and proportions; in fact, they disappeared almost completely after 1950. This confirms yet another of Frey's findings to the effect that localism in national politics has increased and that the older elite of bureaucrats and army officers has lost power, see my "The Anatomy of Social and Political Change : Turkish Parties, Parliaments, and Elections," *Comparative Politics*, Vol. 5, No. 4 (July, 1973).

affect the historical tendency of Turks to rally around two major political parties.

A second and more basic factor lies in the very nature of the economic and social developments in Turkish life over the past half century. One of our findings was that the members of the provincial executive committees of the major parties had middle-class origins rather than having risen from the peasantry. On the other hand, the occupational distribution of these individuals differed sharply from that of their fathers. The latter tended to be based in moderate-sized agricultural enterprises or in artisanship and small trade. Higher educational facilities were not generally available to them. Today, university and professional schooling is far more widely available, though still insufficient to meet the demand. Hence the appearance of an increasing number of professionals in the smaller towns and provinces. But perhaps even more significant is the growing number and variety of businesses and occupations, paralleling the rapidly developing national economy. Rising income levels and growth and extension of communications and transport facilities have been prime factors in this connection. They have brought in their wake new businesses and occupations, such as garages and automobile service stations, sales agencies, and repair services for household appliances. These new professionals and businessmen invariably form organizations of their own, and do not hesitate to speak out when their interests are at stake. Links between them and the political parties, though not by any means uniform, exist and are exploited alternatively by both sides.[1] With increasing variety and with increasing experience, these groups are more and more exerting their influence outside of the parties as well. Their growth and development is bound to further weaken the hold of the traditional elites in the provinces. Indeed, this may be another reason why the large landowners have apparently followed suit by beginning to utilize their own organization (the Farmers' Unions) in similar fashion.

The challenge of this increasing pluralism to the traditional elites may be more apparent in the more developed provinces of Adana and Aydın than elsewhere. Thus, there are undoubtedly areas where "leading families... still maintain almost absolute control over the economic,

---

[1] Cases such as that in Aydın, where the Bar Association was a stronghold of the PRP, or Konya, where, according to Karpat, a provincial congress of the Democratic Party was heavily infiltrated by shoemakers, do not appear to be widespread, at least in such blatant form. See Kemal H. Karpat, "The Turkish Elections of 1957," *Western Political Quarterly* 14, no. 2 (June 1961), p. 451n.

social, and political life of their respective communities."[1] Such areas are more likely to be found in the remote and less-developed parts of the country or in those regions in which the new families have established their own supremacy and affect all political and economic avenues of ascendancy, as happened in the later years of Democratic rule. In this sense, Adana and Aydın may be leading cases which show the increasing pluralism which one expects in a modernizing social system. In a nutshell, the argument is that the new groups whose political activities and involvement we have analyzed here are new to the political scene. The hope is that the Turkish provincial town will not merely end up exchanging the domination of one group for another.

---

[1] Karpat, "Society, Economics and Politics," p. 56.

CHAPTER NINE

IDEOLOGY IN TURKEY AFTER THE REVOLUTION OF 1960*

NATIONALISM AND SOCIALISM

KEMAL H. KARPAT

INTRODUCTION : RELATION OF IDEOLOGY TO SOCIAL CHANGE

The military revolution of May 27, 1960, marked a turning point in the ideological development of Turkey. It undermined the social bases of the political balance established in the first three decades of the Republic and helped liquidate the last vestiges of traditional concepts of social organization and government authority. It brought to the surface economic and social conflicts and helped crystallize thought on these issues. The initial aim of the revolution was to restore the rule of law based on democratic parliamentary principles and protect them through adequate constitutional safeguards. These purposes were formally achieved through the Constitution of 1961. However, in the long run the by-products of the revolution in the realm of social thought and the movement of social groups are probably more important than its institutional achievement.

The revolution speeded up two socio-political processes of decisive importance in Turkish politics. The first process concerned the power struggle between two middle-class groups, one associated with the bureaucratic elite of the early days of the Republic, and the other a large, new, rising group rooted in economic occupations and liberal professions. The second process consisted of the rise of a labor class and structural changes among rural groups, and their search for recognition and power based on economic interest.

Ideological developments in Turkey after 1960 reflected the above social processes and were at the same time an effort to interpret and direct them through some sort of political action. Consequently the source and role of ideology in Turkey appear to be intimately connected with social transformation and are both its causes and effect. Turkey has reached the point where the ruling groups associated with early modernization have been successfully challenged by other groups from below, created

---

* A version of this article has been published in *Yıllık* ("Year book") (Ankara, 1965).

or fostered by the very political and economic forces of modernization. The conflict between upper social groups may appear as a struggle between conservatism and modernism. Yet the terms of reference of both groups have become so drastically altered as to make both conservatism and modernism appear in a new modern context rather than as a struggle between the old and new. This was certainly the novel aspect of ideological development in Turkey after 1960. Social and political transformation made imperative a change in the former understanding of conservatism and modernism, and ideology became the medium for achieving an intellectual change from within. Thus, during the initial phase of transformation in a new country, ideology may be used to justify the change in the so-called traditional institutions and mode of life, whereas in the second phase it may help to achieve internal adjustment to a new way of social and political life. Therefore, in the second phase the terms "modern" and "traditional" may lose much of their original meaning. Often what used to be considered "modern" may turn out to be a conservative force whereas the "traditional" may acquire a dynamic, forward-looking aspect.

The *ulema* group may be a conservative force in the initial phase of change. But if it presses for political rights and turns into an entrepreneurial group interested in industrialization it may well become "modern," whereas the reformist intelligentsia looking at the problem from the formal viewpoint of authority may resist this economic-minded group and appear itself as a "conservative" force. During this process the *ulema* outwardly may preserve their garb, attachment to religion, and habits, but their thinking about society, man, and government may be so drastically changed as to make their formal attachment to tradition motivated mainly by economic reasons. This in itself is a fundamental change, since economic motivation is likely to create a chain of reaction among social groups and call for new roles completely different from the past when the *ulema*'s role was mainly religious. (The above suggestion stems from the discovery of this writer that many of the *ulema* and their descendents in Turkey have become, during the last twenty years, landowners, merchants, and craftsmen, or identified themselves closely with these groups).

It seems that the Arab countries are presently reaching the end of their first phase of change. Turkey meanwhile has entered the second. Consequently, such problems as secularism, religious reformation, and emancipation of women, which constituted the backbone of Turkish reform, appear today not as the dividing line between traditionalism and modernism but as normal issues on which there are individual differences of opinion and interpretation intended not to challenge modernization but to adapt to it. These points are illustrated by the changes in the understanding of nationalism, accompanied by fading efforts to preserve its various meanings, and also by the new "individual" ethics sought in Islam, dealt with later in this study.

The ideological developments in Turkey after 1960 will appear meaningful only if studied in relation to the social and political changes and especially to the power shifts among the ruling middle-class groups which occurred between 1946 and 1960.

The civil and military bureaucracies and the intelligentsia (men with formal secondary or higher education) formed the bulk of the middle class which ruled Turkey until the late 1940's. This was originally a revolutionary, nationalist middle class which secured national independence, put an end to Western economic domination, and established a republican regime by ousting the Ottoman dynasty and destroying the political power of its supporting groups, the traditionalist *ulema* and imperial bureaucracy. Internally, the group consolidated its power by associating itself with agrarian and commercial groups in the countryside or creating economic groups of its own through state enterprise.[1]

This bureaucratic middle class derived its social and political outlook mainly from its association with the state rather than from affiliation with any particular social group. Theoretically, the state represented the entire nation, even though the population had not yet become fully aware of its own national identity. In fact it was the state which strove to create a Turkish national ethos according to a secularist-nationalist philosophy that was alien to the folk culture. This was the nationalist ideology of the period; it had limited relevance to social realities. Without emotionally binding ties between rulers and the ruled, without an integrative social and economic process, and with only limited popular participation in public life, the bureaucratic middle class found itself separated from the bulk of society. The nationalism of this class eventually acquired strong conservative tendencies. These manifested themselves in the form of opposition to the upward mobility of lower social groups and rejection of class differences and conflict of economic interests. They emphasized the utmost superiority of the nation and state over the individual and drew considerable strength from the glories of Turkish history.

---

[1] See Kemal H. Karpat, "Society, Economics and Politics in Contemporary Turkey," *World Politics* 17, no. 1 (October 1964), pp. 50-74.

The main goal of this ruling group was the establishment and consolidation of a modern political structure, namely the national state. The need for such a state was not the result of philosophical speculation but rather the outcome of international conditions, the Turks' need for self preservation as an ethnic group, and the power interests of the ruling groups.

The establishment of a national state, completed in the early 1920's, was a major achievement if considered in the light of Turkey's background, rooted in the universalist traditions of Islam and the multinational Ottoman state. Moreover, the political authority exercised on behalf of the national state had a determining impact on future social developments. It provided a modern political framework in which internal developments were contained and eventually regulated in the light of the problems, interests, and aspirations of social groups living within Turkey's well-defined territorial limits. The national state gradually created a way of life in addition to being a form of political rule. Consequently, the political struggle following the liberalization policy initiated after 1945 must be regarded as a movement directed not against the republican regime itself, but chiefly against the power of an elite, the ruling People's Republican Party.[1] This was also a social struggle in the sense that it aimed at securing recognition for the power and the interests of social groups operating within the sphere of the national state, as mentioned before. Formal opposition to the Republican Party originated first within its own ranks over the question of land reform in 1945. The rebels eventually formed their own party, the Democratic Party, in 1946 and then won power in 1950.

The Democrats claimed that the basic justification for strong rule in the past had been the need to preserve the modern reforms connected with the political system. They claimed that these basic reforms had been accepted and that no organized group challenged them since most of the population had become familiar with the new way of life. Consequently the justification for a self-appointed elite holding power as "guardians of reform" had disappeared.

The Democrats' alternative to strong rule was *democracy*. The clue to later ideological development in Turkey is found, in fact, in the meaning they attached to democracy. This meant individual political rights, and respect for private property with proper safeguards to protect it from seizure by the government. Democracy also implied freedom of economic enterprise. This rebellion against the existing strong rule

---

[1] Kemal H. Karpat, *Turkey's Politics* (Princeton, 1959), chapt. 12 and 13.

began in 1945, during a period when new ideas were proposed to redefine statism and to orient it toward social welfare and broader popular participation.

The leadership in the Democratic Party was assumed by landed groups, business and commercial interests, and professionals, whose views on democracy and government were closely related to their own economic status based on the idea of the sanctity of private property. The legal system adopted in the Republic, especially the Civil Code, regulated property relations in the greatest detail but was not supplemented by political institutions capable of checking the government's sporadic violations of private ownership such as the Capital Tax of 1942.

The lower urban groups, workers and peasants suffering from various restrictions and controls imposed as a result of economic statism from 1930 to 1945, favored a liberalized economic regime. Moreover, there was a commonly shared desire for increased economic development or activity, and at this stage few were interested in debating its means. Consequently the rising expectations, which could not be met by the statist policies enforced in the past, made a liberal economic approach the most likely policy for the future. A few scattered apologists for socialism found no acceptance, especially after the relations with the Soviet Union worsened after 1946 as a result of the latter's demand for territory in northern Turkey and bases on the Bosphorus.

The second major determining influence connected with foreign policy came from the West, and especially the United States, through the North Atlantic Treaty Organization (NATO) and foreign aid. The United States favored private enterprise and a general economic policy likely to enhance the rapid growth of the entrepreneurial groups. This policy had considerable political impact on ideological developments after 1960 since the rise to power of an entrepreneurial middle class was viewed by socialist groups as a Western scheme intended to dominate Turkey from inside. The Democrats' economic policy after coming to power in 1950 followed a course determined by the conditions just described.[1] This new economic policy encouraged social mobility and facilitated the rapid expansion of a new middle class of entrepreneurs

---

[1] The economic expectations deriving from, and the far-reaching social meaning of the Democrats' victory at the polls were dramatically illustrated by the publication of several books which hailed the change of government in 1950 as a White Revolution ("*Beyaz Ihtilâl*") : e.g.: Turgut Omay, *Beyaz Ihtilâl* (Ankara, 1950); M. Cavit Ersen, *Hürriyet Mücadelesi, Beyaz Ihtilâl* (Adana, 1953).

from among professionals, the existing entrepreneurial groups, the upper ranks of the peasantry, the services, the lower bureaucracy, and craftsmen in the urban areas. In mentality and method of work, this new entrepreneurial middle class relied on individual initiative, and, somewhat reluctantly, accepted competition resulting from an economy oriented toward the law of supply and demand. Consequently it differed from the commercial and industrial groups created at the beginning of the Republic through state backing and controlled internal markets. Eventually the beneficiaries of the statist policy and the landowning group came to form the upper layer, now referred to as "capitalist," of the new order. However, despite this liberal economic policy, the state's role in the economy increased rather than diminished. The state invested heavily not only in public works (dams, roads) but also in industry, apparently hoping to stimulate activity and speed capital accumulation in the private sector. In this purpose it was, in fact, successful, with a resulting change in the entire rhythm of the old life based on the economic supremacy of the state. The new economic policy and the growing association of politics with economic interests facilitated the emergence of a series of interest groups which exercised growing pressure on political parties in order to secure economic benefits. The initial pressure groups were formed in cities as professional organizations among service groups, craftsmen, and a variety of other occupational groups, bus and car drivers (over 200,000 members), shoemakers, butchers, bakers, and the like. Meanwhile the Industrial and Commercial Chambers, representing the bigger capitalists, became a truly powerful interest group.

The activities of these groups, steadily increasing since 1950, have caused chain reactions. For instance, the building owners' group was able to secure the abolition of rent controls in 1954 (Law 6084) after some intensive pressure on the government. The tenants in turn organized the *Türkiye Kiracılar Cemiyeti* ("Tenants, Association of Turkey") and, with moral support from the press, revised the law to their own advantage.[1] The pressure groups acquired further importance after the revolution of 1960. In fact the Constituent Assembly, which drafted the Constitution of 1961, was organized on the basis of professional representation and thus symbolized Turkey's inner change. It must be noted that the peasantry, though lacking in organization, has acquired the mentality

---

[1] Rona Aybay, "Baskı Grupları," *İstanbul Üniversitesi Hukuk Fakültesi Mecmuası*, 1-4 (1961), pp. 3-16; *Dünya*, January 28, 1961; Yavuz Abadan, "Türkiye'de Siyasi Partiler ve Tazyik Grupları," *Siyasal Bilgiler Fakültesi 100. Yıl Armağanı* (Ankara, 1959), pp. 77-118.

of an interest group by using its voting power to secure material benefits from political parties.[1]

The emergence of voluntary associations based on a modern notion of economic interest is certainly an important development not only for Turkey but for the entire Muslim world. It indicates the birth of new identities and new motives for seeking association with groups larger than one's own family. A new understanding of community and civic responsibility is also developing.

The new economic orientation of Turkey was accompanied by a slow change in the meaning attached to education. Literacy and knowledge ceased to be the monopoly of a few groups and a distinct mark of status.[2] An incipient pragmatic, utilitarian approach to education was evident, as expressed in a report according to which the purpose of schools was to train the "individual to be productive, alert, adaptable and at the same time mastering a skill useful to society." [3]

The rise of a new middle class in Turkey based on economic power was a fact acknowledged even by its bitterest critics. One of them, in a devastating attack on Westernism and Turkey's foreign policy, stated that the most evident aspect of Turkish development in the past fifteen years was the emergence of a bourgeoisie living far above the economic capabilities of the masses. This class attached itself to foreign interests and became its spokesman.[4] The new middle class group lacked polish, appeared avid for wealth, and was utterly lacking at the beginning in social consciousness and responsibility. Having no broad cultural horizon, vision, or ideals, it indulged in all the material pleasure that money could buy. It seemed that men's animal instincts had their way in a country in which inner, traditional, regulatory forces had broken down, and new ones had not yet been devised. But in time this middle

---

[1] I have witnessed several cases which gave a fair idea of the manner in which the peasantry exercised pressure on politicians. In the province of Diyarbakır, the Republican Party candidate, hard pressed for votes in one district, signed a check authorizing the purchase of water pipes for a village well. He tried to convince the village representative that he would build the well after he won the elections but the villager insisted on prompt delivery, saying that this was the decision of his village mates. He had his say. Cf. Howard A. Reed, "A New Force at Work in Democratic Turkey," *Middle East Journal* 7, no. 1 (Winter 1953), pp. 33-44.

[2] On the relation of education to social status see, Frederick W. Frey, *The Turkish Political Elites* (Cambridge, Mass., 1964).

[3] *Türkiye Eğitim Milli Komisyonu Raporu* (Report of the National Committee on Education in Turkey, Istanbul, 1960), p. 74. Also issued in English.

[4] Niyazi Berkes, *Batıcılık, Ulusçuluk ve Toplumsal Devrimler* (Istanbul, 1965).

class instinctively felt the need for some moral precepts to control this spreading materialism. It could not adopt overnight the values, manner, and outlook of Western middle classes, but had to rely on its own cultural resources. True, some of the urban members of this class did adopt a modern outlook, evident especially among their children. But the majority turned to Islam, hoping to find there the ideas likely to restrain the society's material expectations, which instead they unwittingly stimulated. The intelligentsia regarded the return to Islam as a reaction against secularism, whereas in reality this was a search for a new meaning and function in religion. There was no discussion of changing the political framework (except among a few powerless reactionary groups), but of using religion to replenish moral, ethical, and spiritual needs. In any case the social education of this middle class and the broadening of its cultural and professional horizons were the first conditions for its survival.

Meanwhile, inflation hit hard at the salaried groups, especially the civil and military bureaucracies, and lowered their living standards. The rise of new economic groups to power considerably changed the old system of values. Wealth seemed to have become the chief factor in determining social status. Consequently the former ruling elite groups were subjected to a painful social decline in addition to economic hardship.

There is a rather intimate relationship between the rise of social-minded or socialist literature and the transformation in the social status of the bureaucracies. The new school of social thought, which gradually acquired a doctrinaire leftist view, was promoted by intellectuals belonging to the lower ranks of the bureaucracy, teachers, and some marginal groups. Consequently, faced with economic hardship and the deterioration of their social status, the intelligentsia and bureaucracy, apathetic to social ideas until the 1950's, began to show an interest in social justice, economic development, and a rationally planned economy. In fact, the idea of creating a new and just social order became the driving force behind the currents of social thought.

The revolution of May 27, 1960, occurred amid this process of social transformation. We shall leave aside the political struggle between the opposition and government parties which precipitated the military's action and instead concentrate on its social aspects. The military claimed that the revolution was not directed against any group but aimed at reinstating the democratic order on a firmer basis. Politically speaking this contention was correct. But socially speaking many of the measures undertaken by the military indicated distinctly that the revolution was directed against a group, namely against those who had acquired economic and political power under the Democrats.[1] Some junta members openly declared that the Democrats had "taken all kinds of measures in order to destroy the army's place in national cultural life" and "treated officers worse than a step child," [2] and had boasted that their policies created so much wealth that fifteen millionaires could rise in each city district. The arrest of landlords who had supported the Democrats, the establishment of wealth investigation committees (later disbanded), and the heavy taxes imposed on land and real estate were all aimed at the new middle class. A document issued in order to justify the revolution, pointedly stressed that "the State under the Democrats had taken the form of physical force and was used to serve the interest of certain special interest groups." The state consequently became hostile to other groups, such as the army (the real basis of the state), universities, bar associations and the press,[3] all of which had in fact formed the ruling group until 1950. The contributions by various commercial enterprises to the Democratic Party chest showed indeed that money had become an important instrument in Turkish politics and that business enterprises used financial power to further their interests.[4] (See chapter VII)

The revolution also had far reaching constitutional aspects. The fact that the military took over the government by force and exercised authority on behalf of the armed forces with some well-defined social motiva-

---

[1] *Cumhuriyet*, August 28, 1960.

[2] *Cumhuriyet*, July 20, 1960, August 8, 1960 (Views of Orhan Erkanlı and Turhan Yavşın).

[3] *27 Mayıs*, (Istanbul, n.d.), pp. 24-27; *News From Turkey*, May 30, 1960, pp. 6-9.

[4] The funds deposited to the Democratic Party account in the Yeni Cami Branch of Iş Bank alone between March 1, 1960, and April 13, 1960 amounted to T.L. 3,385,000. The total was estimated to be over T.L. 25 million (9 T.L. to a dollar). The donation ranged from T.L. 10,000 to 500,000; among the donors there were the Yapı Kredi Bank and Vehbi Koç's fourteen major enterprises, even though Koç was a member of the Republican Party until March 1960. The Democratic Party collected from 42 banks and enterprises alone T.L. 3,000,000 for the elections of 1957, and distributed T.L. 2,047,000 to provinces in one month. Some of the contributors were Yakup Soyugenç, a relative of the Finance Minister Hasan Polatkan (50,000) and firms such as Bozkurt (100,000), Unilever (150,000), Dumeks (200,000), Ottoman Bank (200,000), Eczacıbaşı (50,000), Verktürk (250,000), and Antalya (500,000). The Republican Party was also the recipient of large sums, which were not made public. But it can be assumed that their receipts were not less than Democrats', since the level of wealth among Republicans was greater than among Democrats, particularly in the provincial organizations.

tions was a total departure from historical precedent. Power in the past had changed hands several times, but always with some legitimizing excuse borrowed from traditional concepts of authority.[1]

Even Atatürk, while enforcing truly revolutionary principles during the War of Independence and later during the Republic, was extremely careful to justify them with traditionalist arguments, as in the case of his speech advocating the abolition of the Sultanate.[2] Mustafa Kemal's own rise to power and the establishment of the Republic, and even some of the reforms, were not carried out ruthlessly but were often explained, justified, and legitimized through popularly acceptable arguments rooted in traditional views of authority. The masses, therefore, preserved the idea that despite changes in leadership harmony between the state and fundamental principles persisted.

But in 1960 the revolutionary officers ignored all the traditionalist concepts legitimizing the assumption of power. First, they were not indoctrinated with such concepts, and second, the conflict was generated by economic forces and a social transformation which had no parallel in the traditionalist era. The state henceforth appeared no longer as the embodiment of divine will but as an institution of worldly power. Consequently, after the revolution many of the political symbols and myths surviving from the traditionalist era were discarded as incompatible with Turkey's true needs. Even the old poetical and often incoherent talk full of allegories, metaphors, and appeal to human situations began to be replaced by more logical, positive, and rational reasoning. To a student of Turkish politics such as this writer, the political developments in Turkey from 1931 to 1960 and from 1960 onward appear different in nature and orientation from previous ones. Increasingly after 1960 there was an earnest intellectual effort to establish a rational relationship, based on a dialectical understanding of power, between the basic concepts of

---

[1] The Ottoman concepts of government and authority, strongly influenced by classical Islamic thought, had been devised in conformity with the requirement of power. The Ottoman rulers seemed to have a realistic understanding of power and of the role of human groups. The Muslim citizen was loyal to the state for it was synonymous with his faith. His readiness to follow state commands certainly was a basic asset in maintaining political authority. Throughout the reformist era, beginning with Selim III and ending with Atatürk, governments in Turkey were extremely careful not to tamper with those essential bonds which tied the Muslim citizen to the state. The durability of the Ottoman Empire, aside from international conditions, was largely due to a continuous acceptance of state authority which was riveted in tradition and faith. See chapters 1, VII.

[2] *Atatürk'ün Söylev ve Demeçleri* (Istanbul, 1945), pp. 261-71.

society, government, and nation, whereas in the past such concepts had been accepted without critical analysis despite and because of their traditional content.

The preceding introduction makes it abundantly clear that the revolution had a unique social background and that this background was bound to reflect itself in politics in the form of new ideas, that is to say, of ideology. The ideological discussions in Turkey after 1960 seem to fall into two distinctive categories : the first has consisted of nationalist concepts which had been in vogue during the past decades, whereas the second category has contained socialist ideas born from the economic and political realities of a newly diversified social order. It is important to note that after the revolution even the military gradually changed into a kind of interest group, as evidenced by such efforts as raising salaries and retirement pensions, or providing housing credits for officers. Economic motivation, be it on an individual or a group basis, was accepted as legitimate and worthy of legal protection. This development in turn had a profound influence on the decision to allow the workers the rights of collective bargaining and strike. It provided also an incipient argument for the entrepreneurial groups to defend the profit motive as a proper reason for economic activity. Some of the extremist nationalist concepts such as racialism were discarded whereas other nationalist concepts were gradually reinterpreted and adapted to new conditions. Socialism appeared also in several shades ranging from Islamic socialism to marxism. Moreover, for the first time in Turkish politics the right and left extremes appeared in full clarity, thus making possible the establishment of a third moderate position which became, in fact, the backbone of the established political system after 1961.[1] The currents of thought to be discussed later in detail, developing amidst these circumstances, were promoted by individuals identified with social groups. The thought, although superficial in many instances and reflecting a passing whim of the echo of half-assimilated foreign slogans, was also the expression of a deeply felt individual desire to understand, explain, and justify events and harmonize them with one's personal life and philosophy. There was the need for a new set of political and cultural values and beliefs which would give meaning and direction but also security to man vis-à-vis

---

[1] The 38 members of the National Unity Committee, the military junta, epitomized well the existing ideological groupings; one group of about five people defended militant nationalism, another group of about seven leaned toward socialism, whereas the rest, although socially minded, preferred a parliamentary democracy.

his society and government. This was, in fact, the ultimate goal of ideology.

TURKISH NATIONALISM BETWEEN CONSERVATISM AND SOCIAL CHANGE

Nationalism in Turkey, if studied in relation to social change and power politics, would mirror faithfully the evolution of Turkey's internal regime from a narrowly based elite to a broader social representation.

Nationalism developed intially from 1908 to 1918 among intellectuals through free discussion, and was instrumental in mobilizing all social groups from left to right around common goals in the War of Liberation. It embraced all ideological groups from leftists to Islamists and eventually united them around the idea of establishing a national state for Turks, in which each group hoped to make supreme through nationalism its own creed. The Republican Party eventually decided to make nationalism a formal principle in 1931, and then in 1937 it incorporated it in the constitution and dogmatized it. Thus, the scope of nationalism was narrowed considerably to the secular, modernist ideas and reforms upon which modern Turkey was founded. The nation was regarded as a community of individuals living within well-defined territorial limits. The uniting links among the people were held to be past memories, future aspirations, and the desire to live as Turks in a political state with a national culture based on the people's own language and local traditions. Nationalism sought national pride, not in Islamic history but wherever in the past Turks had displayed the distinctive characteristics of a national group.

The search for achievement in national history created an unusual interest in the history and the heritage of central Asia and weakened considerably the relation of nationalism to the realities of contemporary Turkey. The Republican government, interested in promoting a secular concept of nationhood, purposely ignored and downgraded the cultural heritage of the Ottoman Empire, chiefly because of the latter's intimate association with Islam and its universalist aims. Political expediency, however, led the government to maintain the traditions of loyalty to the state and respect for authority inherited from the Ottoman Empire. The Republic became an accepted political reality in the people's minds, but the Ottoman heritage, embracing the entire fabric of society, also continued to live in the people's hearts.

Meanwhile the bureaucracy, comprising most of the civil service inherited from the Empire, continued to grow in size and power and eventually absorbed the offspring of Ottoman ruling families and conservative groups. The regime's need for survival led to a rather paradoxical alliance between conservatives and the power-conscious bureaucracy supposedly serving a secular and socially progressive state. The Republican Party in turn discarded by 1935 all pretensions of democracy and became synonymous with the nation and state.

The government insisted on implementing a rigid, artificial, and dogmatic secularism, and socially it became archconservative, conforming thus to the tendencies of the groups in control of power. But much of the ancient social conservatism promoted in the past on behalf of Islamic orthodoxy was preserved even under secularism in the guise of nationalism. The culture of the small town eventually permeated the upper structure, even though the regime's outward form was modern. Consequently the original broad cultural orientation based on Western values was perverted into a limited self-centered concept of national egotism rooted in the elite's concern for its own status and power. The government's decision to transform nationalism into a state ideology and define it in accordance with the understanding of some government bureaucrats controlling educational and cultural policy, further degenerated its content. However, a group of progressive-minded nationalists in the government and in the Republican Party fought to preserve the secular aspects of nationalism. But they overstressed the material aspects of culture and raised positivist thinking to the level of a creed by ignoring totally the natural influence of a traditional background. Thus nationalism harbored two opposite schools of thought, positivism and traditionalism, whose conflict broke out repeatedly in various forms.[1]

The policy of liberalization implemented after 1946 gradually brought into the open the contradictions between the secularist, positivist, and traditionalist understanding of nationalism. The ensuing conflict was best epitomized by two institutions representing the dual understanding of nationalism: the People's Houses ("*Halk Evleri*") and the Turkish Hearts ("*Türk Ocakları*").

The People's Houses (established 1931-32) aimed at creating a secular Turkish national identity based on the folklore, life, and experience of contemporary individuals and communities. They searched for historical roots in the experience of Turks as an ethnic group and were dedicated

---

[1] See Kemal H. Karpat, "Die Geschichte der ideologischen Strömungen und ihre Vertreter," *Bustan*, January 1962, pp. 17-26. A historical analysis of Turkish nationalism by the same author is in the *Cambridge History of Islam* (1970) pp. 551-65.

supporters of secularism. The *Türk Ocakları,* abolished in 1932, were reestablished privately in 1949. They began to receive government support after 1950, and eventually replaced the People's Houses which were closed in 1951. The *Ocaks*, faithful to their original ideas (they had been the promoters of Turkish nationalism since 1911), claimed that between Ottoman history, Islam, and Republican Turkey there was an organic, cultural, and emotional continuity and that the denial of this relationship could undermine the very existence of the state. They accepted as a motto the three slogans of Ziya Gökalp: membership in the Turkish *millet* ("nation"), in the *umma* of Islam, and contemporary civilization. This expressed the three interlocking identities of modern Turks. The review *Türk Yurdu,* republished in 1954 with government support, insisted that the cultural foundations of Turkey were rooted in historical experience. Remzi Oğuz Arık, Osman Turan, the late Mümtaz Turhan, and Cezmi Türk, to mention a few names, agreed that Turkey's modernization in the form of technological development was a basic necessity, but that this did not imply a rejection of the Ottoman-Islamic past. They did not exclude the ancient pre-Islamic history of the Turks but insisted that the real identity of the Turks emerged after their conversion to Islam, and especially after the establishment of political states (Selçuk, Ottoman) which inevitably carried Turkish cultural characteristics. The conquest of Anatolia, after the victory over the Byzantines at Manzikert in 1071, appeared to them the opening of a new period of Islamic-Turkish history, a nine-hundred-year process which shaped and created a Turkish community. The "conscience of history" binding the Turks together consisted of recollections of bravery, victory, and sacrifice on the battlefields for a homeland and collective ideals. The nation, according to this nationalism, was not confined only to territory but comprised also outside groups who felt a historical and cultural affinity towards Turks living in Turkey. They placed emphasis on *soy* ("family and group lineage") and somewhat less on language or folk culture in order to differentiate the Turks from other Muslims who shared a common history and culture.[1]

The state, according to the new nationalist thought, represented national ideas; hence it was desirable that it coincide with the nation. The two were compatible as long as they preserved the original spirit that conceived them both. Therefore the Republican regime had to conform

---

[1] See Remzi Oğuz Arık, *Türk Inkilâbı ve Milliyetçiliğimiz* (Ankara, 1958), pp. 6 ff.; Cahit Okurer, *Ideal Milliyetçilik* (Istanbul, 1961).

to this spirit. The technological modernization of Turkey was to be entrusted to an elite educated in the modern science of the West.[1]

It must be pointed out that the leaders of this nationalism were university professors and writers with considerable influence. This brand of nationalism also included mystics inspired by Sufi teachings, such as Nurettin Topçu, as well as liberals such as the late Ali Fuad Başgil, who had rejected racialism.[2] Their writings appearing in reviews, such as *Türk Yurdu* (Turkish Homeland), *Türk Kültürü* (Turkish Culture), *Tohum*, (Seed), were relatively well organized, logical, and occasionally persuasive.

The nationalism oriented toward the Ottoman-Islamic past had also a militant, reactionary wing represented in the main by the disciples of Riza Nur (1879-1942). Born in the conservative town of Sinop, Nur was a close associate of Atatürk but turned against him and left Turkey. His five writings on nationalism, donated to the British Museum, became available to the public only in 1960.[3] Nur's piecemeal writings, however, were known and read by his disciples, for in addition to a philosophy he furnished also the blueprint for a nationalist organization, the *Party for Turkey's Resurrection*. Riza Nur accepted a Republican form of

---

[1] Mümtaz Turhan, *Garplılaşmanın Neresindeyiz?* (Istanbul, 1958); see translation *Where Are We in Westernization*, trans. David Garwood (Istanbul, 1965). Turhan, appearing outwardly as a modernist, gave a series of lectures in the *Aydınlar Klübü* ("Intellectuals' Club") in 1962, on the modernization of Turkey and Japan. His basic idea was that Japan was successful in rapid modernization chiefly because she maintained her national identity in all its historical and cultural aspects. Turhan's lectures were supposed to be a refutation of my articles published in *Milliyet*, January-February 1962. These articles were based on the papers presented to the Social Science Research Concil conference on the modernization of Turkey and Japan held in New York in 1962. See Robert E. Ward and Dankwart A. Rustow, *Political Modernization in Japan and Turkey* (Princeton, 1964).

[2] Başgil wrote that "we (Turks) are not Central Asiatics, either by spirit or body structure, even though linguistically we are related to Central Asia. On the contrary we are a special nation, a synthesis of races, living a life of its own in a country ringed by Islam." Başgil was considered for the Presidency by the Justice Party in 1961 but was opposed by the military. In another article Başgil declared that Islam and nationalism are identified with each other since both form a "united front against a common enemy; communism, atheism or godlessness and cosmopolitanism or *soysuzluk*" ("without a lineage") (*Yeni Istanbul*, November 30, 1963). Later Başgil was elected a deputy from Istanbul but his popularity diminished after a new wing of moderates took control of the Justice Party.

[3] See Cavit Orhan Tütengil, *Doktor Rıza Nur Üzerine* (Ankara, 1965); *Cumhuriyet*, March 9, 1964; *Kitap Belleten*, October 1, 1964, pp. 3-5; and Ziya Yücel Ilhan, *Sevenlerin Kalemiyle Dr. Rıza Nur* (Istanbul, 1962).

government but also Islam as the official religion. The old alphabet was to be restored and used together with the Latin one. The sects were to be reestablished as missionary organizations to disseminate Turkism. The Caliphate was to be reinstated. Nur opposed industrialization, fearing its disruptive effects on social organization, but advocated a modernized agriculture. Women were to be returned to home life. A dedicated racialist, Nur advocated the reunion of all Turks into a confederation in which the Anatolian Turks would hold the key position. Bitterly opposed to Atatürk, he made a special point of proposing to give positions to Rumeli Turks (those born in Balkan countries) only proportionate to their number.[1] Although theoretically not opposed to a multiparty system, he proposed to dissolve the Republican Party and replace it with a fascist type of nationalist organization which would assume supreme power. Nur has been hailed by nationalists as having expressed the true feelings of Anatolian Turks. These ideas, including his denunciation of Atatürk (he proposed to destroy his statues), have become today the chief source of inspiration for a variety of nationalist militant currents.

The nationalism oriented toward the Ottoman past (the racialist views had little appeal for them) found wide support among the upper and middle classes pursuing economic occupations. It appealed emotionally to them but also strengthened implicitly their social position by upholding the traditional belief in the immutability of the social order. In practice, however, as mentioned before, this new middle class was the main source of disruption of the old social organization even while trying to maintain its symbols. The study of the Ottoman past has lately appealed to the leftists because it was a laboratory of social experience showing the society's evolution toward socialism.

The first reaction to the rise of traditionalist nationalism and its conservative orientation came from the secularists. These began to search for deeper meanings in *Atatürkçülük*, ("Ataturkism") and shaped it into a movement seeking to reassert Turkey's initial secularist-nationalist principles. The secularist nationalists eventually organized the *Türk Devrim Ocakları* ("Turkish Reform Hearth") early in the 1950's and attracted various liberal and social-minded groups, including the grad-

---

[1] In the late 1950's another militant group publishing the *Serdengeçti* and a variety of tracts repeatedly attacked the "unfaithhful" Rumelians from Salonica (e.g., Atatürk) for having imposed secularist ideas which undermined the spiritual Islamic purity of Anatolian towns. The militants would go as far as to demand the full rehabilitation of the Ottoman dynasty. See M. Raif Ogan, *Sultan Abdulhamid II ve Bugünkü Muarızları* (Istanbul, 1956).

uates of Village Institutes. The organization opened branches in a few cities and exercised considerable influence among university students. The rise of new middle classes coupled with the Democrats' liberal economic policies compelled the secular nationalists (urbanites and bureaucrats) to take a position on economic and social problems. The immediate outcome of these developments was the emergence of a social consciousness which began to manifest itself in a variety of literary works published in *Varlık* ("*Existence*"), *Dost* ("*Friend*"), *Yeni Ufuklar*, ("*New Horizons*"), and *Yedi Tepe* ("*Seven Hills*"). These reviews sponsored the publication of original books and Western translations which formed a sizable percentage of the total number of books published in Turkey. Dailies such as *Dünya* ("World") and *Cumhuriyet* ("Republic") supported this group. Meanwhile the *Devrim Ocakları*, whose number remained limited, gradually turned into cultural clubs where discussions on secularism expanded into economic and social fields. The *Ocaks* leaned toward the Republican Party since many of their members came from the youth branches of this party.

Two groups began to emerge among secular nationalists. The first moderate group contented itself with defending a return to the original secular nationalism under a democratic form of government. The second and younger group sought to give a social interpretation to Atatürk's reforms. It regarded the cultural secular reforms as bound to remain without effect if not supported by profound social change and by a political regime dedicated to this goal. Some intellectuals in this group eventually became the promoters of socialism.[1]

The military revolution of 1960 speeded up and completed the dichotomous evolution within Turkish nationalism. The revolution was, in a way, a victory for the secular nationalists. Their former opposition to the Democrats, and the officers' secular orientation seemed to bring them together, especially with regard to the Democrats' suppposedly anti-reformist policies. Consequently they found themselves opposed to the conservative Islamic nationalists who had received support from the

---

[1] For instance, many contributors to the socialist review *Yön* were the members of the *Devrim Ocağı* in Ankara. The Research Office of the Republican Party was already manned by members of this group. Various publications on Turkey's social problems issued by this office, mainly after 1957, clearly point out the social dimension acquired by secularist nationalist thought. See publications by PRP Research and Documentation Office on Workers, Economic Development, Civil Service Personnel, Social Problems, etc., Ankara 1957-60.

Democratic government.[1] Thus, political change precipitated the significant formal break long in the making between the two groups of nationalists. The secularists gradually became identified with the Revolution of May 27 and its reforms, and supported the military government. The others sympathized with the opposition and identified themselves with the cause of the ousted Democrats.

However, for some time after the revolution the essence of the new nationalism was not yet clear. The nationalist wing of the junta under Colonel Alparslan Türkeş seemed to lean toward the Ottoman past (although in a secular context), chiefly because its historical appeal was deemed necessary to foster national unity. It was reliably reported that Mümtaz Turhan, a conservative, nationalist professor, had been seriously considered for an appointment as Minister of Education, probably to direct the *Kültür ve Ülkü Birliği* ("Union of Culture and Ideals") which was supposed to replace the Ministry of Education.[2] Meanwhile the People's Houses were restored under a new name, *Kültür Birliği* ("Unions of Culture") and only later, in 1963, reverted to their old name. In an interview with some of the social-minded members of the National Unity Committee this writer asked their opinion about the nationalistic measures planned while they held power. They rejected racialism but defended the other measures since these were intended to enhance the sense of national unity and morally rejuvenate society. (The attitude of the military toward nationalism is conditioned by a variety of historical, social, and educational factors beyond the scope of this work.)

In any case, the nationalist policies of the military, coupled with the general freedom of the press, encouraged the conservative nationalists to reorganize themselves further and make full use of their existing associations and publications. The main organization of this nationalist group was the *Milliyetçiler Derneği* ("Society of Nationalists") established in 1953, with the purpose of "preserving and promoting the values which make up our nation and bring up Turkish nationalists in a model fashion imbued with the consciousness of history, scientific

---

[1] The Democratic Party supported some nationalist publications with subscriptions and secret subsidies. Immediately after the revolution this was made public and contributed to loss of prestige for these publications and their editors, including the poet Fazıl Kısakürek who published the ultrareligious-political *Büyük Doğu* ("Great Orient").

[2] See detail in *Öncü*, October 27, November 9-11, 1960. Türkeş's memoirs began to appear in *Yeni Istanbul*, February 10-17, 1962, but were suppressed for attacks on Inönü.

mentality, spirit of sacrifice, abnegation, justice and virtue" (Bylaws, Art. 2). The society originally had only a few branches. After 1960 it opened new branches in the main cities of Turkey in order to fight the spread of communism.[1] The members of country branches were professionals, lawyers, doctors, some teachers, and a variety of other groups associated in one way or other either with the town "intelligentsia" or with the economic middle class. The *Milli Türk Talebe Birliği* ("National Union of Turkish Students," originally established by nationalist students in the 1930's fused later through government pressure into the larger student union but separated again in 1947) represented this current among university students. The *Türkiye Milli Talebe Federasyonu* ("Turkish National Student Federation") was the main student body until recently. Particularly after 1960, it adopted a left-of-center position). Although it participated in the April 1960 demonstrations against Menderes, the National Union has displayed on occasion chauvinistic tendencies such as the antiforeign campaign *Vatandaş Türkçe Konuş* ("Citizen speak Turkish") of August-September 1960.

In addition to these two organizations several other clubs and groups were organized to defend similar nationalist ideas. For instance, the purpose of *Türk Gençlik Derneği* ("Turkish Youth Association") established in 1963 was to "protect... the national values, fight subversive ideologies, especially communism, spread knowledge about great Turks and train youth as true nationalists" (Bylaws, Art. 2). The more recent organization *Komunizmle Mücadele Derneği* ("Society for Struggle Against Communism"), which has more than forty branches, represents the militants of these nationalist organizations. This last organization has been actively engaged in violent demonstrations against the leftists, especially the marxist Labor Party.

The basic cause for the resurgence of this nationalism after the revolution is opposition to social currents. It is defensive and conservative in character. Hence it is prone to oppose any social ideas as being communistic and subversive and exalt traditional virtues found in history and religion.[2] In the economic field it is opposed to state planning. It

---

[1] *Milliyetçiler Derneği Ana Nizamnamesi ve On Yıllık Faaliyetleri* (Istanbul, 1963). The association publishes books, and organizes conferences and seminars : 19 publications and 150 seminars by 1963. Several publishing enterprises were controlled by these nationalists : *Sönmez Matbaacılık Anonim Ortaklığı, Ilim Yayma Cemiyeti, Türkiye Anıtlar Derneği*, and especially *Türkeli Anonim Şirketi*.

[2] Fethi Tevetoğlu, *Faşist Yok, Komunist Var* (Ankara, 1962); Hikmet Tanyu, *Niçin Komunist Oluyorlar* (Ankara, 1958); George S. Harris, *The Origins of Commu-*

tends to defend economic liberalism in absolute form. It supports a parliamentary democracy in the belief that it can control the public vote and oppose the reforms proposed by social-minded groups. Bent on preserving the social structure intact, it idealizes the parochial town mentality and traditional family values as the true foundations of Turkish society. It hails Atatürk as a liberator, but privately some extremists belonging to the Anatolian supremacist current denounce him as ignorant of the spiritual aspects of Anatolian society. In fact, some go as far as to say, wrongly, that he may not have been a "real" Turk since he was born in Salonica outside of today's Turkey. At times the foreign policy aims of this nationalism draw some inspiration from Pan-Turkism in hoping to liberate the Turks living abroad and unite them in one single country.[1] But, its preoccupation with internal problems, or rather opposition to profound social and economic reforms, outweighs by far its interest in foreign affairs.

This conservative wing of traditionalist nationalism can be regarded also as a psychological reaction to the disintegration of the traditional mode of life and value system.[2] There is fear of the common man's awakening, the sharpening of the individual's sense of existence and responsibility, and the shattering of the intelligentsia's own self-created image of social perfection and leadership mission in life. (The same fear of the commoner's rise is evident also among the other wing of the elite: the statist socialists who would like to control the individual through a modern collectivist ideology.)[3]

---

nism in Turkey (Stanford, 1967). The anticommunist literature is quite abundant among this group. See İlhan E. Darendelioğlu, *Türkiye'de Komunist Hareketleri*, 2 vols. (Istanbul, 1961-64).

[1] *Cumhuriyet*, January 19, 1964; A. Nurullah Barıman, *Bizim Milli Ülkümüz, Turancılık Nedir?* (Istanbul, n.d.), p. 15.

[2] The overwhelming majority of these nationalists were trained in modern schools in the semi-racialist nationalism which prevailed in the educational system from 1935 to 1945. During the Democrats' rule this nationalism acquired a religious ingredient, which although present in the past in a variety of forms, was not openly acknowledged. The teachers of history, language, and literature played the main role in imparting this nationalism to the youth in the conservative towns of Anatolia. Today the strongest supporters of this nationalism are *İmam-Hatip* ("clergy") schools which were established to train a modern-minded clergy, but became in fact a politically militant conservative group.

[3] In 1962 one of the most extreme defenders of statist socialism told this writer that he, a married man with a house, car, and children was afraid of his own fate when the masses, awakened to life by economic changes, could no longer be controlled by the existing authority.

The militant conservative nationalists appeal to the commoner's mysticism and his surviving sense of Islamic mission in order to preserve his loyalty to collective values rooted in his faith.[1] Consequently they stress dedication to Islam, respect for ancestral ways of life, veneration of traditions, high morality, love of kin and one's race, and mistrust of foreigners as the best ways to preserve national identity.[2]

The intensive activities and abundant publications promoting conservative nationalism after the Revolution of 1960 were, as mentioned, basically of a defensive character.[3] For the first time in the history of Republican Turkey this militant conservative nationalism was subjected to severe criticism by secular nationalists and especially by socialists. These attached a different meaning to the concepts of nation and Turkish youth and had new ideas on economic and social policy. "The Turkish Youth" according to secular nationalists comprised "millions of young men, town people, villagers, schooled and unschooled workers, rich and poor farmers, government officials and professionals with a million of different personalities and interests, expectations and tendencies."[4] They ridiculed the conservatives' slogan "beware of currents

---

[1] See Cahit Okurer, "Ben Niye İnanıyorum", *Büyük Zafer*, March 6, 1962. The best examples of this thought can be found in the daily letters published in the *Son Havadis* (1962-64) in the column "University Student Corner," and in the essays sent to *Yeni Istanbul* for the competition entitled "The Turkish Youth, How Should it Be?" (1962). See the first three prizewinning essays in *Yeni Istanbul*, November 15-17, 1962 and summary, November 24, 1962. A translation appears in Kemal H. Karpat, *Political and Social Thought in the Contemporary Middle East* (New York, 1968), pp. 367-68.

[2] Some quotations from militant conservative nationalist writings may give a better opinion about their ideas. One youth wrote, "If the noble Turkish Youth were to regard history with the deepest respect and enthusiasm, he would find out that the power that secured endless victories, and made the Turks masters of the world... was the dedication to God, the attachment to religion and readiness to sacrifice life for these truths." Another urged Turkish youth to "remain loyal to Islam, fulfill its commands and recognize God and His Prophet. This nation ran from one victory to the other as long as it remained loyal to Islam and its commands...Turkish youth must remain loyal to its traditions, for if a nation deserts its own customs and traditions it is bound to disappear." See letters sent to *Son Havadis* and *Yeni Istanbul*, footnote 30 above.

[3] Several of these publications, some appearing sporadically, provide good insight into the content of conservative nationalism. See the weekly *Düşünen Adam* ("Thinking Man"), the literary *Toprak* ("Earth"), *Yol* ("Road"), and rabid sensational tracts such as *Birlik* ("Unity"), *Yeni İstiklal* ("New Independence"), *Hür Adam* ("Free Man)", or *Milli Yol* ("National Path").

[4] *Cumhuriyet*, August 19, 1960.

with roots abroad" since nationalism itself was of Western origin, and Islam was taken from the Arabs. Even Ziya Gökalp, the father of Turkish nationalism, was rejected as being out of date, and criticized as having erred in his definitions of nation, culture, and civilization. Already as early as 1958, Emin Erişirgil, identified once with elitism and extreme nationalism, declared that Turkish nationalism had entered a humanist phase.[1] The search for foreign writings praising the Turks was criticized, as was the reluctance to accept outside criticism and persistence in the idea that the world was a great admirer of the Turks.[2] The minorities, including Greeks and Jews, were described as being loyal to Turkey and this was the sole reason for extending them equal treatment and consideration.[3] The ideas and myths of Islamist racialist nationalists were attacked by secular or social-minded dailies such as *Cumhuriyet*, *Milliyet*, *Dünya*, and *Vatan*. Falih Rıkı Atay, the publisher of *Dünya*, coined the much-used term *Kara Milliyet-ilik* ("dark nationalism") to condemn the religious-minded nationalist. *Vatan* in a series of articles described the love of country as a natural feeling common to all human beings. Extremist nationalism on the other hand was depicted as a reaction to the downfall of an empire and disintegration of feudalism. It was mystical, racialist, unethical, intolerant, antimodernist, and uncreative; it produced no major work of art or truly great man.[4] Secularists claimed that whereas Atatürk wanted to use nationalism within national boundaries as a means of modernization, now nationalism had deviated from Atatürk's concepts by becoming chauvinistic and aristocratic, and fed itself upon self-invented tales of past grandeur.[5] In reality, Kemalist Turkey was the first true Turkish state, whereas in the past Turks had established states under a different identity and served universalist goals. The socialists, particularly Çetin Altan in his column in *Milliyet* —later he wrote for *Akşam*—led the attacks on racialist nationalists. These were accused of ignoring the poverty-stricken masses of Anatolia and indulging in utopian dreams about the land of Turan in Central

---

[1] Emin Erişirgil, *Türkçülük Devri, Milliyetçilik Devri, İnsanlık Devri* (Ankara, 1958).
[2] Melih Cevdet Anday, "Kendi Kendimizi Eleştirme," *Cumhuriyet*, June 3, 1961.
[3] *Ulus*, Janaury 10, 1961 (Statement by Bülent Ecevit).
[4] A. N. Kırmacı, "Türkiye'de Aşırı Cereyanlar. Milliyetçilik, Irkçılık, Turancılık," *Vatan*, November 24-27, 1960. The article appeared during Ahmet Emin Yalman's editorship; after he left —actually he was ousted—the paper leaned to the left.
[5] See essays in *Atatürkçülük Nedir?* (Istanbul, 1963).

Asia.[1] "True nationalism" for Yaşar Kemal, the socialist novelist, "consisted of preventing a minority from exploiting a majority." [2]

The secular, social-minded nationalists reinterpreted Ottoman history. The Ottoman rulers according to them consisted of a group of cosmopolitans who felt no identification with any social group or national culture and used even Islam as a justification for holding power. (This theory, which originated in the early nationalist movement in the nineneenth century, has acquired a social orientation and exercises far more influence on Turkish minds than this brief reference may indicate).

In conclusion, it may be said that nationalism, whatever its forms and shortcomings, achieved its mission in creating a national state and sense of Turkish national identity. However, its mysticism and subjectivity proved unable to face the challenge of social change, and eventually became an obstacle to further modernization. The increasingly modern and complex society needed new ideas and horizons, a new vision of man and society, which the old form of nationalism could not provide. The secularist thought itself needed drastic revision, for its rejection of Islam actually was a direct consequence of the rejection of all religion, of man's spiritual needs, and his desire for belief in moral values. The secularists' idealization of Atatürk created a personality cult of vast proportions which was as "unscientific" as the Islamists' blind rejection of modern science. In any case, the diverse ideas on nationalism indicated that Turkish intellectual life was ready to enter a new phase based on a pluralist system of thought. Turks were no longer satisfied with the political slogans and the isolationist mentality of the old nationalism which prevented them from joining mankind in name and spirit.

The Constitution of 1961 gave a clear indication of the stage reached by nationalism in Turkey. The preamble stated that "...the spirit of Turkish nationalism... aims always to exalt our nation in a spirit of national unity as a respected member of the world community of nations enjoying equal rights and privileges."

However, the Article 2, defining the characteristics of the Republic, refers to the state as being national,[3] democratic, secular, and social.

---

[1] The conservative nationalists answered by saying that the foes of Turanism hesitated to show the same sympathy for the Turkic peoples of the Soviet Union as they did for the people and leaders (e.g., Lumumba) of former colonial territories of Africa (*Yeni Istanbul*, May 6, 1963).

[2] *Cumhuriyet*, August 21, 1960.

[3] *Milli* ("national") in the Turkish version of the Constitution appears as "nationalistic" in the official English translation of 1961. This is puzzling since I remember very distinctly that as a member of the translating committee, I corrected it to read *national*.

The term "national" in Article 2 was subject to a long heated debate. The military and some politicians in the Constituent Assembly wanted to define the state as nationalistic. They were opposed by secularists and socialists who thought that nationalism had achieved its mission and if inserted in the Constitution as a principle it would, besides creating division and restriction, perpetuate the old parochial philosophy. "National" on the other hand would include any ethnic group and permit the birth of other currents of thought. A compromise was reached by alluding to nationalism only in the Preamble and keeping it out of the text.

The latter developments speeded up the synthesis in the conçept of nationalism and clarified the atmosphere.[1] The extremist nationalists seemed to have abandoned their opposition to social reform. Their opposition to socialism and communism has acquired new organizational forms and a more realistic understanding of the forces which generate extreme social currents. They seem to accept a diluted form of land reform, economic planning, workers' rights, and a variety of other social measures. Moreover, they have also discarded much of the old mystical militant approach. The extreme nationalists attempted to take control of the Justice Party, but failed, and left this party to moderate-minded professionals from the middle classes. Meanwhile Colonel Alparslan Türkeş, the leader of the nationalist wing in the junta, returned from his assignment abroad and joined the Republican National Peasant Party. He became chairman of this party and together with several of his former officer followers entered the new National Assembly elected on October 10, 1965. His party held only a few seats in the 450-member Assembly of 1965-69.[2] Eventually he adopted a new name for his party, *Milli Hareket Partisi* ("National Action Party").

Several of the critics of conservative nationalism went farther to the left and joined the Labor Party. Secular nationalism presently seems to be grouped chiefly around the Republican Party, although the program of this party is leaning heavily toward a moderate form of welfare socialism. The other emerging characteristics of nationalism are evident in

---

[1] The tendency to stress patriotism instead of nationalism was part of this development.

[2] Türkeş was backed by Gökhan Evliyaoğlu, the militant nationalist organizer, but Türkeş failed to support him for a seat in Parliament. Although with the 1969 elections the percentage of total votes of Türkeş's National Action Party increased from 2.2 to 2.8, it holds only two seats in Parliament as a consequence of the revised election system. For the political views of Alparslan Türkeş see his *Türkiye'nin Meseleleri* (Istanbul, 1969).

foreign policy and in the new attitude toward Westernization. The failure of the West to support unconditionally the Turkish position on Cyprus has led to a reconsideration of the alignment with and the total commitment to Western policy. Consequently the need to chart a new independent foreign policy is considered essential for the better protection of national interests and for acquiring a clearer understanding of Turkey's internal life without the bias of foreign alignment. This development is of capital importance, for it conforms to a line of thought long in the making, namely the desire to judge and appraise Turkey's internal problems in the light of her own conditions and establish goals accordingly. There is also the desire to end the imitation of foreign models and assert the Turk's own personality. This idea of independence is the new facet of Turkish nationalism and it may well symbolize the fact that Turkey has reached a mature stage in her development as a national state where she can take a new critical view of her modernization. But there is also the mounting leftist effort to turn this sense of independence into a movement against the West under the guise of antiimperialism and anticapitalism and thus radically change Turkey's foreign policy, parliamentary democracy, and Western cultural orientation.

Socialism : A Means For Development or Power?

Socialism in Turkey, as in the rest of the Near East, is part of the general movement of modernization. If often appears associated with nationalism and expresses the latter's economic and social aims. Social ideas in Turkey were incorporated in the national goals at the beginning of the Republic. These were gradually ignored, and eventually replaced by purely nationalist ideas. The group in power, preoccupied primarily with political matters, had not grasped the full complexity of the economic and social aspects of modernization. After the Revolution of 1960, socialism emerged as a distinctive ideology rejecting culturally the Islamic racialist and Ottoman facets of nationalism. It also opposed the rise of the middle classes and proposed central planning based on state authority as a rapid means of development.

The beginning of modern social thought in Turkey may be traced to the Young Ottomans in the 1860's, then to Prince Sabahaddin's ideas, to the Socialist Party and clubs in the Young Turk period, and to a variety of marxist and socialist organizations in the Republic. However, it was only after the Revolution of 1960 that socialism appeared as a major current of thought and attracted a large following. Moreover, it was partly legitimized by the emergence and acceptance of socialist political organizations.

Socialism in Turkey appears concerned with economic development, social justice, taxation, industrialization, workers' rights, education and a variety of welfare problems. It is a modern current as far as its goals are concerned. There are, however, two aspects of socialism both in Turkey and elsewhere in the Near East which require closer scrutiny. The first aspect concerns the ethical and philosophical sources inspiring this socialism. These cannot be divorced from the movement itself. Socialism seems to derive at first sight from some Western ideas. However, it seems to this writer that socialist ideas in Turkey, like nationalist concepts previously borrowed from the West, have lost much if not all of their Western essence. Hence one is inclined to conclude that, while the term was borrowed from the West, much of its spirit came from traditional cultural sources, including the social ethics of Islam. (The wide ideological gap between a Shaikh Khalid M. Khalid and a "modern" socialist in Egypt is considerably narrowed when one leaves aside the terminology and considers the essence of their thought.)

The second problem raised by socialism concerns the method of advancing it. The overwhelming majority of socialists in Turkey as elsewhere in the Near East are statists, that is to say they accept chiefly an authoritarian form of socialism based on state authority. Obviously the present economic and social conditions in the developing areas impose great responsibilities on the government, the only agency which has the organization and controls the skills capable of coping with the technical and financial aspects of large-scale development. Yet classical Western socialism, even in its extreme forms, recognized a role for voluntary associations and regarded the state as the tool of the dominating classes. The idea of the state "withering away" has not been mentioned by Near Eastern socialists. These have pinned their hopes of materializing their social aspirations on the state and have not bothered with theories concerning the role of modern government. Their first expectation from the state is social justice. Paradoxically enough the achievement of "justice" has been the basic goal of traditional Islamic governments. The modern concepts of politics have supplied the intelligentsia with the practical arguments of modernity to consolidate their traditionally dominant position in society by restoring the government to its supreme position.

The socialists in countries like Egypt and Turkey with a continuous tradition of organized government are definitely more statist than those in Muslim countries which for one reason or other have not had such governments. However, overriding all these background influences are pressing problems arising from the need to modernize the production apparatus, introduce new methods of social organization, raise living standards, and achieve general material welfare. The problem, therefore, is to determine whether these goals can be reached through institutions which have preserved much of their traditional outlook, including the very government expected to modernize society.

The question of leadership is intimately connected with statism and socialism, for both rely on elitist concepts. The elitist philosophy is still powerful in the Near East and is manifest largely in the relations between government and subjects. Elitism ignores man's inborn ability to grasp issues and learn how to govern himself by associating freely with his fellow men. The socialist finds in social justice the necessary ethical arguments to justify his elitist claim to absolute state power. There is no built-in philosophical conviction capable of limiting this power. Vague Western liberal ideas have lost their influence following liberation from the political rule of the West. The traditional Islamic idea of opposition to tyranny, which on occasion had a limiting effect on governments in the past, has lost its force partly because of secularism but chiefly because the state's socialist policy was described as conforming to Islam's social commands. Consequently, once the use of state power was thus justified there were no grounds for opposing it.

Unavoidably one comes to the conclusion that state power in the Near East can be limited only if and when power groups can emerge to oppose the ruling group. It seems that each major political change in the modern Near East has been followed by the rule of the elite leading the movement for change. The subsequent phase of political life seems to consist of a struggle against the ruling group, and this gradually involves other segments of the population. This process may lead to a stage whereby all government relations may be visualized as power relations and thus conform to the nature of the national power state. A socialist government may in the long run create individual self-consciousness by means other than formal political indoctrination, and against its own wishes. Presently, however, Near Eastern socialism does not seem concerned with such problems. If the government were to achieve some success in establishing a measure of welfare, it could thus justify on behalf of modernism the perpetual rule of the bureaucratic elite which controls it.[1]

---

[1] These problems have been explored, with reference to original texts translated

Turkey, however, unlike other Near Eastern countries, witnessed the birth of socialism after 1960, in an atmosphere that was relatively favorable to free discussion, group organization, interplay of conflicting interests, and to political activity. It was also free of pressure from outside. This atmosphere permitted the influx of new ideas into the "socialist" thought and broadened its scope. Moreover, the new Turkish socialism was born after a period of state capitalism which had often been dubbed socialism or statism. The material achievements of this system from 1930 to 1945 were rather insignificant in relation to its cost and to the bitter, popular opposition it created. Consequently Turkish socialism, despite some theoretical aberrations in favor of totalitarianism, was forced to take note of the people's democratic yearnings if it wanted any following at all. Thus, the idea began to develop that the individual's relations with the state and government did not consist solely of an exercise of authority but also of a joint effort to satisfy man's material needs. The intense debates on social and economic issues stimulated by the emergence of socialism in Turkey initially had a diluting effect upon the extremist aspects of statism. For instance, the five-year development plan has received considerable popular support after the government sponsored a campaign to explain its potential benefits to the populace. Even villagers have realized that the government would be unable to satisfy all their demands, and have begun to use their individual initiative and ability to better their own lives. Some sections of the population at least have begun to regard the government as an association born from their consent and need and have developed their political philosophies accordingly.

We have implied throughout this study that socialist and nationalist ideologies in the Near East are linked to the political and cultural traditions of their respective societies even though they may have modernist aims. This attitude may stem from practical considerations such as the necessity of building a bridge between past traditions and future goals in order to achieve popular acceptance for a specific regime. It may also derive from the simple fact that the promoters of change share to some extent the very traditions and habits they want to change and that continuity in society is a force as strong as change. Ideology, being a system of values with deep psychological roots, is bound to reflect the struggle between the old habits of mind and beliefs surviving in the subconcsious and the ideas consciously borrowed from outside. A Near Eastern man

from Arabic and Persian, in Kemal H. Karpat, *Political and Social Thought in the Contemporary Middle East* (New York, 1968).

may exalt the virtues of modernism and change and the next moment proudly prove with factual data his nation's ability to preserve its ardent personality and traditions. This attitude is not a contradiction as some shortsighted students tend to believe but a rather basic law of society which makes change possible without destroying one's group or national personality.

The case of change and continuity is evident in the relationship between socialism and religion in Turkey. Secularism has been successfully applied for more than forty years. The modern social forces have overwhelmed the vestiges of the past. Yet, even in Turkey there have been serious intellectual efforts, though not comparable with Arab-Islamic socialist ideas, to link socialism to Islam. The powerful Islamic socialism defended by the review *İştirak* ("Participation") during the Young Turk era apparently left its impact. Even the *Yön*, the first organized effort to disseminate socialism, has published articles linking Islam to the modern socialist doctrines. Aside from this calculated appeal to religious social thought there have been genuine Muslim socialists in Turkey who upheld the egalitarian commandments of Islam and specifically referred to the social measures undertaken by the Prophet, and especially by 'Umar, in land legislation and taxation. One wrote :

> Socialism is one of the modern political forces which strives to change the world ...by abolishing inequality...The unjust actions by capitalists in some countries have compelled people to rebel. Without effective measures to cope with this situation it would be impossible to preserve order and stability and prevent revolutions. Everyone can be satisfied by recognizing as sacred and implementing properly the Islamic laws concerning participation [*iştirak*, from Arabic *iştirakiyya* or "socialism"], justice, and equity.... Islam has sternly prohibited the exploitation of man by man, and the use of others through force of capital. The Koran has described all property as being "emanetullah" [in custody]. Since property is given by God in custody [to man], everyone has a right to it. The exploitation of property and its use for everyone's benefit through the state, is accepted as an essential principle...If the revolutionary socialists have taken a position against religion they do not actually aim at the faith proper but at the use of religion as a means by ruling groups to exploit the masses...between the human purposes of Islam and the claims of socialism there is an almost perfect resemblance.[1]

---

[1] Faik Bercai, *Islamda Sosyalizm* (Istanbul, 1946), pp. 3-4, 49-51. The author according to his bibliography has read works by Western socialists along with works by Arabs. He seems to rely, however, on social works written in Turkish some thirty or forty years earlier, such as Kilisli Ismail Hakkı, *Hakikat-i Islam*, and Musa Kâzım, *Külliyat-ı Şeyhulislam*. See also A. Cerrahoğlu, *Islamiyet ve Osmanlı Sosyalistleri* (Istanbul, 1964).

Another work dealing primarily with contemporary socialism in Turkey begins by describing Islam's early period, in the days of 'Umar and 'Ali, as a social struggle against the upper classes.[1] Eventually the writer ties this struggle with the popular social movements in Anatolia and with their leaders, particularly with the important Simavnalı Şeyh Bedreddin's socio-materialistic teachings.[2]

Any study of socialism in Turkey must devote some attention to those Islamic social ideas which have survived in customs, folklore, and traditions, and have indirectly prepared an atmosphere for egalitarian "modern" socialism. Egalitarianism seems to be the strongest feature of Turkish socialism.[3]

The rise of socialist currents in Turkey after the Revolution of 1960 was preceded by the development of a strong current of social realism in literature.[4] The basic structure and power changes underlying this development have been considered in the Introduction. Indeed, late in the 1940's and early in the 1950's Turkey witnessed the growth of literary writings dealing with the plight of the peasantry. These stimulated interest in the fate of the villagers and helped broaden the intellectual's social horizon.

The Democratic Party, which showed unrelenting opposition to socialist doctrines, reacted rather mildly to the village literature, for it helped justify the party's rural policy of bettering the peasants' lot, even though

---

[1] Hilmi Özgen (Halim Köylü), *Türk Sosyalizmi Üzerine Denemeler* (Ankara, 1963), pp. 12-13; also *idem*, *Türk Sosyalizminin Ilkeleri* (Ankara, 1962). This work, although of limited significance, was described by a recent Soviet article as the beginning mark of the postrevolution, socialist current in Turkey. It is highly significant that the author is a highly placed bureaucrat, a former finance inspector.

[2] Sheik Simavnalı Bedrettin provided Nazım Hikmet, the communist poet who died recently in the USSR, with material for one of his most powerful epic poems. On Bedrettin see A. Gölpınarlı, *Simavna Kadısıoğlu Şeyh Bedrettin* (Istanbul, 1966); and *Der Islam* 11 (1921).

[3] The Islamist-nationalists, who idealize Islam's concepts of political and social organization, have ignored the ideas of Muslim socialists. They are prepared to support at most the Islamic principle of charity but reject violently any discussion regarding property. In fact, they use arguments drawn from Islamic literature to support the concept of the immutability of the social order. See for instance the tract *Hakkaniyet* ("Equity") by M. Raif Ogan and Izzet Mühürdaroğlu. But there are other clerics who, on the basis of the Koran, reject the supremacy of landlords and chieftains; see Mehmet Emin Bozarslan (the Mufti of Kulp-Diyarbakır), *Islamiyet Açısından Şeyhlik-Ağalık* (Ankara, 1964).

[4] See Kemal H. Karpat, "Social Themes in Contemporary Turkish Literature," *Middle East Journal* 14, nos. 1 and 2 (Winter and Spring 1960), pp. 29-44 and 153-168.

the Democrats' interest in villagers was inspired by practical rather than ideological reasons.

The attitude of the Republican Party to social ideas, on the other hand, was affected by the same literature and came out in part as a reaction to the Democrats' economic policy. The Republicans gradually broadened their narrow social outlook and in 1953 accepted within their party even the workers' right to strike (in 1936 they had passed the most rigid antilabor legislation). At the same time they began to sponsor the cause of groups affected by inflation and unplanned economic development, the salary and wage earners, as well as the peasants, despite failure to win popularity with the latter group. The Republican Party's new social and economic outlook seemed to have emerged by the time elections were held in 1957, when it attempted to formulate a platform corresponding to the needs of social groups which it proposed to defend. The elections resulted in an increase of four times the number of Republican deputies in the Assembly, despite the Democrats' frantic appeals to voters to completely eliminate the Republican representation in Parliament.[1] This encouraged the Republican Party to devote full attention to social and economic problems. Consequently the Research and Documentation Office of the party, manned by young intellectuals some of whom later promoted socialism, began to publish a series of studies on civil service, workers, economic development, and a variety of other social problems.

The bimonthly review *Forum* (1955) meanwhile became one of the most influential publications of the period. It was a democratic-minded review interested in social problems. It appeared under the direction of Aydın Yalçın, Osman Okyar, and several other intellectuals leaning basically toward English social thought. Many of the members in the Republicans' Research Office contributed to the *Forum*. The review was one of the most serious publications ever published in Turkey. The *Forum*, although critical of the Democrats, did not propose radical social or economic changes but defended the idea of a rational economy and the broadening of the political democracy into the social field.

Meanwhile Cemil Sait Barlas, ex-Minister of Trade, influential

---

[1] Kemal H. Karpat, "The Turkish Elections of 1957," *Western Political Quarterly*, June 1961, pp. 436-59. The Republican success was also the outcome of dissatisfaction among the lower ranks of the Democratic Party, mainly among those who were instrumental in establishing the first organizations of this party in 1946. The "reassertion of the spirit of 1946" became their slogan in the sense of opposing the rise of a new power elite.

member of the Republican Party and scion of a rich family of notables from Qaziantep, began to discuss openly in 1958-59 in his review, *Pazar Postası* (Sunday Mail) the question of "socialism". He translated socialist articles from European publications and published a variety of letters and short stories with social content.[1] Other literary reviews were doing the same. Social tendencies in the Republican Party seemed to be so evident that Ismet Inönü was accused publicly of having reverted to his old socialist, statist views as expressed some twenty-five years earlier.[2]

In reality both the socialism of the Republican Party and that of Barlas were slightly amended forms of statism. They placed emphasis on production and to some extent social justice, but avoided reference to a change of social structure. Nevertheless, the word "socialism" coming from the Republicans whose loyalty was above discussion helped dispel some of the pathological fear it had radiated.[3] Consequently, by 1959 the younger generation of secular nationalists began to lean definitely toward socialism. These came closer at the same time to the intellectuals from villages (institute graduates) and labor groups. The social gap between village and city or the higher and lower class of intellectuals narrowed in proportion to their identification with the national social problems of Turkey.

The period between 1957 and 1960 may be rightly considered the sentimentalist, universalist, and humanist phase of Turkish socialism. It appeared during this period as a search for a means to achieve general social mobilization for economic development, welfare, and progress rather than a proposal for a new political regime. Soon afterwards the younger generation manning the press, which became a powerful intellectual force, moved rapidly to the left, not by any overt defense of socialism but through stories, headlines, and omission or manipulation of news as the case might be. (Recent evidence concerning the opposition of the press and intelligentsia to the Democrats' dictatorial policies early in 1960 indicates that the newly rising socialist groups played a leading part in it).

---

[1] Cemil Sait Barlas, *Sosyalistlik Yolları ve Türkiye Gerçekleri* (Istanbul, 1962).

[2] See the session of the Republican Peasant National Party convention on January 18, 1959, when speakers referred to Inönü's article published in the statist socialist *Kadro* in the 1930's.

[3] It was reliably reported that the police were so shocked by the open advocacy of "socialism" that they thought of taking some measures against Barlas. However, the relative stature of the man and the Democrats' hope that this would discredit his party in the public eye prevented any action against him.

The Revolution of 1960 brought the first official recognition of this thought defined as socialism. Speeches by some National Unity Committee members indicated that they had definite social aspirations. Finally General Cemal Gürsel, the Head of State, alluding to a newly formed small but insignificant socialist party, declared: "There is a socialist party in Turkey. I have allowed it to operate. I am of the opinion that a socialist party is not harmful but could be very beneficial as long as it does not have malicious intentions." [1]

Encouraged by this statement, the accumulated social resentment against the Democrats, already evident in the press, came out violently in the form of criticism of landlords, and of the groups enriched during the Democrats' term. The peasantry's plight was dramatized, although the villagers were criticized for their support of Menderes. Some intellectuals openly advocated a voting system which would give each citizen three or four votes according to the level of his education and thus balance the peasantry's numerical superiority and prevent it from committing further political errors. However, the peasant, as a junta member described it, while benefiting from political freedom and retaining his religious outlook had also developed new "modern" material wants. The peasant, according to him, expected the government to respect his religious feelings and traditions, but also to satisfy his economic needs and establish an impartial bureaucracy. This was, he declared, "the [basic] yardstick in Atatürk's time and has remained the same since. But now, in addition, people want to study, to receive better care for the sick, to have real shoes ... to sleep in a real house rather than together with their beasts, to listen to the radio, to have electricity, roads, employment, and income. In résumé they want those things which a European peasant possessed 150 years ago." [2]

On the other hand some officers and intellectuals lamented the disintegration of the middle class by which they meant the old ruling bureaucratic group, and proposed to revive it and make it the foundation of the forthcoming democratic regime.

The discussions of social problems were clearly converging toward the idea of social classes and particularly class struggle. The full establishment of freedom of the press immediately after the revolution enabled the marxists to express their own opinion, often in the form of oversimplified social slogans but definitely aimed at causing class conflicts.

---

[1] *Akşam*, August 10, 1960.
[2] Orhan Erkanlı's memoirs, *Milliyet*, June 24, 1962.

This was evident in the conflict caused by an amended press law enacted by the military.[1] The law definitely favored the employees. Subsequently nine major newspapers protested the law as interference with freedom of the press and suspended publication for three days.[2] Their action produced the first social clash between newspaper owners and their employees. The latter organized meetings and published their own paper *Basın* ("Press") protesting against the press *ağas* ("landlords") and their unscrupulous exploitation of employees. Large numbers of city intellectuals sent as teachers to villages during their military duty discovered the rural dimension of their country and brought tales of poverty, ignorance, and exploitation in villages. The daily *Milliyet* chose as the title for an essay competition in 1962 "The Realities of Turkey" based on these experiences.

Some writers devoted serious thought to discovering the social causes of Turkey's economic backwardness. Aziz Nesin, the social satirist, attributed the economic instability and the weakness of the entire social structure to the lack of a modern concept of property. "The main security in life," he wrote, "is property. If this security disappears, individuals would seek security elsewhere, and thus become *kapıkulu* [slaves or servants of the state]. We all, and all our classes, are *kapıkulus*. When a a peasant clothes himself with the uniform of the gendarme, he butts first with his rifle his village fellows, knowing too well that one day he will be at the receiving end. ... The uniform transforms him into a *kapıkulu*. This is still valuable currency today. Look at the press. As soon as the government makes a decision they praise it." [3]

Actually the term *kapıkulu* was put forth orginally by Ahmet Hamdi Başar, who claimed that Turkey was ruled by the same groups—bureaucrats, merchants and professionals—who had held power in the Ottoman Empire and relied on the state for a living. The criticism of *kapıkulu* mentality pointed to the lack of moral courage and integrity to stand by one's own convictions regardless of government policy.[4] Gradually

---

[1] The title is "Law...concerning the regulation of relations between employees and employers in the profession of journalism" (Law 212 of January 4, 1961, *Official Gazette*, no. 10703).

[2] *Akşam, Cumhuriyet, Dünya, Hürriyet, Milliyet, Tercüman, Vatan, Yeni Istanbul, Yeni Sabah*, January 10, 1961. Of these, at least four later became supporters of socialism.

[3] *Akşam*, March 13, 1961. Aziz Nesin was building his case in favor of collective property.

[4] Ahmet Hamdi Başar, *Yaşadığımız Devrin Içyüzü* (Ankara, 1960), pp. 39-40.

the rich middle classes became the main target for attack, for their wealth was deemed to have been unjustly accumulated. The investigative committees established by the military to discover the manner of enrichment had so alarmed some of the wealthy middle class as to make them consider leaving the country altogether to escape from "enmity to wealth." [1] The wealth inquiry committees were eventually disbanded since economic life had come to a standstill and the economic middle classes regained power through political parties. But the middle classes preserved the agonizing fear of expropriation which came so close to being a reality in 1960. This attitude was basic later not only in seeking formal legal safeguards against leftism but also in thinking of new economic and social methods to combat it from within.

The demands for agrarian reform, for a literacy campaign, and for an expanded system of social security continued to mount without a definite program to materialize them, especially since the reestablishment of the parliamentary system seemed to turn things back to where they had been on the eve of revolution. Vedat Nedim Tör, a former marxist and co-founder-member of the statist review *Kadro* (1932-4) summarized the situation:

> A poor and backward nation like us, has neither the time nor the energy to play the game of European democracy. We are yearning for the régime which will take us to social economic and cultural development by the shortest and fastest road.[2]

The question was to find a social group capable of leading the nation toward rapid economic development. The leadership as expected fell again to the intelligentsia. Consequently the old theory of elites was gradually reshaped in the light of new socialist-statist ideas. The guiding light on elite theory came from some members of the School of Political Science (established 1853) in Ankara, the backbone of the bureaucratic elite order which had ruled Turkey for a century. It was asserted that Turkey needed to entrust her fate to a brain trust or a new elite with expert knowledge of government affairs and technology, and having the values of the modern age.[3] This elite was to replace the old one consisting of

---

[1] *Milliyet* stated, "We are not the enemies of property but of wealth accumulated unjustly. We are the enemies of thieves, not of property" (November 24, 1960).

[2] Vedat Nedim Tör, "Rejim Buhranından Kurtulabilecek miyiz?" *Forum*, August 15, 1960, pp. 7-8. For similar views see also Nihat Türel, "Toplumsal Gerçekler ve Beklenen Reformlar," *Vatan*, October 7, 1960 : Ceyhun Atıf Kansu, "Halk Devleti," *Ülke*, October 1960.

[3] See Mümtaz Soysal, "Planlama ve Demokrasi," *Planlama*, Autumn 1961,

simple bureaucrats, the military, and landlords (this elite has already been replaced by the new middle classes).

The publisher of *Dünya*, disappointed that the revolutionaries did not bring to power a secular elite group but seemed interested instead in a parliamentary regime, found it necessary to translate and publish in installments Ortega y Gasset's *Revolt of the Masses*. The point was that the masses had no creative or leadership ability and had to be led—a rather commonly shared belief among intellectuals.[1] The People's Republican Party, meanwhile, following the lead of its younger social-minded members declared through the then Secretary General, Ismail Rüştü Aksal, that the party would devote closer attention to social problems since it was already social-minded, but refused to openly adopt socialism as party ideology in order to placate the conservatives.[2] The Republican Party's social orientation resulted in part from conviction but also from a desire to win over the intellectuals and the military by assuring them that their social aspirations would be met if the Republican Party came to power. The promise of social reform aimed also at undermining the efforts of a small group in the junta who advocated a strong regime in order to carry out such reforms. The ousting of fourteen members of the junta on November 13, 1960, eliminated eventually the danger of a strong regime. It also opened the way for return to civilian rule, most likely, as it appeared at the time, under the Republican Party.

The recognition accorded to labor and the establishment of a State Planning Organization are two other major influences which affected

---

p. 65; Bülent Daver, "Siyasi Elit ve Reformlar," *Cumhuriyet*, January 23, 1964. Ziya Gökalp's famous article "Güzideler ve Halk" ("Elites and People") became popular again.

[1] A socialist book found it necessary to allude to Ortega y Gasset in discussing the question of social balance. See Mehmet Altın, *Türkiye'de Siyasi Hareketler ve Sosyal Yapı* (Ankara 1961). Incidentally, the foreword to this book was written by Cihad Baban who only a few years earlier had declared that socialism was materialism and preoccupation with food.

[2] *Vatan*, August 30, 1960. The newspaper *Vatan*, which after ousting its liberal editor A. E. Yalman openly embraced the cause of socialism, commented, "The PRP with most of its leaders, deputies and a powerful organization all over the country, is the party of the rich and the notables. The deputies who won the elections in 1957, were mostly landlords. Many of these were sons of deputies...a deputy seat in the PRP, based on land ownership and personal influence, is transferred from father to son. Despite its statist principles, the structure and ideas of its leaders are such that the PRP cannot become socialistic" (*Vatan*, August 1, 1960); see also *Tanin*, August 12, 1960.

the development of socialism in Turkey. The military recognized labor as a social group and lifted various restrictions imposed upon their freedom of organization. By 1964 the trade union membership rose to about 300,000 people organized in a national labor confederation, *Türk İş Konfederasyonu*. Labor was interested in welfare legislation but refused to associate itself en masse with any of the existing parties. (The Republican Party was instrumental in enacting many labor laws but the majority of workers as individuals still tended to support the Justice Party as they had the Democrats in the past. The explanation for this attitude must be sought not only in the bad memories of the old statism enforced by the Republicans, but also in a certain belief among workers that they could not talk and bargain with the authority-minded Republicans.) The recognition accorded to labor as a social group created interest among politicians and the socialists. The first regarded it as a source of votes and the latter as a potential vehicle to power through revolution. However, labor, although politically minded, showed little sympathy for statist socialism. The relative lack of information and education on social problems, the fear of repression, the bad public repute of socialism, the superficial character of most previous socialist parties, and the commoner's mistrust of the state may explain somewhat labor's apathy toward socialism. (See chapter IV)

The State Planning Organization (SPO) was established in September 1960 (Laws 91, 99, 340), with the initial purpose of assisting the government to locate resources, determine economic and social objectives, achieve economic cooperation and prepare plans for economic development. Intellectually, the SPO represented a major effort toward rationalization, systematization, and a scientific approach to economic problems. However, soon some members of the High Planning Committees of SPO asked for extensive political authority. The planners, mostly unknown people from the lower ranks of academia, were described by their own supporters as capable of turning Turkey into a bountiful country if given full power to enforce their magic, economic know-how. Eventually SPO assumed a middle-of-the-road philosophy and continued to exercise a very healthy and much needed influence on the Turkish economy and on general thought as well, but not before establishing the idea that government planning was the great discovery of the age. The productive groups, originally distrustful of authoritarian planning, gradually came to regard general democratic planning in a more objective fashion and to accept it.

The period between 1960 and 1961, analyzed above, prepared the ground for the second organized phase of socialism. The reinstatement of freedom of activity for political parties in the summer of 1961 undermined completely the hopes for a strong social regime. The forthcoming elections of October 15, 1961, confronted the Republican Party, the Justice Party, and the New Turkey Party (the last two were successors of the banned Democratic Party) with the vital problem of securing a majority of votes at the polls.

The latter two parties favored liberal views and capitalized on the discontent caused by the rather inefficient military rule and the fear of a strong regime. The Republicans, however, faced great difficulties. They had adopted the social ideas born of the Revolution of 1961, and took a leading part in electing the Constituent Assembly which drafted the Constitution of 1961 and defined the regime as being "social." It seemed certain that the Republicans would succeed the military to power. The statist-socialists in the Republican Party remained loyal to the organization, hoping for an election victory so as to have a legitimate basis for enforcing a social program.[1] Of these, Bülent Ecevit, Turhan Güneş, and Turhan Feyzioğlu (he left the party in protest against its socialism in 1967 and established his own Güven ["Reliance"] Party) were influential in the party's central organizations, but advocated a more realistic and pragmatic approach and opposed an extreme statist-socialist orientation lest the voters be frightened away.

The party convention held in Ankara on August 21, 1961, resulted in the defeat of the second group represented by Kasım Gülek. But at the polls on October 15, 1961, the Republican Party failed to receive a majority of votes and was forced subsequently to form first a coalition government with the Justice Party and then two other coalitions with minor parties with liberal views, and eventually was left out of government. Consequently the Republicans had to amend their social program considerably and eventually agreed to limit the authority of the State Planning Organization. The statist-socialists' hopes for power were dashed. Some of those not involved in the party leadership eventually resigned, combined forces with groups at large, and embarked on the ambitious project of organizing a socialist movement. An immediate outcome was the publication of the review *Yön* ("Direction") on December 20, 1961.[2] The publication had the purpose of welding together various socialist ideas into a coherent theory and giving them a practical orientation. The

---

[1] *CHP XV. Kurultayına Sunulan Parti Meclisi Raporu* (Ankara, 1961).
[2] The founders were Cemal Reşit Eyüboğlu, Mümtaz Soysal, and Doğan Avcıoğlu.

declaration published in the first issue of *Yön* and signed by several hundred intellectuals defined the new statist-socialist philosophy.[1] It stated that democracy and modernization which were the goal of Atatürk's reforms could be achieved only through rapid economic development, and that full modernization was possible only by reaching the West's level of economic development. Poverty was the main obstacle to democracy, and this necessitated the unity of all social groups around a development philosophy. The groups in power had no such philosophy and, despite the pressing economic needs of the people, they refused to undertake serious social reforms. Lasting results could be achieved through overall planning by the State Planning Organization. There were also other voices which openly defended an economic development based on freedom and democracy and offered a new definition of statism.[2]

The "development philosophy" proposed by *Yön* called for "mobilizing all economic resources, intensifying investments, planning of economic life in its entirety, achieving social justice among masses, abolishing exploitation and bringing democracy to the masses." *Yön* proposed to preserve the mixed economy but place the main emphasis on the state sector since private enterprise was wasteful, slow, and unable to achieve social justice. The new statism proposed by *Yön* would plan all investments and create large units of production. Statism was also the means of eliminating social injustice and bringing about true democracy.

The signatories condemned the system which allowed speculators and middlemen to earn more than high government officials, scientists, and scholars. Trivial as it may appear, this last idea epitomized the basic motive of this statist socialism: reinstatement to power and income of the old ruling groups on behalf of social justice and economic development.

---

[1] *Yön*, December 20, 1961, pp. 12-13. An English translation by Frank Tachau appears in *Middle Eastern Affairs*, March 1963, pp. 75-78, and Karpat, *Political and Social Thought*, pp. 334-38. See also the *Socialist International Information* 13 (June 1, 1963), p. 17. A rough breakdown of the first several hundred signatories shows over 100 writers, newspapermen, and intellectuals at large, 60 academics, 75 school teachers, 35 engineers, 25 doctors, 30 lawyers, 25 trade unionists, 25 officers, 10 judges, 20 economists, 4 life-time senators (ex-members of the NUC), and 4 deputies. Özgen, *Türk Sosyalizmi*, p. 41.

[2] The *Barış Dünyası* ("*World of Peace*") (April 1962, pp. 18-22), published by Ahmet Hamdi Başar, issued its own declaration but was superficially abused by *Yön* as defending the capitalist viewpoint. Aydın Yalçın was branded a pseudosocialist friend of capitalists, and *Forum*, which tried to maintain a balanced view, was described as a follower of McCarthy.

As usual there was no allusion to the ways and means of assuring popular participation in the economic proces. *Yön* was reminded that the review *Kadro* in the early 1930's had defended the idea of a classless society led by an elite and that this scheme was actually implemented without its social content.[1] *Yön* answered dogmatically that since its basic social philosophy was different it would not commit the errors of *Kadro*.

The socialist doctrine proposed by *Yön* reinterpreted the three principles of Kemalism : reformism, populism, and statism, and described Atatürk as a socialist.[2] In reality *Yön* took these ideas out of their historical context and arbitrarily adapted them to its own doctrine without paying attention to the completely different conditions prevailing in 1962. *Yön* gradually rejected the parliamentary regime based on a party system and capitalized on state supremacy.[3] It advocated implicitly revolutionary methods to reach power and rejected the West as a model for Turkey's modernization.

Yön's circulation reached 30,000 copies, then dropped to 5,000 and was closed in 1963 under the authority of martial law. It reappeared later and adopted a definitely radical leftist orientation but ended its publication in 1967 for lack of readers. It vehemently attacked the United States as an imperialistic power exploiting Turkey, and condemned everything associated with the West while publicizing the achievements of Eastern Europe under socialism. It had abandoned its objectivity and like many other reviews in Turkish history lost its usefulness. It showed a regrettable hurry to solve Turkey's problems through solutions imposed from above and therefore ignored the actual social and historical forces which conditioned the birth of social thought.

Yet, one cannot ignore *Yön's* influence on thousands of intellectuals, teachers, army officers, and university students. It came at a turning point in Turkish political history and shaped their social viewpoint.[4]

---

[1] Melih Cevdet Anday, "Açıklığa Doğru," *Cumhuriyet*, July 7, 1962.

[2] Fernand-Wilhelm Fernau, "Courants sociaux dans la deuxieme République Turque", *Orient*, November 23, pp. 17-19. A popular book on the socialist ideas of Atatürk, though superficial and biased, is Çetin Altan, *Atatürk'ün Sosyal Görüşleri* (Ankara, 1965).

[3] For a lengthy analysis of *Yön's* views in the light of Turkey's social background see Kemal H. Karpat, "Yön ve Devletçilik Uzerine," *Forum*, December 15, 1962, January 1, 15, 1963, and translation in Karpat, *Political and Social Thought*, pp. 342-56. Also see Yıldız Sertel, *Türkiye'de İlerici Akımlar* (Istanbul, 1969), pp. 215-93.

[4] Influential newspapers such as *Milliyet* and *Cumhuriyet* originally supported the socialists. The latter, in fact, chose socialism as the topic for its essay competition

It also helped crystallize social issues and forced groups to formulate their own social views.

Early in 1963, the socialists also established the *Sosyalist Kültür Derneği* ("Social Cultural Society") with the purpose of providing a socialist education for intellectuals and workers within the framework of "nationalistic-patriotic democratic and libertarian ideas".[1]

Socialism according to the society was "a method of thought and action based on scientific study of social and economic relations in society, and a search for their regulation in accordance with the laws of reason." Socialism started from a world view above individual and group interests and relied on people to achieve a social order for the people.[2]

The formal emergence of socialism caused a violent reaction among conservative groups who assaulted it in their own publications and in Parliament as being communistic and subversive in purpose.[3] The controversy between the secularists and socialists on one hand, and the conservatives and the Islamist, racialist nationalists on the other, involved various groups in every field of endeavor.[4] The *Türk Devrim Ocakları*, The Village Institute graduates, and the Teachers' Federation sided with the first groups in publicly debating various social issues. The university students were also divided and often fought each other on ideological issues. The state security organization, alarmed by these debates, issued a report in 1963 asserting that the confused ideological atmosphere bred extremist currents such as communism, Islamism, and Kurdish nationalism.

Meanwhile the new middle classes began to show an organized reaction to socialism, partly by siding with the conservative nationalists

in 1962-63. Eventually these papers adopted a social democratic attitude and deserted *Yön*. However, other publications, *Sosyal Adalet* ("Social Justice") and *Eylem* ("Action"), came out defending socialist views.

[1] The head of the society was Osman Nuri Torun, the former head of the State Planning Organization. Other members were Sadun Aren, Türkkaya Ataöv, Doğan Avcıoğlu, Nejat Erder, Ilhami Soysal, Reşit Eyüboğlu, Şükrü Koç, Mümtaz Soysal, and several others, some of whom had been associated with SPO and *Yön*, and later with the Labor Party. The society had two main branches in Ankara and Istanbul, but was rather passive.

[2] See *Socialist International Information* (June 1, 1963); Cahit Tanyol, "Bir Bildiri," *Cumhuriyet*, February 8, 1963.

[3] See a good account in Julien Le Moyen, "Les difficultés de la Turquie," *Le Monde*, weekly edition, (February 7-13, 14-20, 1963).

[4] The *Imam-Hatip* ("clergy") schools and the students of the High Islamic Institute proved to be the militant supporters of the latter group.

but mostly by informing the public and especially the working classes of the complexities of production and distribution which socialists ignored.[1] The private banks and entrepreneurs, in an effort to counteract the socialists, organized research institutes and conferences, with the purpose of presenting the problems of economic and social development in an allegedly more objective and balanced fashion. The idea of inducing greater numbers of people to participate in economic enterprise and enabling them to benefit from increased production seemed on its way toward replacing the old static economic concepts prevailing in the public mind.

The growth of socialism, as expected, helped clarify the stand of political parties on economic and social policy. The Republican Party gradually shifted to the left in order to capture the leadership of the social movement. After intensive discussions it decided that its ideological stand was "left of center" as stated by Ismet Inönü, the party leader, during the election campaign of 1965. The party has clearly indicated that it does not accept any dogmatic social ideology but remains faithful to Atatürk's ideas. The Justice Party, the main opponent of the Republicans and chief spokesmen for the middle classes, also adopted a moderate social viewpoint as a response to pressure from socialists. It accepted agricultural reform rather than *land* reform, economic planning, and welfare measures, but without relying on extensive government authority.

The social and economic views of these two parties are best expressed by their interpretation of *Karma Ekonomi* ("mixed economy"), which is a constitutional principle defining Turkey's economic and hence social policy. The Republicans proposed to expand the state sector in order to achieve public welfare, whereas the Justice Party regarded the government as an institution of public service and as an auxilliary supplement and supporter for private enterprise.

In fact, the Justice Pary program adopted in November 1964, and its election platform of 1965, indicated clearly that this party's ideological stand conformed to the social philosophy and economic aspirations of the middle classes which controlled the party. It drew its support not only from rural areas but also from cities and towns as the representative of the small businesses and manufacturing interests, craftsmen, and shopkeepers. Thus, both the Republican and the Justice parties have accepted the idea of increased social welfare and economic de-

---

[1] Namık Zeki Aral, "Memlekette Sosyalist Cereyanı," reproduced in *Yeni Istanbul*, February 7, 1963. Also see *Komunizme Karşı Hürriyet*, Publication of the Union of Trade and Industry Chambers, (Istanbul, 1965).

velopment but differ with regard to the scope and role of the government. Both accept private property and enterprise, and qualify basically as middle-of-the-road parties.

The development of socialism in Turkey has been analyzed above in a generic fashion without dealing specifically with marxist groups which played a major role behind the scenes. Marxist socialists made common cause with secularist nationalists and social-minded groups at the beginning and then came out in support of socialist publications and organizations once their existence was legally recognized. Several of them were also influential in the Republican Party. Acting at the beginning as democratic-minded social reformers, they gradually revealed their true identity under the guarantee offered by constitutional freedoms, and the hope of success rooted in the growth of social consciousness.

Marxist thought in Turkey has developed steadily in the last fifty years, taking advantage of periodic liberalization.[1] The two socialist parties, the Socialist Party of Turkey of Esat Adil Mustecaplıoğlu and the truly marxist Turkish Workers' and Peasant Party of Şefik Hüsnü Değmer established in 1946, were closed that same year. Several underground organizations were discovered during the following decade and their leaders and members jailed since communism was outlawed.[2] Yet, underground activity supported by various organizations abroad continued.

The revolution created new conditions. Articles 140-142 of the Criminal Code, prohibiting organizations and propaganda designed to promote class struggle or communism which was defined by the Code as the establishment of the supremacy of one class over the other, were rendered inoperative by the outburst of social currents which confused further the already vague differences between social democracy, socialism, and

---

[1] The scattered works on marxism in Turkey consist mainly of translations from popularized versions in the West. But Turkey had nominal marxists, and at one time between 1934 and 1936 there were even societies aiming at popularizing marxist ideas. The contemporary socialists have read Marx from foreign sources and probably from second or thirdhand interpretations. Actually marxist ideas in Turkey seem to have spread by word of mouth more than by writing. Hence some socialist writings seem to be an elaboration of marxist slogans rather than an analysis of Marx's works. Marxist ideas acquire dogmatic forms in intellectual thinking and make a travesty of democracy and economic development. See Kemal H. Karpat, "Socialism and the Labor Party of Turkey," *Middle East Journal*, Spring 1967, pp. 157-172, and *idem*, "The Turkish Left," *Journal of Contemporary History* 1 (1966), pp. 669-86. See also George S. Harris, *The Origins of Communism in Turkey* (Stanford, 1967).

[2] Karpat, *Turkey's Politics*, pp. 357 ff.

marxism. Moreover, the leftist intelligentsia's and bureaucracy's opposition to the entrepreneurial middle classes and to capitalists, coupled with the spread of interest consciousness among social groups, destroyed all criteria for distinguishing marxist thought from democratic socialism. But on the other hand, it seemed that without a strong directional command the developing social thought could strengthen the ideological position of a middle-class political party, possibly the Republicans, and thus help consolidate the social democratic order rather than create a truly marxist regime.[1]

These tactical considerations were probably instrumental in the establishment, on February 13, 1961, and especially the orientation of the *Türkiye İşçi Partisi* ("Labor Party of Turkey"). The party was established by leftist trade union leaders but in 1962 the leadership passed into the hands of Mehmed Ali Aybar, a lawyer, a relative of Nazim Hikmet, and a French-educated scion of a wealthy family from Istanbul. Soon it gathered around leftist intellectuals and a variety of marginal urban elements, some of whom were rather wealthy. Despite strenuous efforts, the overwhelming majority of workers did not support the Labor Party. The Confederation of Labor rejected formal affiliation with any political party and its leaders were called in true marxist tradition "traitors to the labor cause." Actually the law on collective bargaining and strikes, of July 7, 1963, which recognized extensive rights for the workers, turned their attention to securing economic gains and strengthened their tendency to become an interest group.

The Labor Party program condemned imperialism and described its organization as belonging to the labor class, and to those groups who followed the industrial workers' leadership: agricultural workers (*"ırgat"*), small farmers, wage earners, craftsmen, small merchants, low income professionals, progressive youth, and social-minded intellectuals. The working masses were considered the source of all production and the essential force for social development.[2] The workers' full acquisition

---

[1] The favorable political atmosphere brought about a proliferation of "socialist" parties. Alaettin Tiridoğlu's party, established in 1959 to combat communism through some social reforms, proposed to expand its activities. A tiny Labor Party ("Çalışma Partisi") established in 1961 combined with that of Tiridoğlu but showed little activity. Meanwhile the leaders of the Socialist Party of Turkey (closed in 1946, reinstated after acquittal in 1952, and then closed once more by the government) were acquitted after eight years on trial. The news concerning these socialist parties is in *Vatan*, January 12, 1959; *Akşam*, October 3, 1960; and *Cumhuriyet*, March 4, 1961.

[2] See *Türkiye İşçi Partisi Kimlerin Partisidir?* (Istanbul, 1962). The present party

of rights and of proper living means, and the full modernization of Turkey were regarded as being two related and mutually dependent problems. The party condemned landlords, capitalists, and all other groups who opposed development.[1]

The method for achieving rapid development was socialism, which the Labor Party defined as participation by all working groups in administration and production. The party program did not openly reject private enterprise but proposed to absorb and liquidate it while all industry was slowly appropriated by the state. The Labor Party wanted to eliminate the differences between village and city and between manual and intellectual workers, to provide employment for everyone, and to end forever the system based "on the exploitation of man by man." It also advocated a foregin policy in accordance with the principles of the Turkish War of Liberation, by which it meant antiimperialism and greater independence from the United States. It accepted a parliamentary system and proposed to assume and leave power by popular will.

The party evaluated events in Turkey and abroad from the viewpoint of the labor class and the masses. It denounced the government coalitions, opposed Turkey's affiliation with the Common Market, and launched an unsuccessful campaign to abolish Articles 141 and 142 from the Criminal Code.[2] The Labor Party leaders did not associate themselves with the Republican statist socialists at the beginning. In fact there was mutual distrust between them. Mehmed Ali Aybar, when interviewed by this writer in 1962, dismissed *Yön* and its leaders as being dilettantes concerned only with power, who had borrowed socialist techniques in order to achieve their ambitions.

However, at a later date in 1962 and in 1963 *Yön* found that it had no support among any social group and began to show increased sympathy for the Labor Party. Later several of the statist socialists associated with *Yön* and the Socialist Cultural Society joined the Labor Party along with a few members of Parliament, students, and university professors. Thus

---

program was adopted at a party convention held in Izmir on February 10, 1964. See *Türkiye İşçi Partisi Programı* (Istanbul, 1964).

[1] The leaders elected in the convention of August 20, 1962, consisted of: Chairman, Mehmet Ali Aybar; Secretaries, Rüştü Güneri and Orhan Arsal; Central Executive Board, İbrahim Denizciler, Kemal Türkler, Ismail Topkar, Rıza Kuas, Cemil Hakkı Selek, and Kemal Sülker (the executive board is made up mostly of trade unionists). Some of these resigned from the party.

[2] See the declarations of July 8, 1962, and September 15, 1963.

the party seems to have become the symbol of intellectuals' social aspirations, as well as their potential vehicle for power. But its reliance on the elite curtailed the party's popular appeal, as indicated by results obtained in the municipal elections of November 17, 1963. Despite an extensive preelection propaganda campaign it received barely 34,301 votes, whereas the Republican and Justice parties' total was over 7.5 million.

The failure of the Labor Party to attract the workers and arouse popular interest led to a change of tactics and philosophy. The dogmatic, narrow, class view was replaced by a more general approach intended to appeal to all classes and to all men "siding with labor." The new party program of 1964 stressed the economic backwardness of Turkey and proposed comprehensive scientific planning for the welfare of everyone and an end to exploitation. It capitalized further on nationalist feelings aroused by the failure of the West to back fully the Turkish stand on Cyprus. It concentrated its attacks on the Justice Party, which was described as the tool of the West and the spokesman for the vested interests of Turkey. NATO was denounced while friendship with the Soviets was implicitly praised. The Republican Party, on the other hand, assuming that the Labor Party propaganda would undermine the popular appeal of the Justice Party, its main rival in the forthcoming elections, appeared to condone the Laborites' ideas. Moreover, the Republicans' definition of their own ideological stand as being "left of center" strengthened the conviction that they associated themselves with the Labor Party in forming a united social front. Consequently the Labor Party as an extreme and militant leftist party appeared as the leader of this social front and therefore was able to attract the Republican Party's younger, dynamic and social-minded elements. During the 1965 election campaign the Labor Party chose to make Turkey's foreign policy a main issue. It entered the election of October 10, 1965, in practically every province but elected only two deputies, although at the end the number of its deputies went up to 15 as a result of the cumulative election system. It received 276,101 votes or 3.7 percent of the total votes cast while the Republicans won 2,675,785 votes, a drastic loss in comparison with past elections. The Justice Party, which denounced communism and defended private enterprise, increased its votes to 4,921,235 or 52.9 percent of the total (as compared to 34.8 percent in 1961), or enough to form a government by itself. The workers seemed to have overwhelmingly backed the Justice Party whereas the Labor Party's votes, aside from about 59,000 in Istanbul, were spread thinly throughout the country. The votes cast for the Labor Party came from such varied groups as to make the party appear the least homogeneous political organization of Turkey. Later from 1967 to 1969 the party was shaken by internal fights between its intellectual and "Laborite" wings. (In the 1969 elections the Labor Party's total votes fell to 2.8 percent and it could retain only 2 seats in Parliament).

The 1965 elections, nevertheless, led to an important political alignment in the Assembly. It created one small extreme left (Labor Party), one small extreme right (Alparslan Türkeş's Nation Peasant Party, later National Action Party, with 11 seats), and a large number of middle-class groups (Justice 239 seats, Republican 134, National 31, New Turkey 19).

The elections of 1965 thus resulted in the victory of the new middle classes, clarified substantially the stand of political parties and thus concluded an important phase of social and ideological development in Turkey. It isolated extreme socialism, even while the social demands of the population have been steadily rising along with a firm determination to maintain political freedom. The success of social policy in Turkey, therefore, lies in its ability to achieve its ends by conforming to democratic ideals.

CONCLUSION

Ideological development in Turkey since 1960 has closely followed the diversification and stratification of the social structure. It was, therefore, a direct product of forces within society rather than being imposed from the top. The absence of a government committed firmly to an ideological stand permitted a natural growth of ideas rooted in the prevailing conditions in society.

The ideological monopoly of nationalism was terminated through the emergence of social ideas which in turn attested to the birth of a pluralist social and intellectual order. It is quite possible that the overlapping and conflicting ideas of nationalism and socialism may become further compartmentalized and narrowed in scope so as to permit the growth of other ideas which may not fit into either category. Political and economic development presently are being rationalized and explained through systems of thought rather than being passively accepted as the product of forces beyond the control of the human mind. A rational and systematic way of thinking, linking social causes to their political effects, is gradually spreading to the masses. Thus the elites are losing their exclusive monopoly of education, and together with it their basic claim to leadership. Economic and social forces intensify mobility and create new aspirations and loyalties centered around large, integrated and impersonal organizational units. The older forms of organization have tended to disintegrate, leaving men earnestly in need of a new rationale for understanding and obeying the rules of society and government. Ideology explains the role and place of authority in relation to these new conditions and organizations and tries to legitimize their observance. In terms of modernization this second endeavor is vitally important not only in preserving but also in perpetuating material achievements. Consequently, as a result of ideological development, Turkey has acquired a clearer understanding of her social and economic goals and gained confidence that she can reach them.

Turkish ideological development certainly has not arrived at a final synthesis. It has, however, concluded the first and most difficult phase in giving expression to social thoughts, resentments, and hopes accumulated during fifty years of forceful and guided change. If the democratic process had broken down between 1960 and 1965 as it often threatened to do, and if one single social group had acquired absolute control of power instead of having power reside in several mutually balancing social groups, the expression of accumulated social resentment would have easily resulted in the establishment of a strong extremist regime.

Future ideological developments of any significance may be expected to come about not from the right or left extremes but from the middle, that is to say, the middle classes. And this would further strengthen the existing democratic social system.

Since the above was written and updated in 1969, some drastic changes have occurred in the Turkish leftist movement. Though these require extensive treatment, we shall limit our observations here to a few general points. An amendment to the election law neutralized the Labor Party as an effective group in Parliament since it reduced the number of its deputies from fifteen to just two. Moreover, the controversy over the criticism of Soviet intervention in Czechoslovakia by the chairman, Mehmet Ali Aybar, produced violent reaction on the part of the pro-Soviet wing headed by Saden Aren and Behice Boran.[1] Eventually Aybar retired from the party and Boran was elected chairman. By this time the party had lost its popularity since the moderates had become displeased with its emphasis on foreign policy and dogmatic Soviet orientation, while the extremists found it too conservative. Thus, the Labor Party

---

[1] See *Yeni Gazete*, October 14, 17, 1969, (editorials). For intellectual discussions also see Muzaffer Sencer, *Osmanlı Toplum Yapısı*, Istanbul, 1969.

ceased to play a central role as the gathering point and coordinator of leftist movements in Turkey. Subsequently the center of gravity of leftist action shifted to the universities and the press. The School of Political Science, the Middle East Technical University, and somewhat less the Hacettepe University, all in Ankara, became the centers of student activity. These three institutions, which are among the most modern and socially conscious institutions of Turkey, came to be dominated by two groups : the *Sosyal Demokrasi Derneği* ("Society for Social Democracy") which is a close affiliate of the People's Republican Party, and the *Devrimci-Gençlik* ("Revolutionary Youth") which is an outgrowth of the old *Sosyalist Fikir Kulubleri* ("Socialist Thought Clubs") and has a predominantly maoist orientation. The rightists represented by the *Ülkü Ocakları* "Patriotic Hearths" have been dutifully eliminated from the places in which the leftists were dominant.

The leftist groups and their publications mushroomed so that one was at a loss to follow their ideology and points of difference from each other. For instance, *Aydınlık* appeared as two publications bearing the same name, both calling themselves the representatives of the revolutionary proletariat, one more authentic than the other. There were in addition other leftist publications such as *Ant* ("Oath"), *Emek* ("Labor"), and *Işçi-Köylü* ("Worker-Villager") which defended the views of small groups and had their faithful followers. The common general characteristics of these groups were their sectarian attitude, the opposition shown to them by both the peasant and worker masses, and their failure to realize that they had become isolated from the population at large, despite their frantic efforts to prove the contrary. But these groups, some of which were headed by young faculty people in the lowest ranks of academia, have been instrumental in translating and printing a large amount of socialist writing, ranging from Western socialist books to the works of Lenin, Stalin, Mao, Minh, and other lesser names among Asian and African socialists.

The rightist-religious groups have also translated practically all the major works of Islamists and nationalists in the Arab countries. The moderate, democratic-minded groups, after flirting with socialism, actually social democracy, for a while, have pulled away from extremism.

Special mention should be made of the weekly *Devrim* ("Revolution") published by Doğan Avcıoğlu, a marxist-nationalist educated in France. This review placed its emphasis on nationalism first and promoted socialism-marxism as a means to achieve the goals of nationalism, such as economic development and total independence. Bitter anti-Americanism and constant appeals to youth and intellectuals to rid Turkey of American "tutelage" was one of Avcıoğlu's points which endeared him to other leftist groups and permitted them to tolerate his ideological aberrations from orthodox marxism. *Devrim* had chosen the young officers as potential agents of socialist revolution and had directed its efforts to indoctrinate them with socialist ideas under the guise of nationalism, since nationalism-patriotism proved to be the best channel to recruit a following for socialism. The review also secured a rather large following among school teachers, whose concern with national problems, with development and independence, and modernization in general is part of their ideological upbringing.

The memorandum presented by the Joint Chiefs of Staff to Premier Suleyman Demirel on March 12, 1971, asking in effect for his resignation, was in good part the result of the unrest created by ideological differences among the intelligentsia and the lower ranks of the army. The inability of the government through its own loss of prestige to stem the unrest caused military intervention. Although Parliament and the political parties were allowed to perform their legislative functions, the government was entrusted to Nihat Erim, a former university professor and veteran member of the People's Republican Party. One of the first acts of the new government was to suspend the leftist publications and arrest some of the most oustpoken leftist representatives and publishers, including Doğan Avcıoğlu. These were eventually brought before courts for inciting class warfare and rebellion against the established order. Thus, one may say that a major phase in the history of social and political thought in Turkey came to an end in March 1971. It was a crucial phase not only for having brought to public attention some of the most important social and economic problems of Turkey but also for having challenged the fundamental principles of the political system and its criteria for selecting the leading cadres. Extreme leftism came to an end for having espoused violence and anarchism and for its indiscriminate use of every idea and every device in an effort to bring down the existing system and all that had entered into its making during the past fifty years of Republicanism.

This outline of the latest ideological developments may not do full justice to the actual evolution of thought in Turkey and its possible consequences for the country's political future. But a full and adequate analysis of these latest developments transcends the immediate purpose of this study and must be dealt with elsewhere in a different context.

INDEX OF NAMES

Adalet Partisi (see Justice Party)
Abdulaziz (Sultan), 46
Abdulhamid (Sultan) II, 99, 102, 105, 114
Adana, 287, 290, 292, 293-305
Afghanistan, 94
Agency for International Development, 143, 173, 175
Ağrı, 287
Agricultural Bank, 143
Albanians, 97, 105, 116
Alican, Ekrem, 242, 258 n. 2, 259. 260 n. 1, 261
Alişar Village, 200
Almond, Gabriel, 19, 62
Altan, Çetin, 338
Anatolia, 115
Ankara, 74, 182
Antalya, 200
Arık, Remzi (Professor), 296 n. 1, 330
Armenians, 95, 97, 105, 193
Association for the Defense of Rights of Anatolia, 186
Association of Foundry Operators, 141
Atatürk, Mustafa, Kemal, 47, 55, 103, 104, 105, 106 n. 1, 111, 113, 118, 119, 120, 151, 186, 187, 293 n. 1, 298, 326, 332, 336
Athenagoras, Patriarch, 245 n. 2
Avcıoğlu, Doğan, 365, 366
Aybar, Mehmet Ali, 260 n. 2, 360, 361
Aydemir, Talat (Colonel), 255, 257 n. 3
Aydın, 287, 290, 292, 303 n. 1, 305-312

Balıkesir, 290
Barlas, Cemil Sait, 347
Başgil, Ali Fuad, 250, 331
Bayar, Celal, 55, 245 n. 2, 262 n. 1
Baykam, Suphi, 302
Beyazid (Sultan) I, 31
Beyazid (Sultan) II, 36
Berger, Morroe, 135
Bismarck, 95, 112

Black, Cyril E., 22
Bulgaria, 54
Bursa, 287

Cavour, 112
Cebesoy, Ali Fuat, 103
Central Bank, 143
Cevdet, Abdullah, 107, 114, 120
Chamber of Commerce, Istanbul, 138, 139, 141
China, 94, 95, 96, 107
Christians, 95, 117
Cilician Gate, 293
Common Market, 260
Çorbaci-djorbajis, 38, 39
Craftsmen's Association (Esnaf Dernekleri), 140
Çukurova, 293, 295, 296, 301, 304
Cutright, Phillip, 16
Cyprus conflict, 111, 164, 193, 262, 341, 362

Danıştay, administrative court, 7
Değmer, Şefik Hüsnü, 359
Demirel, Súleyman, 7, 61, 300 n. 1, 366
Demirsoy, Seyfi, 165, 168
Democratic Party, 55, 58, 59, 60, 77, 84, 152, 156, 188, 198, 217, 229, 231, 233, 234, 239, 243, 245, 247, 248 n. 1, 257, 264, 290, 295, 297, 306, 325 n. 4, 333, 347, 349
Demokratik Party, 280
Deutsch, Karl, 15, 16, 18
DISK (Confederation of Revolutionary Trade Unions), 174, 175, 176
Doğan, Avni, 249 n. 1

Ecevit, Bülent, 345
Economic and Social Research Foundation, Istanbul, 141-142
Egypt, 96, 97, 99
Eminsu (Retired Revolutionary Officers), 248

INDEX OF NAMES

England, 18
Erim, Mehmed (Yurdakul), 106
Ereğli, 127, 128, 129, 143
Erişirgil, Emin, 338
Erim, Nihat, 7
Eylem (Action), 268

Faris, Robert, 130
Farmer's Union, see Adana, 302
Feyzioğlu, Turhan, 237, 260, 354
Five Year Development Plan, see Subject Index
Forum, 347
France, 18
Free Party, 55
French Enlightenment, 206
Frey, Frederick W., 22
Fuad Pasha, 108

Galbraith, John K., 21
Galip, Reşit, Minister of Education, 212
Gâzi, 110
Gâzi Teacher Training Institute, 209
Gedik, Namık, Minister of Interior, 310
Gemerek, 221, 222, 223
Gökalp, Ziya, 206-207, 330, 338
Goltz-Pasha, Colmar von der, 98
Grand National Assembly, see Parliament in Subject Index
Greece, 97, 99, 193, 287, 307 n. 2
Gülek, Kasım, 243, 302, 354
Gümüşpala, Rağıp (General), 242
Güneş, Turan, 266, 354
Gürsel, Cemal, 236, 237, 250, 252, 262, 349
Güven, see Reliance Party

Hagen, E. E., 24
Halk Bankası, 144, 145
Halk Partisi (see People's Republican Party)
Hapsburgs, 95, 108
Harbiye, 108, 219 n. 5, 223
Hatay, 304
Hoselitz, Bert F., 17

Inalcık, Halil, 186
Inan, Şefik, Minister of State, 234

India, 112
Industrial Development Bank, 143
Inönü, Ismet, 111, 113, 120, 243, 249 n. 1, 257, 258, 261, 262 n. 1, 358
Institute of Business Administration, Istanbul, 133
International Labor Organization, 173
Ipekçi, Abdi, 259
Iran, 94, 95, 96
Işçi Partisi (see Labor Party)
Iştirak ("Participation"), 345
Izmir, 287, 290, 306

Janissary, 32, 96, 98
Japan, 18, 94, 107, 113
Jews, 117, 338
Justice Party, 6, 80, 84, 169 n. 2, 175, 242, 244, 247, 248, 252, 253, 254 n. 1, 255, 256, 257, 258, 261, 262, 267, 279, 280, 290, 291, 292, 296, 301, 303, 307, 310, 331 n. 1, 358, 362, age and occupations of members, 81-82

Kadirli, 299, 300 n. 1, 311
Kanunname, 32
Karaosmanoğlu, Fevzi L., 91-92
Yakub Kadri (Novelist) 118
Kara George, 41
Keleş, Ruşen, 191, 200
Kemal, Mustafa, See Atatürk
Kemal, Yaşar (novelist), 300 n. 1, 339
Koç, Vehbi, 259, 325 n. 4
Kocatopçuoğlu, Şahap, 275
Konya, 245 n. 2
Korutürk, Fahri (President), 252
Köy Yatı Mektepleri, see free boarding schools (elementary)
Küçük Said Pasha, 109, 120
Kühne, German education advisor, 212
Kuznets, S., 21, 24

Labor Party, 90, 168-169, 174, 175, 260 n. 2, 262, 268, 305, 306, 311 n. 1, 335, 340, 361, 362
Lausanne Treaty, 55
Law Faculty, Istanbul University, 238
Law of Collective Bargaining, 156, 157
Lerner, Daniel, 22-23, 195

INDEX OF NAMES

Lebanon, 18
Lavantines, 116
Leyli meccani, see free boarding schools in Subject Index
Lipset, Seymour M., 16
Lise, see free boarding schools, secondary, in Subject Index

Macedonia, 111
Mahir, Ismail Effendi, 207
Mahmud (Sultan) II, reforms, 42, 48, 98, 101, 104, 105
Makal, Mahmud (novelist), 118
Malatya, 290
Mannheim, Karl, 230
Mehmet (Sultan) IV, 103
Mehmet (Sultan) I, 31
Mehmet (Sultan) (the Conqueror) II, 32, 110
Melen, Ferit, 259
Menderes, Adnan, 84, 103, 104, 106, 244, 248 n. 1, 264, 276, 297, 300, 306, 309, 349
Menderes, Yüksel, 310
Mersin, 296
Merzifon, 245 n. 2
Mexico, 113
Middle East Technical University, 365
Midhat Pasha, 102, 119, 209
Milli Birlik Komitesi, see National Unity Committe
Ministry of Agriculture, 190
Ministry of Education, 213, 217
Ministry of Labor, 155
Moltke, Hellmuth von, 98
Moore, Barrington, 15
Mosul conflict, 111
Mudafaa-i Hukuk Cemiyetleri ("Associations for the Defense of Rights"), 47
Muhammed Ali, 97, 98
Mülkiye, 109
Murat (Sultan) II, 32
Musa (Sultan), 31
Mustecaplioğlu, Esat Adil, 359

National Action Party, 340
National Party, 169 n. 2

National School, 110
National Unity Committee, 188, 234, 237, 248-9, 251-3, 327, 349
National Union of Turkish Students, 335
N.A.T.O., 321, 362
Necati, Mustafa, Minister of Education, 209 n. 3
Needler, Martin C., 25 n. 1
Nesin, Aziz, 350
New Ottomans, 102, 105
New Ottoman Society, see Society of Union and Progress
New Turkey Party, 169 n. 2, 242, 244, 247, 248 n. 1, 258, 279, 306, 354
NUC, see National Unity Committee
Nur, Riza, 331-332

Obrenovich, Miloş, 41
Okyar, Fethi, 55
Okyar, Osman, 347
Orbay, Kâzim, 252
Organski, A.F.K., 21
Orta Okul, see free boarding schools, secondary
Osman, Gazi (Sultan) 29

Paris, Treaty of (1856), 44
Party for Turkey's Resurrection, 331
Peasants' Party (*Köylü Partisi*), 396 n. 1
People's Houses (*Halk Evleri*), 187, 329, 334
People's Republican Party, 47, 55, 80, 103, 107, 112, 124, 156, 188, 197, 217, 239, 243, 244, 245, 247, 258, 261, 291, 294, 295, 296, 299, 303, 304, 306, 310, 328, 329, 347, 352, 358, 362; ideology, 55; age and occupations of membership, 81-82
Polatkan, Hasan, 244, 325 n. 4
Progressive Party, 103

Ramazanoğlu, 300
Reformation, 94
Reliance Party, 260-261, 354
Renaissance, 94
Republican National Peasant Party, 169 n. 2, 188, 258, 260 n. 1, 261, 291, 340
Republican Party, see People's Republican Party

Riza, Ahmed, 101, 104
Rize, 287
Robinson, Richard D., 56, 200
Romanovs, 95, 108
Rousseau, J.-J., 120
Russia, 94, 97, 107, 111
Rustow, Dankwart A., 21
Rustow, Walt W., 20, 24

Sabahaddin (Prince), 102
Sanders, Liman von, 98
Satır, Kemal, 302
Schumpeter, Joseph, 4, 24
Selim (Sultan), III, 41, 42, 48, 96, 98, 99, 114, 119
Seljuk Turks, 29, 31
Sirmen, Fuad, 252
Sıvas, 290
Şinasi, Ibrahim, 100, 119
Social Cultural Society, 357, 361
Society for the Struggle Against Communism, 335
Society of Nationalists, 334
Society of Union and Progress, 100, 101, 112
Stara Zagora, 54
State Planning Organization (SPO), 258, 259, 352, 353
Sunay, Cevdet, 249 n. 1, 250, 252
Swiss Code Civil, 49

Tansel, İrfan (Air Force Chief), 249 n. 1
Tanzimat, 99, 100, 102, 108, 119, 229
Teachers' Federation, 268-269
Tedbirler Kanunu, 257
Tenants Association of Turkey, 322
Tohum (Seed), 331
Toker, Metin, 249 n. 1
Topçu, Nurettin, 331
Trabzon, 287, 290
Trade and Industrial Chambers, 235, 253, 259, 261
Treaty of Sèvres, 105
Tunç, Halil, 163, 165, 168
Turan, Osman, 330
Turgut, Mehmet, 267
Turhan, Mümtaz, 330, 331 n. 1, 334

Türk Kültürü (Turkish Culture), 331
Türk Ticaret Bankası (Commercial Bank) 144, 145
Türk Yurdu (Turkish Homeland), 330, 331
Türkay, Orhan, 191, 200
Türkeş, Alparslan, 291, 334 n. 2, 340, 363
Turkish Hearths (*Türk Ocakları*), 187, 329, 330
Turkish Management Association, 141
Turkish National Student Federation, 335
Turkish Reform Hearth (*Türk Devrim Ocakları*), 332-333
Turkish Youth Association, 335
TÜRK-IS (Confederation of Turkish Trade Unions), 153, 154, 158, 159, 160, 163, 164, 165, 168, 169, 170 n. 2, 172, 174, 176, 270, 272, 273, 274 n. 3

Ulay, Sıtkı (senator), 251, 252
Union and Progress Committee, 47, 104, 112
Union of Culture and Ideals, 334
Ürgülü, Suat Hayri, 169 n. 2, 252

Village Institute, 211, 212, 213, 214
Voice of America, 193

Weber, Max, 230, 245
Workers Insurance Organization, 270
Workingmen's Party (*Çalişanlar Partisi*), 272

Yalçın, Aydın, 347
Yapı ve Kredi Bank, 325 n. 4
Yassıada Trials, 194, 243, 254
Yön (Direction), 268, 345, 354, 355, 356, 361
Young Ottomans, 45, 341
Young Turks, 46, 47, 100-101, 114, 117, 206, 208, 341
Yüregir, Remzi, 293 n. 1

Zorlu, Fatin R., 244

INDEX OF SUBJECTS

Agriculture, 58, 67, 69
—, mechanization of, 58, 67, 68, 69, 199-199-200
Ahis, 29
Arabs, 95, 103, 116, 117, 338
Army, agent of change, 33-34, 51, 52, 60, 82, 131, 133 (*jandarma*, 194), 236
—, military reform, 95, 98, 112, 117
—, military schools, 98, 117
—, and party politics, 249-252, 255, 257, 265
Associations, 140, 141, 282, 287, 313, 323
Ayans, 36-39, 42, 186, 229, 299, 300

Balkans, 115, 116, 117
Banks, 143-145
Businessmen, see Entrepreneurial Groups

Caliphate, 111
Capitulations, 116
Census, 1913 and 1915, 53
—, 1921, 54
—, 1927, 54
—, 1932-1939, 56
—, 1960, 152
Civil Servants, 236, 268
Classes, see Economics, Elites, Entrepreneurial Groups, Intelligentsia, Labor, Social Classes
Code of Obligations, 49
Communications, 17, 74, 76, 79, 80, 104, 117, 187
Constituent Assembly, 238, 239, 240, 243, 271, 278, 322, 346
Constitution of 1961, 90, 152-153, 218 (structure and philosophy, 237-243, 244, 279), 317, 339, 340, 354
Coups of 1962 and 1963, 255-256
Credit, financial, 143, 144, 145-146, 148

Democracy, see Political Parties in Index of Names
Development, administrative-political, 186-189

—, economic, 189-192, 195
—, govnment agencies of, 190, 201, 310, 333
—, Five-Year Development Plan, First, 157, 161, 261, 271
Devşirme, 30, 32

Economics, 2, 10, 51-57, 61, 62-86, 192, 228-9, 268, 342, 353-6
Economic Groups, see Elites, Entrepreneurial Groups, Labor Unions
Education, 17, 45, 77, 78, 100, 218
—, as a factor in political party membership, 285-286, 290, 292, 295
—, special schools, 44, 50, 203
—, see also Free Boarding Schools
Elections, 243-249
Elites, 1, 2, 7, 25, 63, 74, 79, 227, 229, 233, 234, 236, 240, 242, 254, 267, 282, 283, 319, 351, 352, 357, 363 (*Zinde kuvvetler*); coalition of elites, 27, 243, 254
—, bureaucratic, 125, 126, 130, 131 (historic role of, 132)
—, conflict with masses, 91-92
Entrepreneurial Groups, 3, 4, 51-62, 90, 134-147, 200, 228
—, farmers, 138, 200
—, see also Elites, Intelligentsia, Social Classes

Farmers, see Entrepreneurial Groups, Peasants
Foreign debt, 234
Free Boarding Schools, 203-223
—, elementary, 211-213
—, secondary, 213-216
—, university, 216-219, 221-223

Halkçılık, see Populism
History, stages of development, 5, 6
—, use of, 11-12
Ideological struggle, 227, 239, 254, 266
Ideology, after the 1960 Revolution, 317-366

—, conservatism, nationalism, and social change, 328-341
—, and social change, 317-328
—, uses of socialism, 341-363
Income, 126, 128, 129
—, of civil servants, 134, 135-137, 143
Industrialization, 51-62, 191, 293
Intelligentsia, 6, 44, 45, 48, 62, 69, 92, 227, 254, 256, 263-269, 280
Intelligentsia-bureaucracy, see Elites
Islam, Islamism, 107, 114, 193, 265, 318, 336 n. 2, 337, 342, 343

Jelali rebellions, 34

Labor, agricultural, 52, 142, 151
—, collective bargaining, 158, 162, 273, 275, 360
—, industrial workers, 269-275
—, legislation, 151, 153 (history of, 155-157), 158, 259, 275
—, in politics, 165-170
—, protests, 153, 158, 179, 273-274
—, social reform, 170, 171, 259, 270
—, unions, 156, 157, 158, 161, 162, 172, 173, 174, 175, 177-178, 235, 238, 294, 313, 322, 353
—, wages, 180-181, 271 n. 1
Land, *miri*, 43
—, private property, 49
—, reform law, 43, 229
—, tribal, 43
—, *vakf*, 43
Lise, high school, 77, 79, 286
Literacy, 22, 23, 77, 79, 198
Literature, 118
Local Party Politics, see political parties in Index of Names

Maoism, 6
Marxism, 6, 359, 360
Military, see Army
Migration, 54, 58, 115, 191, 287
Millet System, 33, 183
Miri, see Land
Modernization, 1, 3, 5, 11, 67, 93, 94, 96, 102, 104, 120, 182, 206, 220, 221, 231, 318, 331, 339, 341, 355

—, development of stages theory, 20-25, 26
—, theory of structural change, 12-13, 14-20, 57, 72, 80, 229

Nation formation, 1, 2, 17, 51, 111
National consciousness, 111
National Unity Committee (NUC), see Index of Names
Nationalism, 7, 46, 95, 103, 106, 114
—, see also Ideology, Political Parties, and names of individual political parties in the Index of Names
Newspapers, 77, 193, 235, 242, 254, 255, 256, 264, 274 n. 3, 279, 333, 338, 348, 350
Notables, 102, 105, 123
Nomads, 31, 300

Occupational Differentiation, 62, 63, 74, 80
—, by sex, 64-65
Ottoman (Empire), 12, 17, 19, 22, 26, 108, 110, 112
—, army, 32, 35
—, bureaucracy, 32 (transformation of, 44, 48), 45, 109, 116
—, economics, 28, 29-32
Ottomanism, 102, 105

Party Politics, see names of principal parties in Name Index
Peasants, 29, 33, 80, 107, 152, 228, 235, 263, 275-281, 349
Politics, development, 53, 72
—, groups, 330, 331, 332, 333, 334, 335, 340
—, leadership, 80, 83
—, reviews and publications, 330, 331, 333, 337 n. 3, 345, 347, 348, 356, 365
—, transformation, 61 (basis of, 62; indicators, 62, 69, 70, 71, 72, 74, 77, 85-89)
Political Parties, membership data, 284-285, 288-289, 291, 359, 360
—, in province politics, 282-316
—, see also individual parties in Name

Index, especially under Adana, Aydin; Demokrat Parti, Demokratik Party, Justice Party, Labor party, National Party, National Action Party, New Turkey Party, Peasants' Party, People's Republican Party, Reliance Party, Republican National Peasant Party, TIP
Political Precincts (*ocak* and *bucak*), 276, 277, 278, 279
Population, 72, 73, 74, 75, 191, 196
Populism, 49, 206-208
Press, see Newspapers, also Politics (reviews and publications)
Press *agas* (landlords), 350
Professional schools, 210, 211, 351
—, see also Free Boarding Schools

Quantitative Growth Indicators, 62, 69, 72-90

Radio, 77, 129, 193
Railroads, 192
Revenue, 72, 73
Reforms (of May 27), 243, 252
Republican Turkey, birth of, 47
Reserve Officer Teacher Program, 188
Revolutions (1960), 60, 61, 90, 151, 152, 188, 189, 194, 217, 231, 248, 251, 257, 272, 276, 341, 346, 349
—, causes, 231, 232-237
—, impact on villagers, 275-281

Secularism, 50, 51, 106, 237, 265, 303, 318, 329, 345
Servet beyanı (wealth declaration), 235
Sipahi, 32; function, 31-32, 33, 34
Social Classes, groups, 3, 45, 46, 48, 60, 62, 67, 74, 84, 130, 228, 244 (villagers, 275-281)
—, middle, 2, 4, 16, 56, 57, 59, 62, 194, 220, 235, 236, 312, 313, 317, 322, 323, 349, 351 (the new middle class, 126-130)
—, mobility, 3, 20, 58, 162, 221-223, 238, 290, 292, 295, 307, 319, 363
—, urban strata, 57, 60
—, see also Army, Elites, Intelligentsia, Labor, and Peasants

Socialism, 69, 148, 254, 305, 327, 341, 359-60, 365
—, Islamic and cultural origins, 345-346
—, in literature, 333
—, see also Ideology, and Political Parties in the Index of Names
Soy (family or group lineage), 330
Squatters, 57
State, modern, 17, 18, 19
Statism (see introduction), 48, 49, 55-60, 227-228, 333, 341, 343
—, see also Entrepreneurial Groups, Elites

Taxes, 234, 235, 244, 253, 259, 278
—, Income law, (1960), 235
Technology, 14, 20, 51, 53-55, 355
Telegraphy, 104
Timars, 30, 33, 34, 35
Trade, 39, 41, 49
Trade Unions, see Associations and Labor (unions)
Transportation, 74, 76, 117, 192, 199

Ulema, 99, 102, 318, 319
Urbanization, 17, 21, 22, 72, 73, 74, 75, 80, 191
Uç Beyleri, 29

Vakf, see Land
Village, Law of 8 March 1924, 187
—, social change in, 188, 193, 194, 195, 196-199
—, see also Development: administrative-political, economic, government agencies of
Villagers, see Peasants
Vocational Schools, 210. See also Free Boarding Schools
Voting, 79, 83

War, of Independence, 103, 109, 197, 229, 326, 328, 361
—, World War I, 96, 97, 98, 110, 287, 293, 307
—, World War II, 95, 111, 229, 270
—, Ottoman, 97, 108
Westernization, 341

Yörük (nomads), 300